Exporting the UK Policing Brand
1989–2021

CLARENDON STUDIES IN CRIMINOLOGY

Published under the auspices of the Institute of Criminology, University of Cambridge; the Mannheim Centre, London School of Economics; and the Centre for Criminology, University of Oxford.

General Editors: Mary Bosworth and Carolyn Hoyle
(*University of Oxford*)

Editors: Alison Liebling, Paolo Campana, Loraine Gelsthorpe, and Kyle Treiber
(*University of Cambridge*)

Tim Newburn, Jill Peay, Coretta Phillips, Peter Ramsay, and Robert Reiner
(*London School of Economics*)

Ian Loader and Lucia Zedner
(*University of Oxford*)

RECENT TITLES IN THIS SERIES:

Penality in the Underground:
The IRA's Pursuit of Informers
Dudai

Assessing the Harms of Crime:
A New Framework for Criminal Policy
Greenfield and Paoli

Armed Robbers:
Identity and Cultural Mythscapes in the Lucky Country
Taylor

Crime, Justice, and Social Order:
Essays in Honour of A. E. Bottoms
Liebling, Shapland, Sparks, and Tankebe

Policing Human Rights: Law, Narratives, and Practice
Martin

Normalizing Extreme Imprisonment:
The Case of Life Without Parole in California
Vannier

Respect and Criminal Justice
Watson

Neighbourhood Policing:
The Rise and Fall of a Policing Model
Innes, Roberts, Lowe, and Innes

Respectable Citizens – Shady Practices:
The Economic Morality of the Middle Classes
Farrall and Karstedt

Advocates of Humanity:
Human Rights NGOs in International Criminal Justice
Lohne

Exporting the UK Policing Brand 1989–2021

Georgina Sinclair

Great Clarendon Street, Oxford, OX2 6DP,
United Kingdom

Oxford University Press is a department of the University of Oxford.
It furthers the University's objective of excellence in research, scholarship,
and education by publishing worldwide. Oxford is a registered trade mark of
Oxford University Press in the UK and in certain other countries

© Georgina Sinclair 2022

The moral rights of the author have been asserted

First Edition published in 2022

Impression: 1

All rights reserved. No part of this publication may be reproduced, stored in
a retrieval system, or transmitted, in any form or by any means, without the
prior permission in writing of Oxford University Press, or as expressly permitted
by law, by licence or under terms agreed with the appropriate reprographics
rights organization. Enquiries concerning reproduction outside the scope of the
above should be sent to the Rights Department, Oxford University Press, at the
address above

You must not circulate this work in any other form
and you must impose this same condition on any acquirer

Public sector information reproduced under Open Government Licence v3.0
(http://www.nationalarchives.gov.uk/doc/open-government-licence/open-government-licence.htm)

Published in the United States of America by Oxford University Press
198 Madison Avenue, New York, NY 10016, United States of America

British Library Cataloguing in Publication Data

Data available

Library of Congress Control Number: 2022941537

ISBN 978–0–19–874320–0

DOI: 10.1093/oso/9780198743200.001.0001

Printed and bound by
CPI Group (UK) Ltd, Croydon, CR0 4YY

Links to third party websites are provided by Oxford in good faith and
for information only. Oxford disclaims any responsibility for the materials
contained in any third party website referenced in this work.

General Editors Introduction

The *Clarendon Studies in Criminology Series* aims to provide a forum for outstanding theoretical and empirical work in all aspects of criminology and criminal justice, broadly understood. The Editors welcome submissions from established scholars, as well as manuscripts based on excellent PhD dissertations. The Series was inaugurated in 1994, with Roger Hood as its first General Editor, following discussions between Oxford University Press and Oxford's then Centre for Criminological Research. It is edited under the auspices of three centres: The Centre for Criminology at the University of Oxford, the Institute of Criminology at the University of Cambridge, and the Mannheim Centre for Criminology at the London School of Economics. Each supplies members of the Editorial Board and, in turn, the Series General Editor or Editors.

Exporting the UK Policing Brand 1989–2021 draws on a wide range of primary and secondary material, including interviews, to document how the UK government successfully exported its policing model abroad. In adopting an historical lens, this book contributes to a lengthy tradition in the UK of policing studies, while its oral histories place it at the intersection with more straightforwardly criminological accounts. Interspersing testimonies with documentary analysis, Georgina Sinclair explores the changing form and nature of international policing, while tracing its effect back to practices and rhetoric in the UK. From peacekeeping assistance to privatization, she demonstrates how the international stage has offered numerous opportunities for the police, along with some risks as well.

As the title suggests, Sinclair argues that in deploying its police abroad, the UK government has sought to extend the reach of a particular 'brand' of policing. The UK Policing brand, however, is not uncontested, and is also not unchanging. While originally rooted in a particularly 'English' vision of the past, and the so-called 'Peelian' principles of policing by consent, the UK police brand, she suggests, has shifted in response to corporate opportunities, Brexit, as well as other more local visions from Scotland and Northern Ireland.

In the post-Floyd era, the police brand everywhere has been brought into question. Little attention, however, has been paid to the role or implications of international policing. In mapping the extensive engagement of British police abroad, Sinclair opens new avenues for analysis of long-term questions about the police in terms of their purpose and legitimacy. She also advances our understanding of the relationship between the police and the nation state. As a work of recent history, this book provides important and novel evidence of an under-scrutinized field of government policy and demonstrates conclusively that it should be given far more attention. We are pleased to include this account in the Clarendon Studies in Criminology.

Mary Bosworth and Carolyn Hoyle
General Editors
Centre for Criminology, University of Oxford
May 2022

Acknowledgements

There has always been considerable public interest surrounding policing, and the police are often in the media spotlight for one controversy or another. Yet our knowledge of many aspects of police history remains incomplete as does our understanding of the *doing of policing*. I hope that this book will shed further light on the internationalization of UK policing, fill in some of the gaps in relation to the police and their overseas activities, and at the very least point readers in a direction where more research is needed.

This is a book that I have wanted to write for a long time: the genesis stemmed from discussions with Graham Ellison that began almost a decade ago. Graham was instrumental in providing much of the inspiration behind the building of a theoretical framework that is reflected within subsequent chapters—this book would not have come to pass without him.

Exploring what police do on the ground through oral testimonials and 'field' research has provided a bridge between the theory and the practice, the historical and the contemporary. It gave me a far greater understanding of what international policing was all about. Simply put: this book would not have come about without all those UK police who candidly shared their views 'at home and away', as well as military personnel, government and intelligence officials, and police from many other parts of the world. Huge thanks to that cast of hundreds. I would, however, personally like to thank Maureen Brown, Paddy Tomkins, Andy Goldston, Colin Port, Ces Dunster, Andy Pritchard, Jackie Gold, Jason Hogg, Ed Henriet, Dean Henson, Pedro Da Silva Nogueira, Jan Leenslag, Paul Dutton, Gary White, Steve Hartley, Rod Hansen, and Alistair Eivers. Patrick Radbourne and Mark O'Donoghue read and commented on many of the chapters as did Joe Napolitano, who has always provided a valuable sounding board for all things policing over the years.

In studying the police and policing, I have been fortunate to engage and benefit from the guidance of many colleagues. My last 'full-time' academic post was at the Open University where I was able to move away from my earlier interest in the history of colonial policing to the contemporary period, and examine the internationalization of UK policing. Without the support of colleagues in the history department this would not have been possible. I remain deeply grateful to Chris A. Williams, Paul Lawrence, and Anne Laurence who supported my forays into the world of international policing. As I write, reflecting on my time at the Open University is tinged with sadness with the loss in 2020 of my mentor, close colleague, and friend Clive Emsley. Clive more than any other police historian encouraged and grew my sense of history and he is greatly missed. The past few years have also seen the passing of Tank Waddington and Mike Brogden: both encouraged and debated with me in equal measure and showed me how to view the police and policing through a very different lens—they are also greatly missed.

As I began my writing journey in March 2020, I benefitted from the guidance of Richard Hill another close academic mentor and friend. Richard provided ongoing support often with considerable humour, and encouraged the book writing process as it collided with my professional world—I owe him a great deal. Many other colleagues, past and present, have discussed aspects of the book as it emerged from its cocoon and refined much of my thinking—often without realizing it. My thanks in particular go to Philip Murphy, Nick Fyfe, Cornelius Friesendorf, Athol Yates, Lawrence Ho, Peter Manning, Hervé Dubois, Keith Ditcham, Alexander Babuta, Paul O'Neill, Tom Gillhespy, and Dane Rogers. Rohan Burdett has over the past six years enlightened me on so many aspects of international criminal justice, and I thank him for reading and commenting on earlier sections of this book with his customary patience and kindness.

Writing a book is a solitary and challenging enterprise and I have more often than not been absent from friends and family as I disappeared deep into my writing cave. However, simply asking how 'the book was going' often sustained me on this arduous journey. A huge thank you to you all and in particular to the entire O'Donald family: Lewis, Jane, Freddie, Anna, and Lucy for all the fun and laughter when it was needed most and to Beatrice Gonzalez, Trina McCluskey, Sally Turner, Roger Longman, Sylvia McGill, Howard Gardener, Guillaume Vivaux, Marina Kuechen, Pauline and Dennis Banks, Susie and Ralph Saunders, Matt Thomas, Bertie Hadfield, Sarah Emes and, to my three canine companions who accompanied me daily on this journey.

I would also like to thank my publishers at Clarendon Series at OUP and in particular Kate Plunkett for her patience and support throughout as well as to the OUP reviewer who made many helpful suggestions and inadvertently confirmed my own theory as to where changes were needed. Any errors in this book are entirely of my own making.

During those final months, my former colleague and trusted friend, Declan O'Briain, provided critical feedback as I edited the draft manuscript and then encouraged my thinking as I drafted the postscript. I owe Declan an immense debt of gratitude.

It has been the unfailing support of my husband James and sister Anita over the years that has sustained my interest in policing and police research projects, particularly when my professional journey took me in a very different direction. This book is for you both with my love.

Contents

Table of Figures	xv
List of Abbreviations	xvii
The Export of UK Policing	1
Theoretical underpinnings	5
Historical framework of analysis	6
Policing as brand management	7
Reading policing and police history	9
Police voices	11
A note on sweeping generalizations: models and typologies	13
Book structure	15
Chapter 1	15
Chapter 2	16
Chapter 3	16
Chapter 4	16
Chapter 5	17
Chapter 6	17
Chapter 7	17
Chapter 8	18
Conclusion	18
1. Conceptualizing the International Policing Agenda	19
Investigating the Western research literature	22
Transnational policing	23
Global policing	24
Security sector reform	26
Policing concepts within SSR: a mingling or a muddle?	28
Multilateral policing assistance: peacekeeping and peace support operations	30
Capacity building and capacity development	32
'Back to the futurism': a historical framework	33
Pre-1989 UK policing brand development	33
Security sector reform, aid, and development	34
Corporate security sector growth	35
Concluding comment	37

2. The UK Policing Brand in Historical Context: Myth and Reality — 38
- The 'New Police' — 40
- The Irish Constabulary — 42
- The British colonial police — 44
- The Ceylon Police — 45
- Whig and revisionist histories — 49
- Policing by *mutual* consent — 51
- Policing in England: an end of a golden age — 54
- Divided society policing in Northern Ireland — 57
- The internationalization of UK policing — 59
- Post-war police missions — 61
- Twenty-first century brand(s) — 63
- Concluding comment — 65

3. From Peacekeeping to Statebuilding: 'Conflict Entrepreneurs' — 66
- International peacekeeping: Bosnia and Herzegovina — 69
- Bringing the Northern Irish experience to the Balkan context — 73
- Revisiting divided society policing — 76
- Armed policing capability — 79
- Police–military co-operation — 81
- Ministry of Defence Police (MDP): international 'niche' policing — 82
- UK police in East Timor — 85
- Sierra Leone—'back to the futurism' — 89
- Concluding comment — 92

4. UK Policing in Afghanistan, Iraq, and Libya: After 9/11 — 93
- Afghanistan — 96
  - International disunity and disarray — 96
  - 'Access and influence'—training, mentoring, and advising the ANP — 99
  - MDP military integrated approach to MMA — 103
- Iraq — 106
  - Post-invasion planning and policing — 106
  - Training and advising the Iraqi police — 109
  - Pre-deployment preparation — 111
  - Police corruption — 115
- Libya — 118
  - UK policing with strategic intent — 118
  - Post-intervention stabilization — 120
  - Concluding comment — 124

5. The Rise of Police and Security Contracting   127

    The growth of the private military and security industry   130
    Towards private sector regulation in the UK   133
    Hybrid networks: the connection between public and private policing   137
    Hard security and strategic advising: police contracting in Iraq and Afghanistan   139
    Building intelligence management systems in Iraq and Afghanistan   144
    International opportunities after retirement   150
    Police contractors in Abu Dhabi: strategic advising and community policing   151
    Concluding comment   157

6. Promoting the UK Policing Brand: Coherence and Fragmentation   159

    Building international policing strategy and doctrine   160
    National Policing Improvement Agency   164
    College of Policing   166
    Building international policing strategy   168
    UK police in South Sudan: a missed opportunity   172
    Joint International Policing Hub: 2015 to 2021   175
    International Policing Response Cadre   177
    Capacity building through the JIPH   179
    Concluding comment   182

7. Police Scotland and PSNI: New International Policing Agendas   183

    Promoting Police Scotland Internationally   184
        The advent of Police Scotland   184
        A Scottish international development agenda   187
        The Sri Lanka police   190
        The Malawi police   193
    The 'new' Northern Irish policing brand   195
        From RUC to PSNI—reform and transformation   195
        Policing with the community   197
        PSNI as a template for post-conflict change management   199
        Supporting police reform in Bolivia and the Philippines   202
        Concluding comment   206

8. **'Global Britain' and the Future of International Policing Assistance** — 208
 - 'Homeland First'? New challenges for UK policing in the twenty-first century — 209
 - Exiting the European Union — 213
 - UK policing within EU, NATO, and UN missions — 215
 - Government mergers and overseas funding cuts — 218
 - Broadening military capabilities — 220
 - Police engagement as a cross-cutting capability — 225
 - Maintaining the UK policing brand — 227
 - Growing the UK policing brand — 229
 - Concluding comment — 231

Concluding Observations — 233
 - Police histories and 'back to the futurism' — 234
 - The guardians of the UK policing brand? — 237
 - The rise of overseas contracting — 238
 - The UK police brand and the international policing agenda — 241
 - International UK policing: a fractured memory? — 242

Postscript — 245

Appendix: Examples of UK police mission deployments — 251
References — 253
Index — 289

Table of Figures

4.1. MDP—Operation Herrick—Concept of District Level Operations   104

List of Abbreviations

ABP	Abu Dhabi Police
ACC	Assistant Chief Constable
ACPO	Association of Chief Police Officers
ACPO IA	Association of Chief Police Officers—International Affairs
ACPOS	Association of Chief Police Officers Scotland
ACRO	A Criminal Records Office
AFP	Australian Federal Police
ANA	Afghanistan National Army
ANDSF	Afghanistan National Defence and Security Forces
ANP	Afghanistan National Police
ARLEMP	Asia Region Law Enforcement Management Programme
BAPSC	British Association of Private Security Companies
BBC	British Broadcasting Corporation
BiH	Bosna and Herzegovina
BPST—A	British Peace Support Team—Africa
BRAIM	British Aid Mission (Vietnam)
BSOB	Building Stability Overseas Board
BSOS	Building Stability Overseas Strategy
CC	Chief Constable
CCSSP	Commonwealth and Community Safety and Security Program
CENTREX	Central Police Training and Development Authority
CIA	Central Intelligence Agency
CID	Criminal Investigation Department
CIVPOL	Civilian Police
CO	Colonial Office
COIN	Counter-Insurgency
CONOPS	Concept of Operations
CoP	College of Policing
CPA	Central Provisional Authority
CPAT	Civilian Police Advisory Team
CPT	Community Policing Team
CSDP	Common Security and Defence Policy (EU)
CSSF	Conflict Stability and Security Fund
CSTC	Combined Security Transition Command
CSTC—A	Combined Security Transition Command - Afghanistan

CSTCA—I	Combined Security Transition Command Afghanistan Intelligence
CT	Counter Terrorism
CTLO	Counter-Terrorism Liaison Officer
CVE	Countering Violent Extremism
DCC	Deputy Chief Constable
DCI	Detective Chief Inspector
DFID	Department for International Development
DI	Detective Inspector
ECRIS	European Criminal Records Information System
EDA	European Defence Agency
EEAS	European External Action Service
EGF	European Gendarmerie Force
ESRC	Economic Social Research Council
EU	European Union
EUBAM	European Union Integrated Border Management Assistance Mission Libya
EUCAP	European Union Capacity Building Mission in Mali
EUJUSTLEX	European Union Integrated Rule of Law Mission in Iraq
EULEX	European Union Rule of Law Mission in Kosovo
EUMM	European Union Monitoring Mission in Georgia
EUPCST	European Union Police and Civilian Services Training
EUROPOL	European Union Agency for Law Enforcement Cooperation
FBI	Federal Bureau Investigation
FCAS	Fragile and Conflict Affected States
FCDO	Foreign, Commonwealth and Development Office
FCO	Foreign and Commonwealth Office
FMI	Financial Management Initiative
FO	Foreign Office
FOI	Freedom of Information
FPU	Formed Police Units
GDP	Gross Domestic Product
GNI	Gross National Income
GNR	Garda Nacional Republicana (Portugal)
HEAT	Hostile Environment Awareness Training
HMG	Her Majesty's Government
HMIC	Her Majesty's Inspectorate of Constabulary
HO	Home Office
HQ	Headquarters
HR	Human Resources
HUMINT	Human Intelligence
IA	International Affairs
ICAI	Independent Commission for Aid Impact

ICC	International Coordination Committee
ICDT	International Cooperation and Development Team
ICoCA	International Code of Conduct Association
ICT	International Capabilities Team
IDP	Internally Displaced People
IFS	Institute for Fiscal Studies
IG	Inspector General
INGO	International Non-Governmental Organization
INL	International Narcotics Law Enforcement
INTERPOL	International Criminal Police Organization
IPAB	International Police Assistance Board
IPAG	International Police Assistance Group
IPAS	International Policing Assistance Strategy
IPCB	International Police Coordination Board
IPCC	International Crime Coordination Centre
IPRC	International Policing Response Cadre
IPS	Iraqi Police Service
IPSO	International Police Secondments Office
IPTF	International Police Task Force
IR	Integrated Review
ISAF	International Security Assistance Force (NATO)
ISRT	International Stabilization Response Team
ISSAT	International Security Sector Advisory Team
JFHQ	Joint Force Headquarters
JIPH	Joint International Policing Hub
KFOR	Kosovo Force (NATO)
LOFTA	Law and Order Trust Fund Afghanistan
MAGI—I	Ministerial Advisory Group—Interior (Afghanistan)
MDP	Ministry of Defence Police
MODPGA	Ministry of Defence Police and Guarding Agency
MENA	Middle East and North Africa
MINUSMA	United Nations Multidimensional Integrated Stabilization Mission in Mali
MMA	Monitoring Mentoring and Advising
MNDSE	Multi National Division South East (Iraq)
MNSTCI—I	Multi National Security Transitional Command Iraq—Intelligence
MOD	Ministry of Defence
MOI	Ministry of the Interior
MOU	Memorandum of Understanding
MPS	Metropolitan Police Service
MSU	Multinational Specialized Units
NATO	North Atlantic Treaty Organization

List of Abbreviations

NCA	National Crime Agency
NGO	Non-Governmental Organization
NI	Northern Ireland
NICO	Northern Ireland Co-operation Overseas
NOIP	Non-Operational Policing Assistance
NPCC	National Police Chiefs Council
NPIA	National Policing Improvement Agency
NPIAIA	National Policing Improvement Agency International Academy
NSC	National Security Council
NSS	National Security Strategy
NTC	National Transitional Council
NTMA	NATO Training Mission Afghanistan
ODA	Official Development Assistance
OECD	Organization for Economic Co-Operation and Development
ONUC	United Nations Operation in the Congo
OSCE	Organization for Security and Co-operation in Europe
OSCT	Office for Security and Counterterrorism
OSJA	Overseas Security and Justice Assistance
OT	Overseas Territory
PC	Police Constable
PCC	Police and Crime Commissioner
PJHQ	Permanent Joint Headquarters
PM	Prime Minister
PMC	Private Military Companies
PMSC	Private Military and Security Companies
POC	Protection of Civilians
PPA	People's Police Academy
PRT	Provincial Reconstruction Team
PSC	Private Security Companies
PSNI	Police Service of Northern Ireland
PSO	Peace Support Operations
PVE	Preventing Violent Extremism
RCMP	Royal Canadian Mounted Police
RIC	Royal Irish Constabulary
RSM	NATO Resolute Support Mission
RUC	Royal Ulster Constabulary
RUSI	Royal United Services Institute
SB	Special Branch
SCEG	Security in Complex Environment Group
SDSR	Strategic and Defence Security Review
SIA	Security Industry Authority
SIS	Schengen Information System

SLP	Sri Lanka Police
SMART	Support Monitoring Advising Report and Training
SME	Small Medium Enterprise
SOC	Serious and Organized Crime
SOCA	Serious Organised Crime Agency
SPA	Scottish Police Authority
SPU	Special Police Units
SSDAT	Security Sector Development Advisory Team
SSNPS	South Sudan National Police Service
SSR	Security Sector Reform
STARS	Science, Technology, Analysis, Research and Strategy
SU	Stabilisation Unit
SWAT	Special Weapons and Tactics Team
TCG	Tasking and Coordination Group
TNA	The National Archives
UAE	United Arab Emirates
UK	United Kingdom
UKOT	United Kingdom Overseas Territories
UN	United Nations
UNAMSIL	United Nations Mission in Sierra Leone
UNDP	United Nations Development Programme
UNDPKO	United Nations Department of Peacekeeping
UNFICYP	United Nations Peacekeeping Force in Cyprus
UNMIK	United Nations Interim Administration Mission in Kosovo
UNMISS	United Nations Mission in South Sudan
UNPOL	United Nations Policing
UNSCR	United Nations Security Council Resolution
UNSMIL	United Nations Support Mission to Libya
UNTAET	United Nations Transitional Administration in East Timor
US	United States
USA	United States of America
USAID	United States Agency for International Development
US DoD	United States Department of Defense
USMC	United States Marine Corps
WO	War Office

The Export of UK Policing

> The police force of Great Britain is a tremendous asset because we were the original democratic community-based policing. The Peelian principles of policing are so heavily enshrined and indoctrinated into our police force I think it is an asset. If you're to look across Team UK and think, 'What are we good at?' well, policing is definitely one of them and it is only, I feel, sensible to share that. It is a strength.
>
> Think about the policemen's helmet: it's not just symbolic, it is actually cherished by other nations. If you see one of these coming down the street it's only ever going to be a police officer underneath it and because of the 250 years of British policing you know you can trust the person who's underneath it. It is the physical reputation of the British policemen going down the street.
>
> **Former Chief Inspector,
> Sussex Police deployed to Afghanistan, 2011**

In 2010, I visited Hampshire Constabulary to 'interview' Detective Chief Superintendent Jason Hogg, one of many British police officers who have shared their international policing experiences with me over the past decade. Jason had deployed to Iraq in 2005 as part of a United Kingdom (UK) policing cohort in support of international stabilization and reconstruction efforts. By 2005, police drawn from across many UK police forces had been involved in post-conflict theatres including the Western Balkans, Timor Leste, and Afghanistan. Why did Jason volunteer for international policing? By that time, he had over ten years' service in the police and an experience of a wide variety of roles, but felt that 'one of the frustrations of policing' was how localized policing always seemed to be. Jason wanted the challenge and experience of a very different policing world, one that was not tailored to his current role as a criminal investigator. However, he admitted at the time that he was not really aware of what the 'job' entailed in Iraq, only that Hampshire had a tradition of sending officers overseas—the former Chief Constable Paul Kernaghan had been the international affairs portfolio holder—and that there was support and encouragement for those police who volunteered.

During the course of that day, Jason discussed his policing experiences in Iraq. He talked about the good, the bad, and the ugly of international policing! He was struck initially by the 'absolute chaos of the place' post-invasion which was unlike anything he had witnessed in the UK. Jason was sent to Basra to the British Consulate where he worked alongside UK police as well as other international police and military, private security companies, and international development contractors. While his selection had been partly on the basis of his skills and expertise as a criminal investigator, he was also expected to support broader police training and mentoring. All the work undertaken, he reflected was 'self-generated' and required a considerable amount of 'thinking on one's feet'. And then there were 'constantly hugely sensitive issues' to grapple with when working with the Iraqi security actors that hinged on issues relating to 'corruption, violence, linkages with local militias and terrorist organizations'. Notwithstanding the multiplicity of international military and policing providers supporting training and mentoring, 'almost like a conveyor belt of people ... dropping police officers and military into situations to do some work ... to do some good, almost in the belief that they are just doing some good by being there without there always being a real sense of what was needed'. Yet Jason returned to the UK, reinvigorated by the policing challenges he had faced and that the opportunity he had seized to 'do something differently policing-wise with a UK flag on my shoulder' had been a worthwhile 'career choice' and a 'sacrifice worth making' (Author interview with former Detective Chief Superintendent Jason Hogg, Hampshire Constabulary, August 2010).

In recent years, I have revisited international policing with some of those earlier police interviewees and asked them to reflect further on their international experiences. Had their views altered with hindsight? In December 2020, after almost a decade, I met with Jason Hogg for the second time to ask that question. Almost his very first reflection was that over the years he had often thought about his time in Iraq. It had left a mark on his twenty-five years of professional service as a UK police officer. Why?

That international experience had provided new and better professional and personal skills about the 'doing' of policing, had forged resilience, provided leadership skills, and a 'truer understanding of human engagement'. These issues had been instrumental in supporting his inner core belief in the 'good' of UK policing, a policing brand that Jason perceived as one that typically encompassed concepts of 'discretion, integrity, scrutiny in relation to uses of force and an upholding of the law without fear or favour'. When I asked about what he had taken forward in his policing career from that time in Iraq, Jason replied that international policing had allowed him to understand that policing was a vocation, that it had value and purpose as a 'mission through partnership with others' (Author interview with Deputy Chief Constable Jason Hogg, Thames Valley Police, 21 December 2020).

I have always been an avid collector of 'police stories' whether oral testimonials or written police memoirs. Since 2009, as my focus shifted from colonial policing towards contemporary international policing history, I began a collection of oral histories which set a course for an exploration of fundamental questions: How has UK policing internationalized? How did this internationalization develop and morph the UK policing brand over time? What is the nature of the UK policing brand? What has that international journey revealed about UK policing from the perspectives of practitioners who generate policing history *on the ground*? How do UK police 'police' at home and away? It is these broad perspectives and my analysis thereof that I hope to colour and bring to life within the chapters to come.

Ultimately, this book provides a broad-brush study of the export of UK policing and the ongoing development of the UK police brand that occurred post-1989; the 'biggest year in history since 1945' that brought the cold war and the short twentieth century to an end. 1989 saw the demise of communism in Europe, the unification of East and West Germany, the emergence of the European Union, the enlargement of NATO and several decades of United States (US) supremacy and globalization (Garton Ash, 2009). This chain of events heralded an era of interventions that are woven into the *story* of international UK policing and reflected within this book.

Charting this history highlights a number of important through lines in the development of a distinct UK police brand from the pre-1989 era to the present. First, that the internationalization of UK policing has been integral to its overall evolution across history. These processes of internationalization contributed to the emergence of a UK policing brand, one that is founded from two original concepts: civil and semi-military. And second, that the brand has retained quintessentially British characteristics that owes as much to the mystique surrounding UK policing in popular discourse as it does to reality on the ground.

As my earlier research has helped demonstrate, the pre-1989 history of UK policing can be seen as a multilayered, complex, and dynamic overlapping of styles and activities that circulated within the British Isles, across the empire and commonwealth and back home. Mike Brogden's earlier contributions to the history of an emerging UK police highlighted the importance of policing experiments that occurred within the British empire and how those experiences found their way back home (Brogden, 1987a, 1987b). This awareness became what Chris Williams and I termed 'two-way traffic': an outward and inward flow of policing personnel, skills, and knowledge (internationalization) which became integral to the historic journey of UK policing (Sinclair and Williams, 2007). From the early part of the nineteenth century, the choice lay within two broad models: the so-called civil (English) and the semi-military (Irish-colonial) (Sinclair, 2006, 2008, 2011b). These models sat on a continuum relating broadly to uses of force and engagement with the community: from the 'softer' policing by consent to the 'harder' policing by coercion. British policing, in its broadest sense, had similarities with the continental police forces in the nineteenth century which operated systems of semi-military (gendarmerie) and civilian police models (see Emsley, 1999). However, the UK has had a long (and for some contentious) history of exporting its policing models and styles within the international arena (Anderson and Killingray, 1991, 1992; Brogden, 1987a, 1987b; Ellison and O'Reilly, 2008a; Sinclair, 2006, 2008). UK police were involved in both *policing* overseas (the operational) as well as providing international policing in an advisory and assistance capacity (the non-operational) although with considerable interlinkage. A period of colonial rule, which saw the widespread creation of colonial police forces, decolonization, and the policing of the commonwealth implanted 'British' policing far and wide (Sinclair, 2006, 2011a). International policing assistance evolved after the Second World War as UK policing supported efforts to reform policing in post-war Germany and Italy. Thereafter UK police joined the United Nations (UN)-led early missions to Cyprus, the Congo, as well as a continuing outward flow of British police as advisers, liaison officers, and diplomats. As a UK policing influence spread globally, so an international reputation was forged.

This reputation has stood the test of time, and across this history certain 'myths' about and surrounding UK policing have taken root. Official rhetoric has reinforced the idea that UK policing (at home) has rested on nineteenth century Peelian principles of 'policing by consent' and that the 'police are the public and the public are the police'. Yet contrary to official rhetoric the 'UK Police PLC' *brand* has never been homogenous but in practice has been multifaceted and drawn from a range of policing histories and styles that evolved across the British Isles—from the early dichotomy, outlined above, between the English/civil and Irish/colonial models.

As this book will show, these core themes—a vivid and long-lived international history and an enduring mythology surrounding the UK policing brand—have ensured its resilience and continue to colour and shape its adaptation since the end of the Cold War. The interventions that occurred from the early 1990s in the Western Balkans following the collapse of the Soviet Union saw a goldrush of international peacekeeping policing. During the subsequent era of interventions, the UK joined other Western nations as they rushed to provide 'expeditionary' policing (Stoker and Westermann, 2018). Support within fragile and conflict affected states (FCAS) greatly increased post-9/11 in support of international military and other civilian actors. International policing, throughout this contemporary period, gained in importance as both an activity and a form of assistance within the wider security and development spaces. Across a wide range of contexts— geographical, political, economic, social—UK police have continued their tradition of international policing, adapted to a twenty-first century context. As we shall see, the earlier reality of a multifaceted brand has recreated itself as well, encapsulated by the modern divergences between Northern Ireland's PSNI, Scotland's Police Scotland, the forty-three constabularies within England and Wales as well as a cluster of niche police including the Ministry of Defence Police (MDP) and the British Transport Police.

What has helped UK police succeed internationally when it did and if at all? How has the brand adapted to the new post-Cold War era of interventions and invasions? And what challenges lie ahead for the UK policing brand as we move into a new era of a post-Brexit Global Britain? It is questions such as these that the book sheds light on, from the perspective of those police practitioners who have helped to build, reshape, and create the UK policing 'brands' over time.

Theoretical underpinnings

This book aims to place the rich and varied viewpoints of UK police deployed overseas within a theoretical framework drawing on multidisciplinary perspectives to help support an understanding of UK police brand development. Although ultimately a work of history, I draw on sociology, criminology, international relations, and development studies, as well as tapping into economics, marketing, and communications as part of a broader social science research approach.

Historical framework of analysis

I have delineated three discernible trends to describe why and how the UK policing brand developed in the way that it did and how that development was managed. First and foremost, and as already discussed above, the development of UK policing through the nineteenth and twentieth centuries included important processes of *internationalization* as a result of colonization, imperial rule, and subsequent decolonization. UK policing effectively globalized, and the history of how that globalization occurred matters to how the brand has recreated itself in the contemporary era.

This early history combines with two features of the contemporary era to shape post-1989 UK policing overseas and produce the current manifestation of the UK police brand. First, the huge growth in the international development sector since the 1990s as a result of US hegemony and a period of post-Cold War interventions. Development has since that time co-existed with international policing assistance. Over the past three decades, there has been a growth in Western support for aid and development assistance programmes under which sits broader police reform and security sector reform (SSR). UK policing was increasingly sought after by overseas governments and state institutions (including police) throughout this period. This occurred across official multilateral police missions and operations, including the European Union (EU), North Atlantic Treaty Organization (NATO), and United Nations (UN); international secondments from the UK government; bilateral requests for assistance and inclusion within dedicated UK (police) development programmes including police, security, and justice reform, and ad hoc arrangements between UK constabularies and overseas police. Secondly, the rise of neoliberalism, global insecurity and post-2008 austerity not only increased Western interventions and by extension, SSR, but created opportunities for a flourishing corporate sector and the rise in the privatization of security and policing. Overseas interventions, reconstruction, and development have generated a growth in international policing *services* by the private sector.

By weaving these three trends together—the UK's history of police internationalization, the rise and professionalization of the international development sector, and the privatization and commodification of policing—this book hopes to support our understanding of why the UK police brand has taken the form it does today.

Policing as brand management

In essence this book understands UK international policing and its growth as a form of 'brand management' whereby UK policing has been projected onto an international stage as part of a wider UK government strategy. International policing as part of the evolution and journey of the UK policing brand internationally sits at the core of this book: policing 'as [an] export business has a long history' (Brogden and Ellison, 2013: 85). Over time UK policing has acquired a veritable brand value as evidenced through the global commodification of its policing activities, and a revenue generated from commercial sponsorship and licensing, particularly within the domestic market. All the while, elements of both myth and reality surrounding the brand have persisted within official, police, and popular discourse. To capture key aspects of this multifaceted policing brand development, I have provided reflections throughout this book on how police personnel who formulate policy have understood the brand; how the brand has been delivered by those who do international policing, and how this might be articulated.

So how should we understand brand management as applied to policing? Public services (including policing) have typically become commodified and accredited with a brand value. Academic attention has only relatively recently focused on what is termed public sector branding; that is the application of corporate branding techniques to a public service (Temporal, 2004; Chapleo, 2010). This has aligned with the concept of 'geo-branding': 'the ways that in [an] era of globalization, modern states seek to enhance their image and reputation' (Ellison and O'Reilly, 2008a: 335). Until the late twentieth century branding was synonymous with advertising and was associated mainly with physical objects such as consumer goods (Aaker and Joachimsthaler, 1999). However, branding has become linked to efforts to create a particular identity and personality for a product, service, organization, or state (see Ellison and O'Reilly, 2008a, Keller, 1993). Developing a brand's image (or personality) can impact on how the consumer evaluates and buys into a product or service and, therefore, the consensus within the marketing literature is that brand value is a key asset within any organization (Aaker, 1991, 1996; Keller, 1993; Kapferer, 2004). Generating a brand value as a marketing concept has more recently led to an increase in the range of organizations and markets to which it can be applied, which has included, for example, the Metropolitan Police Service (MPS) (Smith, 2009). This transformation is reflected in, amongst others, a change in the law in the mid-1990s that permitted UK police forces to generate revenue from commercial sponsorship and licensing.

As an example, consider Scotland Yard's brand development, as a feature of the UK police brand. The MPS licensing of the New Scotland Yard brand to a number of commercial firms is an example of working with merchandizing licensing partners to raise funds in support of frontline policing, staff training and recruitment, and improving the image of the police (Brownsell, 2008). A licensing agreement with brand licensing company The Point.1888 ran until May 2021 potentially contributed to the shortfall in MPS revenue. New Scotland Yard branded as 'quintessentially British, [conjuring] up thoughts of mystery, excitement, strength, justice and determination' within its worldwide reputation (License Global, 2008), which has leveraged those Peelian qualities rooted in the nineteenth century.

UK policing more broadly has developed a brand image over time. The earlier Association of Chief Police Officers (ACPO) articles of association under the Companies Act (2009) permitted engagement in a range of commercial and promotional activities. As such the ACPO undertook corporate activities and its brand name was assumed to be recognized globally as a 'mark of excellence in policing' (ACPO ACPOS, 2012). ACPO was replaced by the National Police Chiefs Council (NPCC) in April 2015 and the ACPO-NPCC brand has continued development through the College of Policing's (CoP) International Faculty (previously the Police Staff College (Bramshill). It has acknowledged a key aspect of its work is to 'support the development of professional and accountable policing throughout the world by delivering effective learning and training assistance in the fields of operational policing and police leadership' (College of Policing, 2020). This has been observed through the College's revenue generating activities (and previously the National Policing Improvement Agency (NPIA) and international academy at Bramshill that Sir Ronnie Flannagan termed 'entrepreneurial policing' (Ellison and Sinclair, 2013) and has demonstrated that the brand has provided an important lens through which to view UK policing.

Arguably, the UK policing brand has been integral to *brand UK*, a sometime key contributing factor in what the UK can and does offer, or impose, internationally to meet national strategic, defence, development, and commercial interests. The recent political, economic, environmental, and social events since 2008 have, however, impacted UK international policing, as this book will demonstrate in later chapters, and have ramifications for its future direction of travel.

Reading policing and police history

Exploring the police and policing through historical and sociological research has flourished over the past fifty years and has 'developed into a thriving field that has expanded in multiple directions' (Johansen, 2017: 113). Yet as Mike Brogden and Graham Ellison (2013) highlighted, this has remained a 'debate without resolution' for there are limitations in the extent to which the theory and the practice can be observed and interpreted. Policing they argued, in the literature remained 'an oxymoron of a concept and confusing—mainly because few have ever grappled with what exactly is the police function. The term is open to many differing interpretations' (Brogden and Ellison, 2013: 15). This, as Anja Johansen reflected, may have left us in a position where we can never fully understand what constitutes a 'police organization' and what is 'policing', despite considerable research undertaken since the 1960s and the 'increasing diversity in police studies across time periods and geographical areas as well as disciplines involved …' (Johansen, 2017: 118). Research into the police and policing, as Otwin Marenin noted, requires a 'complex, multi-level, multi-disciplinary analysis of the conditions that have led to various conceptions and practices of policing, their institutions and symbolic representations and their societal consequences' (Marenin, 2005: 99). While being fully cognizant of these challenges, I aim through this book to make a contribution to this wider field of *police studies* using an historical lens to explore international policing.

The export of UK policing has been part of a lengthy historical process. An examination of nineteenth and twentieth century history has demonstrated the sharp contrasts between traditional (Whig) and revisionist interpretations; the former more often than not aligned with the views of the establishment and police institutions and the latter emerging from the critique of policing research scholars (Emsley, 1999). However, 'history' as Emsley (1999) reflected 'does not write itself. It depends on historians posing questions about the past, and seeking to answer these questions through the critical examination of those traces of the past left in the form of primary source material.... [and] the conclusions and assertions of other historians' (Emsley, 1999: 9–10). The difficulty in managing 'history' may be that its manifestations are always far wider than a single historian can realistically consider. To study the police and policing has always presented the historian with an array of choices that draw on differing theoretical and methodological traditions which require a different level of support and interpretation' (Greene, 2014: 196), and which may feed off and into other academic disciplines. For the historian, the appeal of policing may lie not only in the interpretation of these differences, but also in applying different historical interpretations (for example Whig, revisionist, popular) in describing policing activities that correlate to a particular method across historical time and place. This can also be true of the 'uses' of history by the members of the establishment and police where revisionists earlier poured scorn. However, as this book will show, a myth for one can be the reality for another and therefore not necessarily a falsehood aside from whether it is empirically true *or not*. In essence, the study of police and police work has always been presented as a complex, contradictory, and confusing set of concepts (Reiner, 2010), which no doubt is part of the attraction to the historian. Policing both appeals and challenges in equal measure, as the historian cuts through swathes of theory and evidence, disentangling 'police' (the institution) from 'policing' (police work) (Sinclair, 2016c). Yet, as I have sought to distil mountains of oral testimonials to glean history, I see how those histories can indeed 'arguably [be] the best method of enlarging an experience' (Gaddis, 2002: 9), and particularly from the perspective of a police historian.

Any professional group (including the police) will build a shared identity; a common ethos that emerges from any number of professional, social, and cultural experiences that have occurred over time as that organization developed a corporate memory. While to outsiders that group's interpretation of particular events may be perceived as inaccurate and wholly subjective, they are retained by that institution as a common experience of the past: a *history* (Tosh, 2010: 1). Police history (as interpreted by members of the government and police) has endured as one possible 'history' available to scrutinize and one that has allowed for their *better* history to be used time and time again. At a local, national, and even at an international level, the UK police have interpreted, created, and (re)created their history, drawing on traditions, experience, and culture to appeal to a wider audience. I suggest that the Whig/traditional interpretation of history has been a useful tool for the UK police to project a particular vision of policing across their historical landscape; to continually enhance their legitimacy; and, to maintain common ground with a general public where these values can be shared and their role legitimized (Mawby, 2002). The institution that is the police has continued to recognize that 'Peelian principles' have remained embedded within English policing folklore and latterly discussed as a 'key reference point for thinking about the fundamentals of modern British policing' and how this has been communicated (Report of the Independent Police Commission, 2013: 29). While future police reform will bring shifts to these earlier Whiggish interpretations (see Loader, 2020), for the here and now these values remain embedded within a British police philosophy and culture, have served as a barometer of their institutional past and present and, may serve as a guide for future activities. The UK police voice, however, has always offered I believe an *insider* view of policing and the characteristics that have shaped the UK policing brand.

Police voices

> I think the UK police service does have a good reputation.... [it] seems to be held in quite high regard and I think the integrity and the reputation of the UK police service goes across the world. People talk about Scotland Yard because everybody tunes into Scotland Yard, but it's much broader than that. It's the UK police service PLC ... (Former Chief Superintendent, West Sussex Police, 2017).

I have collected oral testimonies and observed UK police in an overseas capacity since 2010. Raw *oral history* has provided unique insights and in so many ways has allowed me to make some sense of an active relationship between the past and the present, between individual memory and public traditions, and perhaps between historical myth and reality. The practitioner 'voice' has been key in supporting the historical trends that frame international policing. For 'the discrepancy between fact and memory ultimately enhances the value of the oral sources as historical documents. It is not caused by faulty recollections ... but actively and creatively generated by memory and imagination in an effort to make sense of crucial events and of history in general' (Portelli, 1991: 26 quoted in Tosh, 2010: 202). In the course of my 'open' discussions with police practitioners, many issues were repeatedly raised without any prompting and included: Why volunteer for an overseas deployment? What happens 'on the ground' during a mission? How are UK policing skills used if at all? Which policing knowledges transfer well and which do not? How do police adapt (if at all) to high-risk environments? How do they learn (if at all) cultural awareness and sensitivity? How do UK police interact with other international policing and local police? What new learning do they bring home (if at all)? What does it tell us about policing 'the other' (not the West but the 'rest' (Johansen, 2017)? And what has it revealed about their perceptions of UK policing on the international stage and back home?

In writing this book, I have revisited 175 *primary* and *secondary* interviews, some amounting to over 20,000 words. This collection of oral histories has been drawn primarily from the 'traditional' constabularies (England, Wales, Scotland, and Northern Ireland), as well as the 'niche' police, in particular the MDP and a very small number of British Transport Police and Services Police. These interviews have included practitioners of all ranks from constable to chief constable. By primary interviews, I am referring to those that were transcribed and conducted as a formal 'interview'.[1] I have adopted what might be termed a policy ethnography to survey UK international policing in terms of a 'top down' and 'bottom up' perspective: That is, from the perspective of senior officers who devise policy and strategy, as well as from the perspective of rank-and-file officers or private security operatives who were tasked with operationalizing such strategies on the ground. Not only have there been interviews but also discussions and encounters with UK police over time, which have been enhanced through more recent professional activities and overseas field trips. Overall, I have had access over the past decade to many UK police personnel (and others) who have engaged in overseas missions and/or who have been instrumental in the promotion of the UK policing brand.

Each and every practitioner provided snap shots of their international policing experiences (and often in considerable detail) which were more

---

[1] The data has been drawn from a number of research projects (since 2011) that have surveyed the landscape of UK international policing (e.g. Emsley and Sinclair (2011). Author interviews with serving and retired UK police officers, government officials and private security contractors were undertaken between 2009 and 2014. In the author's current professional role, since leaving full-time academic employment in 2014, data collection has not ceased.

than often of the 'warts and all' variety. This was often on the proviso that their anonymity was preserved; many are still serving police officers; others have moved into the corporate world and some work in highly securitized environments. On the basis that it would be difficult to disentangle those who had request anonymity from those who had not, I have, in the main, given only basic details of rank, UK police force, and overseas mission. However, I should add that my database of material generated (respondents also provided primary and secondary source material) has filled several shelves and would require multiple volumes! Inevitably I have had to be highly selective in order to compress the material that I had and to feed this into the case study chapters, which comes back to the challenges facing the historian. This has forced difficult choices and greater dissection than I would have liked, but I have attempted through this process to provide a balanced and enlightened understanding of the delivery and *doing of international policing* and what it can reveal about the UK policing brand. Additionally, the many interdisciplinary exchanges with scholars and practitioners working in neighbouring fields of 'international relations' and 'development' have supported a broadening of these historical perspectives and encouraged the view of policing through different social, political, and cultural lens. This has supported a 'multifaceted, subtle analysis of the dynamics, power relations, boundaries, practices and motivations that shape both in the internal functioning police forces, but also the engagement between police and wider society' (Johanssen, 2017: 117).

A note on sweeping generalizations: models and typologies

At this juncture, I would like to highlight the reasons for my use of what appears to be 'sweeping generalizations' relating to the use of 'model' in this book. The term 'model' has always presented challenges in its use for researchers and police alike. Robert Reiner noted this stark ambiguity and posited: 'is it intended as a neutral analytic word referring to a fundamental structure, a blueprint; or normatively, pointing to an ideal which should be emulated?'. Yet it may have utility as an analytical device with which to identify policing's essential characteristics (Reiner, 1995: 16). I concur. Policing 'models' are both a methodological tool and a prism through which the observer can observe the essential characteristics at a particular moment *in time* or *across time*. Emsley (2014) reflected:

My own position is that types and models are tools for exploring the past, not things for the historian to pursue slavishly, and not something into which past institutions should be forced and hence distorted. But for the historian models and types should never be more than a starting point, a means of establishing frameworks that can be used to explore similarities and differences, and how different regional, national, imperial circumstances and structures inter-acted with other elements to produce variations in forms and practices. If historians ignore broad types, they are restricting their vision, and too much history fails to look beyond national confines (Emsley, 2014: 22).

I consider policing models as a necessary starting point to discuss the evolution of the UK brand from the nineteenth century through its international journey (Emsley, 2009; 2011, 2012; Sinclair, 2006, 2008, 2011b, 2012). Furthermore, the distinction that I have employed between the English and Irish models has been accepted by historians of colonial and commonwealth policing to explore the outward trajectory of UK policing (see, in particular, Anderson and Killingray, Brogden, 1987a, 1987b; Emsley, 2014; Fedorowich, 1996; Sinclair and Williams, 2007). Policing typologies have also proved useful when considering the development of nineteenth century policing and the circulation of policing styles across empire and commonwealth. Emsley's original typology of nineteenth-century police has served to identify historic patterns and changes and to support national and regional differentiation while keeping the historical focus on one country (Emsley, 2014). This simple typology (Emsley, 1999, 2014) was divided into three: state military, state civilian, and state municipal, and has retained resonance in the contemporary period (Emsley, 1999, 2014).

When considering the emergence of models and typologies of policing that emanated across the 'British Isles', it appears that the use of the term 'British' is sometimes interchangeable with 'English'. This was particularly apparent when referring to the advent of the so-called 'New Police' in direct contrast with the adjectives 'Irish', 'Scottish', and 'Welsh'. While Britain (or its adjective British) is the official short form of 'United Kingdom of Great Britain and Northern Ireland', (UK), I found interchangeable use of UK policing and British policing from the late twentieth century. 'British' can refer to a blend of national and regional identities that existed above all others (Colley, 1992). Yet while 'British' may be referring to the *UK* national government and its institutions, there has never been a national British *police* institution which is a complicating factor (Emsley, 2009). Charles Reith, the architect of Whig policing history referred to the 'British' Police in his 1938 and 1943 works though made no direct reference to either Northern Ireland or Scotland. While England and Wales still retain forty-three constabularies, both Northern Ireland and Scotland now have a 'national' police force. In Scotland, for example, the idea of one national force was discussed from the 1850s with rising concerns of civil unrest and disorder, although 'it remained an anathema' and 'ahistorical to assume that a single police service in Scotland was inevitable (see Chapter 7) and the creation of a single service 'Police Scotland' came only on 1 April 2013 (Davidson, Jackson, and Smale, 2016: 88).

I have used both 'British' and 'UK' to pick up on specific references made within official or police discourse and documentation. The early historiography, in particular, introduced a fluidity in the language used to describe the UK's four geographical pillars. Each have contributed, to a greater or lesser extent, to the emergence of a multifaceted UK policing brand. Certainly, the emergence of a single police force in Northern Ireland (from 1921) and Scotland (from 2013) has further generated *their* policing brand; characteristics that are either unique or integral to the wider UK policing brand. There has been recognition that national identifies (including Britishness) can be 'constructed and reconstructed' within an historical context (Ward, 2004). With the UK's departure from the European Union (EU), rising nationalism within the four-nation state, further localization and fracturing of policing may impact upon the use of the terms UK/British which have their foundation in nineteenth century policing.

Book structure

Chapter 1

This chapter begins by introducing the reader to the character of 'international policing' as part of a larger process of development, under which sits police reform and SSR. It sets out the historical and theoretical backcloth to the book in order to explain and problematize the dynamics of the international policing agenda. It provides further detail to the historical trendlines mentioned above: pre-1989 police history, international aid and development, and the commercialization of policing.

Chapter 2

This chapter explores the myths and realities of the UK policing brand through an historical lens across the nineteenth and twentieth centuries. In spite of its manifest contradictions, the 'official' rhetoric of the brand has continued to be discursively framed within a specifically 'English' notion of policing with historical links to its pseudo-Peelian origins. The paradox, however, is that while the official rhetoric of the 'brand' may be constructed from the strands of a somewhat reified 'English' model of policing, in practice it owes just as much to the *other* UK policing tradition—a model that developed in Ireland and circulated across the British Isles, empire, and commonwealth. Over time both models cross-fertilized, internationalized, and have become part of the UK policing offer post-1989.

Chapter 3

The 1990s ushered in a new period of peacekeeping policing. This chapter explores the rise of international policing through case study examples drawn from the Western Balkans and East Timor. The deployment of RUC–PSNI and MDP police cohorts demonstrated the need for securitized approaches; the Northern Irish elements of the UK policing brand were of greatest value as well as requests for civil/English approaches to bilateral police reform and state-building programmes in Sierra Leone. This demonstrated the historical continuity of a pick-and-mix approach within the UK policing brand.

Chapter 4

This trend continued with the continuing rise of international policing assistance during the Western-led interventions in Afghanistan, Iraq, and Libya. No one particular aspect of the brand was exported over another, although RUC–PSNI and MDP were sought after for their earlier experiences of hostile environment policing and civil-military co-operation. International policing led to a growth in commercial opportunities for police retirees and particularly former RUC–PSNI.

Chapter 5

An additional historical trend occurred at this time with the emergence of a large private/corporate security sector, encroaching upon UK serving personnel in several conflict arenas (Afghanistan, Iraq). This chapter discusses 'entrepreneurial policing' whereby former police moved seamlessly from the state to the corporate policing world to promote particular dimensions or aspects of the British 'brand' within global markets, which would become *the* major conduit by which UK policing was exported. Through the case studies of Iraq, Afghanistan, and the United Arab Emirates (UAE), I consider the impact of the privatization of security and policing upon international policing.

Chapter 6

Since 2010 there has been a UK police-led drive to further professionalize international policing through the standardization of policy and attempts to develop a government-owned international policing strategy. International policing (UK) has undergone a rebranding exercise first with the creation of the Association of Chief Police Officers International Affairs (ACPO IA) and then in 2017, the advent of the Joint International Policing Hub (JIPH). This chapter outlines the challenges faced in promoting cohesion within government and across UK policing to halt fragmentation within the delivery of international policing.

Chapter 7

The challenges in promoting international policing as a whole-of-UK policing are considered in this chapter through the entrepreneurial activities of PSNI (since 2000) and Police Scotland (since 2013) and the development of their own policing brands. The drive towards the devolution of political power encouraged the provision of policing services as a commodity at home and overseas. Both Scotland and Northern Ireland have developed an international policing agenda which has (re)shaped the UK policing brand.

Chapter 8

This chapter turns to the future of international policing and assesses the challenges faced by UK policing, nationally and internationally, following the UK's departure from the EU, a period of continuing austerity and rising public security threats and a global health crisis. These factors will have implications for the UK's development agenda in the future as well as the UK's re-pivoting within its foreign, security (including policing), defence, and development agendas. International policing assistance through the state sector will remain limited for the foreseeable future within multilateral missions, although greater integration with defence engagement may bring opportunities and newer forms of blended state-corporate assistance. UK police retirees and the corporate sector will continue to provide the bulk of international policing and as such may become the main guardians of the *UK policing brand*.

Conclusion

This book seeks to locate the UK police brand historically, conceptually, and through case studies by drawing upon wide-ranging interviews and documentation to discuss the delivery of policing in the international arena. It charts the myriad ways in which UK policing has been promoted and projected internationally across a diverse range of security contexts from the 1990s to the present (2021). The emphasis has been on the *doing* of international policing; what individual police practitioners, policy makers, and government officials aim to achieve in a range of scenarios, and how these are often justified and legitimated by way of reference to assumed cultural and symbolic understandings of British/UK police histories. Equally, however, it is argued that international policing is a prism which permits reflection on a number of core themes that have emerged in policing studies in recent years, with the expansion of the private/corporate security sector in the international arena as a pertinent case in point.

1
Conceptualizing the International Policing Agenda

> International policing is a means by which the UK can project global influence ... be that working with international law enforcement bodies, building capacity, or delivering training to share UK policing skills and expertise. Engagement at all levels demonstrates the UK as a dependable partner, and allows us to build linkages with key organisations and overseas states to better tackle issues of mutual concern. We use the UK police brand to export our policing expertise.
>
> **Former Chief Constable and NPCC Lead for International Policing, 2017**

This chapter sets out an historic framework to understand *the what of* international policing; the types of activities that it has provided, and how this has been investigated within the Western literature and from the perspective of the 'practitioner'.[1] The terminology and the concepts that have encapsulated international policing more broadly have often been contested or used interchangeably by theorists (academics) and police practitioners which I now explore.

What is *international policing*? From a UK practitioner perspective, this has remained an umbrella term that encompasses *international policing assistance, international policing activities,* and *international police co-operation*. However, theoretically a distinction is made between *policing*

---

[1] By practitioner I refer to those police personnel, security, non-security, and government actors who develop and formulate policy and strategy and engage with the broader activities of international policing.

internationally and *international policing*. Policing internationally typically refers to the *operational* within all UK operations and investigations and described as 'travel abroad in pursuit of an operational <u>need arising within the UK</u> [sic] (Home Office (HO), 2004: 18), or where there is a specific request from an overseas territory for operational assistance. Policing internationally is more generally referred to as *operational police assistance* and has included judicial and extradition co-operation and the sharing and provision of case-specific intelligence and information. The officially agreed use of definitions within the practitioner space has remained problematic and subjected to change as UK policy shifts in line within international and previously EU frameworks and processes. It is now widely accepted that the UK should not diverge too far from the definitions proposed by international institutions including the UN (Joint International Policing Hub (JIPH), 2020).

Overall, international policing has remained primarily although not exclusively *non-operational*, and has often been referred to international policing *assistance*: indicating that there is a distinct provider and receiver in an (unequal) international exchange of policing related to services or goods (for example, equipment or infrastructure) (ACPO Association of Chief Police Officers Scotland (ACPOS), 2010, 2011, 2012). Typically, although not exclusively, this is associated with development activities that has included components of capacity building: scoping visits, training, monitoring and evaluation, mentoring and advising, crisis response, bilateral programmes, training exercises, and the 'sharing of best practice and the building of relationships which improve operational capability both at home and abroad' (HO, 2012: 2). Occasionally this may spill into or include operational tasks that are not part of UK operations (i.e. support/replacement policing, joint patrol, and investigative support) for example to the UK Overseas Territories (UKOTs) and in support of UK national security interests. From a terminology perspective there have been recent references in the policy documentation to 'non-operational international policing assistance' (NOIP), which has confused matters somewhat as many practitioners have expressed a view that there is a linkage between the operational and the non-operational within an international environment (Author interviews with UK police who have deployed internationally, 2010–2020).

International policing assistance, however, does not include UK police participation in missions led by international institutions including European Union Agency for Law Enforcement Cooperation (Europol) or Interpol. While there is deemed to be mutual policing assistance, this occurs within an institutional framework and is referred to as international policing co-operation (JIPH, 2020). A former ACPO lead for international policing (2008) defined international policing co-operation as 'activities and structures designed to assist the police forces and agencies of different states to tackle criminality that crosses international borders more effectively'. Such co-operation can also assist police professional development in the participating states (Paul Kernaghan, 2008: 150). Professional development, exchange of good practice, and lessons learning within this context can also be referred to as international police co-operation and, may include support to peace operations, security, and justice assistance and 'help[ing] fragile countries to access the best of British policing expertise' (Marsh, 2017: 1).

More specifically, the MDP employed the term 'support to international policing' when referring to international 'tasks' including: monitoring, mentoring, and advising; community and marine policing; humanitarian and compliance training; training for specialist operational support; support to UK military; executive policing; training for infrastructure development; community policing and policing in support of UN/EU missions (MOD, 2012). The Stabilisation Unit (SU) when referring to the international policing (services) it provided distinguished between police (civil institution of a state responsible for the protection of life and property, prevention and detection of crime, and the preservation of order); policing (the activities carried out by policing actors), and policing actors (referring to the range of security actors providing policing within an overseas environment (SU, 2014). Overall, the 'practitioner' discourse on international policing has been theoretically discussed in ways that are not generally reflective of *operational policing* but of *non-operational* policing as demonstrated through the volume of 'guidance manuals', 'toolkits', and 'field manuals' currently available. Within these (see, for example, FCO, 2007a, FCO, 2007b; HO, 2004, HO, 2012) there have been references to activities that have included:

- Assistance to Peace Support Operations (PSO) including: conflict prevention, post-conflict stabilisation and recovery, peace enforcement and peace keeping, and medium to longer-term training, reform and development;
- Assistance to Security and Justice Sector including: training, reform and development activities, supporting overseas state police agencies and government authorities;

- Assistance to other Countries including: training, operational development and advisory support/development; investigative assistance in response to requests from foreign governments/police; building institutional capability and capacity in response to requests from foreign governments/police;
- Assistance to the Department for International Development (DfID) including: covering assistance under contract to DfID;
- International engagement to share good practice, develop doctrine and support and develop networking assistance to UK police forces and agencies;
- Police Advisers including: long term, embedded and short-term advisors (serving and retired officers) to support capacity building, diplomatic engagement, strategic advice within bilateral and multi-lateral missions and,
- Other Overseas Police visits including: official visits encompassing research and/or scoping visits; personal visits to visit, undertake academic research, lecture etc.

Investigating the Western research literature

The Western research literature has directly referenced three strands: *transnational*, *global*, and *international*, which can include the framing of subsets of policing styles or activities that have included, for example, 'democratic policing', 'peacekeeping policing', and 'stability policing'. Overall, the literature has been slower to emerge than the material developed by UK government and police agencies, and has manifested a greater degree of slippage and blurring across the three key concepts. Yet this has provided a prism through which an analysis or critique of *international policing* can be explored from abstract concepts to 'on the ground' scenarios.

Published material (including the research-led variety) has mushroomed particularly relating to SSR, police reform, conflict management, and peace building. Documentation has originated from either non-government directed and publicly available research on particular issues published by academics, research and policy think tanks, and police practitioners, or from commissioned works including monitoring and evaluation reports, strategic reviews, policy development papers, and guidance doctrine relating to the application and implementation of police reform (Peake and Marenin, 2008). This has been referred to as a global community of practice encompassing the full range of security and non-security actors across the public-private sectors (Marenin, 2005). It has engendered interest across the disciplines including police studies, police history, criminology, sociology, international relations, security, and development studies which has always had the potential for a book in its own right let alone one solitary chapter!

Transnational policing

The starting point, however, when considering international policing within the extant literature has been *transnational* policing, which has related to any form of policework that crosses national boundaries (see, for example, Bowling, 2009; Goldsmith and Dinnen, 2007; Marenin, 2005; Sheptycki, 1998, 2000, 2002, 2010). In some respects, the study of transnational policing had an earlier genesis than international policing (see in particular Sheptycki, 1995—but in this case with greater theoretical rather than practical orientation). A number of earlier transnational policing texts concentrated on the organizational structures of those policing institutions and histories of *international police cooperation* as well as crime-control across national borders (e.g. Andreas and Nadelman, 2006) and, the specific problems this posed for national police organizations in an increasingly globalized environment where transnational crime was often linked to cross-border cooperation (e.g. Deflem, 2004; Koenig and Das, 2001). James Sheptycki (2010) outlined the complex nature of transnational policing and how it shifted beyond national boundaries (true of international policing) in that 'police cooperation takes place on different levels and in divergent forms, and partly because it has developed in an informal atmosphere, outside formal policing and legal frameworks' (Sheptycki, 2010: 39). Within a specifically European context this was also demonstrated within studies that focused on European police co-operation (e.g. Brown, 2010; Verhage et al., 2010), and, attempts to promote transnational policing through the activities of Europol following the watershed events of 11 September 2001.

In the US, Nadelman (1993) has been concerned with many of the same issues, albeit in the US context, but somewhat confusingly refers to these processes through the rubric of internationalization. Furthermore, Nadelman (1993) argued that internationalization is in practice indicative of Americanization whereby foreign governments are encouraged to accommodate forms of US criminal justice within a transnational space. In a later publication, Andreas and Nadelman (2006) focused on the 'growth of international crime control' (2006: 3), but again the thrust of the argument was heavily oriented towards US developments. Nevertheless, whatever the terminology adopted, an emphasis on police co-cooperation across national borders, and the practical problems thrown up by such cooperation (organizational accountability, jurisdictional authority, and international criminal law) dominated much of the early literature in this area.

Global policing

More recently, the term 'global policing' has been advanced in preference to transnational policing (see in particular Bowling, 2009; Bowling and Sheptycki, 2012) with Ben Bowling and James Sheptycki (2012) positing the need for 'an integrative inter-disciplinary theory of global policing'. A distinction they argued was needed for 'in recent times co-operation and collaboration have become increasingly ambitious to the extent that some forms of policing now claim a global reach' (Bowling and Sheptycki, 2012: 3). The 'great globalization debate' (Held and McGrew, 2007: 1–50) outlined the need to think much more broadly about the impact of globalization on policing practices. Global policing was defined as 'policing entities that have a global reach' (2012: 25) with 'the capacity to use coercive and surveillant powers around the world in ways that pass right through national boundaries unaffected by them' (Bowling and Sheptycki, 2012: 25, 8). Bowling and Sheptycki (2012) developed a useful typology to frame this wider global 'strategic effort' which they termed: (1) global; (2) regional; (3) national; (4) glocal. These definitions drew on an earlier thesis of the 'contemporary global system' (Mann, 1997) that considered five 'ideal-typical, socio-spacial networks of interactions' (Bowling and Sheptycki, 2012: 24–5). These were: (1) local; (2) national; (3) inter-national; (4) trans-national ('passing right through national boundaries'), and (5) global (covering ' "most" of the world' (Mann, 1997: 475)). Over time this has contributed to the notion of a global policing architecture including Interpol and on occasions the UN Police Division as well as EU organizations: that have included Europol and the European Border and Coast Guard Agency (Frontex).

However, global policing as part of a wider contemporary policing terrain is Western-centric and skewed rather more to US rather than European developments. Contemporary policing, argued Jan Hönke and

Markus-Michael Müller (2016) not only has a global *reach* [sic] it is globally *made* [sic]:

> The 'global making of policing' is the circulation of both policing techniques and practices, which together lend to the global (re)making of policing within the international realm ... [they] are more complex than usually depicted. Policing models and practices are not simply globalized, as is often assumed, through diffusion from a supposed (liberal) centre to seemingly marginal spaces, in which they get translated at best. Instead, core global and domestic police institutions and practices are co-constituted by various actors and experiences from across the globe. Seemingly marginal places in our postcolonial world have played a crucial role in these processes ... the often hidden presence of the margins—as an idea, encounter and agent—in making policing a global reality (Hönke and Müller, 2016: 1–8).

In extending Bowling and Sheptycki's original thesis, Hönke and Müller suggested pushing research towards non-Eurocentric security studies (see, for example, Barkawi and Laffey, 2006; Hönke and Müller, 2012). The realities of that global policing exchange from the perspective of the practitioner have extended beyond a global North/South to include South/South, South/North policing encounters (Sinclair, 2016a). Increasingly within the literature there has been reference to how global policing today is emerging as much from Western as from the wider global south, which may account for the hybrid policing practices that occur within international missions (Hönke and Müller, 2016: 2).

From a UK perspective, references to global policing have complicated rather than simplified government and police practitioner terminology, where there has been a demand for clear references to *international* policing (assistance) or policing *internationally* for UK operational requirements (HO, 2012). Practitioners do not necessary perceive the latter as necessarily 'transnational' (although it can be international police co-operation), and many have perceived this as an extension of domestic policing in an international environment.[2] Terms that emerged within the scholarly literature such as 'glocal' policing (1998) with inference that globalization processes for policing created flexibility between the local and the global (Bowling

---

[2] These comments have been made during the course of author interviews undertaken with UK police 2010–2020.

and Sheptycki, 2012) have not appeared within the practitioner or policy literature. Hence more broadly international policing has been seen by practitioners as an historical characteristic of UK policing as well as an activity embedded within police reform and SSR.

Security sector reform

It has generally been accepted that SSR means transforming a security sector system, which includes all the actors, their roles, responsibilities, and actions, to enable collaborative working in order to manage and operate the security system in a manner that is more consistent with democratic norms and sound principles of good governance (see OECD DAC, 2007). Until relatively recently there were few academic critiques (although see in particular, Bowling and Sheptycki, 2012; Brogden and Nijhar, 2005; Duffield, 2007; Ellison and Pino, 2012). Graham Ellison's and Nathan Pino's survey of policing and overseas development assistance concluded that the practitioner literature lacked a 'solid theoretical and methodological backcloth'. Few studies they noted provided a sufficiently 'holistic and conceptually grounded analysis of police reform endeavors' to provide an objective judgement of either success or failure, and perhaps practitioners should become more 'reflexive' about their impact upon beneficiaries (Ellison and Pino, 2012: 1–3).

Aside from these scholarly perspectives, there has been an international drive to improve aid effectiveness through adequate monitoring and evaluation. The Paris Declaration (2005) provided a practical roadmap to bring about an improvement in the quality of aid delivered and its impact upon development, by ensuring that donors and recipients held each other to account. The subsequent 2008 Accra Agenda for Action reaffirmed the earlier commitments to the Paris Declaration and proposed further areas for improvement, which was followed in 2011 by the Busan Partnership Declaration outlining a set of common principles for development, and subsequently adopted by many governments and international organizations. The UK government, more recently, mandated that all overseas aid and development programmes required regular internal and external reviews (see Independent Commission for Aid Impact (ICAI), 2015, 2018). As an aside, many Western states that contribute to peacekeeping and broader capacity-building missions have invested in dedicated pre-deployment training programmes with accompanying training manuals (see in particular guidance material from the Folke Bernadotte Academy (Sweden); Osland, 2017). The increasing complexity, range, and multidimensional nature of police mandates within SSR, stabilization and crisis missions has moved the focus from monitoring to mentoring, training, and capacity building, requiring 'high quality experts and senior leaders' (van der Laan et al., 2016: 1). Moreover, the expertise required internationally has broadened out to encompass human rights, gender and diversity issues (e.g. SU, 2014, 2019), as well as preventing violent extremism (PVE), counter violent extremism (CVE), and a greater emphasis on counterterrorism (e.g. Betancourt et al., 2019).

The interventions and subsequent withdrawals in Iraq and Afghanistan brought a flurry of publications within academic, government and media circles. While the focus has typically been on the military approaches undertaken by the US and UK in particular (see, for example, Akam, 2021; Barry, 2020; Friesendorf, 2018; Johnson and Clack, 2015; Fairweather, 2014), some academic works have considered the range of effort by Western police actors (e.g. Ashraf, 2007; Friesendorf, 2012, 2018; Sinclair, 2015, 2016a, 2016b, 2016c; Sinclair and Burdett, 2018) with some discussion of the division of labour between the military, gendarmerie, and civil police (Friesendorf, 2018; Sinclair, 2015; Thruelsen, 2010). The focus, however, has been on the 'West's' lack of strategic vision and effective planning, in both Iraq and Afghanistan, and the failure to exploit good practice and lessons learned from decades of Western-led police reform (see in relation to Iraq: Ashraf, 2007; Byman, 2008; Deflem and Sutphin, 2012 and Hoffman, 2006 and, Afghanistan: Friesendorf, 2011, 2018; Koski, 2009; Murray, 2007; Schmeidl and Karokheil, 2009; Schmidt, 2008; Skinner, 2008; Thruelsen, 2010; Wilder, 2007). The UK government faced criticism for a dearth of suitable security and policing strategies and planning in Iraq and Libya (see Report of the Iraq Inquiry (Chilcot), 2016; House of Commons Foreign Affairs Committee, 2016).

The SSR space has become increasingly complicated by the overwhelming number of donor participating countries (Brzoska and Law, 2006). SSR *outside* peacekeeping missions had an earlier tendency to be donor-driven and often rested on the advancement of specific SSR programmes as a precondition of wider aid and development assistance (Born, Caparini, and Fluri, 2002; Diamint, 2002; Ellison and Pino, 2012). This emphasized the degree to which the export of policing reflected the ultimate strategic interests for the donor state, whether in commercial terms or in relation to national security objectives (Bowling and Sheptycki, 2012; Brogden and Nijhar, 2005; Ellison and Pino, 2012; Hendrickson and Karkoszka, 2002; Hinton and Newburn, 2008; Huggins, 1998). Over time, however, there have been repeated calls for international donors to adopt a more holistic approach (Hendrickson 1999; Hendrickson and Karkoszka 2002) and, to address what Ellison and Pino (2012) described as 'geo-political hegemons [who] use economic, political, and security sector reforms to influence the behaviour of other states in the world system to influence events and assuage risks that they feel threatens their own security' (Ellison and Pino, 2012: 231–2). Some scholars have judged those policies imposed or transferred from the outside will rarely be implemented as intended and then often only on a superficial basis (see Brogden and Nihar, 2005; Duffield, 2007; Ellison and Pino, 2012). The SSR paradigm may only, therefore, provide broad-based principles by which international policing can contribute to 'reform' and 'development' for the theoretical aspiration behind SSR; for example, transforming a police force into a police service may not easily match the practical reality, despite attempts at locally-driven development programmes. Paradoxically, while much of the Western academic debate has focused on SSR and wider security concepts, governments globally have become increasingly concerned with issues relating to hard security resulting from the globalized nature of crime and conflict (Bowling and Sheptyicki, 2012; Integrated Review (IR), 2021). This has included issues relating to borders and migration, conflict and post-conflict human rights violations, criminal justice, gender and diversity issues, and uses of force (see, for example, Seely and Rogers, 2019).

Policing concepts within SSR: a mingling or a muddle?

Over the past three decades, theorists and practitioners have used a range of concepts to theorize and operationalize SSR, with democratic police reform, democratic policing, and community policing taking central stage. Democratic policing has been *the go-to* approach when applying *Western* democratic police reform in advanced and transitional democratic societies (Ellison and Pino, 2012: 9) but no consensus has been reached as to its meaning or to what it should look like in practice (Aitchison and Blaustein, 2013; Brogden and Nijhar, 2005; Ellison and Pino 2012; Manning 2010) despite considerable earlier theoretical discussions (see in particular: Bayley 1997, 2001, 2006; Diamond 1999; Fielding 1996, 2001; Marenin, 1998; Mastrofski and Lum, 2008; Reiner, 2000 and Shearing, 1997). The existence of democratic policing, as Peter Manning (2010) observed, has been retained by 'the bearers (North America, the UK, Australia, and New Zealand) of the Peel legacy—the notion of a visible, reactive, bureaucratically organized means of state-based resolution of conflict with minimum force' (2010: 3). With the dominance of Anglo-American models of policing within SSR it became a 'historically-legitimated model for export' (Brogden and Nihar, 2005: 3), the success of which has been questioned (see Brogden, 2005; Brogden and Nijhar, 2005; Pino and Wiatrowski, 2006; Ellison, 2007; Goldsmith and Sheptycki, 2007; Manning, 2010; Ellison and Pino, 2012). The policing reality in many post-conflict environments has been that this democratic policing experiment has largely failed where there has been neither a 'police nor democracy' (Manning, 2010: 9). This has been synonymous with the wider challenges of SSR and whether Western-operated policing principles, values, and activities can be translated into a set of policing characteristics within a democratic (and community policing) paradigm, where an emphasis has been placed on the concept of a 'service not a force', one that is accountable to the law and the citizen and remains 'people centred' (Mathias et al., 2006: 4).

Democratic policing (as part of democratic police reform) has remained a theoretical aspiration and became the foundation from which theoretically the necessary political and social conditions for *community policing* (or for some community-oriented policing) could be created (Brogden and Nihar, 2005: 233). While the international transfer of community policing has more often than not been discredited (see Brogden and Nihar, 2005; Ellison and Pino, 2012; Brogden and Ellison, 2013), the UK has been committed since the 1980s to the development of suitable community policing strategies including neighbourhood policing (local) and reassurance policing (countrywide) (Brogden and Ellison, 2013). As such policing programmes have cross-fertilized with other public services (including social services, education, housing, and health) in an attempt to promote community safety and security as well the principle of community engagement (Home Office, 2019).

Yet this theoretical mingling of democratic policing (within democratic police reform) and community policing has created something of a muddle for practitioners. Certainly, the operationalization of so-called democratic policing (through the development of policy focused on police reform) fermented some discussion amongst international practitioners in the 1990s although more recently the term been dropped in preference for community policing (Denney and Jenkins, 2013). That concept, however, has largely remained rather more of a 'headline terminology' encompassing a range of different community policing *approaches* that have included zero tolerance policing, intelligence-led policing, as well as a broader philosophy within an organization in preventing and managing crime (Denney and Jenkins, 2013: 5).

Faced with a plethora of concepts, the practitioner material has sought to standardize, operationalize, and emphasize the principles, lesson learning, and development of good practice in order to make sense of police and security sector reform and particularly democratic policing and community policing (e.g. OSCE, 2008: 7; SU, 2014). This has resulted in an ever-expanding range of guidance material and handbooks produced locally and by international institutions and even host-state governments and police. Community policing and engagement has become a euphemism over the past decade within Western police for a myriad of other concepts including *community* safety, community security, community resilience, policing vulnerable communities, policing displaced communities, policing and local ownership, and countering and preventing violent extremism (see, for example, DCAF-OSCE, 2009; Denney and Jenkins, 2013; FCO, 2007; Koncak (DCAF), 2018; OSCE, 2008, 2014; Rao, 2013; Saferworld, 2006; Service (Cognita), 2017; SU, 2014, 2019; van der Laan et al., 2016; Vernon, O'Callaghan, and Holloway, 2020). The concept of community engagement has been integral to multilateral policing assistance.

Multilateral policing assistance: peacekeeping and peace support operations

The study of international peacekeeping policing has increased with the proliferation of FCAS in recent years and has spanned the Anglo-American literature (see, for example, Grabosky, 2009; Levine, 2014; Perito, 2010). Peacekeeping's genesis came in 1948 when a team of observers was deployed during the Arab-Israeli War. Later, in 1960, the UK supported the UN Operation in the Congo (ONUC) and following the withdrawal of Ghanaian Police, a Nigerian police unit including British colonial police officers was deployed (Sinclair, 2006). Officially 'UN Civilian Police' or CIVPOL emerged from the 1964 UN Peacekeeping Force in Cyprus (UNFICYP) to differentiate 'civilian' from 'military police' (Bayley, 2006; Greener, 2009; Perito, 2010). According to UN doctrine, peacekeeping is a mechanism designed to 'preserve the peace, however fragile, where fighting has been halted' in order to implement peace agreements. It has relied on the collaborative working of military, police, and civilian components (UNDPKO, 2008: 18). Peacekeeping *culture* evolved primarily as a set of practices within UN peacekeeping, contributing to organizational development and the maintenance of legitimacy within a state (Rubinstein, 2010: 457). Peacekeeping has been distinguished from *peacemaking* (diplomatic outreach to resolve conflict) and, *peacebuilding* (longer term diplomatic and political approaches to prevent further conflict and enable police reform). The activity of peacekeeping has been conceptualized as an attempt to fill the public security gap created by conflict and ideally requires the use of civilian police (Perito, 2004). Peacekeeping (in its broadest sense) has been described as reliant on the *consent* of the local population: the 'societal acceptance of the peacekeepers' presence and their coercive powers' (Levine, 2010: 22) That consent is typically held by a minority alone has necessitated a lengthy phase of 'peacebuilding' to strengthen the 'host society' and the 'future implementation of community policing practices' (Grabosky, 2008: 101–5).

Theoretically, the military have provided stabilization to allow civilian policing to occur through which community engagement can begin through the empowerment of local community groups and institutions, which theoretically can enable inclusive participation (Haider, 2009). While stabilization has been recognized as integral to the establishment and maintenance of order and the provision of community security (SU, 2018), the 'green' does not move on to the 'blue', rather there has always been a co-existence of military and policing activities to ensure *police keeping* (Day and Freeman, 2003). This has included the widespread use of gendarmerie forces; hybrid police organizations with varying semi-military capability and capacity who have been an essential component of all PSOs (Friesendorf, 2018; Sinclair and Burdett, 2018). Over the past decade, NATO has developed a doctrine of *Stability Policing* within 'stabilization and reconstruction' missions (NATO Centre of Excellence, 2016), which has drawn on lessons learned from much earlier peacekeeping missions.

The UK government has recognized civilian police as a key component in PSOs. The term was originally used to describe an 'organised international intervention in a country affected by conflict', with recognition that most PSOs would necessitate a military presence to 'establish and/or ensure stability following a peace agreement to allow a period of reconstruction and development to take place (FCOa, 2007: 10). The term 'peace support' used within some guidance manuals has been largely at odds with the language used by some UK police practitioners who have described their *activities* as: 'conflict prevention', 'peace-making', 'peace enforcement', 'peacekeeping', 'peace-building', 'humanitarian operations', and 'policing the peace' (Author interviews with UK police who have deployed on PSOs, 2010–2015).

Capacity building and capacity development

More recently *capacity building* and *capacity development* have been included in the practitioner and development specialist lexicon as 'the engine of development' (UNDP, 2009: 5) gradually replacing *democratic policing*. The term capacity building may be one of 'enormous generality and vagueness', but it can be useful in framing a typology of the policies of development within international institutions including the UN, EU, and OSCE (Caparini, 2014: 2). Additionally, it has been suggestive of technical assistance and infrastructure development: the building or rehabilitating police stations and related infrastructure (training academies, police headquarters, police stations, and police barracks) (Bayley, 2001: 36 and see Bayley, 1999). Since 2003, the terms 'capacity', 'capacity building', and 'capacity development' have been used within UN peacekeeping 'operations' and 'special political missions' in relation to 'reform, restructuring and rebuilding' (UNDPKO, 2008: 3).

Capacity development (as distinct from capacity and capacity building) has been defined as 'the process through which individuals, organizations and societies obtain, strengthen and maintain the capabilities to set and achieve their own development objectives over time' (UNDP, 2009: 5). Unlike the term capacity building, which implies that capacity is yet to be built, capacity development assumes existing capacity, with a focus on improvement rather than creation from scratch. For external stakeholders, capacity development has typically involved a suite of activities targeting both individual and organizational capacity, including (but not limited to): the provision of additional financial and physical resources; technical assistance; training; systems improvement (e.g. financial and personnel management); the provision of policy and strategic advice; constitutional and legislative reform (to create an enabling environment); organizational redesign; and the development of performance incentives (Morgan 1998: 712). Capacity building and capacity development have rested on the principle that 'the community based policing concept is regarded as key to effective policing' (UNDP, 2009). Embedding and implementing a philosophy of community policing has remained a gold standard however opaque a concept and integral to police reform and SSR.

'Back to the futurism': a historical framework

International policing can be broadly understood as having demonstrated a variety of goals and aims, and practised by recourse to a range of strategies, tactics, and activities which have been influenced by key historical trends that relate to the history of UK policing from the nineteenth to the early part of the twenty-first century. This book uses an historical analyses of UK policing to suggest that there is a sense of 'back to the futurism' in how UK international policing has (re)created itself in the post-1989 world. More precisely, UK policing has imported elements of its colonial and postcolonial era 'brand' to the contemporary period but has been forced to adapt those earlier models to the realities of our current era. Two features of this era—the rise in the international aid and development sector and the rise of the corporate security sector—have been particularly formative in shaping the brand.

Pre-1989 UK policing brand development

The concept of two broad *policing models* that developed from the early part of the nineteenth century across the British Isles is critical to our understanding of the post-1989 era: the 'civil/English' model and the 'colonial/Irish' model. These two models (and their variant styles) were arguably the genesis of the UK policing brand that is in evidence today. Police personnel, policing approaches, skills, and expertise moved across the British empire and commonwealth and back to the metropole. This was never a one-directional flow but a complicated two-way traffic (home and away) whereby UK police interacted with police others sharing styles, ethos, culture, and expertise (Brogden, 1987a, 1987b; Sinclair and Williams, 2007). This circulatory flow of police personnel and skills and policing contributed to the *internationalization of UK policing* through the nineteenth and twentieth centuries. It has shaped the character of UK policing and built a framework for the export of the UK policing brand.

Throughout this period a bucolic image of British policing: 'the bobby' became an icon of Britishness (Emsley, 2003; Loader and Mulcahy, 2003), *the* model of policing to which the Colonial Office (CO) aspired during the period of decolonization to ensure a civilianization of colonial police forces in preparation for independence. Yet colonial policing (while quasi military) 'paralleled and reflected' less-noted features of the Metropolitan civil model although certain English county constabularies bought into the Irish model (Brogden, 1987a). The colonial emergencies and general crises of decolonization became more often than not too challenging for this idealized approach to policing reform and in many places colonial police forces simply (re) militarized—paradoxically this style was adopted by many of the new governments at independence (Sinclair, 2006, 2008). This served as a reminder of the thin line separating civil and colonial styles of policing where Irishness and Englishness cross fertilized and diluted to varying extents, and contributed to a multifaceted policing brand; these histories, myths, and realities have continued to be reified, as well as adapted, into the contemporary era and manifested through international policing (see chapter 2 for an examination of the history of UK policing and its internationalization).

Security sector reform, aid, and development

International policing gained momentum post-1989 and benefitted from the rise of SSR within wider international aid and development programmes. Practitioners and theorists have acknowledged that conflict and insecurity have impacted on development; security and development are closely interconnected (Duffield, 2006: 1; Jackson and Beswick, 2018). SSR has included a wide range of policy interventions aimed at establishing democratic control over security forces. Financial aid has supported development programmes under which SSR has been used to reform the security sector: 'those organizations and institutions that safeguard the state and its citizens from security threats [and transform them] into professional, effective, legitimate, apolitical and accountable actors' (McFate, 2008: 1). As such the classic SSR model was founded on the principles of a responsible, accountable (and effective) security sector (including policing) (e.g. Bayley, 1998, 2001) that contributed to poverty reduction and democracy (OECD/DAC, 2005; Short, 1998).

In the UK, New Labour's international development policy emerged in 1997 (see DfID, 1999, 2000; Duffield, 2006; Michalopoulos, 2020), partly driven by cooperation among Western states on global issues (including world poverty), as well as the rise of overseas development assistance (Chanaa, 2002; Michalopoulos, 2020). Poverty reduction was embedded within international assistance discourse, formalized in the legislation, and popularized by Clare Short as the first Minister for the new Department for International Development (DfID) in 1997 (Short, 1998).

Despite the practical challenges in linking security approaches within development programmes (Jackson and Beswick, 2018), the importance of 'policing' was acknowledged in peace support operations and overseas development assistance as part of the wider SSR strategy. Within policy circles (e.g. DfID) it was taken as axiomatic that the development of a professional, responsive police sensitive to human rights concerns was an absolute requirement if a transition was to take place from a militarized to a civilian regime (DfID, 2007). Since that time, SSR has aligned with the UK's foreign and security policy objectives, and has been enshrined within the National Security Council (NSC) objectives for national security, which has included international aid and development (see HMG, 2010, 2015, 2018; Sedra, 2010). Over time, security and stability concerns have stiffened in parallel with NSC objectives: 'because development reduces poverty and hence the risk of future instability, *it also improves our own security*' [sic] (Duffield, 2006: 2). Indeed, UK policing, in their official pronouncements have been clear that they regard British policing exports as aligning just as much with domestic security interests as with training and assistance (set within wider democratization) in the recipient nation more generally (ACPO ACPOS, 2012; National Chief Constables Council (NPCC), 2017). This, however, has necessitated the ever increasing support of the corporate sector.

Corporate security sector growth

The corporate security sector has increasingly provided international security (and policing) assistance in convergence with the public sector. The growth in the corporate security sector has been driven by neoliberalism and the structural conditions of inequality that can increase crime, ethnic conflict, terrorism, issues around human and food security, and other social problems that have implications for policing (Ellison and Pino, 2012). This led to an increased focus on global (in)security (Brodeur, 2000; Ellison and Pino, 2012), which elevated 'security thinking', generating new police capacity and capability, and a post-9/11 Western view of security through a counterterrorism lens (Sedra, 2010: 21). While the original geographical focus of this global war on terror was Pakistan and Afghanistan (Loewenstein, 2015) it spread outwards; the combination of neoliberal economic policies and a global war on terror created 'a hothouse for private security entrepreneurs' (Klein, 2007; Weiss, 2008) who have flourished in post-conflict zones (Loewenstein, 2015).[3]

The private security literature (more broadly) has held considerably more interest in the activities of 'mercenaries' and private military companies (PMC) (as distinct from private security companies (PSCs) and their 'fulfilment of foreign policy objectives by proxy' (Ellison and O'Reilly, 2006: 1; and see Nossal, 2001; Muthien and Taylor, 2002; Serewicz, 2002; Singer, 2003; Whyte, 2003). PMCs and PSCs theoretically provided different levels of training and assistance within much earlier interventions and their activities in Iraq and Afghanistan bolstered the global security market (see in particular Ellison, 2008; Ellison and O'Reilly, 2008a, 2008b; O'Reilly, 2010; Percy, 2009) and further complicated the public-private relationship within high-risk environments. Conor O'Reilly (2010) highlighted 'the myriad of services these companies provide [which] can further complicate an industry that is far from straight forward' and 'the degree to which both behaviour and techniques traverse the state-corporate nexus' (O'Reilly, 2010: 59). This has involved UK police retirees contracted by the UK government, private military security companies (PMSC), or development consultancies and other international governments where there remains a lack of analyses and an understanding of the relationships between high level corporate security and state security actors (O'Reilly, 2010 with reference to Goldsmith and Sheptycki, 2007: 396). While some commentators have suggested that the challenges and risks presented by an increased private sector engagement have outweighed the advantages and have pointed to questions relating to accountability and governance (see, for example, Ellison and O'Reilly, 2008a, 2008b; Loader, 2002; Loader and Walker, 2007), from a government perspective, overseas interventions (and

---

[3] The governance of security in late-modern society and the changes that have occurred as a result have been well documented in the academic literature (e.g. Johnston 1992; 1999; Loader 1999; Johnston and Stenning, 2015; Shearing and Stenning 1983; 1987). This has resulted in a new and emerging policing 'family' with greater heterogeneity, inclusive of a range of partners drawn from across the public-private space (Johnston and Stenning, 2015). The concept of public-private partnership has been recognized as a valuable tool to deliver public services and infrastructure through the private sector. Behind this, developments in the pluralization, marketization, and commodification of policing and security have contributed to a mixed economy of provision (Crawford, 2006).

subsequent SSR) have been increasingly reliant on the private sector despite an absence of government regulation (Sedra, 2010).

Concluding comment

This chapter has set out the what and the why of international policing by examining the types of activities provided through an investigation of the Western literature, and an observation of the perspectives of practitioners towards the terminology employed. The trajectory of international policing emerged from the nineteenth century policing of the British Isles and its early internationalization to which I now turn in chapter 2.

2
The UK Policing Brand in Historical Context
Myth and Reality

> The work of colonial police officers was adapted to suit extremely diverse conditions across the British empire. Colonial policing was set up as an armed semi-military force to prevent and detect crime, repress internal dissent and defend the colony against external aggression ... these fundamental principles were based on the history of an established British (and Irish) police force as an impartial civilian body to maintain the rule of law without fear or favour.
>
> **Ted Eates, Former Commissioner Hong Kong Police, 1998**

This chapter considers the historical dimensions of UK policing through the development of two broad policing models that developed within the British Isles and spread across the empire and commonwealth. I suggest that there are five key historical trendlines that have contributed to the emergence of a multifaceted UK police brand:

1. The brand stemmed from two core models that developed in the nineteenth and twentieth centuries: the English/civil and the Irish/colonial.
2. The brand emerged from both historical realities and myths.
3. The brand is multi-faceted and complex.
4. The brand's internationalization strengthened and consolidated its reputation and influence both at home and overseas through the nineteenth century.

5. The brand further extended through the late twentieth and early twenty first centuries and has more recently become fragmented.

It has been widely acknowledged that the UK brand has been recently represented by police institutions including Scotland Yard, the MPS, and the National Crime Agency (NCA) among others. Its character has hinged upon commonly held beliefs including 'policing by consent', 'Peelian principles', 'community policing', and a strategy of minimum force (see in particular Reiner, 1985: 54–6). All of the aforementioned are rooted in the historic myth *and* reality of policing though the uniqueness in the case of UK policing may lie in how this has endured over time. I suggest that the early transplantation of the nineteenth-century *models* across the empire and commonwealth contributed not only to UK policing's rapid spread but also grew its international reputation, which in turn promoted its value and purpose back home. In addition, the cross fertilization that occurred between the models within the domestic and international environments has created and continues to build 'brand value' to the present day (Sinclair and Williams, 2007).

Any interpretation of the policing brand has been complicated by what Ian Loader and Aógan Mulcahy (2003) described as 'a mismatch between public and governmental/public discourse in relation to what we can reasonably expect policing institutions to accomplish and, the hopes and expectations of the police' for policing is both 'made and imagined'; 'a complex of institutional power, practices and technologies'. Those who are affiliated with that institution that is the police (both inside and outside including government, other public bodies and the citizen) have to 'make sense of that past, form judgements on the present and project various imagined futures' (Loader and Mulcahy, 2003: 39–40). This discourse has been partly based upon the myths spun and realities maintained creating 'a deep emotional attachment to the authoritative social magic of policing' which has endured over time and broadly supported the emergence of the UK policing brand (Loader and Mulcahy, 2003: xiii, xiv).

The development of UK policing benefitted (at least up until the end of the Second World War) from the public's strong and positive identification with the institution and culture of policing. As Reiner noted a period of 'detraditionalization' and 'diversification' occurred within British society shifting the public's gaze away from the police who were no longer 'a servant of the locality' (Reiner, 1985: 37), and from the 1950s, the so-called golden age of policing entered a period of demise (Loader and Mulcahy, 2003).

While we should be wary of any vast over-simplification of the realities of British policing (Cockcroft, 2015; Reiner, 1985, 1992; Williams, 2011), the decline of local 'bobbying', centralization of policing within urban areas as well as a gradual transformation in the ethnic and cultural diversity of British society were key contributors (Reiner, 1985). Public priorities, however, may still arguably be influenced by twentieth, and even nineteenth century ideas about the 'doing' of policing: 'for most people, the police still principally exist to respond quickly, to deter crime (largely by their physical presence), and investigate when it occurs' (Higgins, 2020: 23). Even recent austerity measures and concerns emerging about 'the health of the police 'covenant' [sic] with the public (NPCC, 2018), as well as increasing disparity between the public's view of policing and their 'traditional' expectations 'and what the police feel compelled to prioritise' (BMG Research, 2019: 5) have not dispelled the nineteenth century foundation.

The 'New Police'

The institutions that we refer to as 'police' today were the creations of the bureaucratic nineteenth-century state. An obvious legislative starting point in England is Sir Robert Peel's 1829 Metropolis Police Improvement Act. While early British Whig historiography considered the foundation of London's Metropolitan Police (MPS) as the 'first' modern (and professional) police; the lesser-known City of Glasgow Police was founded in 1800 and the Edinburgh City Police in 1805. The Metropolitan Police, a force of some 3,000 men 'took to the streets' of the capital between September 1829 and May 1830 (Emsley, 2010: 235). The City of London remained a separate jurisdiction and introduced its own London City Police in 1832, which became the City of London Police in 1839 (Harris, 2004: 132–53). The concept of a 'New Police' originated at this time and formed the basis of what I describe as the English/civil model of policing (see subsequent sections), and has been employed ever since to describe the 'wholesale reorganisation' of policing (Lawrence, 2011).[1]

---

[1] The term was initially used using lower case letters and this then changed to capitals in an 1830 article in the *Morning Chronicle* which carried the headline 'Murder of a New Policeman by a gang of burglars'. *Morning Chronicle*, 18 August 1830. New Police was used throughout the nineteenth century to refer to any of the new forces set up in response to the Police Acts of 1829, 1839–40 and 1856 or, collectively all of them (Lawrence, 2011).

The New Police 'marked an important development in law enforcement in modern Britain' (Taylor 1997: 5) and their arrival has been widely discussed amongst police scholars (see in particular Emsley, 1991, 1999; Reiner, 1985; Taylor 1997). In theory, Sir Robert Peel intended for the first duty of this organization to be the prevention of crime and, secondly the maintenance of law and order. This would facilitate an engagement between the new Metropolitan police officers with the capital's communities through a concept of 'policing by consent' (Emsley, 1991). This aspirational notion of how police officers should go about their day-to-day activities has remained a constant source of debate amongst academics. The traditional historiography made the clear suggestion that law and order maintenance was carried out through a process of minimum force (see, for example, Reith, 1938, 1943a, 1943b). This view was challenged by revisionists who demonstrated the tension between consent and coercion (force) within the activities of the New Police, a *force* designed to provide more effective mechanisms of social control (Taylor, 1997: 5 and see, for example, Storch, 1975). Emsley (1991) in a wide-ranging survey outlined the multifaceted powers of coercion available to the police under the law in which they operated (Emsley, 1991). Yet the conditions in which the British police have *policed* have to some extent dictated the style of policing to be adopted and the question of use and type of force. Emsley, when referring to the earliest experiences of the New Police, noted that all officers could be armed. MPS inspectors carried pocket pistols from 1829 and arms were always available for use in London's police stations. While edged weapons were more common—the MPS and many rural constabularies continued to train and drill with swords during the nineteenth century—cutlasses were also made available for police in 'dangerous' areas or issued when police were dealing with serious disorder. As such it was 'frequently suggested to organise the Metropolitan Police *militairement* [though] always repudiated' (Emsley, 1985: 59).

However, while the New Police were readily employed from the nineteenth century, the organization established as Paul Lawrence (2011) noted 'certain conceptual distinctions which were readily adopted by both the public of the nineteenth century and early historians of the police'. This was an important marker in weaving the historic myth of policing for the 'discontinuity between 'old' [sic] and 'new' [sic] was less acute than might be assumed. The term *new* was heralded within official discourse as an improvement on what had come before. The New Police were described as 'both more efficient and effective' and yet the development of policing at this time 'was far more complex than the simplistic 'out with the old in with the new' mantra of early police historians (Lawrence, 2011: xi–xii). This concept of 'newness' within the doing of policing created part of the mythology around policing in England and Wales. Yet while the *new* Metropolitan Police model dominated in England and Wales, it was not the only tried and tested one. Many counties and larger boroughs also looked to the Irish model to recruit their senior officers (including Gloucestershire and Staffordshire) to ensure the necessary policing experience.

The rationale for this was that nineteenth-century police reforms were arduous and plagued by disputes between central and local authorities; this was true of all areas (for policing reform in Wales see Jones, 1983; Parris, 1961, and in Scotland see Barrie, 2008). In England (outside of London), a gradual legislative reform of policing in the boroughs was initially precipitated by the national 1833 Lighting and Watching Act and the 1835 Municipal Corporations Act granting local authorities the means to improve their daytime watches and night patrols. In the rural areas the 1839 Rural Police Act gave permission to the country magistrates to establish (or not) rural police. Police reform outside the metropole stumbled slowly forward through the 1840s and 1850s although, it was not until the 1856 Country and Borough Police Act that the establishment of police forces became a requirement at local government level within all counties and boroughs (Hart, 1955, 1956; Jones, 1983; Parris, 1961). By approximately 1870, most provincial authorities had established New Police (Lawrence, 2011). Ironically, this was also true of Ireland where after the 1801 union, political and social tensions and the conflict that ensued provided an impetus for a further *model* of policing within the British Isles.

The Irish Constabulary

The British establishment saw the policing of Ireland as needing to curb 'the wild Shamrock manners of the Irish' by containing political and agrarian unrest and introducing Anglicization and modernization (Ellison and Smyth, 2000:15). Ireland, Peel's first policing experiment (although the first organized police force in Ireland was the Dublin City Policing in 1786 (see Palmer, 1988)). Security concerns were linked to a 'new wave of ribandism' that had been poorly managed by the Peace Preservation Force (created in 1814), and the need to reduce the cost of keeping large numbers of military in country who were unsuited to policing duties (O'Ceallaigh,

1966). In 1822, this was partly addressed through the creation of a Country Constabulary, a permanent national police force, which operated alongside the Peace Preservation Force and dealt with public order maintenance until their amalgamation in 1836. The 'new' Irish Constabulary effectively created a style of policing that would continue through the nineteenth century (Ellison and Smyth, 2000). Subsequently, the reform of policing in Ireland brought far ranging organizational and cultural changes. While the Irish Constabulary (which became the Royal Irish Constabulary (RIC)) was a designated 'civil force', its operational style and culture led it to be described as a 'regiment trained as light infantry' (Fulham, 1983: 94); a quasi-military police *force* (see in particular Brewer, 1990; Curtis, 1871; Hawkins, 1966; Herlihy, 2005; Malcolm, 2006). The Irish Constabulary remained armed: the right to bear arms was perceived in Ireland at the time as 'the mark of a gentleman, a jealously guarded prerogative of the landlords in a garrison state' (Fulham, 1981: 105). As a result, a quasi-military model of training modelled on prevailing army standards for light infantry was set up at the Constabulary Depot at Phoenix Part in Dublin (Sinclair, 2006). Describing the programme in 1853, the Inspector General Sir Duncan McGregor commented: 'we make them soldiers as far as we can.... the drill I believe to be nearly the same' (Report of the Commissioners, 1866 cited in Fulham, 1983: 100). So, while this body was armed and deployed along the lines of a 'gendarmerie', the British Government preferred the term 'constabulary' when creating the necessary legislation (Palmer, 1988: 242). The Irish Constabulary was subsequently described as a force of 'proven discipline and efficiency'; and in official parlance perceived (rightly or wrongly) as key to London and Dublin Castle's ability to govern Ireland, albeit up until partition in 1921 (Fulham, 1981: 106).

The nineteenth century Irish Constabulary created a hierarchical division between officers and all other ranks, which would have a bearing on the structure of colonial police forces (Emsley and Clapson, 2002). Officers were drawn from the gentry and were typically better educated; 'gentlemen cadets' were preferred when recruiting to the inspectorate 'because they were thought to command the respect of the ranks by virtue of their class (Fulham, 1981: 100) and, in contrast to London's New Police, the Irish Constabulary was lodged and organized within barracks (rather than police stations) the largest numbers deployed to rural areas and a smaller force in constabulary barracks in the cities. A reserve force that typically comprised mounted sections of veterans was held on standby to ensure that the right mix of experienced and inexperienced officers could be deployed in the 'maintenance of peace', the force's principal duty or on patrol in areas requiring additional support. Following the 1836 Reform Act, the government's overriding impression was of a reliable policing organization, and as such the Constabulary was entrusted with a range of additional duties and responsibilities that included: the collection of the decennial census, annual agricultural statistics and census, inspection of weights and measures, issue and collection of the election voting papers of Poor Law guardians, dog registration, enforcement of statutes regulating vagrancy, fisheries, and illicit distillation (Curtis, 1869: 93). The types of duties undertaken by the Irish Constabulary were mirrored in the colonial police, in an attempt to bring the police closer to the population through visibility, 'eyes and ears', and intelligence gathering (Sinclair, 2006). There has been an interesting footnote to the history of the RIC that related to a suggested gradual erosion of their semi-military nature—referred to as a 'gradual domestication'—as the establishment became 'more truly representative of the Irish population' [and] was attached to home as its duties became more routine, more akin to house-keeping than peacekeeping; and it was tamed because its ability to use force was greatly diminished...' (Lowe and Malcom, 1992: 27). The RIC by this time was able to perform two core duties: one quasi-military in relation to the 'preservation of the peace' and the other of a more 'civil' nature. This reflected a degree of cross-fertilization with the quasi-civil model of policing employed on the mainland.

The British colonial police

The model of policing that developed in Ireland came to be known in government discourse as 'colonial policing' (Jeffries, 1952: 9), and can be categorized using Emsley's typology as a 'state military force' (Sinclair and Williams, 2007). The concept of a distinctive 'English' and 'Irish' model was laid out by Sir Charles Jeffries (Deputy Under-Secretary of State for the Colonies) at the Colonial Office (CO) who believed that an alternative system of policing was required overseas for 'the first demand was for administrators and police, to lay the foundations of law and order...' (Jeffries, 1938: 18). Jeffries later noted the suitability of the Irish model in allowing the Colonial Police to evolve through three phases: the securitization of law and order; the establishment of semi-military constabulary forces to preserve the peace and suppress crime; and, at a much later stage toward colonial independence, a 'conversion of these semi-military constabularies into civilian police forces, following in most essentials the British pattern of police organisation' [could occur] but [crucially] 'still retaining certain continuing supplementary functions of a military character' (Jeffries, 1952: 33). As the case study chapters will demonstrate, Jeffries's 1952 description of these three phases bears some semblance to the Western international efforts (military and policing) within post-conflict environments (including Iraq and Afghanistan) where an attempted phased approach was undertaken.

British colonial policing was always complicated by the pre-existence of earlier policing institutions and local rulers with their own policing styles. In theory, 'indirect rule' provided for what was called 'native authority' policing framed within local law and custom. This allowed the traditional rulers to maintain control providing they worked *with* the colonial administration and left criminal dealings with expatriates to the 'European' colonial police (Sinclair, 2006). In some cases, these institutions were reorganized in line with recommendations from the Colonial Office (see Jeffries, 1952 for an historic survey of the CO and colonial policing).

Across the empire (and commonwealth) while senior officers experimented with elements of both the English/civil and Irish/colonial model, there was far greater emphasis on retaining a semi-military model. This was particularly true during periods of local unrest, political dissent and importantly during the 'long era of decolonization' and subsequent colonial insurgencies. To return to Jeffries's (1952) point 'the really effective influence upon the development of Colonial Police forces during the nineteenth century was not that of the police of 'Great Britain' [sic] but that of the RIC' (Jeffries, 1952: 31) although resistance to its transfer demonstrated a historic trajectory of what rapidly became a multifaceted policing brand.

The Ceylon Police

The Ceylon Police, established in 1834, experimented with both the English and Irish models depending on the background of senior police and their vision for police reform (Pippet, 1938; Dep, 1969). The very earliest reforms were undertaken by a Metropolitan Police sergeant, John Colepepper, responsible for Kandy district in 1840. He was inspired by the MPS (English) policing approach which included unarmed policing. This was overturned in 1845 by Thomas Thompson, a former Irish Constabulary officer who became superintendent of police in Columbo (Herlihy, 2005: 298). Thompson was not in favour of Colepepper's earlier reforms and rearmed the police changing the colour of their uniforms from metropolitan blue to Irish green. When Thompson retired in 1848, he was replaced by another ex-Irish Constabulary officer, William Macartney who continued in an Irish vein and further militarized the Ceylon Police (Dep, 1969). This brought resistance from the Ceylon administration (Police Commission, 1864) who were doubtful as to whether an Irish model was suitable:

> [We] cannot concede that the Irish Constabulary is at all an analogous Force [sic] to our Ceylon Police, and we would here beg leave to express our opinion, that it would have been more conducive to the efficiency of our Force ... if the English Metropolitan Police had been preferred as a model to work from, instead of a Force, however admirable in its own country, so unsuited to our requirements as would appear to be the Irish Constabulary (Dep, 1969: 1).

The real debate here lay between the colonial administration and the police commissioner and focused on the extent and nature of militarization; whether the Ceylon Police should be trained in drill and use of arms, whether the police should be routinely armed and issued with the types of weapons used, and how should force would be employed. Arguably this reflected the view of senior police chiefs in the nearby Indian Police Service who had a tendency to mix the English and Irish models to suit their purposes (Arnold, 1986).[2] In the event, many of Thompson and Macartney's reforms were retained and the views of senior police seemed to prevail with the selection in 1866 of yet another former Irish officer, George Campbell, who had also served in the Indian Police (Jeffries, 1952; Dowbiggin, 1928). Campbell introduced additional Irish (and also Indian Police) features included the adoption of the title Inspector-General (IG) rather than Chief Constable and, increased military training and drill with the argument that this would allow for a reduction in the number of troops stationed on the island (Jeffries, 1952: 32). However, Campbell was not entirely averse to an English character of policing providing the context permitted. As

---

[2] An early commissioner of the Madras Police, Lord Harris, was drawn to unarmed law enforcement, though this was overturned by the Madras government itself, which considered a model based on the Irish precedent to be more to their liking when 'policing a colony' (Arnold, 1986: 27–8).

Jeffries theorized, the third phase of colonial policing would bring about the emergence of a civil style police. By 1879, the Ceylon Police was being described as 'a Civil Police with a semi military training. It is armed with Snider Rifles and Swords and drilled, but the men carry only batons when on duty other than Treasury, or Convict or Gaol Guard' (Campbell, 1879 quoted in Dep, 1969: 126). By the early part of the twentieth century there was a drive to recruit directly from English forces rather than Ireland to support attempts at civil style reform though these were largely unsuccessful (Dep, 1968).

It was not until the 'Grand Old Man of the Colonial Police Service' (Jeffries, 1952), Sir Herbert Dowbiggin, became Inspector-General in 1913 (until 1937) that widespread reform was undertaken to transform the Ceylon Police into 'civilians in uniform' to reflect the 'good image of British Police' (Dowbiggin, 1928). This included changes to the police training curriculum, the carrying and use of arms, and greater emphasis on the detection and prevention of crime through the creation of CID (Sinclair, 2006). However, whether the Ceylon Police was then modelled solely along English (and perceived civil lines) is highly questionable. Rather it emerged, as elsewhere, as an amalgamation of different policing styles (from the nineteenth century English and Irish models) that suited the Ceylon context and aspirations of the Ceylon administration and police chiefs while retaining a strongly colonial character.

Overall, a cross-fertilization of approaches could be seen across the empire with a higher dependency on the original Irish model. This was reflected in a higher number of former Irish police who accepted overseas postings and were particularly sought after to control 'settler' populations. Within the commonwealth, particularly within a 'frontier' setting where 'pacification policing' was central to the government's social-control imperatives during the nineteenth century (Hill, 1995)—this included Australia, New Zealand, and Canada—military and semi-military techniques were 'borrowed' from the Irish Constabulary, and also occasionally from the French Gendarmerie. In New Zealand, for example, a semi-military force was set up in 1867 to police the frontier against the Maoris (for an authoritative history of policing in New Zealand see Hill, 1986, 1989, 1995). Yet within an urban context there were attempts to minimize the use of force wherever possible: 'we keep a baton, but seldom use it; when we do, its application should be scrupulously apportioned to the need' (O'Donovan, address to the New Zealand Police Force (1920) cited in Hill, 2019). Australia saw the creation of a Metropolitan-style of policing within the urban centres of Sydney and Melbourne and the use of beat patrols (Finnane, 1990). However, within rural areas there was a preference for the Irish model, not least because of the presence of a large and sometimes Irish settler population that could be controlled more efficiently through quasi-military policing. A similar approach was taken when creating Canada's police forces which gradually developed a three-tiered system with city and town police forces using an English model while the provincial police forces in rural areas, and the national police force that emerged to support the dominion government, adopted Irish practices. The most well-known has remained the Royal Canadian Mounted Police (RCMP), the successor to the North West Mounted Police and which is today responsible for the enforcement of federal statutes in all ten provinces and in the three territories (Sinclair, 2006).

Within twentieth century police discourse there was discussion relating to the character of the 'British' colonial police forces, acknowledged as 'semi armed' (Dunn, 1951); 'semi-military' (Jeffries, 1952), requiring 'soldiering' (with specific reference to Palestine) (Duff, 1938: 19), and with the occasional reference to a 'Foreign Legion' during the period of small colonial wars (Hewitt, 1999). As the former Inspector-General of the Uganda Police wrote in 1961, with regards to colonial policing:

> We should bear in mind its history and constitution and its character which is somewhat military ... it was formed in the first instance to protect the Administration and provide a means of enforcing Government Policy [sic]. Against this Imperial background an officer of conservative mind might express gratification with the rate of progress and the transition to a protective service for the whole community. But to a modern and democratic mind ... is still to be found'.... [If] the colonial police forces were permitted to develop on democratic lines, it would render an excellent account of itself (Harwich, 1961: 149–51).

Indeed, many former colonial police officers maintained that there was always a CO-led aspiration to revert to and engage with English/British civil approaches to policing if and when the right conditions prevailed, outside colonial emergencies and public unrest (Sinclair, 2006). The desire to transform from a semi-military to a preferred model of civil policing has become part of the historic folklore of British policing to which I now turn.

Whig and revisionist histories

The earlier Whig histories showed policing as a linear story of progress where the New Police were described as having made a necessary contribution to societal change (Emsley, 2014). This reading of police history, I would suggest, has lingered on within some police and government discourse. It has contributed to a *sense* of their official history, tradition, and nostalgia that presented the universally acknowledged 'bobby' as an iconic symbol (Brunger, 2014; Emsley, 2014; Loader and Mulcahy, 2003). The many policing approaches adopted since the nineteenth century (including policing by consent, discretion, routinely unarmed policing, and latterly community policing (Brogden and Nijhar, 2005: 63) have fed into police culture and built the foundations for an internationally recognizable brand (Ellison and Pino, 2012). How did this come about?

Emsley (2011) wrote that 'once upon a time it all seemed so simple. Until the early 1970s the history of policing remained the preserve of enthusiasts who were often former police officers or who had cordial connections with the police .... The history tended to be congratulatory' (Emsley, 2011: xi–xii). These early police historians were members of the British Establishment (see in particular Ascoli, 1979; Critchley, 1978; Reith, 1938, 1940, 1943a, 1943b, 1952, 1956) who took an interest in ensuring that the 'British' police were perceived as a force of progress and, an institution that functioned with the consent of the general population. Charles Reith, the founding father of Whig history and inspired by his experiences of the Second World War, perceived the police as 'preventative' to 'solve the problem of recurring war among nations' (Reith, 1940: viii), by protecting 'the weak against the powerful'. Key was that 'the police and the people are one', a 'principle' that Reith considered had been fully adopted in 1829 (Reith, 1943: 7–10). Moreover, Reith posited that in a few decades, 'Britain' had established not only a professional and effective police force but the 'best in the world'; and that the Metropolitan Police experiment 'was copied throughout the entire area of the country, and of the empire, in the short space of thirty years' (Reith, 1952: 20). The foundation for this 'police ideal of service to the public' was the law: the police officer (the 'bobby') was 'the servant of law, but he [sic] is regarded by law as a citizen who is responsible to it for his actions, and these are not covered, and cannot be excused (Reith, 1943: 23). Indeed, for Whig historians, the New Police was the result of an entirely rational response of public-minded reformers to real societal problems and crime that had been poorly managed in the past (Emsley, 1985, 1999, 2011; Lawrence, 2011).

So, the official rhetoric and promotion of the UK brand rested on an *assumed* Peelian tradition drawn from a particular reading of policing history.[3] Yet there has been a lack of evidence that these Peelian principles originated in 1829, or indeed had been conceived by Peel or either of the first Metropolitan Police commissioners: Sir Charles Rowan (1829–1850) and Richard Mayne (1829–1868). Rather, it seems likely that they were given their first significant formulation in the work of Charles Reith (1938, 1943 (Emsley, 2014: 11). In addition, there has been some suggestion that these nine 'principles' could also be attributed (in part) to Melville Lee's much earlier work: *A History of Police in England* published in 1901 (Emsley, 2014: 13).[4] However, the British police establishment has over time posited itself as unique, not only in the detail of its organization but, more particularly, in the principles which it adopted and evolved: the 'nine Principles of Police' (Reith, 1943a: 3) that endorsed the 'British Bobby' and his [sic] 'value and virtue' (Emsley, 1999: 7). The Whig tradition was often binary viewing police history through the prism of individual forces (particularly the MPS) with few comparisons made across the wide range of forces in England, Wales, Scotland (though see the history of police in England and Wales between 1974 and 2010 written by former Chief Constable Timothy Brain (2010) and T. A. Critchley (1967)) (Williams, 2011).

Any challenge to this early orthodox interpretation did not present until the 1970s, when revisionist studies critiqued the earlier 'cop-sided' and celebratory accounts (Reiner, 1985). Nineteenth century policing was then examined through the eyes of the citizen; coercion rather than consensus was evidenced as the more likely policing *modus vivendi* particularly of the working classes (see in particular Brogden, 1982; Philips and Storch, 1999; Reiner, 1985; Reynolds, 1998; Storch, 1975, 1976, and Taylor, 1997). The arrival of the New Police represented a 'significant extension into hitherto geographically peripheral areas of both the moral and political authority of the state' (Storch, 1975: 61). While these earlier revisionist debates were

---

[3] The 'General Instructions' provided to police officers since 1829 (known as the Peelian Principles) contain a set of influential ideas that still provide the foundations for policing in Britain and many other countries. The principles emphasize crime prevention over enforcement, the maintenance of public co-operation and consent, minimal use of force and police impartiality before the law (see Home Office, 2012).
[4] A third edition of *Policing in America* published in 1999 identified twelve (rather than nine) policing principles identified from much earlier historical sources and has continued to underpin approaches to policing in contemporary USA (Chaires and Lentz, 2007).

later to be contested (see, for example, Emsley, 1991), their value remains in the issues raised that relate to the state's control of different elements of British society. Emsley in particular demonstrated how historical methodologies could be used more widely not only to inform the history of nineteenth century policing but all subsequent sociological concepts (Emsley, 2014). This included the police officer as a citizen in uniform, who through legal accountability, a largely unarmed approach performed a 'service role' as well as crime prevention, law enforcement, and public order duties in order to achieve the highest possible levels of public consent to policing (see in particular Reiner, 1985, 1992, 1995; Loader and Mulcahy, 2003).

Policing by *mutual* consent

From the very beginning, Peel and the other early architects of British policing attempted to pacify London community's 'fear and distrust' through the development of a traditional model of policing by consent (Reiner, 1995: 29 as cited in Miller, 1977). As posited, a central tenet of traditional Whig theory was that the police enjoyed the support of society based on consensus ('policing by consent'). Thus, the police became accepted and indeed admired by the population; a form of 'kin' police as opposed to those in continental Europe (Reith, 1952: 20). The practice of consent centred upon society's ('the community's') endorsement of a police presence and the subsequent building of a police/citizen relationship. This has resulted in the well-oiled phrase: the 'police are the public and the public are the police' that has often been projected onto an *English* policing landscape.

Policing by consent has been likened to the 'police version of the Magna Carta'; integral to the values and purpose that make up policing though it often appears vague and opaque as a concept (Author interview with former Chief Constable, Lothian and Borders Police, August 2019). Policing by consent assumes that the public or a member of the public gives their consent to a police officer without resistance. Perhaps a more accurate way would be to describe this (theoretically) as *policing by mutual consent* as there is a requirement for a *mutual* agreement between the police officer and the citizen to a specific course of action: a social contract to resolve a problem or misunderstanding in a civilized manner. Police officers have often described the term 'by consent' as suggestive of stasis and passivity and not necessarily inclusive of both parties (Author interviews 2010–2019). Despite anecdotal evidence, the official discourse has remained largely supportive of a fundamentally 'Peelian' notion that in generating public approval by acting respectfully, behaving with decency and fair play towards members of the public, the police build legitimacy and a sense of 'moral alignment', which can trigger consensus and co-operation (BMG Research, 2019 with reference to, for example, Tyler and Jackson, 2013; Bradford and Jackson, 2011).

Yet there has always been considerable debate amongst police historians and sociologists as to the extent to which the 'original' New Police operated by consensus or through coercion. This came with the knowledge that force was legitimately authorized and had become integral to the culture of policing (Emsley and Clapson, 2002) and, represented the complex reality that is policing surrounding consent and coercion as P. A. J. Waddington (1991) explained:

> Unlike the police of many other countries, it is often asserted, the British police do not need to be armed, ... because the British public willingly complies and does not have to be coerced. In short, the British public *consent* to being policed. The term though is misleading and a better description is that the police 'act with *legitimate authority*'.... Ultimately their [the police] task is to tell people what to do, and if they do not comply, to force them to do so ... the police officer possesses ... *authority*: the power he or she wields is recognized as legitimate by those who are subjected to it. The result is that people *conform* [author's emphasis] to the instructions of the police, whereas they are likely only to *comply* [author's emphasis] with those of a thug (Waddington: 1991: 4).

The tension between consent and coercion remains I suggest a key historic (and probably legal) dilemma and owes much to this mythological image of the essentially 'non-threatening' character of British policing (Waddington, 1991: 6, Tyler, 2006). While the authority to deter and detain has been used since the nineteenth century, 'coercion' used by the holder of the ancient office of constable was held to be legitimated by the state *as well as* by the community: police-public co-operation (and by extension legitimacy) has always been posited as necessary in order to maximize social control (Emsley, 1991; 2009; Waddington, 1991). Yet this question of police legitimacy remains a complex mix of individual, organizational, and institutional issues that are theoretically upheld by the beliefs and actions of the citizen (Bottoms and Tankebe, 2012). It rests on the belief that the citizen has a fundamental *respect* of criminal justice institutions to determine what is legally right and wrong, and to trust when there may be a need for 'coercive force'. While those earlier Whig histories regarding policing by consent are now partially discredited, some of the original theory appears plausible when a police officer's discretion (legitimate or otherwise) to decide on the appropriate course of action. The MPS establishment in 1829 was in reality very small (some 3,000 officers) for the area of London to be covered (minus the City of London Corporation). 'Discretion' in the handling of those who had fallen foul of the law often meant that leniency was the easiest course of action and guaranteed the safety of the officer and allowed him to complete his beat in good time (Emsley, 2009; Inwood, 1990). Stephen Inwood (1990: 142), in his vivid portrayal of nineteenth century London demonstrated how the police developed 'a practical compromise between middle-class ideals and working-class realities':

> Certainly the hand of the law fell most heavily on the poor and the ragged, those who did their drinking, fighting, gambling, playing, fornicating and pilfering on the open streets, rather than in clubs, offices and comfortable homes. But the Metropolitan Police was not a bulldozer able to flatten working-class culture, institutions and expedients for survival wherever they offended delicate middle-class sensibilities. Social control models, especially when they are simplified and generalised by repetition do not do justice to the complexity of the circumstances and attitudes involved in the policing of the metropolis.... [The Commissioners] also wanted their constables to be able to walk alone at night and lightly armed, in London's most dangerous areas, able perhaps to call upon other citizens to help them if necessary. This would not be possible if the police set themselves against all kinds of working class environments, as rate payers and clergymen often pressed them to do ... the beat system, the unarmed constables and the effective policing of poorer areas depended upon it (Inwood, 1990: 142–3).

British police have continued (since the nineteenth century) to use their discretion when *doing policing* and it remains a 'key manifestation of police culture' (Cockcroft, 2013: 46), of 'deep symbolic relevance' for police officers and has been integral to their work (Klockars, 1985) although increasingly challenged by process-driven policies. Simply put, the police have never been able to enforce every piece of legislation and the use of discretion, when an officer has local intelligence and context awareness, may allow for a better application of the law (Brogden and Nijhar, 2005). But the police's use of their discretionary powers is also reliant on the *public's discretion*: the citizen uses his or her discretion to decide whether or not to involve the police and the police can take action (or not) regardless of the rights or wrongs of this (Cockcroft, 2013). While there has been a myth surrounding 'policing by consent' it continues to be the 'dominant ideological underpinning of the British policing model' (Jackson et al., 2013, 19, and concept drawn from oral histories, 2010 to 2019). It has fed into community policing approaches (see, for example, Home Office, 2012; Walton and Falkner, 2019: 9), which have a particular value internationally and have become integral to the UK policing brand offer.

Policing in England: an end of a golden age

British policing has a 'distinctive historical place' (Miller, 1977: ix) and 'considerable residual faith has remained in this particular state institution (Newburn, 2011: 1). There is a linkage to the early histories where the image of the 'bobby' suited the Victorian, Edwardian, and interwar British view of those who served in the oft claimed 'best police in the world' (Emsley, 2009). Within official circles, the bobby can easily be resurrected with 'a harping back to the "olden days"; a golden age of policing; when policing by consent was the Dixon of Dock Green mantra of legitimacy' (Mawby, 2013: 189). British policing institutions (including Northern Ireland) became an 'explicit reference point', a benchmark against which policing in other countries could be measured (Sharman, 1983: 233). The paradox has been that the UK policing brand accrued a renewed market value overseas in the latter part of the twentieth century as the British public's affection for that 'symbol of national pride' (Reiner, 1985) was in decline.

Typically, the British public's trust in policing is understood as embedded within the concepts of consent and legitimacy. Trust (and confidence) in policing has declined since the 1970s with a continuing downward trajectory (Jackson and Sunshine, 2007): the police are no longer perceived as 'sacred' but 'profane'; yet another public service where public confidence is now '… tentative and brittle … to be renegotiated case by case' (Reiner (2000: 162). There are wide-ranging and complex explanations posited for this decline that emanate from the societal, political, economic, and cultural shifts that have occurred (see in particular Brogden and Ellison, 2013; Loader and Mulcahy, 2003; Reiner, 2000).

The police, for example, became increasingly embroiled in industrial and social unrest in the 1970s and 1980s, and came into confrontation not only with their traditional support base but wider societal groupings. As the institution became more bureaucratic and regionally centralized so local visibility and accessibility (the bobby on the beat) declined (Hough, 2003), which coincided with rising levels of crime perceived by the public to have been poorly managed (Garland, 2001). By the early 1980s any 'golden' gloss of policing had evaporated and the police were exposed to radical attempts by the then Conservative government to improve efficiency and cost saving by pursuing the Financial Management Initiative (FMI). An amalgam of FMI, growing privatization, Home Office Circular 114 (1983), and later 106 (1988) that gained further control over policing, an expansion of the Common Police Services budget and the advent of the National Criminal Intelligence Service further squashed localism creating a de facto national police force (Reiner, 2010). An application of private sector management methods and imposition of market disciplines without adequate consultation with the police representative bodies further dented police morale. Policing strategies adopted at the time (and now generally referred to as 'policing by objectives'), forcibly cut police expenditure without 'any real concern about the effect this [might] have on policing' (Rawlings, 2002: 46), raising questions as to how budgetary constraints and growing privatization would impact policing (Rawlings, 2002).

Public confidence in the police and criticism of policing by this time had reached an all-time low spurned on by revelations of police corruption and a spate of miscarriages of justice, including the 'Guildford Four' (1989), the 'Birmingham Six' (1991), and 'the Maguire Seven' (1991). The murder of Stephen Lawrence that followed shortly after and the widely recognized reluctance of the Metropolitan Police 'to promptly arrest those suspected … and the stonewalling of the subsequent investigation' further discredited wider British policing (Brogden and Ellison, 2013: 149). Not only did this highlight the failings of the MPS to focus on wider police-community relations, and respond to accusations of discriminatory treatment of ethnic minorities, but further demonstrated that the police had not engaged with issues of policing and race raised by Lord Scarman (1981) following the Brixton riots and New Cross fire (Rowe, 2007). The subsequent Stephen Lawrence inquiry, chaired by Lord Justice Macpherson, publicly elevated issues of police discrimination; Macpherson was 'hugely critical' of the MPS and policing in

England and Wales generating official and public debates (Souhami, 2007: 66–7).

In the course of the twenty-first century, erosion of public confidence in policing has continued as fiscal and budgetary measures have taken their toll on police effectiveness. More recently the societal divides brought sharply into focus by post-2010 austerity and a legacy of the neoliberal global market economy have increased (Brogden and Ellison, 2013). Following the 2008 global banking crisis, sustained reductions in public spending, including a call for police budgets to be cut on average by twenty-two percent, impacted upon public service delivery particularly for frontline policing (Sindall and Strugis, 2013). Arguably the police were having to deliver a more complex level of service as the types of crime (including cybercrime), mental health provision, and home-grown terrorism attacks grew, necessitating an increase in the numbers and skills of specialist teams. Moreover, the organization and structure of policing has further changed with the emergence of 'quasi' police officers (including Police Community Support Officers) (Millie and Bullock, 2012) with a new governance structure of Police and Crime Commissioners (PCCs) and 'pressures upon greater private sector involvement in the delivery of police services and provoking (insatiable) [sic] public expectations and demands for greater front-line public policing....' (Crawford, 2014). Crawford's notion (2014) of an 'extended policing family' may not prove, as Brogden and Ellison (2013) earlier suggested to be a useful one-size-fits-all solution to contemporary policing where 'policing for profit' (private sector) collides with a public service agenda (Brogden and Ellison, 2013: 150). The 'residual "golden" memory of a harmonious social ordering agency' may be further declining (Brogden and Ellison, 2013: 146) along with police morale and general dissatisfaction. On 5 July 2019, five former Metropolitan Police Commissioners (1993–2017) and other senior officers (2002–2018) wrote in a letter to *The Times* warning that cuts to police budgets were a contributory factor to the 'feeling of lawlessness' that prevailed and called for a royal commission on policing as the 'only way to encourage fresh thinking, challenge outdated working practices and develop a new framework to help to deliver lasting reforms: *British policing was once the envy of the world. No one would claim that now*'. [authors emphasis] (BBC News, 5 July 2019; *The Times*, 5 July 2019). Aside from England and Wales, the history of policing in Northern Ireland has been particularly challenging.

Divided society policing in Northern Ireland

The history of policing in Northern Ireland has been marred by turbulence and conflict, one through which the myths and realities of the Irish policing model have endured but also fractured and changed following the emergence of PSNI. At the core of Northern Irish policing and lodged within what Edna Longley described as a 'cultural corridor', was a space through which both Irishness and Britishness travelled and intermingled, which resulted in a lengthy and violent sectarian-political conflict referred to colloquially as 'The Troubles' (Longley, 1993 cited in Murphy, 2013). Policing 'occupied a contested space' within society and became a divisive and emotional issue that stood between the Catholic and Protestant communities. Police reform was integral to the establishment of a political settlement in a bid to soothe the Catholic community's historic angst towards the RUC (and RIC that came before) (Ellison and Pino, 2012: 137–8, and see Ellison and Smyth, 2000; Mulcahy, 2006; Weitzer, 1995).

The RUC adopted a concept of so-called divided society policing, which has continued to attract scholarly attention. Much of the original focus has been directed towards Northern Ireland (see Brewer, 1991; Ellison and Smyth, 2000; Hamilton and Moore, 1995; Hillyard, 1979, 1997; Weitzer, 1985, 1987, 1997), which Ellison and Smyth (2000) termed the 'divided-society model of the North' (Ellison and Smyth, 2000: 182). This concept can be understood as a society that 'privileges divisions based on ethnic, religious or national division' and, where the police and policing are often a product of those social divisions, conflict and power distribution (Hillyard, 1997: 163). As a consequence, policing was both political and politicized and linked to the state (Ellison and Smyth, 2000). Wide-ranging issues relating to policing policies, the structure of the police and the administration of the wider criminal justice system were central to the polarization of Northern Irish society contributing to the societal divide. Broadly Protestant (Unionists) saw this arrangement as necessary to maintain the constitutional status quo faced with what they perceived as the threat of militant republicanism, while the Catholics (nationalists) understood this as the sectarian nature of the state (Ellison and Smyth, 2000; Hamilton and Moore, 1995). Minority groups within divided societies typically challenged police legitimacy without which the police encounter is often ineffective and conflicting, which can potentially erode public safety (Nanes, 2018).

From the perspective of former RUC officers, the sheer size of the organization (13,500 at its peak) and the relatively small population of Northern Ireland meant there were few Protestant families without some personal link and to the loss of colleagues. This remained a highly emotive subject. Many had accepted the need for broader police reform: an emphasis on building community safety through community-police partnerships and statutory oversight bodies. When a noticeable shift from the quasi-military and counterterrorist styles of policing that had dominated policing approaches from the 1970s to the 1990s came (the British government introduced a policy of police primacy in 1976 which placed the RUC at the forefront of combatting terrorism), many agreed that community engagement should *and* could be embraced (Author interviews with former RUC, 2008–2011). Arguably the RUC 'made progress towards modernization' moving from divided society policing to 'universalistic policing' from this time. As an organization it was suggested that it moved towards greater even-handedness in its 'dealings with Protestant and Catholic suspects alike and it embrace[d] a fiercely anti-political ethos' (Weitzer, 1987: 88). Evidence of the attempts to bridge the divide through community engagement approaches were frequently expressed in discussions with former RUC–PSNI officers, despite an acceptance that maintaining social order in deeply divided societies is a contested activity particularly when considering a return to perceived normality (Mulcahy, 1999). Later the Patten Report recommendations 44 to 51 addressed the strategy of 'policing with the community' stating that this 'should be the core function of the police service and ... every police station' [para 7.9, Patten Report, 1999]. Policing with the community was seen to underpin the process of institutional transformation and reform to PSNI (Saferworld, 2014: 1) (see chapter 7 for further details relating to the Patten reforms).

For some RUC officers, the attraction of an overseas deployment was greater than employment in the *new* PSNI and many were quick to apply for further overseas secondments. Others seized the 'Patten package', a lucrative financial severance package and moved into the corporate security world (Author interviews with former RUC officers, 2010–2011; Ellison and O'Reilly, 2008). However, these former RUC–PSNI officers contributed to a refining and modernization of the post-1989 UK policing brand. Those who deployed to peacekeeping (and later peacebuilding/capacity building) missions brought a *Northern Irish* experience of semi-military and divided society policing as well as a familiarity with civilian-military co-operation and later counterterrorism and counter-intelligence experience. Post

Patten, an additional facet was added: an experience of institutional and cultural policing reform as the RUC transitioned to the PSNI (Ellison, 2008; Ellison and Pino, 2012; Sinclair, 2012).

The internationalization of UK policing

The UK policing brand has strong global resonance (Reiner, 1992) which began with a circulation of police personnel, policing styles, and skills from the nineteenth century (Sinclair and Williams, 2007). From that time there was national and international toing and froing, as senior police officers in the English, Welsh, and sometimes Scottish provinces, brought in 'men to show how things should be done' who might typically take up a future posting overseas. The MPS excelled from early on in establishing a cadre of police experts that other forces could draw upon at home and overseas creating a professional and social policing network. Alfred John List joined the MPS cadre and, as a result moved from London to take command of the Scottish county of Haddingtonshire (East Lothian) in 1831, where there had been particular concerns about vagrancy and rising levels of crime. He was said to have been the 'most influential police officers of mid-nineteenth century Scotland' (Emsley, 2009: 92). With burgeoning colonial and commonwealth police forces from the nineteenth century, came rising demands for police assistance, which was directed towards the Irish Constabulary or the MPS. One of the earliest international assistance deployments was an inspection undertaken in 1834 by Inspector Francis Mallalieu (MPS) to advise the Barbados Police on police structure and reorganization. Throughout the 1830s MPS officers were deployed to Jamaica, Ceylon, Canada, Australia, and South Africa where demand for their skills was ever increasing (Sinclair, 2006: 13).

The appeal of English (and particularly MPS policing), however, was overshadowed by the Irish police, whose experience of managing public disorder and political dissent were highly sought after. Following the partition in Ireland, further career opportunities opened up for many former RIC officers (and Irish military) overseas; the newly created Palestine Police was one prime example (Anderson and Killingray, 1991; Brogden, 1987a; Fedorowich, 1996; Jeffries, 1952; Sinclair, 2006, 2008). However, Irish (colonial) and English models of policing melded in new ways from the 1920s with the expansion of policing as a technocratic profession uniting police across the English-speaking world. An international community of policing practice was reflected, for example, in the pages of the *Police Journal* (established in 1928) which was dominated by a discourse of science and of policing standardization (Sinclair and Williams, 2007).

Throughout the early part of the twentieth century, senior police advisors circulated across empire, commonwealth, and further afield providing technical assistance and support for police reform. After the British army landed in Sicily in 1943 Arthur Young, who at thirty-one had been the youngest chief constable ever (for Leamington Spa), arrived with sixty British police officers to reorganize the police system in Italy. Young was dynamic and brought a 'British' style to police reform without seeking to change the basic structure of Italian policing, divided as it was between the military Carabinieri, the rather less military state police, and the local *Vigili* (Emsley and Sinclair, 2011). Young's international career would later see him deployed to Malaya and Kenya during the colonial emergencies in the 1950s and then lastly to Northern Ireland as the first RUC Chief Constable in 1970 (Sinclair, 2006). The reconstruction of Germany's post-1945 police provided the British and Americans with an opportunity to implement what could be described as an early version of democratic police reform (see, for example, Reinke, 2009). The British approach to police reform within their German zone of influence was far closer to a 'civil' than a 'colonial' model of management: the mantra being to 'decentralise, denatizify, demilitarise and democratise' by extricating the police in North-West Germany from their longstanding policing traditions. Decentralization involved the removal of all centralized police structures that had been in place since the Nazi regime and aligned to the different branches of the Nazi police and state security apparatus in Berlin. Key was to move the concept of 'order' as inherent within German policing from its central European root to an 'Anglo-Saxon' approach. This relied (in theory) on the development of an 'independent' police force, politically disentangled from government and the earlier mechanisms of accountability established during the Weimar Republic and Nazi Germany. This 'new' police (as perceived by the British government) became a symbol of a new political order, where many of the extraneous policing duties and responsibilities that would not been out of place in either nineteenth century Ireland or within the British empire had been removed (Reinke, 2009).

Post-war police missions

Reforming the police in post-war Germany and Italy ran parallel to other policing missions in Europe and included a British police mission to Greece (1944–1952), led by an RUC Inspector General, Sir Charles Wickham, who had in the 1930s advised on police reform in Palestine. The British police were specifically tasked with training the 'town police' (Athens Police) and 'county gendarmerie' (outside Athens), advising on police reform, recruitment in the gendarmerie, and 'sorting out' the internment camp on Makronissos Islands (*The Times*, 1949). The British government's selected Wickham for his Northern Irish experiences of managing armed policing units and an understanding of gendarmerie models of policing. Wickham presented a candid opinion of the different UK policing models and clearly distinguished between the 'armed' or 'unarmed' and, he was not averse to the use of a gendarmerie as he had been in Palestine. However, he clearly distinguished between the military and the police advising that 'our aim is to turn [the Greek Police] into a lightly armed police force (civil) … not a military outlook for the less they play at soldiers the better' (The National Archives (TNA) War Office (WO), 1945).

The post-war bilateral missions followed different approaches to police reform and the selection of one or other policing model often highly dependent on the background of the senior officers involved as well as the mission brief. The British police mission to Columbia (1950–1953) provided a very different example to Greece. Following a formal request by the Columbian government for 'British' police officers to redesign their police selection and recruitment processes and to develop suitable training courses for the Columbian national police, an initial mission comprised nine UK police officers (mainly MPS) was deployed led by Sir Douglas Gordon. The Columbian government's brief was that 'the various British systems of police' be 'meld[ed] into the Colombian penal and judicial system'. Yet there was no explanation in the initial brief of how the Columbian government understood British policing and which aspects they were looking for, and, why they considered that this style of policing could or indeed should align with their wider systems of criminal justice (TNA Foreign Office (FO), 1950). This apparent lack of clarity resulted in the mission running quickly into difficulties; Gordon commenting that the 'Columbian Police are still subject to political influence favourable to the government', which was not the case in the UK and that it proved very difficult to negotiate police to police. The UK government became frustrated with the situation with a senior FO official (1953) denigrating British policing approaches to overseas reform stating that:

> While British police methods are the envy of the world ... experience in many places (most recently the bi-zone of Germany) has shown that they do not travel well ... many are obnoxious about our post-Peel ideals about the function of the police (FCO, 1952).

The pick-and-mix approach to overseas police reform included both broad models of policing, which were selected according to whether a civil or semi-military approach was required. However, the UK government arguably preferred to rubber stamp British policing with 'Peelian qualities' rather than the Irish/colonial variant, where the latter may have been a more preferable option within the international transfer of a UK policing style.

The post-colonial and Cold War period saw British police continuing their involvement in Asia. By the early 1960s—Malayan Independence occurred in 1957—the US commitment to Vietnam had escalated through special missions and training provided to the South Vietnamese army and police. In 1964, the little-known British police mission to South Vietnam (1964–1967) was deployed to Saigon to replace the British aid mission to Vietnam (BRAIM), which had included five former colonial police officers from the Malayan Police, selected for their earlier counter-insurgency expertise. The US military had earlier observed colonial policing on the ground during the Malayan emergency and had the intention of implementing a similar policing approach in South Vietnam (Comber, 2008: 4–5, 196). Independent of BRAIM, the UK had supported the South Vietnamese police prior to 1965 as a result earlier police linkages between the Malayan Police and the South Vietnamese Police (Author interview with Leon Comber, February 2014). General Headquarters Far East Land Forces had been running a services training assistance programme which included police training courses for the South Vietnamese Civil Guard and had been delivered by UK, Australian, and New Zealand police trainers. Neither the Malaysian nor the British government had wanted this programme of police assistance to become public knowledge and South Vietnamese police were routinely routed through the military airfield at Butterworth (Malaysia), rather than the international airport at Kuala Lumpur. Between 1962 and 1965, approximately 700 South Vietnamese police received public order, 'jungle warfare', and intelligence services training which drew on the recent counter-insurgency experiences of the Malayan Police (Thompson, 1978). BRAIM and indeed all subsequent missions to South Vietnam sought to recruit former colonial police officers and mission details described as 'civilian' police mentoring were kept under wraps (FO, 1964).

The internationalization of British policing continued throughout the early cold war period with a pattern of retaining or recruiting former colonial police. Officers 'stayed on' in countries that included Kenya, Nigeria, Botswana, Ghana, and Tanzania and often in very senior advisory roles providing advice to the newly independent governments (Sinclair, 2006; Author interviews with former colonial police officers, 2000). In the early 1960s, there was an appetite for former colonial police to join police forces in the Gulf States and serve as senior advisors to the Ministry of the Interior (MOI). Examples included Derek Franklin and Ian Henderson who had served in the Kenya Police as special branch operatives (Author interview with Derek Franklin, January 2000 and Franklin Private Papers (unpublished), 2008). The operational realities of 'overseas' policing that continued through the Cold War and post-Cold War necessitated elements of a security-focused, counter-insurgency and then later a counterterrorist policing approach. While this may, theoretically, have dispelled traditional Peelian images, the brand for export remained an official construct of the English/Irish models. Increasingly it became multifaceted, encompassing key policing institutions including the MPS, Scotland Yard, the National Policing Improvement Agency (NPIA), and latterly the National Crime Agency (founded 2013), and the National Security Cyber Centre (operational in 2016) (Author interviews with UK police 2010–2019).

Twenty-first century brand(s)

In the twenty-first century the UK brand has reshaped and arguably there are now three different policing systems that each align and are integral to the British policing brand although Police Scotland and Northern Ireland have become increasingly distinctive in relation to internationalization approaches and brand offer.

In Northern Ireland, the RUC became increasingly active overseas from the mid-1990s, which included the Western Balkans, Iraq, and Afghanistan (Sinclair, 2012). Exporting lessons learned in counterterrorism, counterintelligence, and hostile environment policing from the Troubles period was 'pursed with vigour by elements within the Northern Ireland policing establishment'. This developed the UK international policing expertise more generally and fed into the organization's global brand, providing a new career for retired RUC officers (Ellison and O'Reilly 2008a: 337). Following the Police (Northern Ireland) Act 2000, the PSNI underwent a 'dramatic and radical reform' through an erosion of a quasi-military model in favour of a state civilian model (Mulcahy, 2013). This transformation was an opportunity to develop a new facet of the Northern Irish brand by sharing lessons and good practice overseas relating to institutional, organizational, and cultural reforms. Weber Shandwick engaged by the organization as public relations consultants sought to brand the PSNI at two level: the introduction of the 'new' organization, and in relation to Northern Ireland's geo-branding, multiply 'efforts to enhance its reputation status internationally' (Ellison and O'Reilly 2008a: 336). This public relations agency put in place a clear strategy to communicate all RUC to PSNI changes to PSNI personnel and Northern Ireland's community particularly in relation to the symbolic value of the new name, badge, and uniform (Murphy, 2013). The PSNI's highly recognizable name and badge remained unchanged until June 2020 when the Chief Constable, Simon Byrne, released draft images to the media of a possible (re)branding from the organization's 'Police Service Northern Ireland' to Police Service NI. These proposals were turned down and in June 2021, PSNI introduced much smaller changes to its branding with a typeface alteration emphasizing the 'Police Service' in PSNI rather than using the term 'Police Service NI' (Hughes, 2021).

Scottish policing has followed a similar path to RUC/PSNI following the establishment of Police Scotland in 2013. Scotland transformed to a national system from eight regional police forces necessitating a radical overhaul of the structure, organization, and governance of the organization (Fyfe and Terstra, 2019). A (re)branding of the organization followed, which all police officers have been encouraged to support and rests on the values of policing for a 'safe, protected and resilient Scotland' (Police Scotland, 2020). Branding guidance was developed specifically for Police Scotland officers with detailed instructions on how the organization's brand personality should be upheld to 'evoke emotions of confidence, inclusion, freedom and security' (Stenson, 2015). The advent of Police Scotland aligned with a drive to promote the brand internationally independently of *as well as* in conjunction with UK policing as a whole.

Concluding comment

As we have moved into the twenty-first century, UK policing has continued to internationalize. No one particular aspect of the brand has been exported over another and the contemporary internationalization of British policing (1991–2021) has often provided a sense of 'back to the futurism'. As with the nineteenth and twentieth centuries, the export and take up of UK policing has been governed by a 'pick-and-mix' approach that could theoretically be 'hard' (Irish) or 'soft' (English)—or a combination of both—depending on local exigencies and circumstances. Arguably what was in the Whig tradition mythologized as the best history of British policing has impacted upon the evolution of police work on a global level (Ellison and Pino, 2012; Sinclair, 2012). By 2021, international policing has been delivered from across English and Welsh constabularies as well as Northern Ireland and Scotland (see chapter 7) and has contributed to post conflict peacekeeping and international development. There has been a rise in the delivery of UK policing by both the official state sector as well as a growing corporate sector (see chapter 5), both having benefitted from the original models developing in the nineteenth century. I now turn (in chapter 3) to a series of case studies to chart international policing as it developed from the early 1990s.

3
From Peacekeeping to Statebuilding

'Conflict Entrepreneurs'

> International policing seemed more strategic and gave me far more responsibility. You feel the difference that you make is much greater and that you are making a much bigger contribution to policing than at a local level. It was a great opportunity to go to Bosnia ... an experience I thoroughly enjoyed. But it was hard, it was tough going at times, it was hard being away from the family, it was hard working in a different culture, it was hard ... the working conditions were really, really hard but, despite all of that I learned so much about myself and about policing and I came back a better cop.
>
> **Former Det Chief Inspector MPS, deployed to Bosnia, 2014**

There were three categories of officers who chose to go on missions: 'missionaries, mercenaries and misfits'. I added a fourth one which was medal collectors! The 'mercenary' is what an individual can get in allowances and screw out of the system. 'Missionaries' really do what they can to support other countries and bring their policing expertise—individuals who do it for the right reasons. They put a lot of energy into trying to achieve things. They are people who really want to bring about change and who have a level of integrity and standards that a lot of countries don't possess. This may sound ideological but there are those who

do actively put themselves out to do things at their own expense. These are the officers that we should be highlighting not those who go because they have been told to go, will get promotion or will benefit from overseas allowances. 'Misfits' often go overseas to escape trouble at home and can end up going back earlier and 'medal collectors' collect missions!
**Former Chief Supt MPS and
Head CIVPOL UNAET Mission, 2011**

The term 'conflict entrepreneur' (Barth Eide and Tanke Holm, 1999) has summed up the professional engagement of many UK police who engaged with international policing. Within these case study chapters, I provide snapshots to explore the historic trajectory of UK international policing and what it has revealed about the UK policing brand's characteristics. From the early 1990s, UK police cohorts were deployed in support of traditional UN peacekeeping in BiH, Kosovo, and Timor Leste and senior UK police supported the more complex task of state-building in Sierra Leona. The UK policing brand provided sufficient characteristics to allow for a 'pick-and-mix' approach through the two broad policing models on offer. However, the challenge lay within there being sufficient capacity across UK policing to meet international demand. In BiH and Kosovo, there was availability of RUC and MDP officers to provide armed capability while in East Timor there was not.

The post-Cold War period was 'unique' in British history; the UK's continuing global influence and wealth (though no longer as an imperial power or concert power) provided some opportunities to determine the new world order (Burleigh, 2017). The fragmentation of the Soviet Union and a shift to an unregulated market economy was accompanied by growing conflict and crises and the struggle to rebuild governmental and other institutions. This created an unprecedented demand for third party intervention (Bayley, 1999). Internationally assisted police reform became integral to post-conflict peace settlements as intra-state conflict escalated following the disintegration of former Soviet states (Barth Eide and Tanke Holm, 1999; Heinemann-Gruder and Grebendschikov, 2006). The UK at this time continually 'punched above its weight' through a period characterized by an unpredictable security environment (Author interview with Major

General, British Army, June 2014). Post-1989 ushered in a new period of 'peacekeeping' policing accompanied by a 'significant expansion' in policing activities as a result of an augmentation in UN, NATO, and EU multilateral missions (Home Office, 2007a; Grabosky, 2009: 101).[1] Throughout this era of interventions, the UK embarked on a series of significant foreign *military* and *civilian* interventions including BiH, Kosovo, Sierra Leone, Afghanistan, and Libya, a myriad of smaller overseas capacity-building programmes as well as domestic operations in Northern Ireland.

When considering the international policing landscape within each mission, it can be hard to fathom the contribution of each country. Arguably more scholars than not have found little evidence of its effectiveness (particularly in relation to community policing) (see in particular Brogden, 2002; Brogden and Nijhar, 2005; Ellison and Pino, 2012; Pino and Wiatrowski, 2006), and robust approaches undertaken by gendarmerie and military forces through community securitization have met with varying degrees of success in the short to medium term (Friesendorf, 2018; Sinclair, 2015, Sinclair and Burdett, 2018). Certainly, there has been a thread between the provision of community security and the use of harder policing approaches that included semi-military and gendarmerie style forces. This has included the recent NATO concept of stability policing (NATO, 2020).[2] A simple explanation posited for this approach is that a certain concentration of coercive power is necessary to ensure that a process of developmental 'compromises' can occur in the future (Van Veen, 2020:1).

Putting scholarly cynicism aside, there has always been a chasm between theoretical concepts and on-the-ground activities. I suggest international policing as understood by UK police is generally framed by the notion: that an officer perceives this as international policing *assistance* (which can be an activity, approach, or co-operation); situated within a process of change

---

[1] The term Peace Support Operation (PSO) was used by the UK 'to describe an organised international intervention in a country affected by conflict. Most, but not all, PSOs have a strong military component. A PSO's main purpose is usually to establish and/or ensure stability during the period following a peace agreement, so that reconstruction and development can take place' (FCO, 2007a: 10).

[2] Stability Policing is an approach developed by NATO (in collaboration with police and military stakeholders) to address three security challenges within FCAS: the deployment gap, the enforcement gap, and the institutional sustainability gap which can necessitate robust policing (gendarmerie) to ensure interoperability with the military. Filling the stability gap can theoretically be undertaken through a transition from an initial larger-scale military presence to the use of stability policing police units and has resulted in some EU gendarmeries (for example, the Gendarmerie National (France) and the Carabinieri (Italy) developing integrated police units (Stingo, Dziedzic, and Barbu, 2012).

(that may or may not be underway); that support for that process of change is given through the establishment of good policing practice (whatever this may be) and through a process of knowledge transfer and exchange. Typically, within FCAS the reform processes have relied on the provision of community security and engagement and may align with Ellison and Pino (2012):

> Perhaps the most we should (or can) realistically expect of a police reform process in transitional states is that citizens are protected *from* [sic] the coercive machinations of the state and its control apparatuses ... for the *real* [sic] solution to development solutions lies in transforming political structures ... citizen safety should not be divorced from this (Ellison and Pino, 2012, 80).

International peacekeeping: Bosnia and Herzegovina

The concept of 'peacekeeping' (policing) was introduced by UN Secretary-General Dag Hammerskold 'to maintain quiet' (securitization and stability) and provide a breathing space to create political solutions (Greener, 2009). The creation of a civilian unit: United Nations Department of Peacekeeping (UNDPKO) in May 1993, was tasked with the planning and coordination of policing within UN peacekeeping missions and, further consolidated the importance of the role of police alongside other civilian and security actors (Hansen, 2002: 21). Policing activities over the following decade deepened and broadened with the traditional support, monitoring, advising, reporting, and training (SMART) model becoming outdated. UN police personnel were drawn into executive policing functions in Kosovo and East Timor and towards the three 'R's: reform, restructuring, and rebuilding (Hansen, 2002; SU, 2014; UN, 2000).[3]

The conflict in BiH from 1992-1995—'Europe's bloodiest conflict since the Second World War'—led to NATO's Implementation Force intervening following the 1995 Dayton Accord to end the war. The UN provided the

---

[3] In 2000 the United Nations Panel on Peace Operations called for a 'doctrinal shift' in the use of civilian police in UN peace operations, to focus primarily on the reform and restructuring of local police forces in addition to traditional advisory, training, and monitoring tasks (UN, 2000b).

mandate for BiH (and Kosovo) and deployed military and police missions alongside NATO and the EU (Friesendorf, 2012: 39–40) onto what would become an increasingly cluttered security and development landscape. The UK initially sent 1,200 troops to relieve the besieged Bosnian capital, Sarajevo in support of the UN in 1995. Defence Secretary Michael Portillo suggested that despite the nefarious situation there should be an emphasis on peacekeeping rather than warfighting (BBC News, 1995). In terms of managing the BiH police this was particularly problematic. The war had left three police forces: Bosniak, Croat, and Serb each with its own jurisdiction, a legacy of ethnic cleansing and having been employed as a key instrument of state brutality (International Crisis Group, 2005). The UN International Police Task Force (IPTF) had deployed late; its officers were unarmed and did not have an executive mandate and relied on the support of these local security forces: peace was a long time coming. Richard Monk who became UN IPTF Police Commissioner in BiH in 1998 was asked by the then Home Secretary, Michael Howard, to respond to 'constant demands by the American to add British police officers to the UN mission in Sarajevo' to support the Dayton Peace Agreement. He visited the region commenting (2011):

> After three days, I was convinced of the humanitarian need and that the UK [police] was conspicuous by its absence. The Foreign Secretary was supportive but of course the trick was selling the idea to HM Treasury. We managed to raise thirty officers from UK Police Forces and subsequently another thirty after I had made an assessment of the effectiveness of the first. I had already been appointed in my own right to inspect the UK Sovereign Base Area in Cyprus so I knew something about overseas policing but this was a whole new experience.... I became the third Commissioner of the United Nations International Police Task Force (IPTF), responsible for re-building and reforming the police forces in the Republic Srpska and Federation of Bosnia Herzegovina. The diplomatic community were trying to make up their minds about what the rule of law really meant and how the police forces were going to break free of the local political influence. I kept questioning what is it that the international police force should be doing?... (Monk, 2011).

The early years of international policing assistance in BiH and then Kosovo were underpinned by ad hoc approaches to recruitment and selection procedures, pre-deployment training, and the mission's operational policing requirements (Author fieldnotes, BiH, 2010).[4] At the time of the early deployments to Bosnia, one week of rudimentary 'hostile environment' training was provided with official overseas policing manuals not produced until 2004 (HO, 2004; FCO, 2007a, 2007b). While officers were drawn from a range of UK constabularies including Devon and Cornwall, Dorset, MPS, City of London, Kent, Surrey, Staffordshire, South Yorkshire, Lincolnshire, West Midlands, and Merseyside and the RUC-PSNI, the initial approach focused as much on policing styles as it did in ensuring UK policing availability, rather than selecting officers with prior international experience. There was also a sense that the UK government was 'spreading the load' across the different constabularies with the larger forces supplying more officers: the MPS provided around eight annually for example (Author interview with former Det Inspector MPS deployed to BiH 1998, May 2011).

The UN's initial brief to international police present largely revolved around 'the establishment of law and order, policing the agreement, and maintaining high profile visibility' as described further by this former RUC-PSNI Superintendent (2010):

> On the ground this was partly about ensuring that Bosnian, Serb and Croatian police policed in a fair way ... We would go into the police stations and check, how were they receiving the public, we would check the cells and look at how the prisoners were being treated, we would see what level of security they provided the community, we would enable the return of Muslims and Serbs to their own areas ... we monitored all aspects of policing that were really very contentious—that is during our early deployments (1998) (Former Supt RUC-PSNI, then Regional Commander, Banja Lucca, January, 2010).

Yet the overriding impression of the UN mission from the perspective of many UK personnel interviewed was one of 'chaos' (Author fieldnotes, 2010). First the range of policing activities was far wider than expected or intended. An example often given were the 'specific goals' to be attained known as 'certification' whereby internationals worked alongside the local

---

[4] The HO and ACPO originally planned for there to be a sufficient number of police volunteers for deployment 'in response to an emergency situation overseas as part of an international group: At 7 days' notice a small group of 10 officers to liaise with mission planners at UN/OSCE/EU headquarters, then deploy to theatre to establish the field headquarters and train incoming personnel. At 30 days' notice a group of 40 officers to deploy to theatre to form the operational core of a newly established civilian policing mission. This following an advance risk assessment co-ordinated by the International Policing Unit' (HO, 2004: 46–7).

police to ensure that they 'performed to a specific level—there was a huge long list of activities that you had to tick in order for that local officer to be certified' (Author interview with former MPS Supt, January 2011). A lack of detail within the Dayton Accord in relation to policing activities certainly contributed to this (Friesendorf, 2012) as well as poor mission leadership, planning, and operational support provided to local police. The view of many UK police was that this led to a 'distinct lack of interest and sensitivity' on the part of some internationals (as well as the local police) as this former MPS officer (2014) commented:

> Somebody had to be in the police station to deal with complaints from the public and some of us (UK police) volunteered as others did not. We would go out and look at the incidents they (the local police) were dealing with and try and help. There was this one... they'd heard a bang in the night, nobody from the local police went to look to see what had happened. We went out the next day and saw that a guy had laid down in the middle of the town centre, such as it was, on a grenade and killed himself, deliberately, committed suicide, and nobody had done anything about it. They (the local police) just happened to find his body out there in the morning and we're supposed to be monitoring and seeing that they were developing but it was often so chaotic and they weren't interested...' (Former Inspector, MPS, January 2014).

Certainly, there was clear evidence of the frustrations experienced by UK cohort leaders at the lack of direction within the early years in Bosnia as candidly expressed by this former senior officer (2011):

> I felt a bit at sea with what we were doing and so what I did was I went and met the British Ambassador and I insisted we had a monthly meeting ... I can remember saying: 'What is it you want of British policing out here and why is Britain in Bosnia? What is it we're doing strategically here that you have invested in because it isn't clear? 'A', we've got military still but 'B' we've got UK police officers here, because this is big investment for the UK?' I didn't really get an answer (Former Det Chief Supt, MPS, January 2010).

UK policing assistance in BiH was rapidly followed by the requirement for an international police presence in Kosovo. By early 1999, NATO was embroiled in an effort to prevent further violence perpetrated by Yugoslav President Slobodan Milošević against Kosovars (ethnic Albanians) in Serbia's southern province of Kosovo.[5] On 9 June 1999, NATO and Yugoslavia signed the Kumanovo Agreement, which stipulated the withdrawal of Yugoslav/Serbian forces from Kosovo and the creation of an international security force, NATO's Kosovo Force, which at its peak numbered 50,000 soldiers. The actions of the security forces, the Serbian police, and their special police units, as well as the local militias (for example the Kosovo Liberation Army), were widely condemned for their actions and crimes against humanity (Friesendorf, 2012). Subsequently resolution 1244 (10 June 1999) authorized the UN Secretary General to establish an international civil presence in Kosovo—the UN Interim Administration Mission in Kosovo (UNMIK). From a security (and policing) perspective, UNMIK prioritized securitization (peacekeeping) rather than development (capacity building). In a rupture from SMART, executive policing was authorized allowing international police to carry out full operational policing with armed capability. This necessitated an urgent rethink in Whitehall about the model of policing the UK could provide and where that police capacity could be sourced without impacting local policing (Sinclair, 2012).

Bringing the Northern Irish experience to the Balkan context

The conflict that ensued in the Western Balkans provided an opportunity for RUC officers who had prior experience of the Northern Irish semi-military policing model and had honed their skill sets during the Troubles. These skills became invaluable in BiH and Kosovo and led to the perpetuation of the long-held mythologies surrounding this specific model of UK policing, even during this period of radical transformation in the aftermath of the Patten Report and the transition to PSNI.

As part of the UNMIK mission, RUC,[6] (PSNI), and later MDP *cohorts* were deployed to Kosovo[7] which became the gateway to a future career

---

[5] The term Kosovo refers to the administrative unit in the South-western corner of the Republic of Serbia.
[6] The RUC undertook overseas missions from the mid 1990s to Bosnia, Kosovo, Ethiopia, and the Commonwealth of Dominica. Bilateral programmes undertaken during this period included, for example, support to Mongolia for the Soros Foundation's Rule of Law program to assist in the implementation of a community-policing programme in Ulaanbaatar (Author interview with former RUC Chief Constable, January 2011).
[7] In Kosovo, UK police (drawn from Scotland Yard and other UK forces) sent investigators to prepare evidence for war crimes tribunals (including ethnic cleansing). The UK was one of several NATO countries invited with specific requests for Scotland Yard owing to its

in international security (Ellison, 2008; Ellison and O'Reilly, 2008a). As a former PSNI Chief Constable (2011) explained:

> We [RUC] were far more deployable than many other forces, apart from the MOD who had the same, sort of, immediate skills.... 'A', it helps to have an armed force because many of these deployments, even for health and safety reasons, require some armed capability. The other skill, of course, is they [RUC] were so used to conflict. You had a body of individuals who routinely dealt with the sorts of conflicts and the terrorist threat which is unique, absolutely unique in the UK and all those skills are absolutely transferable actually, in two ways, one is as serving sworn officers, Kosovo, and two is actually retired officers. As you will know, through NICO there's a huge industry in retired officers delivering training as well as security. You still have the security people because that's a different bit of business, but the British brand of policing is very sellable and so when I was in Kosovo, when I was in Iraq ... the number of Belfast accents was overwhelming (Former PSNI Chief Constable, February, 2011).

In July 1999, following Prime Minister Tony Blair's visit to Kosovo, the deployment of sixty RUC officers was announced as part of a future 100-strong UK contingent: an RUC request for volunteers is said to have attracted over 300 officers (Author interview former RUC Chief Constable, January, 2011) in accordance with Section 8 of the Police (Northern Ireland) Act 1998. RUC officers were told the mission would be executive and armed although there had been some discrepancy around this as one officer (2010) explained:

> According to rumour at the time the FCO had pushed for the Mission to be 'unarmed' so as to share the load around other UK forces but the UN wasn't having any of it as the post war/NATO invasion situation in Kosovo was deemed to be too unstable (Former Det Chief Inspect, RUC–PSNI, 10 May 2010).

---

international reputation. UK investigators deployed on multiple assignments during this period including to Lebanon in support of the UN's Special Tribunal following the assassination of Prime Minister Rafic Hariri in 2005 (Author interview with a former Det Chief Supt MPS (Scotland Yard), January 2010).

Initially the UNMIK mission was advertised for one year with three flights home paid for by the FCO. Three weeks of pre-deployment training was provided in Northern Ireland and, following the Patten recommendations for greater cross-border co-operation moved to the Garda College Templemore where international experiences of Bosnia, Slovenia, and Cyprus were shared (Author interview with former PSNI Chief Constable, February 2011). All RUC officers were trained and issued with a Glock-17 automatic pistol as 'part of the thinking was that an automatic weapon offered increased defensive firepower but also because many less developed countries rated a police service on the weapons they carried and a revolver just wasn't going to convince anyone!' (Author interview with former Sergeant RUC–PSNI, 11 January 2011). According to a memo signed by the Chief Constable (CC) on 2 August 1999, officers selected required the 'relevant experience, including handling arms, working alongside military forces and dealing with a divided community' (*The Irish Times*, 2 August 1999). This provided an opportunity for RUC officers who were growing disillusioned with the reform processes back home to apply their unique skill set overseas.

Yet for others the shift that this entailed in terms of an operational and tactical policing culture resulted in something of a personal and professional unravelling as this former RUC–PSNI officer explained and led to his decision to undertake regular international missions (2010):

> There were mixed feelings at the time that is certain. For those of us who served in the RUC, there was a feeling that you would see this through to the end [as RUC], to ensure that the government in Northern Ireland had an opportunity to flourish. Obviously, terrorism had been our number one objective: defeat terrorism whether it be loyalist or whether it be republican. You focused on that so hard, you had great loyalty towards your fellow RUC, great loyalty towards the job and the task at hand ... your personal life and your working life were meshed into one. So, in 2001 when the Patten recommendations were implemented it felt over and done with and immediately then you had to review your own life and really say: well, if that is behind me then where am I going, what am I going to do ... ? (Former RUC–PSNI Sergeant, January, 2010—deployed to Bosnia and Kosovo on UN and EU missions for five tours).

Revisiting divided society policing

While there was no magical transformation towards this policing with the community ethos nor were the historic rifts between communities fully healed in the longer term, RUC–PSNI officers saw their prior experiences of divided society policing as providing valuable lessons that could support other societies in transition (Author interviews 2010–2014; Ellison and O'Reilly, 2008a). During the early deployments to both BiH and Kosovo (1999–2002) there were extreme levels of tension across the communities where 'the style of policing that we carried forward from the RUC was perfect for the environment that is both community based and intelligence led' (Author interview with former RUC–PSNI Sergeant, January 2010). Yet some former RUC officers talked about the levels of mistrust and suspicion they had always felt by Catholic communities in Northern Ireland. In Kosovo, they did not always fare better and neither did other international police who were subjected to hostile and sometimes violent behaviour, which reflected the extreme tension within local communities. On one occasion early in 2000, RUC officers (accompanied by an Albanian translator) reported that they had come 'under attack' by a crowd of Serbians chanting 'go back to London' (and curiously 'go back to Sussex'). Any attempts at crowd dialogue and pacification failed and the handful of UK police present had to be extracted by a French military KFOR unit. This led a PSNI inspector (2010) to consider whether it was preferable to appear as a 'Northern Irish' or 'British' police officer as he explained:

> I wore a Union Jack badge on my uniform as well as an RUC badge. Within a couple of weeks, I ditched the Union Jack so as to avoid the Bill Clinton/Tony Blair jibes and insults from the locals. They then thought I was Irish and that as I lived in the North of Ireland I was under the occupation of the British and I often heard them shout 'IRA good!' At least it bought me a little empathy and allowed me to communicate with them a bit more (Former RUC–PSNI Inspector, January, 2010).

This view was endorsed by another RUC–PSNI officer (2010) who had noticed the extent to which UK policing was culturally 'divided' between British and Northern Irish models:

> A plus factor was that we were not seen as British police but rather Northern Irish police. Perceived as having a Celtic connection did

Revisiting divided society policing 77

wonders in winning over hearts and minds—as did our reputation for being able to consume alcohol without apparent effect! (Former RUC–PSNI Det Chief Inspector, June 2011).

Mitrovica some twenty-five miles north of Pristina presented considerable challenges for the international security community and threats of violence, terrorism, and extremism for minority communities. The town contained approximately half of all Serbs remaining in Kosovo on the southern side divided by a heavily fortified bridge from the Albanian community on the other side (HoC, 2000: 516). The situation confronted by UNMIK and KFOR was often one of instability, serious public disorder, shootings, and bombings and former members of the RUC cohort commented that this was not 'so alien' and a situation they were used to dealing with back home. However, any view the RUC cohort commander may have had was not necessarily upheld either by police from other countries as this officer (2010) explained:

> Some police from other countries swung between total inaction and complete over-reaction.... Decision making was not a problem for the RUC whilst officers from some contingents went into spasm if they thought they had to make a decision and then be held accountable We used our experience to weigh up situations much better ... in the early days when there was a lot of hostility from the Serbs towards CIVPOL, our experience of working in Northern Ireland with hostile communities helped a great deal. Besides there was always the 'them and us' factor that the Northern Irish police could draw upon (Former Inspector, RUC–PSNI, January 2010).

By 1999, the UK had deployed 100 police officers: sixty RUC to UNMIK out of a total of 2,261 police officers drawn from EU, NATO, and other countries (UN, 2000) with a further forty UK police deployed to OSCE to provide technical assistance (training) rather than operational duties. The Foreign Affairs Select Committee at that time deplored the lack of international police to take primacy from KFOR, which had been the UN's goal and queried whether there was sufficient international policing expertise available. An FCO report published in 2000 posited that:

> The diversity of cultures and backgrounds is obvious from the list of 45 countries ... With the best will in the world, some police sent to Kosovo

have simply not been up to the task, we heard from a number of authoritative sources when we visited Kosovo. This has meant that the numbers of effective police are even smaller (FCO, 2000).

Subsequently, the UK then promised a further eighty police for 2001, although it had until that point been reliant the 'first' sixty RUC officers and subsequent rotations of RUC cohorts. The expertise the RUC brought, the FCO noted (2000) was invaluable:

> ... A force with more experience and skill in policing divided communities than any other in the world. Wherever we went in Kosovo, we heard praise for the RUC... we recommend that the FCO explore with the Northern Ireland authorities the possibility of recruiting more RUC officers for service in Kosovo (Foreign Affairs Select Committee, 2000).

Praise for RUC skills and expertise within high-risk environments appeared in a number of official reports during the early years and did much to bolster the organization's international reputation as this anecdotal evidence (2010) suggested:

> A huge test came in March of 2004 when 'extremist' Albanians launched an uprising against Serbian enclaves in Kosovo. Over a three day period 29 churches were destroyed, Serb villages razed and police and KFOR attacked. We received in the North 1200 refugees. The incident actually started on the Main Bridge in Mitrovica when an Albanian crowd pushed into the north. The situation soon deteriorated into a gun battle in which seven were killed and over fifty wounded. Civil disorder broke out all over Kosovo. The International Crisis Group report in April of that year criticized the UN and KFOR for total inaction and loss of control but, in a damning report, it stated that if it hadn't been for a handful of police officers from Northern Ireland the situation in the whole of Kosovo would have been totally lost (there were four of us in Kosovo at the time) (Former Inspector RUC–PSNI, June 2010).

Certainly, the RUC–PSNI's experience and understanding of divided society policing within executive policing raised their profile in BiH and Kosovo and supported elements of gendarmerie and military broader peacekeeping approaches. While 'community policing' remained a theoretical aspiration to return policing 'to the people' and, designate local police officers to engage with communities, the environment required robust policing to securitize communities, prevent further bloodshed and move Kosovo on the path to its independence in 2008. This necessitated the provision of (executive) armed policing.

Armed policing capability

Police firearms capability in England, Wales, and Scotland remains smaller than other European police organizations where the concept of the unarmed bobby has retained an iconic significance. Although as Waddington earlier reflected this has been a 'manufactured myth' (Waddington quoted in Waldren, 2007) as police can call upon authorized firearms officers or specialist firearms officers (who are trained to a higher standard) to attend an incident and, have recourse to the military (Waddington, 1991). However, in Northern Ireland the RUC (and then PSNI) were trained to use firearms and routinely armed on duty and, during the Troubles, RUC officers routinely carried firearms while off duty for their own protection. The Belfast Harbour Police and the Belfast International Airport Constabulary have also been trained and authorized to carry firearms (Author interview with former RUC–PSNI Inspector, January, 2010). In addition, the Civil Nuclear Constabulary are routinely armed as are MDP with the exception of their CID officers. The MDP have played a significant role in international policing and deployed police on rotation to Kosovo, where (as in Bosnia) both the MDP (and RUC–PSNI) carried firearms in accordance with their own firearms policy (MDP, 2012).

The situation as it deteriorated in Kosovo called for police with an armed capability[8] and an experience of hostile environments. The RUC was clearly

---

[8] UN missions have sometimes required that police officers be armed for operational reasons (executive policing) in Kosovo and East Timor and/or for personal protection in Kosovo, Iraq, and Afghanistan and must meet firearms training requirements. Officers in non-executive roles in Kosovo (mentoring and advising) were not required to carry a firearm though many did according to their own country's requirements (Author interview with former Chief Supt. Surrey Police, January 2011 deployed to Kosovo). Support from gendarmerie and formed police units (FPUs) to support public order and operational activities where local police are unable to do so. Multinational specialized units (MSUs) were deployed in Bosnia and special police units (SPUs) in Kosovo and included international police personnel from countries with full-time public order units (gendarmeries). The EU created the European Gendarmerie Force (EGF) in 2005 to improve crisis management and to potentially fill the security gap and NATO has since developed the concept of Stability Policing although this does not formally include UK policing (Author interview with Colonel, Italian Carabinieri/NATO Stability Centre of Policing Excellence, January 2017).

the most attractive element of the UK policing brand and could deliver executive policing (Baker, 2007; Krogstad, 2012; Sinclair, 2012) as explained by this former RUC–PSNI officer (2011):

> The RUC was a big plus for the Foreign Office. We had all the firearms skills, had all the tactical skills and hardship [sic] wasn't going to be as much of an issue. So, you're sending out people who are pre-armed and pre-ready. You brief them about mission circumstances, mission specific circumstances and you have an instant transfer of policing (Former RUC–PSNI Inspector, January, 2011—five tours Bosnia and Kosovo (UNMIK and EULEX)).

Key was the semi-military ethos inherent within the RUC (see Ellison and Smyth, 2000) that many openly have described as a 'gendarmerie style' from both an operational and tactical perspective as this officer (2010) described of his policing role in Northern Ireland:

> I've reconciled my thoughts to two styles of policing, but the first one has been as a member of the RUC which may loosely equate to the gendarmerie style of policing where you were militaristic in style. To do that I was dressed in a bullet proof jacket, I was carrying first aid equipment and I certainly had a revolver and, on occasions, I carried a rifle. Often you made sure you had 16 soldiers around you so that the two of you [RUC] could walk through a difficult area. Or if you were a Duty Sergeant, you'd double check the call, you sent a helicopter up above the Head of the Town, Strabane and you tried your best to be unpredictable (Former RUC–PSNI Inspector, January 2010).

This style of policing approach was formalized within the RUC's military style hierarchy as this practitioner explained (2010):

> Sergeants were powerful and similar to sergeants in the army. They were police officers with a lot of experience with very clear hands-on skills and abilities. They could do the job; they could walk the walk and they could run a section along military lines ... (Former RUC–PSNI Inspector, January 2010).

One issue with which the RUC had had familiarity and experience was a close working relationship with the British army: civil-military coordination has been recognized as prerequisite to successful peacekeeping and capacity building (SU, 2014).

Police–military co-operation

There is a growing literature of the blurring of boundaries between military and police roles (particularly within peacekeeping) framed within the wider security landscape (see in particular Easton et al., 2009; Friesendorf, 2012, 2018; Den Heyer, 2011; Topaktas, 2016). Peacekeeping typically requires military and civilian (including police) actors to operate within the same space. Yet it is also widely accepted that arranging this police-military division of work is particularly problematic when there is an imbalance between the numbers of military and police present (Friesendorf, 2012: 14). Traditionally the military do not undertake 'civilian policing' but this has often become part of their operational modus vivendi to bridge what is widely described as a 'security gap' (Last, 2009). While gendarmerie organizations are widely recognized as filling that security gap and providing semi-military through to civilian policing, deploying their capacity can be limited (Friesendorf, 2018; Sinclair, 2015, Topaktas, 2016).

Civil-military coordination arguably was part of the RUC's DNA and also to some extent the MDP. Former RUC officers talked about how they had worked with the military in Northern Ireland on a daily basis during the Troubles. Indeed, one of the perceived 'successes' was that of military aid to the civil power which translated into operations at a tactical level co-ordinated through territorial co-ordination groups. For the UN this has necessitated ongoing dialogue and interaction between civilian and military actors in relation to co-operation and coexistence (UNHCR, 2021). The military in a subsidiary role typically supported the police in maintaining or establishing public order and providing additional security during hostile encounters involving terrorists, dangerous criminals, and renegade local militias. In Northern Ireland after 1976 when the RUC regained primacy, the military it was claimed 'worked hand in hand with the police to provide street level as well as hostile environment policing in both urban and rural areas' (Author interview with former Det Inspector RUC–PSNI, January 2010). The military essentially provided specialist support to the police: 'both partners doing what they were good at and not trying to turn policemen [sic] into soldiers and conversely soldiers into policemen [sic] (Smith, 2010: 4). In BiH and in Kosovo, civil-military coordination was seen as necessary to prevent any slippage from peacekeeping to *peace enforcement* that would result in versatile (and potentially lethal) uses of force (Friesendorf, 2012: 94).

While civilian-military co-operation was a characteristic of Northern Irish policing, the British army also had an experience of working closely with the RUC since August 1969. Both organizations had a shared interpretation of the concept of 'command' which is central to military philosophy and planning and rests on discipline, hierarchy, and structure (Smith, 2010). In both Bosnia and Kosovo, RUC–PSNI officers were posted to specific towns (for example Banja Luca (BiH) and Mitrovica (Kosovo)) to specifically work alongside the military as explained by a former RUC–PSNI (2010):

> One of my first assignments was to set up a foot patrol unit (Unit Beat) in a particularly damaged area of the town [Mitrovica] with an objective of bonding with the locals and forming a relationship with the French KFOR. I had no problem with that as I recognized that police and military should work together in some circumstances whilst many other police from around the world couldn't make the connection. After a lot of struggles a solid relationship was built with not only the French KFOR but also the locals. The Neighbourhood Unit created as a result eventually spread its tentacles all over the town and built up a good local knowledge—something that wasn't being done by the patrol sections driving about in the jeeps (Former RUC–PSNI Chief Inspector, January 2010).

With a recognition that the future building of a civil police service (in both BiH and Kosovo) would be an arduous route, let alone wider state-building, the need for strong civil-military co-operation was seen by many police officers as essential to fill the security gap and provide a consistent approach among peacekeepers. The MDP were also familiar with the military culture and used their international experiences in BiH and Kosovo as a platform for their missions in Afghanistan.

Ministry of Defence Police (MDP): international 'niche' policing

Since 2000, the MDP, despite having a far smaller establishment than either the MPS or the RUC–PSNI, were significant contributors to overseas policing. Some 612 officers deployed between 2000 to 2015 to approximately fourteen countries and, several mid-ranking MPD were seconded to the SU to manage the UK's response to international policing (MDP, 2012; MOD, 2014). Overall, there has been very little research interest in their overseas activities in comparison with the activities of the RUC–PSNI (see Sinclair, 2015). Here I provide an overview of their brand features and contribution to international policing.

One former Chief Constable (2012) described the MDP as providing 'specialist, niche, high value and top end policing capabilities that defence and other UK departments require but which are beyond the capability or capacity of other police forces (Author interview with former Chief Constable, MDP, 9 November 2011), though an 'integral part of UK Police PLC' (Author interview with former ACC, MDP, and head of international secondments, 9 November 2012). The MDP is a *national police force*, established in 1971 from an amalgamation of the Admiralty War Office and Air Ministry Constabularies, with officers deployed in England, Wales, and Scotland. In 1996 it became a defence agency and expanded to include the MOD Guard Service in 2004 when it was renamed the MOD Police and Guarding Agency (MDPGA). MDP has status under the Ministry of Defence Police Act (1987) which conferred constabulary power on its officers who conform to national policing standards. MDP officers are routinely armed and provide guarding at key defence sites, counterterrorism activities, protection of defence personnel and property, and uniformed general policing. In addition, the MDP criminal investigation department undertakes criminal and fraud investigations for MOD, and provides specialist capabilities such as waterborne security for HM Dockyards and HM Naval Bases; has one of the largest dog sections in the UK (twenty-three sections in 2012), and is the only UK police service able to work fully in a chemical, biological, radioactive, or nuclear environment. At a local level, joint investigations or operations with other law enforcement agencies or other public bodies are commonplace (for example, cross-use of resources such as crime scene investigators, transport, intelligence, and so on as well as routine interaction with other UK police forces). Under the austerity measures that followed the Strategic Defence and Security Review (2010), MDP establishment was cut to around 2,400 by 2016 (MODGA, 2012).

Several key characteristics originally made the MDP an attractive proposition for deployment to Kosovo in 2000. It had armed capability, was part of the MOD (rather than the HO), had an experience of civil-military cooperation, and familiarity with military culture as well as a national capacity.

First, a high number of MDP officers provide *armed policing*, which some MDP officers have likened to a 'quasi military mindset' emanating from their MOD footprint. However, it has been stressed that this should not be confused with the *semi military* policing approaches practiced by the RUC that MDP witnessed in BiH and Kosovo. Few MDP officers had experience of conflict and counterterrorism prior to their overseas deployment although their specialist response teams have provided tactical support in response to national security threats (Author interview with former Det Chief Supt, MDP, January, 2011; former Chief Supt, MDP, January 2011; former CC, MDP, November 2012; former Inspector MDP, January 2011). MPD are routinely armed but also provide 'general' policing duties for example within garrison towns, defence and military establishments or, in support of the military police in areas where there are high numbers of off-duty military present (Author interview with former Det Chief Supt, MDP, January, 2011). As such the MDP had a familiarity with 'military culture, language and all the ways of doing things ... we are comfortable working close up to the military ... just completely comfortable in that environment'. Moreover, a culture of *defence*, being part of the MOD and working closely with the military allowed senior MDP to 'clearly see the defence advantages to overseas conflict being resolved early, to be being prevented and to police being involved in re-stabilization [sic] in the wake of military operations' (Former Chief Constable, 9 November 2012).

MDP involvement in international policing has been described as an 'institutional reflex' (Inspector, MDP, and Head of the International Police Secondments Office (IPSO), 8 November 2012). It was supported by the creation of a dedicated and centralized deployment hub, which until 2008 managed the recruitment, pre-deployment training, deployments, and debriefings of MDP personnel overseas. Yet as with other UK police, the positive experiences of an overseas deployment and skills uptake did not match the return home. Some MPD interviewed were disillusioned by the lack of opportunity to 'try out new skills' on their return home and transfer knowledge accrued. In some instances, MDP returned to 'no vacant posts'—MDP operated a practice of backfilling positions when an officer was seconded overseas—and considered that their 'career would go nowhere'. Some even were told to stay at home until a position could be located (Author interviews with MDP, 2011–2015). Yet the provision of what one former chief constable (2012) described as 'expeditionary policing' to Afghanistan under Operation Herrick, provided an example of 'hot fighting' alongside the military and services police which I return to in the next chapter. MDP also deployed in a range of other capacities in particular providing senior staff officers to NATO and EU missions, intelligence liaison, and investigative services. For some of these officers, retirement from MDP opened up new international security horizons although to a lesser extent than other UK police.

UK police in East Timor

The deployment of UK police to BiH and Kosovo coincided with a request for a British police presence in East Timor.[9] In the run up to the referendum for independence in 1999, the UN deployed 270 *unarmed* police as election monitors including seven UK police who had experience of BiH.[10] The UK government soon voiced concerns that the Indonesian police were failing to protect UN staff from attacks by pro-Indonesian militias intent on disrupting the referendum proceedings. Members of the police contingent pointed out that 'local officials were not cooperating' and that the work of international police monitors was constantly disrupted and dangerous (*The Guardian*, 6 July 1999). The announcement of voting results was followed by a widespread campaign of violence and destruction by pro-integration militias; approximately 750,000 out of a pre-consultation population of approximately 880,000 were either internally displaced or forced to flee across the border into West Timor (UN, 2000). The violence that ensued between August and September 1999 led to the return home of all UN personnel. A subsequent UN security council resolution 1272, (the UN Transitional Administration in East Timor (UNTAET)) on 25 October 1999 set a peacekeeping operation in motion mandated to provide security, maintain law and order, and support all aspects of governance and administration. Civilian police numbering 1,640 were given executive authority to operate alongside the military (UN, 1999).

Two UK police officers were deployed to carry out an in-country risk assessment for the FCO. The MPS UK police contingent leader described (2011) what he witnessed on arriving in East Timor:

---

[9] Six countries (including the UK) were specifically requested to provide assistance: Australia, US, Philippines, and Germany (Author interviews 2012 with UK officers who served in East Timor).
[10] The British contingent was drawn from Suffolk, Humberside Constabulary, Hertfordshire, MPS, Lancashire, Lincolnshire, and Nottinghamshire constabularies. FCO Daily Bulletin, 11 November 1999.

By then [30 October 1999], East Timor had been systematically devastated. On disembarking from the C130 Hercules, we entered an environment more conducive to military than police. Fully equipped troops carried out numerous foot patrols. The local people waited anxiously as they expected the militia to reappear. Not only had the complete infrastructure been destroyed, virtually every house, commercial and government building was totally levelled or seriously damaged. In most remaining buildings all windows were smashed, many had no doors, or roofs. There was no electricity, water, telephones or other amenities. Stories of massacres were abundant and it was then estimated that thousands of people had been murdered, to this day no one knows the full number. In addition, tens of thousands had either fled or been transferred to West Timor and other parts of Indonesia (Former Chief Supt MPS, 2011).

The FCO was clearly faced with a dilemma. Deploying UK police to support UNTAET practically necessitated an experience of hostile environments. BiH and Kosovo had drawn heavily on the RUC where an experience of semi-military and high-risk environments was a prerequisite. As a result, there was little RUC capacity which required volunteers from other UK constabularies potentially without the experience of high-risk environments. Wherever possible, police with prior mission experience were selected. However, of the first fourteen volunteers, only three had experience of BiH.[11] While these officers undertook a 'range of duties' and demonstrated 'flexibility and innovation' (Author interview with former contingent commander, May 2011), they could not operate on a par with the Garda Nacional Republicana (GNR) (Portugal)) or the Australian Federal police (AFP). By 10 February 2000, some 539 CIVPOL had been deployed from twenty-nine countries along with a second UK contingent of just nine officers.[12] This may have demonstrated an interest and willingness among senior police to release officers for an overseas mission but the reality of the East Timorese context necessitated semi-military or gendarmerie experiences.

---

[11] The first UK contingent comprised constables and sergeants. They were drawn from the MPS (4), South Yorkshire (1), Devon and Cornwall (1), South Wales (2), Cheshire (1), Merseyside (1), North Wales (2), West Mercia (1), and Humberside (1).

[12] The contingent commander was from the MPS. Other officers were drawn from Sussex, Leicestershire, Greater Manchester Police, Dorset Constabulary, MPS, Durham, South Wales, and Lancashire.

Partly as a result, some of the UK police deployed were given administrative tasks including logistical support, mapping out police duties and responsibilities, and identifying the necessary personnel: 'this resulted in us police filling the void until alternatives were available and required flexibility and innovation to produce the desired outcome' (UK contingent commander notes to author, 2011: 3). Yet of strategic value to the UK was that one of *their* police had been selected to lead CIVPOL UNTAET (2000 to 2001) and manage the rule of law programme in the face of escalating public order situations. Public protest often became violent confrontations: CIVPOL were *unarmed* and relied on the military as a 'first line of defence' to minimize confrontations with the international police. The UK CIVPOL lead had significant prior public order experience from the UK which he realized he would need to be 'flexibly adapted' to the East Timorese context as he explained (2011):

> Basically, we didn't want the military to shoot local people.... I had all the training and I had all the experience so it was just about putting it into the context of East Timor and a little bit extra—stepping outside the box of the public order manual of ACPO tactics because we were not in the UK and we had to do things that worked ... You are not confronting a group of people with placards, stones, bottles and maybe a petrol bomb ... in the East Timor context you are confronting people with bows and arrows, spears, machetes and potentially homemade firearms. In different cultures, people's flashpoints for becoming uncontrollable are at different levels—in East Timor the crowd would flare up more quickly.... The level of lethal weapons carried was higher....To be frank it was about having the experience to have the confidence and about having the mental agility to say that this would work better in this context than that. It may not work back home but it will work here (Former MPS Chief Supt, and CIVPOL UNTAET commander, 2011).

While British officers spoke of the potential for 'high levels of violence' in the UK that they had encountered in their careers, in East Timor (and this point was also made in relation to all FCAS) a 'flashpoint situation' could occur more rapidly necessitating more 'aggressive tactics' than used back home. In some instances, they drew on the tactics used by *other* international police:

> We had a situation in Dilli where a football match degenerated into rioting and violence. We put out our four-wheel drive vehicles with four cops in each one, went out there and broke up the groups using the vehicles, using aggressive vehicle tactics and so dispersed the groups. That is definitely not in the ACPO manual (Former MPS Supt, 2011).

This point demonstrates the tension within the UK policing brand and the perceptions of robust policing (public order) which would not have been out of place in Northern Ireland (see Ellison and Smyth, 2000). It suggested that the civil UK policing model may not have been perceived as adequate to close the security gap. Scrutiny of PSOs over the past two decades has shown that this gap must be filled during all three phases: deployment, enforcement, and sustainability (Dziedzic, 2003). CIVPOL was unable (in the first instance) to provide the 'amount of muscle needed to cope with the potential levels of violence': the police component relied entirely on the military to escort patrols and public order disturbances (Nebreda Martell, 2016: 106).[13]

The levels of violence created an opportunity for FPUs from GNR and the General Directorate of Gendarmerie (Jordan) to be sent by early 2000: these were units specifically trained in riot control tactics and used as a first response. In East Timor, a lengthy period of both Portuguese and Indonesian rule had soured community police relations and local communities had an expectation of a gendarmerie style of policing. The GNR deployed for decades to East Timor and operated in support of local police to foster better community relations in an attempt to implement community policing programmes (Author interview with GNR senior officers who served with UNAET from 1999–2005, March 2016; see in particular Nogueira, 2012).

---

[13] The literature has referred to other forces that fall between the military and police broadly referred to as 'paramilitary police units' (for example Lutterbeck, 2005). Police SWAT (Special Weapons and Tactics) teams as well as military special forces have evolved since 1989 and anti-terrorist units within civilian police forces. SWAT units may introduce a 'culture of paramilitarism' in the police'. Countries including France, Italy, Portugal, Spain, Canada, Chile, Netherlands, and Germany have integrated different types of militarized police forces within their security architecture: a 'solid and clear legal framework' (Nebreda Martell, 2016: 112–3). With the Good Friday Agreement and the advent of the PNSI, the UK has probably discarded the remnants of gendarmerie or semi-military policing.

Sierra Leone—'back to the futurism'

By the late 1999s, UK police were regularly rotating in and out of UN missions as well as deploying senior strategic police advisors, which included support to the Sierra Leone Police. Rolling back in time to the 1950s, a former commissioner of the Sierra Leone Police had commented on the challenges faced in 'civilianizing' and 'localizing' the police following the 1948 recommendation by the FCO to ensure the transformation of colonial police forces prior to independence away from a semi-military model (Author interview with Ted Eates, April 2000; Sinclair, 2006). Sierra Leone gained its independence in 1961 and joined the commonwealth. By 1999, following a civil war that began in 1991, the state was near total social and economic collapse and the police and wider criminal justice system had been decimated (Ginifer, 2005: 17).

In 1996, the newly elected President of Sierra Leone, Ahmad Tejan Kabbah, who had previously worked for UNDP, sought international assistance to begin a dedicated programme of police reform (Albrecht, 2010: 4; Friedman, 2011). UK-led security assistance to Sierra Leone began in the late 1990s and ultimately included wide-ranging programmes that encompassed the police, military, justice, intelligence, and governance structures (Varisco, 2014). Of particular importance to the UK at that time was the role that the new DfID would play in providing 'comprehensive' SSR and a developing concept of stabilization before it entered popular parlance in UK government circles (Albrecht, 2010; Baker, 2010; Krogsad, 2012). DfID's policy approach in Sierra Leone was that there 'would be little development in the country without security; and that security would not materialize without transformation of the security forces; and that reform had to happen quickly ... (Baker, 2010: 3).[14] Clare Short, then international development secretary, gave her support for SSR and police reform provided that other programmes relating to poverty reduction, humanitarian assistance, and reform of the judiciary and legal systems were developed (HoC, 1999). The subsequent UK financed police reform programmes: Commonwealth and Community Safety and Security Programme (CCSSP), 1999–2004; (Justice Sector Development Programme, 2005 10); and Sierra Leone

---

[14] Peter Albrecht (2010) made a valuable point about how SSR-related programme in Sierra Leone was an early attempt to establish whole-of-government collaboration (FCO, DfID, and MOD) before the Global Conflict Prevention Pool had been established. DfID's comprehensive police, intelligence, national security coordination, and defence programming for Sierra Leone had never been attempted elsewhere in the UK (Albrecht, 2010).

Security Programme was for the UK government and DfID, 'a test bed of its latest thinking on police reform policy and practice'. It 'represent[ed] the single most important effort by the agency worldwide to fundamentally reconstruct a police service in a post-conflict state' (Baker, 2010: 17).

In a manner reminiscent of senior UK police who were invited during the colonial and immediate post-colonial period to take up overseas postings, Keith Biddle, whose prior role had been as Assistant IG at the Home Office was appointed at Kabbah's request. Biddle had considerable international experience particularly within commonwealth countries. He later commented that he 'certainly cautioned against having a Brit as the Inspector-General of the Police.... They weighed the risk and decided to do it. It could have gone awfully wrong. We were very fortunate' (Interview with Keith Biddle, Oral History Program, 5 December 2007). His hesitation lay in 'citing the *risk* of assuming responsibility for a police service torn by war ... The IG [Inspector General] would have to be part of the instrument of fighting, part of the National Security Council or war cabinet. About a third of the police force was actually fighting almost as infantry' (Biddle cited in Albrecht, 2010: 53–4). This hesitation (and the requirement that Short give her assurance of DfiD's support), was different perhaps to the attitude regarding *risk* than would have been posited by senior RUC. In this instance it was assumed that Kabbah desired a civil policing model to emerge from the proposed reforms. Yet in 1998 when Kabbah had announced the Sierra Leone policing charter and a focus on police primacy, the country was still wracked by conflict (Albrecht, 2010: 53). Biddle (2007) although not yet appointed IG, recognized that a period of robust policing lay ahead for which the local police needed to be prepared to manage potential civil disorder:

> Then we came to the risk ... and I remember going to London and saying, 'Look, I need some riot equipment.' There were civil servants saying, 'No, no, no, you can't have any riot equipment, you might fire gas and gas people. Those rubber bullets, they might hit somebody and bruise them. They might hit people on the head with the truncheon. They might smack somebody in the face with a shield.' I'm not joking, this was the level of many of the questions being put.
>
> There was a lot of unease from the professional level and the permanent civil service level. The Secretary of State [Short] herself, she has always been anti use of gas in Northern Ireland and on mainland UK and not very keen on rubber bullets either. She was very nervous, but

they trusted my judgment. I was their man. They trusted my judgment and trusted me to handle it properly and to train people properly. We brought people out to do that training. So, DFID was prepared to take that risk (Keith Biddle, oral History Program, 2007).

In relation to risk, there were several issues arising: Biddle recognized the much wider element of risk to wider government, the 'new' DfiD and also to the integrity of UK policing through support provided to Sierra Leone. While he was prepared to manage that risk, it necessitated the necessary guarantees backed by government at ministerial level, including DfID's support for his wider policing, security, and justice vision over the longer term. In the event, Biddle was given full operational independence to support the Sierra Leone police as their IG including control over the police budget. He became the architect of an executive management board to encourage the development of senior leaders with as many as ten assistant inspector generals: it remained a key forum for decision-making following Biddle replacement by Brima Acha Kamara in 2004 (Albrecht, 2010). Biddle noted that a succession plan called for Sierra Leonean officers to attend training courses at the Police Staff College (Bramshill) funded through the CCSSP, as well as training provision for over 9,000 officers (Meek, 2003: 106).[15] Biddle also supported the development of a community policing approach known as 'Local Needs Training' that his deputy Adrian Horn defined as 'policing that meets the expectations and need of the local community and reflects national standards and objectives' (Adrian Horn quoted in Albrecht and Jackson 2009: 32). As Biddle optimistically remarked in 2000:

Reform is a nice easy word in Britain, it means that we're going to change the way things are done to something better. The better word, to my mind, is development. We're going to develop what's there and improve it rather than change (Biddle, 2000).

Biddle's point more broadly reflected that UK policing was by that period providing assistance from peacekeeping through to state-building which necessitated police reform and SSR and reflected a softer side that was focused around capacity building away from the harder executive peacekeeping policing of BiH, Kosovo, and East Timor.

---

[15] CIVPOL through UNAMSIL also provided support to the Sierra Leone Police.

Concluding comment

Following the collapse of the Soviet Union, the UK entered an age of interventions which began in the Western Balkans. Overseas interventions necessitated both military and policing support bringing a goldrush of security actors from across the globe. In terms of policing this *globality* can be understood in terms of 'transfers—albeit with uneven and sometimes perverse consequences—of policing expertise, models and practices from core to periphery, either by leading states or multilateral state-building and peacekeeping efforts' (Laffey and Nadarajah, 2016). This bolstered the international reputation of a multifaceted policing brand, which from a UK government perspective provided a 'philosophy and an approach that is grounded in international best practice and UK experiences' (SU, 2014: 1). Yet given the forums of intervention within conflict and high-risk environments, it was the RUC elements of the brand (with its Irish/semi-military antecedents) that was the most effective and raised the international policing profile of the UK in BiH and Kosovo. Where the capacity for this element of the brand was not available as in East Timor and fewer UK police were deployed, the UK's policing profile was far less in evidence. As the decade progressed and the international development (and SSR subsector) grew and professionalized, it co-existed with security approaches and operational policing approaches and brought police capacity building (through wider state-building) to the fore. There were several key linkages here that have been framed within chapter 1; first the co-existence with the development sector and secondly the gradual corporatization of security that occurred from this period. Throughout the 1990s, mission experiences certainly sharpened the appetite of many serving officers and built on their professional, personal, and leaderships skills, creating opportunities to enter what would become a global security market (Author interviews 2010–2014). This would grow within the interventions that took place from the early 2000 in both Iraq and Afghanistan to which I now turn in chapter 4.

4
UK Policing in Afghanistan, Iraq, and Libya

After 9/11

> I'm still not convinced that UK Plc has grasped the metal of how to be able to do expeditionary policing in a reliable sustained integrated built in way and I suspect, rather surprised and confused police and military officers have found themselves landed with situations, by surprise, with little preparation, be it Palestine or Kenya or wherever and this pattern just continues and I believe it will continue for as long as we stay with the present ownership governance commissioning model of FCO, DFID, Home Office, ACPO and MoD being five stakeholders with fault lines and different agendas.
>
> **Former Chief Constable, MDP, 2012**

> There is still a tendency for Home Office police to look at MDP not necessarily as equals, shall we say. So, we've tended to be looked at sometimes as second-class police officers. I think that the reality of how the MDP has performed throughout the Balkans and since then has proved to the FCO that that's not the case and that we are a valuable asset and I think we were progressing very well and it wasn't necessarily... it's been partly circumstance and serendipity, it hasn't necessarily been a strategic intent on our part I have to say, but it has worked that we've slowly increased our profile and our footprint within international policing in a very positive way and that, I think, was only increased when we became involved in Afghanistan.
>
> **Former Chief Inspector, MDP, 2013**

As SSR and police reform became integral to the foreign and security policies of the US and European states through the post-Cold War 1990s, so 9/11, the ensuing global 'war on terror' and the US's strategic 'long war' approach further cemented these trends in the early 2000s (Ahrari, 2006). The US-led invasions of Iraq and Afghanistan led to political decisions augmenting the missions beyond purely military counterterrorism (CT) and counter-insurgency (COIN) to ambitious state-building objectives. Their effectiveness remains seriously questionable after two decades (Barry, 2020).

Throughout this period, the UK sustained a limited police presence within conflict hotspots with much wider support given to bilateral assistance programmes. The earlier missions to BiH and Kosovo became a benchmark for hostile environment and post-conflict policing and grew an expertise that UK police could take forward; international policing had become an integral part of what UK policing could offer. The 'war on terror' also provided an 'unprecedented focal point for the transnational interchange of security expertise and knowledge transfer ... not to mention an inestimable volume of informal traffic between policing and security personnel' (Ellison and O'Reilly, 2008a: 396). RUC–PSNI officers remained an attractive proposition for these types of missions with many slipping into the corporate security world, contracted by private security organizations and development agencies (see chapter 5). However, international policing continued to involve the entire spectrum of UK policing including the MDP and military services police. Senior officers were sought after for key strategic level posts particularly within NATO and EU-led missions to Iraq, Afghanistan, and Libya which placed a spotlight on UK policing (Author interviews, 2010–2014).

However, there was failure at government level to prioritize UK international policing assistance within the immediate post-invasion phases to prepare for post-conflict stabilization (Iraq (Chilcot) Inquiry, 2010). While the characteristics of the UK policing brand were in evidence—e.g. civil versus semi-military—the extent to which the UK policing brand had any real influence was debatable. From wide-ranging discussions with police and military practitioners, there were two key drivers that impeded real impact. First, there remained no government-led international policing strategy to fuse an international approach across the fifty-two territorial and three niche police forces (British Transport Police, Civil Nuclear Constabulary, and MDP), the relevant police authorities and supporting government departments, despite 'historically Chief Officers having formed associations' (Kernaghan, 2010: 3). As a result, the planning of international policing and the day-to-day business was often ad hoc and chief officers were directed in a fragmented manner according to the type of mission and the availability of officers (Author interview with former ACPO International Affairs (IA) portfolio holder, former Chief Constable Avon and Somerset, January 2011). At a constabulary level there was little if any official recognition of the value of an international mission in relation to the experience gained and the possibility alignment with a career pathway. Nor were competencies or newly-acquired skills used to their best advantage within a domestic context (see Ashraf, 2007; Author interviews, 2010–2020). Moreover, the extreme environments into which UK police deployed in Iraq and Afghanistan exposed the weaknesses and limitations of UK policing's capacity and capability relating to policing styles as well as issues relating to risk, duty of care, and reward for an overseas deployment. This ongoing lacuna certainly contributed to police moving into the corporate sector and sometimes before their scheduled retirement (Author interviews, 2010–2014).

Additionally, the military retained primary responsibility for security and stabilization with a focus as much on strategy as on the operational (Rand, 2005: 124). Senior police repeatedly identified (and most prominently during the 2010 Iraq Inquiry), how UK policing was left out in the cold at the planning stage of a mission with tensions between military, government, and civilian agencies occurring as a result (Iraq (Chilcot), 2010). Certainly, this raised further questions relating to the identification of suitable elements of UK policing for hostile environment police as compared to bilateral assistance programmes. Civil-military co-operation remained key within these environments but theoretically necessitated the support of those elements of UK policing who had an experience including MDP and RUC–PSNI.

Arguably the drive towards a whole-of-government approach to conflict prevention and post-conflict recovery with the advent of the SU in 2007, the National Security Council (NSC) in 2010 and, the Building Stability Overseas Board (BSOB) in 2011, brought 'together different resources, capabilities and areas of expertise that exist across government' ... and ... 'an appropriately resourced implementation plan' (Building Stability Overseas Strategy (BSOS), 2011: 33). This included an overhaul of available resources and funding including an overseas roster that housed interested parties including police (see chapter 6). Post 2010, NSC strategies and country-specific objectives supported UK government policy towards new interventions in Libya and Syria as well as the continuing engagement in Iraq and Afghanistan (House of Commons Foreign Affairs Select Committee, 2016).

Afghanistan

International disunity and disarray

The 2001 military invasion came in response to the terrorist attacks against the US on 11 September 2001 and triggered the 'war on terror'.[1] Afghanistan through its history has been subjected to long periods of war and civil violence. Following the Soviet invasion (1979 to 1989) and the later civil war (1992 to 2001), multifactional militias and non-state armed group continued to emerge, impacting the lives of local people within one of the poorest countries in the world (Barry, 2020). However, unlike many other international post-conflict interventions, Afghanistan was not seen as a peacekeeping operation but as an intervention that would focus on CT and COIN, while initially marshalling international support for wider state-building through aid, reconstruction, and development (including SSR). The 2001 Bonn Agreement provided a foundation for intensive capacity- and capability-building programmes with five original reform pillars spearheaded by individual countries: military reform (US); police reform (Germany); disarmament, demobilization, and reintegration (Japan); criminal justice reform (Italy); and counter-narcotics (UK). This siloed approach prevented an interconnected approach from the onset and resulted in the 'longest and costliest reconstruction projects in history'. By extension this impacted the attempted reform of the Afghan National Police (ANP) (Jalali, 2016: 7).

The Afghan National Police (ANP) had never been a *civilian* establishment nor had the organization a reputation for effectiveness. Police building had always been a 'poor second to the army in international security sector priorities', which severely hampered Germany's attempt to initiate reform (Suroush, 2018: 9). While Germany had provided the ANP with training, mentoring, and advising in the 1960s and 1970s, the

---

[1] US National Security Advisor Condoleezza Rice initially used this term which she explained as a 'broad war, not a single event'; 'war on terrorism' and 'war on terror' was coined by President Bush, the latter being adopted with the add on 'global' (Farrell, 2017: 46).

police was acknowledged in 2002 to be in a 'deplorable state ... there is a total lack of equipment and supplies. No systematic training has been provided for around 20 years' (Quoted in Farrell, 2017: 129). Germany's approach was to restore the Kabul Police Academy, build police stations, provide equipment, vehicles, training and support for institutional development and, the coordination of all other donor activities relating to the ANP (German Federal Ministry of Interior, 2006). Programme delivery was denounced as inadequate and overall responsibility was given to the US Bureau of International Narcotics and Law Enforcement Affairs (INL), which promptly commissioned DynCorp, a private security company. The quality and sustainability of the training delivered was highly questionable and responsibility was again moved to the US department of defence 'who handed the mission' over to combined security transition command—Afghanistan (CSTC-A) in 2005 (Farrell, 2017: 129). While the ANP from 2002 to 2021received technical assistance and capacity building from approximately twenty-five countries and a myriad of international organizations, the US was always been dominant (Friesendorf and Kempel, 2011). The 2006 Afghanistan Compact theoretically provided a framework for co-operation between the Afghan government and international donor states to improve coordination with a vision to transform the ANP from a semi-military to a civil police force (Government of the Islamic Republic of Afghanistan (GIRoA), 2017). Over a decade later, the Afghanistan national defence and security forces (ANDSF) 2017 roadmap plan to bolster capability and an ongoing reorganization necessitated continued external assistance (SIGAR, 2019).

Within this crowded space, the UK, from 2002 to 2021, deployed both serving and retired police to NATO,[2] EU,[3] and

---

[2] NATO Internal Security Assistance Force (ISAF) deployed in 2001 tasked by the Afghan government and under a UN mandate. On 11 August 2003 NATO took command of ISAF. The other eight provincial reconstruction teams (PRTs) remained under the command of US-led Operation Enduring Freedom (US-led military operation). NATO Resolute Support Mission (RSM) was launched on 1 January 2015 following ISAF's completion when responsibility for security was transferred to the Afghan national defence and security forces (ANDSF). In 2020 approximately 12,000 personnel from thirty-eight NATO member states and partner countries were deployed in support of RSM until drawdowns commenced in 2021 (NATO, 2020).

[3] European Union Police Mission in Afghanistan (EUPOL) was a civilian Common Security and Defence Policy (CSDP) mission established on 23 April 2007. Its aim was to build a civilian police service that operated within an improved rule of law framework and in respect of human rights. The Mission focused on institutional reform of the MOI and on the professionalization of ANP and ended on 31 December 2016. In 2015, it had 156 international staff and 166 local staff thus on a much smaller scale to NATO ISAF and RSM.

OSCE[4] missions, bilateral UK–Afghanistan programmes, MDP support under Operation Herrick as well as a growing private security sector (see chapter 5). Due to the scale and complexity of police capacity building across the donor spectrum, it remained doubtful whether the UK policing brand left any residual traces. However, as with Iraq and later Libya, British police were positioned at the strategic high table wherever possible. Additionally, the rebuilding of the Afghan intelligence agency, the national director of security (NDS), was supported in part by the UK private security sector (see chapter 5) and, the UK National Crime Agency (NCA) and its predecessor the Serious Organised Crime Agency (SOCA) which contributed in no small part to the counter-narcotics programmes (see Koski, 2009 for a discussion relating to pre-2009 criminal justice and policing in Afghanistan).

Within this context, police capacity building and technical assistance saw the cross fertilization of an array of international police and a burgeoning corporate sector complete with their own national and commercial interests, policing styles, and values (see Celik, 2020). To some extent this resulted in 'competing and conflicting visions of police reform ... that are not without their historical patterns' (Heiduk, 2011: 369). The US largely sought to keep the ANP as a semi-military wing of the ANA in support of the counter-insurgency campaign that has waged since 2001. The EU, however, and others (including, for example, the Scandinavian countries) espoused a transformation towards a civil style organization with an emphasis on leadership and management styles (Friesendorf and Kempel, 2011; Friesendorf, 2018). Overall, the judgement has been that the international policing community was well-intentioned and recognized the need for collaboration. The international police coordination board (IPCB) (the main coordination body for police reform) and the law and order trust fund Afghanistan (LOFTA) encouraged some measure of coherence in relation to mission mandate planning, delivery, and transition since 2002 (FCDO, 2020).

Behind the formal structures built to develop international mandates, collaboration, and implementation, has been a global policing exchange (as discussed in a chapter 1 and see Ellison and Pino, 2012). Unity can be enhanced through dialogue, the drive to find a common approach, and a

---

[4] OSCE has provided support since 2003 including election monitoring in 2004–2005. In 2007, following a request from the Afghan government, assistance was given with border security, police training, and counter-narcotics (Perrin de Brichambaut, 2009: 361–8).

clear handover to the next person. Yet there can also be a disjoint in the approaches to mentoring, advising, and training as international police have brought their own agendas, which typically impeded effectiveness, as highlighted (2013) by this UK police officer:

> People would turn up with their national caveats and their national view of what's right.... intelligence is a classic one, you'll have a US Air Force Colonel in charge of intelligence and he or she will decide right, 'It looks like this, that and the other because that's the way we did it in Okinawa'! They'll leave and they'll be replaced by a French person who says, 'Yes, when I was in Côte d'Ivoire, we did this,' and it tacks left and right and the poor Afghans are left there thinking, well, what are we doing? (Author interview with former Det Chief Supt Surrey Police, 1 November 2013).

Having an attitude whereby police took stock of other policing cultures, values, and approaches was described as 'putting the Britishness to one side, standing back and saying there's other policing traditions that have got some very good and valid approaches to problem solving so bring them along ...' (Author interview with former Inspector, Avon and Somerset Police, April 2014, deployed to BiH 2003–2005; EUPOL staff officer to head of mission, 2012–2013). In the context of the early years of the war in Afghanistan, however, such a perspective was not institutionalized and continued divisions and diversions in relation to the leadership of police reform and its implementation persisted.

'Access and influence'—training, mentoring, and advising the ANP

Ongoing debate within academic and practitioner circles has emphasized that police reform should be designed and led at the strategic level by civilian police rather than the military (Friesendorf and Kempel, 2011). One key international policing activity has been the need for senior police to 'access and influence' senior host government officials *with strategic intent*. That is to ensure the host government and police vision for police development aligns with that of the donor country; and in the case of the UK that this should reflect the national security strategy objectives (National Security Strategy and Strategic Defence and Security Review, 2015: First Annual Report 2016). Moreover, international policing assistance has always provided opportunities to peddle UK soft power and influence, which was remarked upon (2011):

> The reputation of British policing stands tall … [which relates] to the more discreet aspect about the projection and protection of our UK assets and interests abroad and the role of policing in doing that…. I know that although my role isn't operational there's a facet of it that is around protecting UK interests in Afghanistan and I think it's absolutely vital that a country like the UK has a footprint here—police can play a part in that. I think we've got to be at the table, there is no way we can't be at the table out here (Author interview with former Chief Inspector, Sussex Police deployed to EUPOL 2011–2012 at Kabul Police Academy, 16 December 2011).

'Substantive' superintendents and those at senior command level were sought for positions in Afghanistan where the UK could have significant strategic influence. The more senior the rank, the greater the degree of influence with the military (and particularly the US military): 'a real assistant chief constable in the 'battlespace' goes down well' noted a former senior police advisor to the NATO training mission Afghanistan (NTMA) (2011). Influence within the military could lead to particular policing approaches being adopted: one of many examples given in this context was the drive to include the National Policing Improvement Agency (NPIA) command and control doctrine that 'suitably impressed the military and showed how good UK policing really is' (Former ACC, Hampshire Police, blog, 27 August 2011). However, community policing doctrine and mentoring was often a less attractive proposition where the military were concerned:

> The democratic (community) policing or police-e-mardomi [sic] has really taken off [in the ANP]. I presented to most of the senior staff here last week and it really messes with the heads of the military. They just don't get it. They think it can't work. What they want is something called the commander's unit assessment tool. This is something those in the field complete about readiness of the people they are mentoring. It is army focused and all about quantity—how many bombs, beans and bullets they have— not quality. —military leading the show… (Author interview with former ACC, 2011).

Overall, the military held sway in Afghanistan. The UK policing brand melded with a myriad of other styles put forward by international security actors—military, gendarmerie, and civilian policing. While UK police considered that 'the British brand is tops ... [and] even the Yanks have a pretty high regard for it' the challenge, they recognized that while 'the brand is strong ... the question is whether we are exploiting it? Are we maximising it? That's a different question as with all of these other countries we are *a bit player*'... (Author interview with former Det Supt Avon and Somerset Police, 27 May 2014 deployed East Timor 1999, Afghanistan NATO ISAF Senior Police Advisor 2013). The reality, moreover, was always that the UK struggled to recruit and deploy the requisite number of senior officers to match those deployed from other countries at a strategic level.

Yet the challenges faced by international 'Western' police were often one and the same. As with Iraq, tackling corruption was seen as one of the greatest threats to the future success of public institutions within Afghanistan, including the ANP, and a major cause of poor community relations and a lack of legitimacy (Skinner, 2008: 295). The US stipulated in the National Defense Authorization Act stating that accountability and corruption issues within the Afghan MOD and MOI had to be addressed in order for funding to continue (SIGAR, 2017: 61). For some UK police, the failure to tackle corruption dented mission effectiveness and any long-term success as reflected (2014) in this reminiscence:

> So, what went wrong [in Afghanistan]? ... we didn't clear the ground beneath our feet and what I mean by that is the corruption issue that was endemic. Some of the [ANP] officers will skim the lower ranks' wages each month so the lower ranks will get paid $200 a month or whatever and they'll say, 'Right, it's going to cost you $10 to work on this unit a month.' If that person is otherwise a good leader, does not have criminal connections but is just skimming for their own good, bearing in mind they might have 400 people working for them so $10 x 400 they're doing pretty well, an extra 50,000 a year, there's almost a view of actually, they're not perfect but they're as good as we're going to get because the other end of the corruption is there are police officers in Afghanistan who are on the board of directors of some of the drug cartels. They are directing operations. So, it's the whole corruption piece. So, have we failed? No, because I think that the sheer presence for a decade and our anti-corruption attitude must leave some trace of thinking of change.

Have we achieved a fraction of what we could have done? No, I don't think that we have (Author interview with Former Chief Inspector, MDP, 9 February 2012).

One further cause of concern for many UK police (and across all missions) was the difficulties with the recruitment, integration, and progression of female police officers, despite 'gender' being integral to all SSR and police reform programmes. In 2005, there were merely 180 female officers within an ANP establishment of 53,400. By July 2013, this had risen to 1,551 female officers from an establishment of 157,000, and by 2018 to 3,200 officers (Suroush, 2018: 7-8).[5] Female police officers continued to face difficulties when deployed outside urban areas and were targeted by militias and their own families who disagreed with their choice of profession. Repeated incidents of abuse and rape by male police officers were reported as well as the murder of high-profile female officers, including Lieutenant Colonel Malalai Kakar in southern Kandahar province. Anecdotal evidence from UK police highlighted the enormous difficulties women faced in Afghanistan in becoming police officers as illustrated by a former senior advisor to NATO ISAF in 2013:

> The few occasions that we tried to get female police brought up to our area [Bastion], it was openly admitted to us that if there were female police they would have just been raped because they would have been looked upon with contempt by their male colleagues because they shouldn't have been doing the job as police officers. They weren't being good Muslim women. So, they would have been in danger had they actually come up here... there were no female police (Author interview with former Supt Surrey Police, 1 November 2013, served NATO ISAF 2012–2013 mentor/advisor to the General Director of Police Specialist Units to operate within the rule of law).

Arguably ANP reform moved at a glacial pace despite the reconstruction costs running into trillions of dollars (Farrell, 2017). That a space could be created for routine civil style policing alongside the traditional paramilitary

---

[5] Colonel Jamila Bayaz became the first female district police chief in Kabul in January 2014 following a thirty-year career in the ANP though during the Taliban era she had been unable to work (Lamb, 2015).

model progressively gained some traction. Support was provided by MDP in collaboration with the military and services police in Helmand province.

MDP military integrated approach to MMA

Between January 2008 and March 2013, MDP supported 'integrated' mentoring and training to the ANP in conjunction with the British services police forces under Operation Herrick. MDP (as previously described in chapter 3) represented one facet of UK policing; a niche police with armed capability, familiarity with civil-military co-operation, and growing international policing expertise. Operation Herrick stood out as a first for UK policing with training and mentoring provided within a hostile post-conflict environment (Author interview with former Chief Constable MDP, 9 November 2012). Over a five-year period, cohorts of between twenty and forty MDP rotated in an out of forward operating bases at Lashkar Gah, Babaji, Nahre Saraj, and Nad E Ali in Helmand Province while MDP officers were also deployed to NATO ISAF (Author interview with former ACC MDP Head of International Unit, 9 November 2012). 'Bringing blue thinking into a green environment' became a key investment area for MDP. This was crystallized within an international gold strategy policy, which pledged MDP's contribution to the 'Afghanistan effort' and ensured 'the maintenance of the capability to respond and deploy MDP resources to overseas deployments more effectively and quickly than other UK police forces' (MDP, 2010: 1).

This integrated approach was initiated in 2006 with training programmes built around an earlier *know how* and *how to* within conflict zones. All officers participated in field hot debriefings with lessons feeding back into the programme. From 2008, the MDP-military concept of district level operations concept was delivered in support of Operation Herrick.

Figure 4.1 provides an illustration of the conceptual approach to integrated mentoring and training (referred to as monitoring, mentoring, and advising (MMA) in this context) delivered by the military, services police, and MDP which rested on a commitment to information and intelligence-sharing. Operationally, MMA was *not* delivered in silos but across the police-military divide to ensure programme delivery involved *all* ANP ranks (patrol, non-commissioned, and senior officers at both district and provincial levels). Importantly the delivery required that each MMA provider (military, services police, and MDP) worked to their *own* levels of risk

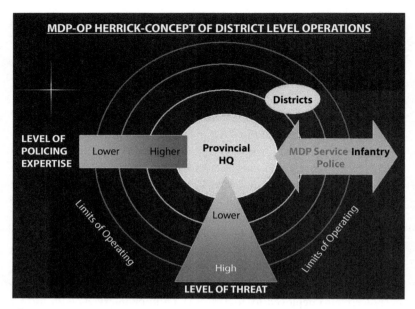

Figure 4.1 MDP—Operation Herrick—Concept of District Level Operations

and their *own* operational limits. These varied according to a dynamic security context and required flexibility to ensure continual progress rather than a 'stop and start' approach as identified within other programmes. The military (and services police) thus operated within the highest level of risk typically at a district (rural) level while MDP tended to remain within provincial police headquarters (urban). This spiralling of effect (both inwards and outwards) is shown within figure 4.1 where MDP (operating at a different level of risk) worked at the core while military and services police operated within the wider vicinity. Identifying with risk within a hostile environment became of increasing importance to MDP when recruiting officers for deployment as illustrated in this following quotation:

> I was part of the interview process and one thing that I personally was extremely strong on was basically selling risk as hard as I could to them [recruits]. We've got officers out there [Sangin] at the moment [2013] and two friends of mine who have both come that close to death. One went out for a cigarette at the back of the building, walked past a contingent of Afghan police, said hi to them, walked round the corner, sat down

and one of the Afghan police had an RPG on his shoulder, was playing silly buggers, pulled the trigger by accident, the RPG went off into the ground and took out his whole patrol. He [MDP] was blown off his chair, suffered a bit of shrapnel wound and that but was first on the scene and was dealing with bits of bodies. That could be the reality … (Author interview with former Inspector, MDP, 3 November 2013).

Regular briefings across all parties clearly identified risk at the local and district levels and allowed for a fluidity in the approaches taken to training and mentoring. Duty of care issues were also under continual scrutiny though MDP operated under different duty of care arrangements than HO police including the permitted use of 'soft shell' accommodation rather than 'hard shell'. The delivery of integrated MMA and variegated training components also ran across multiple layers: from an outer ring where the level of policing expertise required to deliver essentially quasi-military skills was very low as compared to the inner ring where specialist policing skills were required. Theoretically the 'outer ring' provided military led 'green training'; the middle ring provided services police-led training basic policing and investigative skills, and the inner ring MDP focused on institutional and policing reform. In mission the extent of 'problem solving' required within both 'green' and 'blue' training necessitated a meshed approach to MMA to ensure a balance between the delivery of 'harder' green policing skills (outer perimeter) and the 'softer blue police mentoring delivered at the core. This facilitated 'the fullest and frankest' of police-military co-operation which MDP sought to achieve despite the changing and often escalating levels of threat experienced in Helmand (Author interview with former Assistance Chief Constable MDP Head of International Unit, 9 November 2012; Author interviews with MDP secondees to Afghanistan, 8 November 2012).

Following the drawdown from Helmand, MPD delivery for integrated services training ceased and has not been resurrected (though see chapter 6 regarding new civil-military initiatives). The experiences that MDP officers gained within this context should not be underestimated: corporate knowledge of international policing and police-military co-operation grew and had the potential to serve as a useful tool in future overseas deployments. However, by 2020 MDP overseas deployments had dwindled to a mere handful with many of those who went to Afghanistan having retired and far fewer having moved into the corporate security sector than other UK police.

Iraq

Post-invasion planning and policing

The decision taken by the House of Commons on 18 March 2003 to support a US-led invasion of Iraq 'left an indelible scar on British politics': a decade of military operations that followed had a profound effect on UK foreign and security policy and created a reluctance to engage in overseas military interventions (House of Commons, 2016). An international coalition led by the US and UK entered Iraq on 20 March and by 9 April had taken Baghdad. Following US President George W Bush's declaration on 1 May that major combat operations had ceased, a coalition provision authority was installed alongside an interim Iraqi government until the installation of a transitional government following the 2005 elections. The US led military invasion began on 20 March 2003 and the intervention lasted until 31 December 2011; the UK military mission ended in April 2009 (House of Commons, 2016).

Under the direction of the coalition provisional authority (CPA), a 'new' Iraqi police service (IPS) was created as the primary 'public safety and internal security agency', democratically accountable and using state-of-the-art policing approaches. Any vision of a softer policing style was too far removed from the chaos following the invasion (Jones et al., 2005: 12) which necessitated robust policing (White, Iraq Inquiry evidence, 2010). Under the former regime of Saddam Hussein, the Iraqi police had been part of a complicated network of internal security and intelligence organizations that upheld the Ba'ath Party (Perito, 2011). The foundation for Iraqi police had been the former Ottoman and colonial policing structures that left a legacy relating to both the conceptualization and operational practice of policing activities across the Arab world (Gaub and Walsh, 2020). As such the civil police were given responsibility for minor crimes and traffic regulations leaving the other security agencies with far wider legal authority and specialized paramilitary units to manage serious crime, public disorder, and internal security issues. Overall, the Iraqi police were largely considered by the public to be poorly managed, highly ineffective, and corrupt (Ashraf, 2007; Deflem and Sutphin, 2006). Iraq has continued to the present time to rely heavily on international assistance to develop its security forces (including the police) although reform has not yet brought unity nor political independence of policing (Gaub and Walsh, 2020).

Senior UK police were not involved in the pre-planning phase despite this being a US- *and* UK-led intervention. Former Chief Constable Paul Kernaghan, then ACPO international portfolio holder told the Iraq inquiry in 2010:

> I think we [UK policing] frankly should have been consulted, even if it was to say, I'm afraid we can't help. I just think that would have been a professional way to operate ... I was surprised that we were not consulted at all prior to the invasion. I had considered personally whether there would be a requirement for policing post-invasion—need for some police assistance and advice, but there was no approach from Government to ACPO in respect of it. [We] should have been involved at least in the 'post-invasion phase, transition' (Kernaghan, 2010: 12–13).

Douglas Brand, former deputy chief constable of South Yorkshire Police, the first UK police advisor deployed to Baghdad noted that overall 'policing did not appear to have been a major consideration in planning for the post war fighting phase of the conflict' (Brand, 2010: 2) and that there was an assumption that an efficient Iraqi police force would simply 'rise like a phoenix' within months. Indeed, the involvement of UK police was only raised at a cabinet meeting on 10 April 2003 with Kernaghan contacted by the Home Office four days later. Kernaghan then personally approached the FCO on 17 April 'to get a grip of this' copying in the Home Office. In May 2003 (almost two months after the invasion of 19 March) Kernaghan visited Iraq and reported that in his opinion there was:

> **No policing** ... [author emphasis] Iraqi police, what I will call the Green Police, because they wore green uniforms were not there.... the Royal Military Police were trying to recruit people into the police [but] many people were working way above their level with very little guidance or command and control. Some people were not operating in the reality of May 2003. They were in a very utopian land ... (Kernaghan, 2010: 17–23).

Subsequent to Kernaghan's report, the *first formal* request for UK police assistance was made for a 'substantive' Assistant Chief Constable (ACC) resulting in the deployment of Douglas Brand to Baghdad and former PSNI Assistant Chief Constable Stephen White to Basra. Yet neither officer had been furnished with a dedicated US-UK policing strategy that addressed the challenges faced and, the suitability of particular policing approaches view the diversity of policing styles the coalition partners could offer (Kernaghan, 2010: 27, Author interview with Stephen White, May, 2011). It was not, for example, until late July 2003 that a formal request was made through ACPO IA for police with the necessary skill sets (including firearms training) with an agreement by their chief officers for their release, with most deployments occurring from 2004 (Kernaghan, 2010). One exception to this was the MDP, 'the most responsive police organisation in terms of personnel', who were able to deploy officers to coincide with the arrival of Brand in Iraq in October 2003 (Iraq Evidence, Brand, 2010: 3). MDP (as a national organization) had a dedicated international secondments team who could respond rapidly to requests for overseas assistance (Sinclair, 2015).

Overall, the inclusion of UK police in the post-invasion planning phase in Iraq was 'too slow and inadequate' (House of Commons Defence Committee 2005: 56). This was particularly problematic in that the local Iraqi police had all but disappeared following the invasion and there was a reliance on the US and UK military to ensure community security. Moreover, the dearth of planning created misperceptions surrounding the extent of effort that would be required to 'reconstruct' the police and the wider criminal justice sector (Murray and Scales, 2003). The prevailing wisdom was that there would be a relatively benign security environment with sufficient local police remaining in situ to maintain civil order. Yet the emphasis in the early stages pivoted towards humanitarian relief and away from security and the rule of law (Ashraf, 2007; Brand, 2010; Jones, Wilson, Rathmell and Riley 2005; White, 2010). In addition, the provision of international police (including UK policing) was complicated by the UN's refusal to support Operation Iraqi Freedom through the deployment of CIVPOL units. Sourcing additional potential policing resources from other countries (in particular France and Germany) was thwarted by the policing requirements in the Western Balkans and Afghanistan as well as a general lacking of international consensus as to the type of policing required whether semi-military or civil. The design and implementation of the Iraqi police programme therefore became the primary responsibility of the US: in particular the state department's bureau of international narcotics law enforcement (INL) and, the justice department. Further support was provided by the UK, Australia, Canada, and Spain, who were all invited to send senior police.

The delays in seconding police officers overseas meant that even after major combat operations had ceased, there were comparatively few international advisors in-country (Iraq Inquiry, 2016). Given the paucity of international support, the military police were given the policing lead (RAND, 2019: 84) and while the concept of police primacy was much vaunted, this remained a 'military mission', and increasingly so as the security situation worsened (House of Commons Defence Committee, 2005; Kernaghan, 2010). Former Chief Superintendent Kevin Hurley was seconded to Iraq as a senior police adviser. He later submitted evidence stating that 'immediately following and during the combat operations of March and April 2003, there was no plan for the maintenance of law and order amongst the civil population in Iraq ... policing was not part of the strategic military plan' (House of Commons Defence Committee, 2005: 54). It was only when faced with the eruption of widespread lawlessness, sectarian violence, and social disorder that the coalition *then* decided to recruit, train, and equip as many Iraqi police as were possible (Kernaghan, 2010). No doubt this was further prompted by the findings from the US-led Luck commission and national strategy for victory in Iraq, highlighting the importance of rebuilding Iraq's security resilience, which the US president noted required 'a sustained commitment from many nations, including our own: we will remain in Iraq as long as necessary, and not a day more'. (US national Security Council, 2005: 1) Yet it was only two years later that a UK government endorsed strategic task force was created to address issues relating to the recruitment and secondment of UK police.[6] From 2003 to 2005 'there was an absence of strategic policing advice at senior levels in the Coalition while the policing policy was unduly militarised' (House of Commons Defence Select Committee, 2005: para 170).

Training and advising the Iraqi police

Despite initiatives to plan the training and equipping of the *new* IPS 'within weeks' of the arrival of the CPA, the official establishment of a civilian police

---

[6] One possibility raised was the creation of a permanent and dedicated pool of officers available for overseas deployments. UK police could be seconded, in a manner similar to other national secondments, and this would provide an opportunity for career enhancement (Brand (senior police advisor, 2003–2004, 2010 and see chapter 6).

advisory team (CPAT) did not occur until early 2004. By then, the IPS had failed to take control of local criminal and militia activity with spiralling attacks against citizens and police alike (Ashraf, 2007; Kernaghan, 2010). Within the initial stages there was an insufficient number of international police present in Iraq (and Jordan) to support the training and equipping of Iraqi police required (Ashraf, 2007; Author interview with former Det Chief Supt Hampshire Police, 11 August 2010). UK police would go on to provide: *training* for 'generic' policing in Baghdad, Southern Iraq, and Jordan, *mentoring* IPS in the multinational division (south-east) (MND (SE)) and to *support* the 'enhancement of national capabilities including development of a national police strategy' (essentially in Baghdad and Basra).

Training the IPS drew on the majority of policing resources available. At the Baghdad Police Academy, the UK's contribution was the only serving civilian police component (between five and ten officers with a majority of MDP) to the CPA that turned out 3,000 police graduates every eight weeks (FCO, 2005). In the south, approximately twenty-three UK police (both serving and retired officers) provided basic and lower level specialist training to 200 IPS at any one time at the Az-Zubayr Police Academy with commitment to these training programmes lasting well beyond 2005. Outside Iraq, most basic level training was undertaken in Jordan at the international police training centre with approximately sixty UK officers supporting other coalition partners to ensure that 3,000 IPS graduated every three weeks (FCO, 2005). Deployment to Jordan (rather than Iraq) carried far less risk—officers were not required to carry a firearm for self-protection for example.

However, the FCO recognized that more robust approaches to training were needed to ensure a 'hard edge gendarmerie-type capability ... 'an area where the UK has no expertise' (FCO, 2005). While the UK had indeed no official gendarmerie capability, no assessment had been made of the role of RUC–PSNI in Kosovo where they had undertaken quasi-gendarmerie activities on an *operational basis*. Neither had there been any thought given to the experiences of former RUC during the conflict in Northern Ireland and a prior experience of hostile environments (drawn from five Author interviews with former RUC–PSNI who served in Kosovo, BiH, and Iraq). Moreover, an aversion to 'risk' by some chief officers prevented the deployment of police from some UK forces (Kernaghan, 2010; Author interview with former Chief Constable, MDP, 12 November 2012). To compensate with the shortfall, police with the necessary skill sets and experience (including firearms training) were hastily recruited and the FCO contracted out to private security companies and organizations specialized in development,[7] despite having a preference for serving or retired police wherever possible (Ashraf, 2007 and see chapter 5).

Pre-deployment preparation

The lack of a standby pool of serving UK police to deploy internationally (as well as government-led international policing strategy) necessitated chief officer goodwill to release officers for an overseas mission. Constabularies were financially compensated by the FCO yet it was not always possible to replace that person, which alongside risk and duty of care considerations prevented some chief constables from support overseas secondments. As the requests for international missions grew, so the selection of the right candidates may have become less than rigorous (this subsequently changed: see chapter 6). In considering the recruitment processes at this time, there was a sense that a first government paper sift considered prior mission experiences over and above professional experiences and skills sets. Some individuals who had previous mission experience may have been less than suitable owing to personal circumstance and life style choices (particularly alcoholism) while others appeared more interested in financial reward than providing a police service overseas as this former MPS officer (2012) explained:

> There was a mission subsistence allowance of £60 a day. You don't have to be a rocket scientist to work out what that adds up to. When we got to Warwickshire and were told we were going to Jordan and the allowance was going to be £30 a day because it's not so hostile and it's not so dangerous, there was huge uproar and, I guess, that's when I realised not everyone had come for the experience of training the Iraqi police! (Author interview with former Chief Inspector, MPS, 14 April 2012 deployed to Jordan/Iraq)

The time lag between an application for deployment to Iraq and the actual release of an officer varied considerably and in some cases an individual

---

[7] Specialist IPS training and mentoring in Southern Iraq was delivered through FCO contracts awarded to ArmorGroup and by forty International Police Advisors including some retired UK police (FCO, 2005).

waited for between one and two years for release from their home force. Then they were required to undergo pre-deployment training, including hostile environment awareness training (HEAT), which was at the time seen by most as largely irrelevant. An officer who was being deployed to Jordan as a police trainer (2004) remembered that:

> We went to Warwickshire for two days to a hotel where we were given an Iraq specific briefing but no Jordan specific briefing. But we were told very little about the Iraqi Police or about the context but they did talk about battlefield injuries and a bit about hostile environments. We were told even less about why we're there, what our aims and objective were. There was no one actually there from the Foreign Office to brief us and answer our questions and there was no manual of guidance given out … (Author interview with former inspector Northumbria Police, June 2011).

The failure to provide adequate pre-deployment briefings (described by some as abysmal) and ensure safe passage, particularly to those police deploying to a site of military intervention in Iraq resulted in issues that could have damaged the integrity of UK policing as a former MDP cohort commander (2011) remarked:

> When I think back on it, it was shocking because we went there with no brief, no remit, no terms of reference. Not a single piece of paper was given to me about what I was getting into. I went there under the assumption that we were going to be housed with the military working alongside the military and then, goodness me, we actually carried our own weapons on a British Airways flight and when we got to Kuwait, obviously they're in a bag, and they go through a scanner to get out of the airport and this guy said, 'Put them on the scanner.' I said, 'I can't.' 'Yes,' he said, 'Put them on the scanner.' I said, 'I can't, there's something sensitive in there for the scanner.' 'Okay,' he said. I just slipped them through. So, we got them through that way but that was the FCO approach at the time… we had to get on with it (Author interview with former Chief Supt. MDP, 11 August 2011).

UK police trainers were quickly aware of the challenges on arrival at the training establishments in Jordan where the bulk of international police training was undertaken—approximately 32,000 new Iraqi recruits to be trained yearly. One key issue related to the training curriculum that had been 'thrown together' and the lack of an earlier training needs analysis that delivered to the quantity of recruits rather than the quality of training. The curriculum centred on four weeks of 'classroom theory', one week of driving instruction, one week of firearms instruction, and one week of 'officer safety training' and use of force (the use, for example, of handcuffs and batons). For some UK police, the curriculum was too far removed from the needs of the IPS, many of whom were illiterate and could not follow the PowerPoint presentations. Examples given where the material was inappropriate included criminal investigations and wider criminal justice systems (based on a 'Western' rather than the Iraqi model of criminal justice); 'democratic' policing (based on recent experiences from Kosovo); community policing (based on a 'Western' rather than Iraqi model). Moreover, for many recruits, driving instruction was seen as unnecessary given the uncertainty that they would even have access to a vehicle on their return home. (Author interview with former contingent commander, Jordan, 2004–2005, August 2010). Moreover, while the recruitment age was set at twenty to forty years, poor selection procedures in Iraq meant, as one former UK police trainer reflected (2011):

> There were recruits who were I think clearly 13 or 14 years old. There were guys in their 60s because it was a job and back then it was about $140 a month for the training. So, they're getting nearly $300 for being there. It was just desperately sad to see these people. We had completely illiterate people from small villages and tribal areas but we also had people who had before the invasion been bankers, lawyers, senior army people that wanted a job and were desperate for a job (Former Chief Inspector, MPS, September 2010, deployed to Jordan).

Yet by 2004, the coalition had formed a supposed view that the interim Iraqi government perceived their police as a 'community-based force', providing general policing duties, including crime prevention and detection, and leaving the army with the primary responsibility for security (HoC, 2005; Kernaghan, 2005). The hierarchical nature of international donors, the tension between US contractors ('gold rules: he who has the gold makes the rules') meant that many issues were simply not reported up through the chain of command and evidence of a lack of training efficacy remained anecdotal (Author interviews, 2010–2014). Moreover, as 2005 drew on, clearly the UK wished to withdraw. By then the FCO Iraq directorate held just one retired police officer which suggested that: 'By this stage the strategic direction was set. We were not there to transform Iraqi society. We were there to get out' (HoC, 2005: 67).

Aside from the large cohort of UK police trainers, in Baghdad and Southern Iraq, small numbers of UK police held posts as senior 'civilian' police advisors to the MOI operating at a strategic level. By 2005, there were twelve further officers in lesser supporting roles (FCO, 2005) who used their British policing influence wherever possible as Douglas Brand (2010) commented:

> Though our police presence in Baghdad was miniscule, we did try to have a larger than life presence by engaging in activities that had high visibility and importance. For the UK police, the leadership of the Baghdad training academy, the staffing of the TIPS hotline, (a form of Crimestoppers), and the development of the Joint Coordination Centre in the HQ of the 1st Armoured Division were three excellent examples (Brand, 2010: 2).

Within the four MND(SE) provinces (including Basra),[8] police of superintendent rank mentored and advised the provincial police chiefs theoretically to enhance leadership and criminal investigation capabilities though practically to provided operational support alongside the coalition military and CPA governance coordinators. Some of these officers had an 'intelligence background' and were seconded from PSNI while others were drawn from wider UK police working in an intelligence capacity as one officer (2010) explained:

> We were undertaking intelligence stuff... Almost like eyes and ears to find out what was happening within the police in Basra. There was a real problem at the time with police corruption and infiltration of militias into the IPS.... we were trying to work out from that web of who we could work with and who we couldn't work with to try to understand where the root of some of these areas of corruption were. So effectively we were fonts of knowledge about what was happening. We'd brief the

---

[8] The UK provided the leadership of MNF-I's Multi-National Division (South-East) (MND(SE)) which covered the southern Iraqi provinces of Basra, Maysan, Dhi Qar, and Al Muthanna. As well as the UK, MND (SE) included Italian, Norwegian, Romanian, Danish, Dutch, Czech, Portuguese, and Lithuanian troops.

British security services and give briefings to all sorts of people in the Foreign Office who were visiting, ministers and such like (Former Supt (force withheld) May, 2012).

Sometimes RUC–PSNI officers were favoured over and above other UK police for their counterterrorism and counter-intelligence expertise as well as an experience of hostile and divided society policing; Kernaghan described this as a 'fairly high-level capability and indeed at one stage a light armoured capability' (Kernaghan, 2010). Ashraf writing of his personal experiences in Iraq noted that RUC–PSNI officers 'tended to be amongst the most effective in understanding the Iraqi situation ... They understood the threats and pressure that Iraqi officers faced. They also understood the crucial importance of acquiring and using intelligence effectively in a terrorism context, and they knew how to coordinate action with the Army' (Ashraf, 2007: 108). One example of RUC–PSNI policing influence was the adoption of a confidential telephone line known as TIPS in Baghdad and Basra largely based on the Northern Irish model. This allowed the citizen to report illegal activity, crime, and suspicious individuals to the police, boosting intelligence capabilities and going some way to improve public confidence in the local police (Ashraf, 2007; Kernaghan, 2010, Author interview with former Supt RUC–PSNI, May 2010). Stephen White as senior police adviser and director of law and order for the CPA (2003 to 2004) brought an experience of policing Northern Ireland during the Troubles as well as wider policing reform: institutional, management, and cultural post 2000. White returned to Iraq (2004 to 2009) following his retirement from PSNI as head of the EU's integrated rule of law mission in Iraq (EUJUSTLEX) where he continued to draw on his earlier experiences (Author interview with Stephone White, May 2011).

Police corruption

In a similar vein to Afghanistan, corruption within local security forces was perceived as a particular challenge in Iraq by Western police, as well as the high incidence of brutality and torture towards detainees and the inadequate protection of civilians (Author interviews, 2010–2014). While the term 'police corruption' can be used to explore many different activities, there has been considerable scholarly debate regarding the breadth and competing definitions (see Newburn, 1999). Across all Arab countries evidence of widespread police corruption prevails which is largely recognized as a blocker to building trust between the police and community. Broadly police corruption in this context has been described as 'the misuse of authority for personal gain' which exploits or denies routine police work. It is distinguished between three types: 'gratuities' including bribes; 'opportunistic corruption' where police target criminal offenders and, 'process corruption' whereby judicial procedures are influenced in return for personal benefits which may include framing citizens, falsifying evidence, and perverting the cause of justice (Gaub and Walsh, 2020). Corruption in Iraq was seen by UK police as hampering efforts at police capacity building as illustrated (2010) here:

> The police had their fingers in everything and they were the root of corruption as far as we were concerned. Electricity is a good example, the electricity and oil were being protected by the Iraqi police but, of course there was corruption in the Iraqi police and all the tools kept on being stolen, contractors were getting shot at and killed and there were difficulties with supply. Until you sort your police out, sort the corruption out, you're not going to be able to build your power stations or get your trade routes, capacity building, is not going to happen (Former Det Chief Supt Hampshire Police, August 2010).

Yet many recognized that bringing an understanding of corruption in the Iraqi context required a far greater situational awareness and understanding of local culture as this officer (2012) reflected:

> Corruption is not so simple. My view of life, I guess, has been changed by my Iraq experience in that over 20,000 Iraqi police officers have been murdered since 2003. If you've seen what I've seen in Baghdad ... he horror of the bombings ... the impact everything has there and that seven years after we've liberated Iraq, they have less electricity and running water than they did under Saddam, and the police are joining for $300 a month. Many of them are being killed. Yes, some of them make money on the side through corruption, and again, when we come onto the British style of policing, we're going into countries like Iraq and Afghanistan forgetting that ... we expect them to be holy than thou and whiter than white and eradicate all that, and though that's how the country operates and has always operated (Former Chief Superintendent, MPS 11 August 2011 and former contingent commander Iraq).

Improving Iraqi capability to tackle thorny issues that included corruption, necessitated support from international police with access to senior Iraqi police and, influence at the strategic level which could impact the direction of travel, as Douglas Brand explained to the Iraq Inquiry (2010):

> For example, an opportunity to affect the strategic direction and powers of the Iraqi Intelligence Service by introducing a UK police 'Special Branch' system arose, and over a series of meetings with US and UK security interests and myself, the Administrator was persuaded of the utility of the British system. The initiative was lost however, because the UK was unable to second an experienced Special Branch manager to put the structure in place. A similar opportunity was lost in the setting up of an HMIC type standards and inspection unit for similar reasons (Brand, 2010: 1–2).

In preparation for the UK's drawdown from Iraq, a twelve-month duration was set for training giving the military the lead on basic policing and civilian police oversight of specialist capability. All overseas missions would require direction from local government and 'much unfavourable comment' was made about the lack of an Iraqi national police strategy or planning from the MOI as to what areas of expertise they sought (Smith, 2010). Even though Sir Ronnie Flanagan (former PSNI Chief Constable) was seconded to Basra to carry out a review of policing in 2005 in support of future strategic planning, his findings were subsequently reported to Sir John Chilcot (Author interview with former PSNI Chief Constable, January 2011). By January 2005, UK police remained in two priority areas only: MND (SE) in operational training and mentoring roles and, in Baghdad in strategic roles (including very senior posts in Baghdad Police College). Yet a lack of police resources meant that the UK was perceived as a 'small player' even though some officers held key posts including the advisor to the deputy minister of police. Overall, the civilian police advisory team remained under military control despite some attempts to enhance UK policing influence through the provision of technical training courses in investigation, criminal intelligence, and forensics. This included the training of fifty criminal intelligence operatives in Jordan in 2005 led by UK and Czech Republic intelligence advisers (House of Commons Defence Committee, 2005).

Libya

UK policing with strategic intent

The UK's involvement in Libya was something of a departure from Iraq and Afghanistan, and involved senior police as strategic advisors at the political high table. This could be likened to a greater opportunity for brand management of UK policing (in a similar vein to Sierra Leone) and the provision of strategic intent. In both cases (Sierra Leone and Libya), there was an historic backcloth which included policing.

Libya's police have their roots in the Libyan Arab Force, which was created with British support and fought under King Idris al-Sanusi against the Italian occupation during the Second World War. In 1951, when Libya became independent, the Libyan Arab Force was transformed into the Cyrenaica Defense Force merging with the Tripolitania Defense Force to form the Libyan National Police in 1952 and tasked with providing civilian security. The leader Muammar Gaddafi, by the late 1970s had become reliant on his newly created security services and revolutionary committees, and in a similar vein to the Iraqi Police under Saddam Hussein, the Libyan National Police were increasingly purged and marginalized with newly created extra-legal security organizations (brigades) taking over its functions and responsibilities (Cole and Mangan, 2016).

Diplomatic relations were severed with Libya following the murder of MPS officer Yvonne Fletcher in 1984 and were only restored in 1999. A lifting of sanctions in 2003 led to the UK's (re)engagement primarily related to trade, defence, and oil. In 2004 and 2007, PM Tony Blair met Gaddafi to negotiate defence and commercial agreements and a memorandum of understandings relating to criminal justice procedures (House of Commons Foreign Affairs Committee, 2016). This included support to the Libyan security forces through UK military and police assistance. By this time, and in parallel with much of the Arab world, Libyan policing departments were housed in specialized directorates within the general security directorate accountable to the MOI while domestic intelligence was controlled by the internal security organization (Cole and Mangan, 2016).

Through this pre-2011 period, the UK, through the NPIA International Academy (Bramshill) engaged with the core policing departments (including CID, police special forces, riot police, and local police) to deliver multiple training packages (in Libya and the UK). In particular these were related to counter-narcotics, major incident command, command and control, and forensics and passed seamlessly into history unnoticed by the British media (Author interview with former head of NPIA International Academy Bramshill, 20 December 2010). It was not until 2009 with the secondment of PSNI officers to Libya that the 'fury' over their presence was aroused in Northern Ireland and risked becoming a political hot potato. Criticism levied at both PSNI and the Northern Ireland Policing Board centred on whether the two officers in question were involved in 'intelligence operations' (PSNI, 2011) and created a furore amongst unionist politicians seeking compensation for victims of the Troubles period from the Libyan authorities for their alleged support of IRA violence (*Belfast Telegraph*, 2009). Revealing in this case was the suggestion that the provision of international policing assistance was being used to oil diplomatic channels to establish future trade agreements and defence engagement activities. While PSNI had continued to deploy officers (including those from an intelligence background) to EULEX, for example, it was the intervention in Libya that raised the spectre of the earlier conflict in Northern Ireland. The most senior PSNI officers involved (at that time seconded to the NPIA) clarified that the visit to Libya was not an 'an unusual event' as training packages had been provided over the past eighteen months by PSNI officers amongst others:

> The picture at that stage was of an excellent government to government relationship developing and fully supported by the British Embassy in Tripoli and by the FCO.... I took this as the greatest indicator yet that our relationship was working extremely well which had to be for the benefit of wider UK interests.... Moreover, part of the project had been funded by UNDP (Former Chief Inspector, PSNI, May 2010 deployed to Libya 2008–2010).

Yet this had sparked a media controversy with Amnesty International calling for 'rigorous reviews' of PSNI training of 'overseas police forces in the light of the killings of protestors by Libyan and Bahraini police' (Amnesty International, 2009). Some PSNI officers feared that the ensuing media campaign was more about the earlier RUC reputation rather than where they were training and that the RUC had tainted the 'new' PSNI brand (Author interviews with former RUC–PSNI officers 2010–2014). Media pressure had escalated by 2011 with calls on the UK government to re-evaluate whether police training should be provided particularly to the MENA region and Gulf states (including Abu Dhabi, Qatar, and Saudi Arabia) (for example

Amnesty International, 2009; McDonald, 2011; Norton-Taylor, 2011a) and, whether export licences should be granted for public order equipment to Libya including 'teargas and irritant ammunition' (Norton Taylor, 2011a). The NPIA was a not-for-profit organization and maintained that while it sought to ensure financial security, UK policing overseas sought an engagement on critical issues for the UK government including human rights, gender, and diversity which could result in police professionalization within the developing world (see chapter 6 for further details; SU, 2014).

Post-intervention stabilization

The request for UK policing support to Libya provided further evidence of the international perception of the brand built upon an historic (colonial) and near recent relationship between the Libyan police and UK policing. This rested on senior and strategic police advisors operating at the highest echelons of government following the 2011 intervention and, the request for a UK policing model by the 'new' Libyan government. In particular, a small number of British police held responsibility for strategy and planning within the Libyan MOI, which showcased elements of the UK policing brand. Policing with *strategic intent* has been recognized as a UK *policing forte*. EU police partners have acknowledged that UK policing has a particular expertise in planning and supporting the (re)building of police structures and institutions where there are none (Author interviews with EU police 2016–2018). This senior UK police suggested has rested on an understanding within the UK police that operational linkages should always be created between the police, government, public institutions, and the wider private sector, which creates a familiarity and experience in working with and across multiple stakeholders. Within SSR and police reform programmes, working at a strategic level has necessitated an understanding of the host government architecture and an expertise in negotiating and influencing, leadership and management skills across all stakeholders (Author interviews, 2016–2018).

Anti-government protests in Libya began in Benghazi in February 2011 sparked by wider uprisings across the Middle East and North Africa and the growth of political Islamist and extremist networks, which opposed Gaddafi. By this time the Libyan National Police 'were a weak and submissive institution' and despite international policing assistance (including the UK), were largely dominated by other security actors to undertake local security functions. This 2011 revolution resulted in the 'wholesale collapse in policing institutions' with a gradual return of some elements following the demise of the regime and creation of the national transitional council (NTC) which formed as a de facto government for ten months until the August 2012 elections. However, all successive transitional government failed to deliver a long-term vision for security sector reform 'creating significant legal ambiguity over the status and nature of policing' (Cole and Mangan, 2016: 6–8; Author interviews with senior police advisors to Libya, 2018–2020).

The 2011 uprising saw periods of heavy conflict prior to the fall of Gadhafi between pro and anti-regime forces and swiftly the UN security council enforced a no-fly zone and enacted the necessary measures to protect civilians. UNSCR 1973 (17 March 2011) was approved by a coalition of countries and several days later the UK gave its support to military intervention as part of NATO's Operation Unified Protector (House of Commons Foreign Affairs Select Committee, 2016: 6). Europe's 'expeditionary oriented countries' France and UK, took the lead bolstered by their improved security cooperation following a mutual signing of the Lancaster House Treaty (Zandee et al., 2020: 3). For the UK, Libya also marked a turning point in that a 'whole-of-government' approach was adopted, a first since the advent of the 2010 NSC and its sub-committee on Libya which was described (2011) as:

> An effective vehicle for driving the campaign: early decisions helped prevent a wide scale humanitarian crisis and encouraged action by the wider international community; departments moved rapidly to conflict footing and prioritised resources; real time military, intelligence and diplomatic assessment including from theatre gave Ministers an understanding of the detailed context in which to take strategic decisions, as well as to identify areas where further action was needed (National Security Adviser's Review, 2011).

The drive to promote cross-government working had been present since New Labour though the NSC was a real attempt to harness a rapid response to crises. For example, the SU[9] identification of experts from a dedicated pool for post-intervention planning and stabilization, which included

---

[9] The SU co-ordinated and supported cross-government stabilization planning and execution and was tasked early on (24 February) by the MOD and Cabinet Office to facilitate early scenario planning, which later formed the basis for much of the subsequent post-conflict stabilization and recovery planning.

both serving and retired police. Yet somewhat reminiscent of Iraq, the initial planning did not involve senior UK police, was devoid of a policing strategy, and gave the initial brief to the military. It took several months for a senior police advisor to be brought to the planning high table in London, and then to be deployed to Libya in July 2011, following requests from National Transitional Council's (NTC) Minister of the Interior, Fawzi Abdel A'al. Despite this, the UK held several ace cards. First while other European countries had police attachés or liaison officers already present in Libya (who would go on to work closely with UK police and provide considerable technical assistance), the relationship developed between the UK and Libyan police since 2007 was beneficial and, secondly, the 'reputation of British policing' cemented the decision to embed a senior officer within the MOI. Particular elements of the UK policing brand were requested, including Scotland Yard's reputation for its intelligence and investigative capabilities and, the NPIA's expertise in delivering bespoke training packages. It was clear that the Libyan Police 'did not want policing out of a tin' or to be provided with an *off the shelf* bundle of training materials that had been used elsewhere (Author interview with the first senior (strategic) police advisor deployed to Libya, 2011–2012, 4 December 2020).

UK police provided a 'caretaking' role between July and September 2011 in advance of the UN support mission to Libya (UNSMIL). Embedding a senior advisor in the NTC MOI while the conflict was ongoing, allowed the UK to navigate and support nascent police reform and then to coordinate with other EU countries, the US, and international organizations as the NTC moved from Benghazi to Tripoli (Author interview with senior police advisor deployed to Libya 2012–2013, 15 June 2020). The strategic police advisor was tasked with building a relationship with the minister to:

> define what policing in Libya could look like in the future, to look past the fighting .... The perception at the time was that the UK was good at strategic planning in these situations ... The UK policing brand let me into the Libyan MOI and the effort that I made to generate relationships kept the door open. I worked closely with the MOI to consider the Libyan's police future institutional structures, human resourcing issues, budgeting, recruiting, staffing and so on ... (First senior (strategic) police advisor deployed to Libya, 2011–2012, December 2020).

In essence the UK was alone amongst an array of other EU partners in its support of NTC to fill a formal advisory role, and there was wide recognition of the 'usefulness of external technical advice of this nature' (DFID, 2012a: 5). This strategic local buy-in resulted in an 'unexpected level of access and influence [...] in an environment in which foreign technical advice has been treated with extreme caution' (DFID, 2012a: 5). The success of the initial strategic advisor led to a MOI request for additional police advisors further increasing the UK's influence within the Libyan MOI. In parallel, an international stabilization response team (ISRT) comprising eleven international experts[10] drawn from different backgrounds, including security and justice, was sent to Libya to report on stabilization requirements (DfID, 2011a; House of Commons Foreign Affairs Select Committee, 2016: 23). For some this was a novel approach that demonstrated lessons learned from Iraq, the need to plan for stabilization, and aligned with the strategic defence and security review (House of Commons Foreign Affairs Select Committee, 2016: 119). In addition, the ISRT bolstered the activities of the police advisors who navigated between strategic planning and an operational focus on the immediate security challenges, structural reform on the new police, security planning for elections, and wider MOI reforms (DfID Annual Review, 2012b).

Throughout this period the NTC sought to create new institutions to fill the policing gap; the most well-known was the supreme security committee, which in December 2011 officially became a new state security institution with quasi-policing functions and accountable to the MOI, comprising an array of different brigades and militias drawn from across Libya's political and ideological spectrum (Cole and Mangan, 2016; Author interview with the first senior (strategic) police advisor deployed to Libya, 2011–2012). Yet in the June to December 2011 period there was a sense that the UK government' vision was 'cloudy' as to their policing assistance strategy for Libya and which elements of the policing brand could be provided (2011):

> The MOI has expressed an interest in a UK policing style but supported by a strong riot police capability. Others [in NTC] spoken to include functioning and transparent investigation, case management systems, forensic capability, improved intelligence systems and Border Management and Port controls, in this list. There is little doubt that all of these areas will require rebuilding and some form of international

---

[10] International experts were drawn from Australia, Denmark, Italy, Turkey, US, UK, and Canada.

assistance however they would require to be part of a larger SSR package and would not be considered an immediate priority ... (Smith, 2011).

Yet on the ground, robust policing approaches were needed. In contrast to other interventions of the previous two decades including Kosovo, Timor Leste, Afghanistan, and Iraq, there was no international military peacekeeping force in-country. The NTC was wholly reliant on its own security capabilities as the strategic adviser reported in August 2011:

> There is an urgent requirement for the NTC, as part of their identified National Security, to form an armed capability, able, in the near future, to respond professionally, and in accordance with legal arrest procedures and human rights, to public disorder and use of weapons. It may be possible to consider bringing militias or others wishing to join the police organisation into this type of units (DfID, 2011b).

There was a strong sense of the UK's crisis management focus on strategic planning for Libyan police reform and only then would technical assistance be provided within post-conflict stabilization. From 2011 to 2014, the UK attempted a holistic and long-term assistance strategy to build strategic influence and sustainable reforms within Libya's security structures. Support to the MOI and the Libyan police included mentoring and advising, technical assistance covering an array of specialist trainings, and the provision of infrastructure. Yet the eruption of civil war in 2014 saw renewed conflict and violence and more recently new foreign actors diminishing the authority of the UN, US, and EU countries. While the Libyan security sector has undergone attempted reform since 2011, each of the successive transitional governments have instigated a diverging and often competing set of reforms. Civilian policing strategies remain largely dictated by domestic intelligence or defence priorities and its functions and responsibilities remain fragmented and bound by geopolitical considerations (Cole and Mangan, 2016).

Concluding comment

I have used a broad-brush stroke to illustrate examples of where UK policing has intervened following what have been largely US-led interventions since 2001. Fighting a global 'war on terror' to prevent any further erosion of security in the US, Europe, and the wider world through acts of terrorism has been central to these actions (House of Commons Defence Committee, 2012). UK policing contributed (albeit in small part) to these interventions through the deployment of serving officers (FCO, 2004a; 2007). Yet the 'ability of the UK to meet demand' as the missions rose exponentially was severely tested. This was particularly true of the search for senior-ranking officers to fill posts that held strategic priority for the UK, in contrast to UN mission that were rankless. International policing in the main remained the preserve of the few rather than the many. Senior police competed with their EU counterparts for posts which was for some off-putting though more contentious was the lack of enthusiasm by many chiefs to release their officers, and no apparent benefits to the official career pathway and promotion prospects (Kernaghan, 2010).

The limited uniformed police presence in planning and delivery for the post-intervention phase continued to underline a critical gap in the UK government's approach to SSR and police reform, which would be highlighted in both the Iraq Inquiry and lessons from Libya (Kernaghan, 2010; House of Commons Foreign Affairs Committee, 2016). Overall, the military, owing to their expeditionary raison d'être held primacy within overseas missions though their involvement in police reform and capacity building was not well viewed by senior UK police and has remained a source of controversy. The lack of a government-led international policing strategy once again prevented the formalization of international policing assistance. It is also worth reflecting on the UK's lack of a gendarmerie equivalent at that time—the RUC was the only UK police force that had a semi-military capability that proved effective in Kosovo. While the MDP had armed capability, its operational culture and ethos was very different to RUC–PSNI.

UK policing throughout this period continued to compete with a multiplicity of policing providers drawn from across the global north and global south and each with their own 'brand' characteristics. Within the enormity of Afghanistan's multilateral and bilateral missions, for example, the UK policing brand was noticeably subsumed and there are questions as to the appropriateness and sustainability of what was exported over these past decades, by whom, and for what reasons (Pino and Waitrowski, 2006; Goldsmith and Sheptycki, 2007; Ellison and Pino, 2012) and (Author interviews, 2010–2014). As the numbers and complexity of missions have grown, so the numbers of serving UK police deploying have fallen, the market has opened up to the corporate security sector which has swallowed up police and military retirees. It is to the private security sector and their involvement in international policing assistance that I now turn in chapter 5.

5
The Rise of Police and Security Contracting

> There is a definitely an important place for retired officers as they bring policing expertise, credibility and flexibility and they shouldn't be ignored but the preference has been for most receiving countries to have serving officers. If a country is seen as strategically important it is an opportunity for the UK to sell the policing brand, drive its influence in a different way... but there are many challenges as it is not always easy to have people released from active policing service.
>
> **Former Chief Inspector MPS and JIPH lead, 2019**

> What have I been doing here in Abu Dhabi?... trying to identify where we've got some performance gaps, trying to look at then using the committees, and the committees are made up of officers from different Emirates, tasking them to actually look at this issue to have some improvement and trying to pump prime them with good practice from the UK to say, 'Well, this is how it's done in the UK and it's not supposed to be the best, but have a look at it and see if it will work here. If you need then to actually visit the UK to actually see it in action well, you can do that and we'll try and facilitate that and we'll try to identify who's the lead force in the UK so you can go and have a look at that.' It may well be about missing persons, it could be about homicide, it could be about all sorts of things, but it's trying to actually just stimulate that curiosity in respect of let's have a look at somewhere else, see if we can drag that expertise to here.
>
> **Former UK former strategic advisor UAE, 2011**

The private military and security market has become a global phenomenon with an expansion in the use of contractors over the past two decades. This has attracted considerable attention: academic and policymakers have often engaged with questions of regulation and oversight; the media has typically courted sensationalism and revealed the murkier sides while 'the popular author who may have "been there and done that", the objective [has been] to convey a sense of adventure' (Dunsby, 2015: 377). In practice it remains extremely difficult to estimate the true numbers of contractors drawn from military, law enforcement, and intelligence backgrounds.

The focus in this chapter is on *security* and what I term *police* contractors: that is, former members of UK police who have provided a range of overlapping services within the international arena that may overlap. I suggest that the growth in the security industry and the demand for elements of the UK policing brand has reinforced its value internationally. However, there has been a tension between the myth and reality of what overseas governments and their law enforcement agencies are interested in, what the UK government may wish to drive forward, and, importantly, which aspects have been marketed by the private security industry in an attempt to fill security gaps. As outlined within previous chapters, the reality of peacekeeping policing and policing within FCAS called for an expertise in *national security policing*. RUC–PSNI had time-defined skills in hostile environments and intelligence management that were transferred first to the Western Balkans where these skills were further developed. Fortuitously it would seem, the advent of the PSNI and the organizational and cultural shifts away from a semi-military to a civilian policing style coincided with the interventions in Iraq and Afghanistan. This opened new horizons for those police who took retirement. That is not to say that other UK police have not contributed to the longevity of the brand. Across wider SSR there has been a surge in demand for police actors (including the UK) within multilateral and bilateral overseas missions, which typically has included a higher number of police retirees. Moreover, the linkage between the public and private sectors has supported the flourishing of a considerable degree of co-operation and interdependency.

There is an historic backcloth to police contracting. In chapter 2, I referred to the internationalization of UK policing and how serving and former British police moved across the empire and commonwealth. Michael Macoun, who visited seventy-eight countries and British Overseas Territories between 1966 and 1979, was first an inspector general of the colonial police service and then what he described as an 'overseas police advisor'. In retirement he used the term 'police consultant'. Macoun was often tasked with police inspections although these visits coincided with an 'invitation' to advise on other police-related issues (Macoun, 1996: 98). Macoun, like so many others reflected on the varying facets and experiences of UK policing. Yet what they had in common was the *UK policing brand* which as roving advisors (and sometime) contractors they reinforced through British policing values and purpose. However, the waters became increasingly muddied by what Ellison and O'Reilly (2006) noted as 'the opaque divisions between private military companies (PMCs) and private security companies (PSCs) [which] are further obfuscated through a constant process of acronymatic re-branding by those involved in this industry sector' (Ellison and O'Reilly, 2006: 643). Former police have navigated between 'security' and 'police' contracting and some have held management positions across these sectors. However, we should not lose sight of the role of police as compared to military contractors.

The rise of the private security (policing) sector in the UK has linked to the ongoing commercialization of public policing: Sir Ronnie Flanagan referred to 'entrepreneurial policing' in 2008 as the need for police institutions to compete within this market place (Ellison and Sinclair, 2013). Selling policing services has been rooted within the history of British policing. Chris Williams observed from the nineteenth century 'there was never a time when British police were not for hire to anyone acceptable who could pay' (Williams, 2008: 192). Fast-track forward and a post-2008 austerity drive led to a shrinkage in the numbers of police deploying internationally, while increasing the number of police retirees and paradoxically individual forces offering services (Author interview with former head of the JIPH, February 2019). This aligned directly with the broader paradox of a neoliberalist stance since the 1980s whereby government funding was tightened and public sector forced to compete with the private sector. While in many sectors this has been a problematic shift, my research has suggested a fairly smooth direction of travel between the public and private *policing* sectors. The police family is well networked; commercial opportunities arise through personal encounters, the sharing of resources, policy transfer and lessons learning within wider knowledge exchange both nationally and internationally (Author interviews, 2010–2019). This has been particularly true of SSR and police reform which has widened the global security market. Within the UK, the rise in aid and development funding (until 2020 0.7 per cent of GDP) while *state-led* has been largely outsourced to the private sector. Policing has often pivoted around soft power that is the benchmark for capacity-building programmes. Yet there has always been a pick-and-mix approach to what UK policing could offer within the public and private sectors to ensure adequate resources (Ellison and O'Reilly, 2008a; Sinclair, 2012, 2015). This overall growth has been supported by the emergence of DfID security and justice programmes from the 1990s, the advent of the SU, the conflict pool, and later conflict, stability, and security (CSSF) fund in 2015 and, the NPIA and then College of Policing (CoP) that 'holds the brand through the delivery of training courses' (Author interview with senior police advisor, lead for international policing, Stabilisation Unit 15 February 2019). By 2017, there were *multiple guardians* of the UK's international policing brand including the Joint International Policing Hub (JIPH), National Police Chiefs Council (NPCC), SU, Scotland Yard, and the National Crime Agency. One recent addition has been the Home Office International Strategy and Capabilities Unit, which develops and manages overseas programmes, deploying both serving and retired officers (see chapter 6).

The growth of the private military and security industry

The historic backdrop was the post-Cold War revival of an industry better known for its military expertise. For some of these emerging PMCs (including the infamous Executive Outcomes and Sandline) there were blurred distinctions in their approaches to warfare and combat activities versus crime, civil disorder, and political insurgencies with a commercial immediacy to seize market opportunities. Defence Systems Limited, for example, a UK company established in 1981, was contracted by the Papua New Guinea government to advise on the creation of a specialist police unit to protect the country's valuable resources. Defence Systems promoted the use for a police tactical force noting:

> The benefit of engaging DSL [sic] consultants in the formation and training of PTF type units is that the client is buying the United Kingdom Police/Army model—which is a proven, tried and regularly tested set of concepts and responses to violent crime and terrorism. DSL [sic] instructors bring with them operational experience that has been gained in counter-terrorist operations since 1972 in the UK and in all major incidents (Quoted in Dinnen, 1997: 62).

Indeed post 1989 there has been a veritable surge of private military and security contracting within FCAS (Isenberg, 2009) with an accompanying literature that is a minefield of terminology often debating how PMCs or PMSCs[1] can be differentiated from mercenaries (see Isenberg, 2009; McFate, 2015, 2016; Singer, 2004, 2007). In parallel, the growth in private security contractors (PSCs) has been studied (see Isenberg, 2009; Kinsey, 2006; Singer, 2007) and private security *per se* now well documented from global perspectives (see, for example, Nalla and Prenzler, 2018; Sarre and Prenzler, 2000; Shearing and Stenning, 1983, 1987). However, international *policing contractors* have received scant attention (though see in particular Ellison, 2008; Ellison and O'Reilly, 2006, 2008a, 2008b; O'Reilly, 2010). While it is unfeasible to provide a complete survey of corporate security services (see, for example, Montgomery and Griffiths, 2016), the growth is well illustrated by a revenue that will grow in excess of $257 billion by 2022 (Technavio, 2019).

The earlier quasi-informal mercenary groups[2] were largely overtaken by formal corporate bodies. This increase in both demand and supply-side factors has been explained within academic and policy-led research as stemming from the dominance of post-Cold War free market state models and the growing trend to outsource traditional government functions (Holmqvist, 2005). This has been described as an entry point for private security actors to support conflict management and post conflict aid and development (Deitelhoff and Wolf, 2009; Author interview with FCO

---

[1] PSCs can be described as 'firms that employ people who carry weapons to protect their clients and use them when necessary. Such firms have also been called private military contractors although that more accurately refers to firms doing unarmed logistics work.... PSCs for some have been a subset of PMSCs but academics have spent years arguing over terminology. I largely consider it an academic distinction that doesn't have much relevance to real-world discussion of the subject...' (Isenberg, 2009: ix).

[2] There has been considerable academic, policy-driven, and media discussion related to the history and operational role of 'mercenaries'. For interesting and recent insights see UN (2018) 'Mercenarism and Private Military and Security Companies' an overview of the work that has been carried out by the UN Working Group on the use of mercenaries as a means of violating human rights and impeding the exercise of the right of peoples to self-determination. The UN working group contributes to wider international discussions on the regulation of PMSCs through international and legally binding agreements (Van Amstel and Rodenhäuser, 2016). Private military companies (PMCs) (the alleged successors to mercenary outfits) have offered services including doctrine formation to hands-on military assistance through government contracts from across the world since their inception in the 1960s. The first PMC, founded in 1967 by David Stirling, progressed from combat training and support to the provision of Military Advisory Training Teams for foreign government clients in the Middle East and across Africa, Latin America, and East Asia (O'Brien, 2000).

Programme Manager, Afghanistan, 2011).[3] Secondly, as most national armies have declined, so an enormous pool of military personnel has become available for recruitment by the private sector (Holmqvist, 2005). The UK, for example, not only has a dwindling military establishment but has, since the mid-1980s, outsourced military services often with training as a central component. By 2007, for example, the MOD had approved £21 billion of new contracts with the corporate sector over a period of twenty-five years, that included DfID and the FCO delivering international training programmes for police and military (Mathieu and Dearden, 2006).

For former members of the armed forces, intelligence agencies, and police organizations, *security* has become a valuable and valued commodity. Within an FCAS context this might include combat support (intelligence analysis, logistics, guarding key infrastructures and weapons, vehicle and aircraft maintenance, and operational support); security (principally armed) for transportation and close protection, training, mentoring, and advising and broader capacity building and technical assistance within SSR (Isenberg, 2009, Author interviews 2010–2019). As many major Western powers have disengaged with countries where intervention has occurred (including Iraq, Afghanistan, and Libya), so the ensuing security void has provided further opportunities for the corporate world (Holmqvist, 2005). Moreover, security business has many offshoots including a growing 'risk industry' as global risk reduction strategies have become mandated by insurance companies (Carola, 2010: 6). The risk industry has attracted former UK police officers who have the skill sets to analyse security and risk for business and governments alike and have found gainful employment with industry giants across the world (Author interviews, 2009–2019).

It was the intervention in Iraq that brought a flourishing of the private security industry with contracts awarded to UK PMSCs alone rising from £320 million in 2003 to more than £1.8 billion in 2004. Yet as PMSCs became an integral part to a war effort (and subsequent transition and development phases), so the criticism and concerns surrounding the lack of regulation grew (Mathieu and Dearden, 2006). In 2003, the media was flooded with accounts of the abuse of prisoners held in Abu Ghraib prison in Iraq. This included US military police, CIA officers, and two PMSC: Titan

---

[3] Between 2002 and 2012 the FCO awarded contracts valued at a total of £402.5 million to 'PSCs in conflict zones' (including Iraq, Afghanistan, Libya, Yemen, and Somalia). Specific reference was made to the contracts awarded to Armour Group and G4S for the provision of police mentors and advisors in Iraq and Afghanistan (FCO FOIA, 2012).

and California Analysis Center Incorporated (CACI) (e.g. *The New York Times*, 20 February 2006). Government and public concerns escalated following the Nisour Square shooting of Iraqi civilians by Blackwater Security Consulting employees in 2007, mirroring the sporadic allegations of violence and abuse perpetrated by security contractors as well as members of the US military following the Iraqi invasion. All along, the United Nations (amongst others) has called for international regulation and greater 'softer' self-regulatory approaches. These have to date included the 2008 Montreux document, an inter-governmental initiative to drive existing international state obligations and so-called 'best practices' in regulating those PMSCs that participate in FCAS and, an international code of conduct developed in coordination with the host state, the security provider, and civil societies with principles, rules, and procedures to which signatories should adhere (Van Amstel and Rodenhauser, 2016). The UN has continued to drive forward the development of a regulatory framework agenda ensuring that all security providers are registered with the national authorities and licensed to operate overseas, as well as efforts to create the necessary legal jurisdiction for any violation of human rights and criminal misconduct (UN, 2017). Yet there are real challenges in holding this corporate sector to account (Singer, 2004: note 2: 151–69) and linked to this is the dilemma of how some organizations balance their corporate obligations to shareholders with the wider ethical and moral dimensions of SSR. Private security mission creep has occurred which may divert from the original SSR intentions and raise questions relating to value for taxpayer's money for services provide by PMSCs. Besides the revolving door between government and PMSCs, the movement of former officials and members of the armed forces and police to and from the private sector who are able to exercise influence through their connections and insider knowledge has explained the sector's success but has raised questions of oversight and scrutiny (Mathieu and Dearden, 2005; Miller, 2020).

Towards private sector regulation in the UK

Despite being closely associated with the world of private security and military services for almost five decades, successive UK governments have shown little appetite to officially regulate this sector (Mathieu and Dearden, 2005; Miller, 2020). In 1999, private security industry regulation in England and Wales was put forward in a government white paper that outlined licensing and how standards could be improved. While this white paper did not specify *international* security work, it framed the private security industry as a whole and the concerns at a lack of regulation as the sector had expanded (Home Office, 1999). Two years later, the Private Security Industry Act (2001) made some *provision* for the regulation through the development of a security industry authority to facilitate licensing, inspections, and provide monitoring and oversight. In particular, the act highlighted the industry's growth and as a consequence the rise in security occupations (Private Security Industry Act, 2001: 1–32). The 2001 legislation, however, was specific to activities undertaken in the UK. Sandline International (1996) was set up by in London by Lieutenant Colonel Tim Spicer and offered military consultancy services overseas.

Sandline was contracted by the Papua New Guinea government to 'blast the rebel leadership of the eight-year secessionist movement' of Bougainville: it sub-contracted to the South African alleged mercenary organization Executive Outcomes. The so-called Sandline affair went badly wrong when both Sandline and Executive Outcome operatives were forcibly removed from the country by the local military prompting embarrassment for the UK government: 'At the same time their appearance in this ostensibly marginal part of the world served as a reminder of the growth and long reach of private military contractors, as well as their potential for fomenting serious political instability. These events also underlined the ambiguous character of corporate entities that bear little resemblance to the caricature of the old-style mercenary outfit.' (Dinnen, 1997: 52–65). With the government view that 'the dangerous, embarrassing and wholly unacceptable events that became known as the Sandline affair are never repeated', the House of Commons Foreign Affairs Committee put forward a green paper that proposed legislative options for 'the control of private military companies which operate *out of the UK*' [author's italics] through regulation that included both licensing and registration procedures (House of Commons Select Committee on Foreign Affairs, 2002). However, there was recognition that 'in some circumstances, private military companies may be able to provide security services to make a legitimate and valuable contribution to be able to provide security services more efficiently and effectively than states are able' (House of Commons Select Committee on Foreign Affairs, 2002: 5) with the proviso that events like the Sandline 'affair' became ultimately the exception rather than the rule.

The intervention in Iraq brought an escalation in military and security contracting although official regulation did not follow. Several years later the House of Commons Defence Committee was pressing for action:

> It is now three years since the Government published its Green Paper on private military companies. We recommend the Government urgently brings forward proposals for the regulation of the overseas activities of private security and military companies. We do not believe that the current reliance on contracts is sufficient. We are well aware of the complexities involved in a licensing regime for individual contracts not least from our experience of the export control regime. We suggest that the FCO should enter into discussions with the Security Industry Authority to find ways in which its offices could be used. Once a mechanism has been established to regulate these companies, Parliament should consider how best it could undertake the necessary oversight (House of Commons Defence Committee, 2005: para 211).

Since that time the lack of official regulation and reliance on individual contracts between industry and government has created a process of *self-regulation* across security providers. With an acknowledgement by the private security industry that their reputation was being tarnished by scandal (including the Sandline affair), the British Association of Private Security Companies (BAPSC) was established in 2005. BAPSC sought to raise standards through a 'hands off' self-regulatory approach. *In theory*, BAPSC members were required to adhere to strict codes of practice and rules of engagement and to fully comply with the rules and principles of international humanitarian and human rights legislation. In 2010, an international code of conduct[4] for private security service providers was established though this presumed that all PSCs would join BAPSC. *In practice*, however, the lack of official regulation and the gaps with national legislation may fail to prevent the occurrence of a possible future Blackwater incident. Indeed, the intermeshing of state and corporate interests not to mention the revolving door of personnel may have indicated that there is too much vested in maintaining the status quo and official regulation will be a long time in the

---

[4] The international code of conduct for private security providers (ICoC) was convened by the Swiss government and set principles for PMSCs, articulating obligations for operational conduct relating to international humanitarian and human right law. The oversight mechanism for almost 1,000 organizations has been the International Code of Conduct Association (ICoCA, 2020).

offing (Ellison and Sinclair, 2013, Miller, 2020). Besides, any BAPSC drive to 'promote interests [and] regulate activities of UK based organizations that provide armed defensive security services in countries outside the UK' has appeared somewhat out of date. A further special interest group: security in complex environments group (SCEG) established in 2011 'to define, develop and facilitate robust, internationally recognised professional standards for the Private Security Sector operating in complexity' had arguably attracted a far higher number of recent PMSCs as members 'embracing international security standards and protecting human rights ... at the core of their business'. Their website has listed some thirty full and associate members including the most well known in the industry (SCEG UK, 2021).[5] It was appointed by the UK government in 2011 as its partner for the development and accreditation of standards for the private security industry operating overseas and has listed a number of UK government departments including the FCO, MOD, DfID, HO, Department for Transport appropriate 'representatives' to attend SCEG meetings (SCEG UK, 2021; White, 2016).

Anecdotal evidence from both Iraq and Afghanistan has pinpointed sporadic incidents of human rights abuses, criminal misconduct, and violence towards local citizens and other private security contractors as well as breaches of company codes of conduct and contractual obligations (Gaston, 2008; Author interviews, 2010–2019).[6] This can be potentially damaging not only for operational effectiveness but the integrity of the UK. The NPIA and its successor the CoP, for example, have sought to 'support

---

[5] SCEG governance policy guidance dated October 2020 and SCEG staff handbook guidance dated October 2020 outlined the practices and processes which a member PSC operating overseas in fragile states should adhere to. SCEG members are expected to be compliant and aware of current human rights legislation, regulations, and principles. In particular the UN Global Compact, UN Guiding Principles on Business and Human Rights, Voluntary Principles on Security and Human Rights, the International Code of Conduct for Private Security Service Providers, the Modern Slavery Act, and the Montreux Document. The UN has also developed security policy manuals for PSCs that include: UN Department of Safety and Security (2012), 'Armed Private Security Companies'. Chapter IV; UN Security Management System, Security Policy Manual. 8 November 2012; UN Department of Safety and Security (2012), 'Guidelines on the Use of Armed Security Services from Private Security Companies', and UN Security Management System, Security Policy Manual, 8 November 2012.

[6] For example, in 2009 and subsequently in 2011 *The Guardian* reported that Daniel Fitzsimons, a British contractor employed by ArmourGroup as a bodyguard and ex-military, had been arrested in Iraq for allegedly murdering two of his colleagues, British contractor Paul McGuigan and Australian colleague Darren Hoare and wounding an Iraqi translator. It was the second killing in the Green Zone involving contractors in less than three months. Fitzsimons was the first Westerner to face trial in Iraq, served a lengthy jail sentence first in Iraq and was later transferred back to the UK to complete his sentence (e.g. Davies, 2011).

the development of professional and accountable policing throughout the world by delivering effective learning and training assistance in the fields of operational policing and police leadership'. This has included (for the latter) the oversight through accredited training courses that are regularly updated by the college (College of Policing, 2020). However, there is still no government-led accreditation of police retirees who are contracted by police institutions, the government or the corporate sector for international policing services. A 2012 draft business plan outlining the accreditation of third parties in England and Wales (quality assurance mechanisms) to ensure monitoring and oversight of *private policing services*, including law enforcement, policing, and justice services by claiming UK police knowledge, experience of skills by 'associating themselves in any way to the police service or particularly ACPO [sic] did not advance beyond an initial presentation to government departments representative of the International Policing Assistance Board' (ACPO IA, 2012: 3).

In terms of the wider industry, the 2001 Private Security Industry Act, has required contractors to obtain a security industry authority (SIA) licence as a contract for services through the SIA. This requires dedicated training for a licence-linked qualification to ensure the necessary skills and safety requirements. UK police who sought PSC opportunities in Iraq and Afghanistan subscribed to the relevant courses,[7] which included a requirement that they were firearms trained. Where mentoring and advising skills were needed then a teaching accreditation was required. Former RUC–PSNI, MDP, and other UK specialist firearms officers had the necessary skill sets and were contracted by organizations including Aegis Defence Services, DynCorp, and Armour Group (UK). Moreover, a proportion of police who joined in the 1980s had previous military experience which 'made it far easier to cross the line' into a PSC and to engage with former military (Author interview with a former Det Inspector RUC–PSNI, 24 January 2021).

Hybrid networks: the connection between public and private policing

Jean-Paul Brodeur has referred to a 'police assemblage' that is 'diverse formal agencies and informal groups performing public and private

---

[7] Some PSCs organized in-house hostile environment training courses for possible candidates hoping to secure a contract which were paid for personally by the candidates.

policing activities'. Globalization has supported cross fertilization between internal *and* external security apparatus, including 'the knowledge industry' that has housed the private sector (Brodeur, 2010: 17–35). Within this is located the 'hybrid agency' that has the flexibility to operate with elements (intelligence and communications for example) of both internal and external security and particularly relevant to transnational and international activities. At retirement police can glide from the public to the private sector further consolidating knowledge transfer through hybrid networks. For UK government there has been an even greater necessity to share information across the policing spectrum through internal *and* external security mechanisms, augmented by a growth in cybercrime, fraud, serious and organized crime, and other crimes (including terrorism) that can occur within the digital space. Police investment in and adoption of new technology has been criticized as 'quite frankly, a complete and utter mess ... to enable the service to meet the challenges of the 21st century' (House of Commons Home Affairs Committee, 2018: 62). Yet maintaining 'strong policing and security co-operation' following the UK's departure from the EU is key to the UK national interests (House of Lords European Union Committee, 2016) (see chapter 8).

I propose three core manifestations of entrepreneurial policing that are relevant to the discussions within this chapter and show an interlinkage within this police assemblage:

> **Group One:** police retirees who as independent police contractors undertake ad hoc consultancies for government, police institutions, and/or the corporate sector and, those who join police forces outside the UK including the fourteen UKOTs and any other country (including the commonwealth).
>
> **Group Two:** police retirees who establish private security consultancies (often in conjunction with other police and sometimes from other countries) to deliver policing and security services and consulting on behalf of UK and other international governments, police organizations, international organizations, international non-governmental organizations (INGO), civil societies and so on, and those who join small, medium, and enterprise organizations (short to medium term) to provide a range of security and policing services. This includes PMSCs and PSCs as well as the larger corporates who engage with SSR and wider capacity-building and technical assistance programmes within FCAS on behalf of UK and other international governments. These organizations have recruited former military,

Plate 1 (© Joe Napolitano)—Station Commander (RUC) KOSOVO

Mitrovica Bridge, Kosovo, 17 March 2004. Initial flash point of Kosovo-wide violence. UN Police backed up by Jordanian Special Police Unit force back Albanian protesters from the Serbian north bank.

Plate 2 (© Gary White)
PSNI with local police commander working on community policing projects including provision of bicycles to aid patrolling, Santa Cruz, 2006.

Plate 3 (© Joe Napolitano)
Contractor and US Army Military Transition Teams meet with local Iraqi police commander, Baiji Iraq 2008.

Plate 4 (© Jackie Gold)
The ladies of 'The Community Watch Group' with UK CPT UNMISS, South Sudan 2015.

Plate 5 (© Jackie Gold)
Working with the teachers in the POC, UNMISS South Sudan 2015.

Plate 6 (© Paul Dutton)
[Chief Inspector Paul Dutton (IPRC)] JFHQ during Op Ruman Hurricane Irma with Partners Across Government cell (PAGs) and J2 intelligence cell, 2017.

intelligence operatives, *and police* to deliver a range of services overseas and/or in the UK.

Group Three: public (UK) police forces, institutions (including for example the CoP and the NCA) and government departments (including the SU and the HO) who provide a range of assistance within FCAS for UK, international governments, and police institutions that can be in association with medium to large corporations, international organizations (for example the UN), and civil societies who engage with SSR. Police retirees can be contracted to work (privately) with the public sector.

Hard security and strategic advising: police contracting in Iraq and Afghanistan

The UK policing brand has benefitted from the ad hoc initiatives of *police* contractors, and latterly security contractors which included a significant global to-ing and fro-ing of British policing knowledge. These processes have been explored within relevant literatures as policy 'diffusion', 'policy transfer', policy 'convergence', and 'policy translation' (Stone, 2012) and more recently within a wider European context have included lesson learning and sharing good practice (Sinclair and Burdett, 2018). Iraq became the launchpad for PMCs and PMSCs and has generated considerable academic and popular discussions (e.g. Bjork and Jones, 2005; Cotton et al., 2010; Johnston, 2006; Isenberg, 2007; Ellison and O'Reilly, 2008a, 2008b; Singer, 2004, 2007). Following the 2003 invasion, tens of thousands of private security contractors were deployed and when Operation Iraqi Freedom terminated in August 2010, the downward trend in the numbers of contractors was offset by an increase in those deploying to Afghanistan indicative of the relative ease of transferability of contracts (see Isenberg, 2009).

Former RUC–PSNI officers were employed by PMSCs as 'security' and also as 'policing' contractors. While security and policing activities can meld, there is within an FCAS context some distinction between the two. Security contractors[8] typically provided *armed services* which policing contractors often did not, which could include convoy security, security

---

[8] PMSCs have recruited from (1) US nationals; (2) expatriates or coalition nationals including UK, Canada, South Africa, and Australia; (3) third-country nationals; and (4) local nationals (Palou-Loverdos and Armendariz, 2011: 40).

escorts, and personal security detail. Police contractors also tended to support tasking and operational coordination, intelligence analysis, hostage negotiations, and security training. Having an awareness and experience of violent and prolonged conflict was considered key, and former *RUC in particular* were recruited for their familiarity with a style of policing that some described as bordering on 'paramilitary' (Author interview with two former directors, Aegis Defence Services,[9] 15 May 2007). Former RUC–PSNI with a special branch background were also highly sought after for intelligence work (see later section).

There have always been considerable risks for security contractors within conflict and high-risk environments. With estimates of as many civilian contractors as serving military personnel,[10] it was hardly surprising that mortality rates and numbers of serious injury rose steeply. As military drawdown occurred in Iraq (and later in Afghanistan) there were suggestions that the figures were far higher than the official numbers reported and a reliance on contractors may have produced artificially lower fatality rates (Schooner, 2008a: 89). By mid-2010, an investigation into contractor deaths in Iraq and Afghanistan according to a ProPublica analysis demonstrated that 'the risks of war [had] been increasingly absorbed by the private sector' as military drawdown had occurred. The provision of armed security including convoy support had presented the highest risk (Miller, 2010). Official figures suggested approximately 5,531 and 2,008 civilian contractors were killed in Iraq and Afghanistan between 2001 and June 2010 including both locals and internationals. Former military and police (including the UK) who were employed by organizations under contract to the US figured within these statistics. Security providers including Aegis Defence Services reported a total of 29 deaths and 285 injuries; Armor Group International Limited reported 62 deaths and 160 injuries; Blackwater reported 33 deaths and 1,145 injuries; CACI reported 40 injuries; DynCorp reported 73 deaths and 2,777 injuries; Hart GMSSCO Ltd. reported 62 deaths and 134 injuries; and Triple Canopy 15 deaths and 707 injuries (Miller, 2009). The risk to both physical and mental health was high (and similarly across the armed forces) with the highest rates recorded amongst contractors on long-term contracts. In Iraq, contractors reported that they faced 'unique stressors'

---

[9] Aegis Defence Services were one of the organizations that recruited RUC–PSNI officers for security work in Iraq.
[10] In March 2016 there were approximately 28,600 private contractors in Afghanistan as compared to 8,730 US military (Congressional Research Service, 2016).

particularly when there was a perceived lack of overall duty of care from the employer. Data from a RAND Corporation report in 2013 showed overall high levels of alcohol misuse (forty-seven per cent) and daily use of tobacco (thirty-seven per cent). In terms of citizenship the proportion of contractors with probable post-traumatic stress disorder and depression amongst UK contractors stood at thirteen per cent and nine per cent respectively (Dunigan et al., 2013: 40–1). Government outsourcing has remained to the present complex, challenging, and risk prone from a commercial as well as a public policy perspective particularly within conflict environments (Schofield, 2008a; Schooner, 2008b).

Security and police contractors have claimed, and with some justification, that the risks associated with working in a combat or post-conflict environment justified what many outsiders perceived as exorbitant daily fees.[11] Many police contractors *and* serving UK police I have spoken with witnessed serious injury and death not only of local and international colleagues but also of civilians, which was often harder to deal with. Often described were the 'tactically difficult situations' when hostile engagement became a possibility. Additionally, duty of care issues for contractors was hugely variable in relation to the equipment and hostile environment training provided as well as medical care available (Author interviews, 2015–2020). Yet the evidence has pointed to local contractors and those recruited from the 'developing world' who bore the brunt of hostile action as one former police contractor (2020) explained:

> Perimeter security on many US bases in Iraq [2004] was provided by international PSCs using 'third world personnel' [sic] including for example from Angola. They received $800 a month and no leave for 1 year. They were always the first to 'get it' if the base was attacked. I saw less evidence of this in Afghanistan but I did see a lot of Nepalese guys 'doing' [sic] the gates. At least one was killed and many injured when our private camp was attacked by the Taliban. Was this exploitation? The Angolans (from Luanda) were happy as they were getting 8 times more monthly salary than they would get at home. Same for the others … [from

---

[11] From 2003, a day rate for a 'Western' contractor could range from $300 upwards depending on the service provided. From 2010 the average was between $500 and $1,000. Security contractors recruited locally or from the developing world were paid a mere fraction of this—sometimes around $10 per day (reference to armed transportation services provided in Iraq and Afghanistan 2003–2007) (Author interviews with former security and police contractors, 2014–2020).

developing countries] (Former police contractor (Iraq and Afghanistan), May 2012).

As the post-intervention phase moved into transition the need for civilian (security and police) contractors increased. Filling recruitment quotas became almost a tick box exercise rather than a thorough assessment of an individual's experiences and expertise. Colin Smith (see chapter 4) commented during his tour of Iraq (2010) that:

> The UK was fortunate, during my period in Iraq, to have a post-Patten pool of ex RUC/PSNI officers. These deployed to Iraq in large numbers through the civilian contractors. There was a failing within their management to acknowledge difficulties and recruit and deploy experienced senior officers as Team Leaders. The military singularly failed to realise the potential of these officers assessing them more in terms of 'pay packets' rather than capabilities (Smith, 2010: 12).

This emphasis on quantity rather than a focus on ensuring that individuals selected for leadership positions had the necessary vision and skill sets was raised as a particular challenge to the use of the private sector. Inadvertently this posed a threat to the integrity of UK policing and its international reputation. The corporate security goldrush particularly in Iraq led sometimes to some poor recruitment choices as outlined by a serving UK officer deployed to Basra (2011) and suggested possible tensions on the ground between the serving and retired sector:

> X [company name not revealed] was big in Iraq but a lot of their [police] contractors had a reputation for being bloody useless. They weren't all from the UK, we had a lot of Kiwis, Australians, South Africans.... I mean, some of the roles they had and didn't have, it seemed to be a bit bizarre why they had them at all. Again, there was no sense of order. Y [name not revealed] was head of X in Basra ... he was a retired detective constable from X special branch [England] and responsible for a multi-million-pound contract ... no international experience and no management talk. I spent all my time in his office and I'd be telling him exactly what we're doing every day and inviting him along to meetings as well just to get him involved and, in the end ... I was getting complaints from the military because they [X] weren't doing anything, the X people weren't adding value.... I asked the Foreign Office, 'Who is in charge of X?' and

it wasn't clear. So, the Foreign Office have got this multi million pound contract which is not overseen by anybody and they've got police and they're not working with us [serving police] which was frankly unacceptable for British policing and what we stand for and what we were trying to achieve in Iraq (Author interview with former Det Supt Hampshire Police, 9 August 2011).

UK police retirees have deployed since the 1990s as the previous chapters have outlined to combat and high-risk environments as both security and police contractors. Ellison and O'Reilly (2006) highlighted within the security industry orbit 'a more complex and interlinked range of providers within the sphere of *high policing*' [author emphasis]. 'Private high policing' activities they acknowledged as:

A wide range of security-oriented services with the principal objective of protecting client interests from security-related risks … the protection of client interests through expert knowledge and access to the appropriate networks, whether local, national or transnational.… A significant factor within the security consultancy's facilitation of state/corporate symbiosis is the so-called 'revolving door' of high policing, whereby there is increased movement of security operatives from the public to the private sector. The security consultancy industry has extensive ties not only with the military and security establishment but also the political establishment—a fact which is often reflected in the composition of the boardroom (Ellison and O'Reilly, 2006: 646–54).

The increasingly blurred distinctions between public and private security revealed linkages at the highest levels between government, the armed forces, UK policing, and the security industry (O'Reilly, 2010). Moreover, as international development and SSR became a hugely lucrative growth area so it was increasingly corporatized with global consultancy firms such as KPMG International Limited and PriceWaterhouseCoopers expanding their horizons to provide development assistance including reconstruction within FCAS. These organizations have typically bid for government contracts directly using their own personnel or have contracted out to smaller private security consultancies, who may then in turn sub-contract to individual consultants. Security and development contracts have criss-crossed organizations and individuals from a variety of backgrounds, and UK police forces have sought to market their own capabilities through official UK government channels or ad hoc bilateral relationships with overseas police and international organizations to provide technical assistance and training (Author interview with SU senior police advisor, October 2019). The MDP that acquired relevant experience of peacekeeping and hostile environment policing has also considered its 'marketable side' and used defence training reviews to consider wider commercial opportunities including as one MPD (2014) explained:

> We were trying to market … well, we didn't actually have to market we had industry coming to us trying to seek partnership with us for training for example. They were prepared to invest in the MDP and provide, say, firearm ranges and in return they would market the spare capacity from those training facilities and they would also use the MDP name and they could use us as a brand, as a market brand and use that police affiliation (Author interview with former Inspector, MDP, 19 September, 2012, deployed Afghanistan)

Building intelligence management systems in Iraq and Afghanistan

The trend for outsourcing intelligence management augmented from 2001 was partly driven by the US government's intention to remedy previous intelligence failures. During the subsequent interventions in Iraq and Afghanistan,[12] the private sector supported virtually each and every US government agency, including the Department of Defense intelligence activities, with an estimated seventy per cent of the intelligence budget used to purchase equipment and services from the private sector (Voelz, 2009). In what became an 'intelligence wild west' as described by an intelligence operative who served in Iraq, the difficulty in ensuring adequate official cross-agency communication between the US and the UK was compounded by a necessity to ensure that the 'private intelligence community' was 'up to speed and on the same page' (Author interview with former UK intelligence operative, April 2012). Within the operational environments of Iraq and Afghanistan, boundaries became blurred. Private contractors undertook

---

[12] View the ongoing security situation in Iraq and Afghanistan (mid-2021) and continuing security programmes, it has not been possible to name the US and UK private companies involved in the provision of intelligence management programmes.

HUMINT (human intelligence), operating as source handlers and performed a range of functions that included intelligence collection, dissemination and, participation in intelligence briefings that included Iraq military commanders, sometimes overlapping with the official intelligence community and reflecting the hybrid approach to post-conflict security. It is worth noting that a high proportion of these contractors were former military with the necessary security clearance and often had previous training from the intelligence community (Author interview with former UK intelligence operative, April 2021). There was therefore a linkage between both worlds although the risks raised by a lack of government oversight, for example concerns of possible espionage and counterintelligence, raised 'philosophical rather than procedural' issues that related to the integrity of private intelligence contractors (Voelz, 2009).

The private sector has not only supported intelligence functions within the armed forces but also the *development of intelligence capability* in the host country. I now turn to this with reference to a case study where a significant number of former RUC–PSNI developed new intelligence doctrine and provided relevant mentoring and training in Iraq and Afghanistan.

Wider reform of the Iraqi police forces necessitated capacity building across the intelligence systems. By 2008, US military perceived the Iraqi Police as 'an untapped source' which if used would provide the necessary intelligence to better manage ongoing inter-sectarian conflict. US Marine Corps (USMC) then considered suitable intelligence management models which had a 'methodology' (systems, tradecraft, and experience of COIN environments) that could be adapted to Iraq and, would have a long shelf life. USMC 'settled' on the RUC Special Branch (SB) intelligence management model. As Gavin Boyd and Gordon Marnoch (2014) commented 'with the RUC/PSNI having contributed significantly to the development of policing in many countries with a history of conflict, it was logical that former RUC/PSNI officers be recruited to deliver a programme on intelligence management' (Boyd and Marnoch, 2014: 252).[13] The 'logic' arguably was RUC–PSNI familiarity with high risk environments (Northern Ireland), an experience of FCAS (for most BiH and Kosovo), and a high degree of familiarity in working with the military. This no doubt made the Northern Irish element of the UK policing brand far more palatable to

---

[13] A study of an intelligence management capacity-building programme involving former PSNI officers mentoring ANP was published in 2014. In particular the authors consider the 'handover' of principles and practices from the donor to the recipient within a specific local context: Kabul (2010) (Boyd and Marnoch, 2014).

USMC than other English-speaking police forces. Former RUC–PSNI have noted their proven track record in intelligence management to 'counter both republican and loyalist groups in Northern Ireland which was based on hard lessons learned in the furnace of a bitter struggle'; the contract was awarded by the US Department of Defense to a US company which operated 'on the ground' through a British company (Author interview with former RUC–PSNI, intelligence contractor, Iraq and Afghanistan 2008–2014, November 2020).

The intelligence management systems initiated and mentoring provided through this programme in Iraq (and subsequently in Afghanistan) drew on former RUC–PSNI doctrine. Intelligence gathering, analysis, and its wider operational use was a major part of RUC activities during the conflict in Northern Ireland (see, for example, Ellison and Smyth, 2000; Mulcahy, 2006; Ryder, 1989 as well as police memoirs: Barker, 2004; Craig, 2008; Latham, 2001). Mulcahy referred to the importance attached to 'information gathering' including increased surveillance, visible observation posts, questioning at checkpoints, and the use of informants (Mulcahy, 2006: 79). Informants (or sources) included 'converted terrorists' or 'turned agents' motivated by 'jealousy or animosity towards the organization to which he or she belonged' as well as 'ideological disillusionment, resentment and greed'. 'Clean agents' were not affiliated to a particular group but were motivated by the organization they were prepared to infiltrate (Barker, 2004: 138–9). Later in both Iraq and Afghanistan, source motivation was considered to have been for similar reasons and may have facilitated the knowledge dissemination and policy transfer (Boyd and Marnoch, 2014). In Northern Ireland, the informer was typically handled by RUC SB source handlers sometimes referred to as the 'SB divisional branch'. This was linked to a tasking and coordinating group (TCG), a dedicated unit within SB that deployed surveillance and strike units to 'confirm, deny or exploit the intelligence collected by divisional branch'. Former RUC–PSNI SB became part of larger programme to build intelligence capability within the Iraqi Police, which included mentoring and training provided to Iraqi provincial and district intelligence officers by former SB operatives (Author interviews with former RUC–PSNI SB officers, 2011–2020).

2008 was a turning point in US military operations in Iraq as it theoretically transitioned to a supporting role handing back responsibility for security to the internal security forces including the Iraqi Police. Practically, however, continuing COIN necessitated that the US military act *in support* as well as continuing to build capability across all sectors of the Iraqi military, police, and border security units (Dunigan et al., 2013: 145). Former RUC–PSNI SB contractors in partnership with USMC initiated the programme in Anbar province. It was then rolled out to areas that posed a significant threat to the Iraqi government from violent extremist groups including the provinces of Diyala, and Salah Al-Din, the governorates of Kirkuk and Nineveh and Baghdad. Training, mentoring, and advising were delivered 'in the field' (operational) in parallel with courses relating to police intelligence provided at the Taii police academy north of Baghdad. In addition, a 'company liaison officer' was deployed to Baghdad providing a linkage between the PSC and Multi National Security Transitional Command Iraq—Intelligence (MNSTCI—I)[14] that is US Command responsible for the doctrinal delivery relating to the collection and management of intelligence to selected Iraqi police units (Author interview with former RUC–PSNI SB, intelligence contractor, Iraq and Afghanistan, 2008–2014, November 2020).

Towards the end of 2009 the intelligence management programme partly transferred to Afghanistan where intelligence capability within the ANP had been identified as lacking (Boyd and Marnoch, 2014; Author interviews with former RUC–PSNI SB, 2010–2020). PSCs *per se* had been present in Afghanistan since late 2001 as coalition forces came into the country and the embassies reopened. Initially this brought private security organizations including Blackwater and DynCorp to provide guarding at the US Embassy and CIA headquarters in Kabul. As the military created forward operating bases, so security was often provided by local security companies. By 2007 there was a drive by the government of Afghanistan to regulate the private sector and as part of this regularization process, licensing was introduced in 2008 for both international and local companies though subsequent oversight proved controversial (Brooking, 2011). Support to deliver intelligence capacity building to the MOI and dedicated ANP units was awarded through a US DoD contract and delivered by a 'large number of former RUC SB' and former military intelligence personnel.

Afghanistan, however, presented a complex international command structure dominated by the US and NATO ISAF and presented challenges for the programme's oversight with reporting to both Combined Coalition

---

[14] MNSTC was established in (June 2004 to January 2010). Its primary focus was to boost the capacity of the Iraqi military and police to ensure that they would have sufficient capability to undertake security functions following the departure of the US. It also trained Iraqi Special Police in counter-insurgency and counterterrorism as a rapid response unit as well as developing wider intelligence capacity and capability.

Security Transition Command Afghanistan—Intelligence (CSTCA—I) (headquarters) and relevant NATO ISAF brigades ('on the ground'), which impacted the programme's momentum. High police attrition (Farrell, 2018) and bureaucratic holdups relating to the requests for new police personnel and equipment also delayed activities particularly within rural areas. A dedicated programme liaison officer within the MOI relayed requests from intelligence contractors assigned to Afghan units with a drive to fast-track new applications and requested transfers through the MOI headquarters human resources in an attempt to speed up the process. A linkage was also created to other Western intelligence providers including the European Union police mission in Afghanistan (EUPOL) a civilian mission that had been developed in 2007. EUPOL provided basic intelligence training to the ANP. Later elements of the Northern Irish intelligence model (including the 'source reporting' form) were taken up and exemplified by EUPOL as good practice within MOI and became standard practice in Afghanistan.

By Spring 2010, CSTCA—I approached several intelligence contractors with a request to explore the creation of a TCG model, including surveillance operators and a strike unit within the broader intelligence management system, to shore up what the US perceived as a lack of intelligence capability. As a result, a team including special forces from ISAF, CSTCA—I and the Federal Bureau of Investigation (FBI) with former RUC–PSNI SB began the development of a TCG which it was argued benefited not only from UK (RUC SB) policing expertise but that of the US military:

> The Americans had the will and the finance to get the project off the ground and we [former RUC–PSNI SB] had the knowledge and as such the modelling was left almost entirely in our hands including the formulating of Standing Orders and Standard Operating Procedures. The new Afghan Intel [sic] centre, aside from assigned mentors, would be entirely Afghan driven with little or no input from the Coalition so as to ensure its continued functioning following an international withdrawal from Afghanistan. Many US military had already served in Iraq and had seen how many Iraqi security force entities had collapsed after the US drawdown. Those with vision didn't want to see it happen again in Afghanistan. Over the next four years the same small group of contractors provided for the day to day running and development of the Afghan police intelligence operations centre. As Coalition assigned lead advisors came and went the core input remained the same. I think only a private company could have provided such continuity as in general

terms military or civilian agencies would rarely commit personnel to Afghanistan for more than a year—in many instances a rotation is a matter of months. In both Iraq and Afghanistan UK Policing in the form of ex RUC SB were bringing to the table something the US military lacked. It wasn't force or hard policing, the US military had an abundance of boots on the ground and firepower, but the finely tuned and quietly subtle ways of managing intelligence from source recruitment and collection to operations able to exploit actionable intelligence. As part of COIN the US were very keen to stop smashing nuts with a sledgehammer and the RUC model gave them a key (Author interview with former RUC–PSNI SB officer, April 2018).

US endorsement came as four of the UK's police intelligence contractors perceived as 'critical to the overall mission' received US top secret clearance (as compared to normal US Secret clearance). Moreover, most intelligence contractors remained in-country for long periods of time (often in excess of four years), which created greater trust and confidence with ANP as compared to those contractors or serving personnel who rotated in and out on a six-monthly basis (Author interviews with former RUC–PSNI SB intelligence contractors, 2018–2020). This 'degree of permanence' coupled with what was described as a 'relaxed' or 'collaborative' approach in which they would advise and guide rather than dictate created what they regarded as good working relations with the ANP (Boyd and Marnoch, 2014: 261).

Yet the ANP struggled to assume full operational responsibility and develop security resilience through an enhancement in their intelligence capability (SIGAR, 2019) as revealed here:

This Afghan input [in intelligence-led operations] was but a thin veneer and when pulled back clearly demonstrated the Coalition to be providing almost everything up to the point when Afghan units exited the helicopters and moved towards the target.... I attended many meetings where Coalition representatives expressed their frustration at the slow pace of our centre's capacity and capability to progress operations. The military, in the main on short rotations, want to 'get things done'. Perceived 'low tempo' output gave the impression of a burden that wasn't being equally shared between Afghan and Internationals. In a wider picture it was clear Afghan units both from the army and police being pushed into action before being ready.... The military accept by their own admission they shortcut circuits to make things happen—the price is paid at some point down the road long after they have gone (Author interview with former intelligence contractor Afghanistan, 2009–2013, February 2021).

Much of the intelligence capability transitioned to full Afghan command and control in 2016 though intelligence contractors and police mentees have occasionally been deployed to support the ongoing management of the programme. Arguably the 'working knowledge of Afghan culture' and development expertise accrued within this context should in some way be 'archived for future capacity-building interventions in Afghanistan and elsewhere (Boyd and Marnoch, 2014: 270).

International opportunities after retirement

Following retirement, some MDP also joined the corporate world or identified opportunities for a 'new' career within a police institution overseas including the UK overseas territories (UKOTs). MDP were deployed to Pitcairn Islands for example following the investigation into child sexual abuse that began in 2000 until the conclusion of the appeals process in 2006 on four-month rotations. While Pitcairn has no formal association with New Zealand, it provides administrative functions and deploys a New Zealand police officer owing to the geographical convenience (Author interview with former head of IPSO, MDP, 9 November 2011). UKOTS have contributed to the security interests of the UK though their size and geographical locations have historically presented unique challenges. Police assistance has previously fallen within the remit of the FCO, DfID, and the MOD and has included the recruitment of police of retired officers to take up a UKOT posting. Recently, appointees included former CC Nottinghamshire Police Chris Eyre who became Chief Constable of Cyprus Sovereign Base Areas police; Jeff McMahon who served for thirty years with Greater Manchester Police to become Chief of Police in the Royal Falkland Islands Police in 2018; Paul Morrison became Commissioner of the Royal Anguilla Police Force in September 2015 having left Sussex Police as a Chief Superintendent; and the recently retired head of the Dyfed-Powys Police became the new Commissioner of the Royal Virgin Islands Police in April 2021 following a thirty-five-year career. Mark Collins has been tasked particularly with strengthening law enforcement against local and international crime in British Virgin Island and building leadership capacity (Police Oracle, 2021).

In the main, long-term secondments of UK police or larger scale deployments of serving officers to manage serious public unrest are only a last resort (HO, 2012). For example, the somewhat farcical deployment of MPS to Anguilla in 1969 to prevent potential law and order chaos when the island's administration threatened self-declared independence (Sinclair, 2006). A 2012 white paper pleaded to strengthen the relationship between UK government and UKOT governments to tackle threats arising from serious and organized crime and international terrorism. Aside from operational support and specialist support coordinated by the FCO across the UK's law enforcement agencies, there were recommendations to increase police training and technical assistance where needed. Moreover, overseas territories (UK OTs) including the Sovereign Base Areas in Cyprus, which is funded by the MOD though not connected to MDP with independent civil police—the Cyprus Joint Police Unit (the Royal Military Police and the RAF police) have concurrent jurisdiction provided a launchpad for UK operations in Afghanistan, Iraq, and Libya (FCO, 2012).

The linkage between the UK and commonwealth countries has been demonstrated through UK police taking up career opportunities particularly in Australia and New Zealand. I have also encountered several mid-career police who having served on international missions found the lack of interest in sharing that experience with their home force on their return, prompted a resignation and a move to a commonwealth country (Authors interviews, 2010–2014).

Police contractors in Abu Dhabi: strategic advising and community policing

UK police retirees have broadly operated as police, security, and intelligence contractors across the international security landscape. This has involved a wide range of experience and differing expertise from the strategic, to the tactical and operational across the policing space as Ellison and O'Reilly (2008a) noted:

> The role of mentors in capacity building programmes is usually thought to involve 'reflecting on experience' and as a group they bring quite different skills to post-conflict societies than the 'security consultants' who guard and protect, or the 'gurus' hired by coalition forces in Iraq

and Afghanistan, to 'strategise' on policing (Ellison and O'Reilly, 2008a, 416–20).

Police 'gurus' are more often known as 'strategic police advisors' or 'senior police advisors' and refer to a person typically of a chief superintendent rank and above who provides 'counsel, strategy, technical assistance and mentoring' at ministerial and senior police level. These 'advisors' have supported strategic-level planning, and institutional and management chance processes, and can scrutinize their operational implementation within FCAS (Author interview with former strategic police advisor to FCO/SU, formerly MPS Commander, 12 December 2019). However, the oversight of their activities will differ according to whether they are retired or serving officers working on behalf of the British government or as police 'consultants' working on behalf of an overseas government. I now turn to the latter and reflect on the role of police retirees as strategic advisors to the Abu Dhabi government (MOI) and Abu Dhabi Police (ABP) and, as community police (warrant) officers embedded within the ABP.

There is an historic linkage between the UK and the United Arab Emirates (UAE) that has involved the circulation of serving and retired police as advisors, trainers, and mentors in-country as well as courses delivered at the UK's police training establishments (including the NPIA (Bramshill)). Since 2013 the College of Police has been the focal point for the delivery of courses to overseas police forces and this has included the ABP.[15] UK police (serving and retired) have supported the UAE's wider policing initiatives since the 1990s though it was only in 2002 that ABP recruited UK police retirees under contract. By 2015 it is estimated that they comprised some 0.5 per cent of ABP personnel of predominantly Emiratis. The ABP was a relatively young establishment (1957) with a 'paramilitary organizational culture' that focused on the maintenance of 'internal security and stability'. The government's vision was to move policing into the spheres of law enforcement, community policing, and crime prevention (Yates, 2018: 301). To some extent this approach aligned with the wider vision for policing across the Gulf states and an engagement with 'soft projects' derived from community policing principles. In Abu Dhabi, these policing projects included issues relating to gender, youth, and expatriates in an attempt to dampen down the community's perceptions of the authoritarian nature of the state

---

[15] For example, between 2013 and 2018, ABP/Abu Dhabi MOI was charged £318,640 for the delivery of international leadership programmes by the UK's College of Policing (CoP, 2018).

(Ardemagni, 2019). The 'contracted foreign expatriate phenomenon' could be perceived as a government tool to soften the image of the local police and improve relations with the expatriate communities as well as providing high level support to the MOI regarding police reform.

There has been a large Western expatriate presence in Abu Dhabi since the 1960s, this influence has come about partly due to the effect of British colonial rule in the region which ended in 1970. The UAE has a multinational population of approximately eighty per cent expatriate citizens from a wide range of nationalities (AlMazrouei and Pech, 2014). British expatriates have also been part of the UAE's military forces throughout this period although their numbers have varied considerably (Yates, 2016). Athol Yates (2021)[16] has made a close study of the 'lifecycle' of these Western military expatriates:

> ... [T]he vast majority... who have served or continue to serve in Emirati armed forces [and] are engaged as part of a group. These groups can range in size from a handful to over three hundred. The groups always have a number of shared characteristics, with the most common being around work role, nationality, employed arrangements, employing military unit and service backgrounds (Yates, 2021: 1).

This expatriate 'lifecycle' has revolved around several key issues: first an expatriate does not have the right to remain in the UAE without employment as citizenship is never granted to non-Emiratis. Their working lifecycle falls into three phases: 'expatriation, service and repatriation'. Then most expatriates have worked within their dedicated group (of expatriates) created in response to a 'capability requirement'. Yates noted that military expatriates remained in the one group throughout their employment and that these groups were 'not enduring but rather rise, transform then disappear', which was likened to a lifecycle (Yates, 2022). Yates suggested that following his observations of UK police expatriates in the ABP that there could be a similarity between the military expatriate lifecycle with that of police expatriates (see Yates, 2018). This can be demonstrated within the establishment and growth phases that Yates (2022) posited:

---

[16] I am extremely grateful to Professor Athol Yates for sharing data from an ongoing research project during the course of our discussions in February 2021. See Yates (2022): *Invisible Expatriates: The Contribution of Western Military Professionals to the UAE Armed Forces* (currently unpublished).

A group's establishment phase has been demonstrated by a single individual or a small group being engaged to assist in addressing some [military] capability. The decision to engage the expatriates is invariably made by a senior member of a ruling family, commonly a ruler or a crown prince.... The initial expatriates will generally propose a plan based on their professional [military experience], personal observations of the local situation, some discussion with senior Emiratis, and the opinions from those close to the sponsor on what he wants (Yates, 2022: 2).

When the case of the recruitment of UK police into the ABP is considered, the 'establishment phase' began in 2002 and came through initial contacts between senior UK police from the Bramshill international academy and the UAE MOI. Sheik Saif bin Zahed Al Nahyan (Minister of the Interior from 2004) sought support for police modernization through a strategic policing plan. No doubt the connection between Bramshill and the UAE facilitated a meeting between the Sheik Saif and senior UK police and led to the recruitment of former deputy chief constable (Lancashire) Gerry O'Connell. O'Connell as the key strategic advisor supported initial development of the policing plan and by 2005 had moved into the 'growth phase of the lifecycle' which involved the original expatriates securing the employment of others to provide the necessary expertise to deliver the projects under development. In this instance, ten further UK police advisors were recruited to cascade the strategic plan through the different ABP departments. From 2005 to approximately 2015, the number of strategic advisors grew to approximately seventy at any given time (Yates, 2018; 2022). This chimes with Yates's point about 'initial expatriates recruiting their former colleagues and spreading the word via their personal networks' (Yates, 2022: 1–2).

From 2009, the 'formal' team leader and also personal advisor to Sheik Saif Al Nayhan (Minister of the Interior) was Sir Ronnie Flanagan who used his network to bring in more junior ranking former RUC–PSNI as community officers (Author interviews with former UK police, Abu Dhabi, 2011; Yates, 2018). Yet while Yates has posited that the recruitment of former colleagues occurred 'not for nepotistic reasons but because the initial expatriates want to maximise the chance that those recruited can undertake the work that is required ...' (Yates, 2022: 3), there was a sense that the policing family network may not always have provided sufficient recruits with the skills sets required, and the necessary experience to compete with those other policing brands in evidence in Abu Dhabi. Expatriate (UK) strategic advisors were expected to support a range of policing projects in Abu Dhabi and work with stakeholders across the corporate sector. Projects included, for example, strategic planning, performance, and programme management, quality assurance, health and safety, civil defence, and emergency response as well as community policing, serious crime investigation, and traffic policing (Author interview with former Chief Supt South Yorkshire Police, strategic advisor, January 2011). This presented difficulties not only in preserving the highest professional standards of good practice but in attempting to visualize the delivery of policing let alone 'the frustration that I feel in that I am only an advisor ... this is not my country. I'm enthusiastic to get things done but I haven't got the clout ...' (Author interview with former Chief Supt South Yorkshire Police and HMIC, strategic advisor to MOI, 8 January 2011). While Emirati police were encouraged to engage with the UK police advisors they could 'choose to accept an expatriate's advice or not ...' (Yates, 2018: 295).

A memorandum of understanding between ACPO and the UAE formally established information exchange and good practice and facilitated the two-way traffic of police coming from the UK to observe the Emirati police and officers then travelling to the UK to consider 'best practice' (Author interview with former PSNI Chief Constable, January 2011). This could be further facilitated through a British embassy police liaison officer who provided a point of contact 'for intelligence sharing and real time policing co-operation as well as slow time legal requests and extraditions' (Author interview with UK UAE Embassy Liaison Officer, January 2011). The UK has had a reputation for good practice in the management of counterterrorism particularly since 2001 and this has been integral to the marketability of the brand. The ABP (and more widely across the UAE) sought technical assistance to enhance their CT strategy and its operational delivery which became part of the strategic advisors' remit: '... they have a CT strategy which, spookily enough, resembles the UK model ... and also resembles other international models' (Author interview with UK UAE Embassy Liaison Officer, January 2011). Here the myth that support to the ABP was driven by a 'UK policing style adapted to meet their needs' collided with the reality. While UAE leaders may have declared the UK model of policing as a 'preferred choice', it was just one of many offered across the region by EU countries, the US, and Australia. This is suggestive of a pick and mix by the client of what was perceived as 'good' within the UK model (Author interviews with UK strategic police advisors, Abu Dhabi, January 2011) and reliant on the relationship between senior Emiratis and British expatriates (Yates, 2022). Yet it has not been possible to gauge the extent to which a senior advisor shielded potentially sensitive information when working for a foreign government. In practice some may serve as a UK channel of influence to improve the reputation of the UK policing brand and facilitate future commercial engagement.

Similar to other Gulf states, the UAE is heavily reliant on expatriate workers which have accounted for approximately eight-five per cent of the population (Hassan, 2010). In 2009, the ADP began the recruitment of former expatriate police with 'proven backgrounds in community policing' as 'community officers'. Community policing in Abu Dhabi was launched by the MOI in 2003 and became operational in 2005. While these officers were not given full executive powers, they were uniformed and tasked with the management of local issues particularly that related to the English-speaking expatriate community (National, 2008). In 2010, four former RUC–PSNI officers were recruited as 'warrant officers' into the ABP. This is somewhat in a similar vein to those UK police who joined police forces in commonwealth countries and, there has been a growing trend to recruit 'tourist police' to fill a security gap where local police have found international visitors to be particularly challenging.[17]

In Abu Dhabi at that time the focus was on the promotion of community policing within the expatriate community and support to the development of their cultural awareness and sensitivity towards local Emiratis. Each of the four were employed on a contractual basis by ABP with no direct UK (FCO) involvement. While these warrant officers reported directly to a senior ABP officer, there was also a chain of command to Flannagan who had not only supported this initiative but handpicked potential former RUC–PSNI recruits (Author interviews with former RUC–PSNI, Warrant Officers ABP, January 2011). The aim has been to extend the recruitment to different nationalities to ensure that the expatriate communities have a point of contact. In 2016 the 'we are all police' initiative called for volunteer Emiratis and expatriates to receive training in order to liaise with the communities and support the police which was considered fundamental to the policing of approximately 200 nationalities (Ahmad, 2016).

---

[17] This includes Thailand and Malaysia where 'Europeans' have been recruited for tourist hotspots. In Pattaya in Thailand, for example, there are both warranted officers and 'foreign police volunteers' who assist local police with the management of tourists.

Concluding comment

This chapter has demonstrated how the rise of the corporate military and security (including policing) sectors, maintained and even strengthened the UK policing brand. Particular facets of the brand's historical characteristics became popular through this era of interventions. This included the harder security, counterterrorism, and intelligence expertise of former RUC–PSNI in Iraq and Afghanistan alongside the 'other' elements of UK policing and security. Additionally, the post-Patten policing transformation agenda as explored through the UAE case study involved the assistance of RUC–PSNI retirees as senior strategic advisors as well as ABP warrant officers. While it was only possible to provide a handful of case studies, there have been many others (and see chapter 7 in relation to PSNI) and UK policing has continued to be exported through the private sector within FCAS, the developing world, and beyond.

The transfer of policing skills and knowledge has been further facilitated by a close private–public partnership that extends beyond the security and police contractor network. This has raised questions relating to the value and integrity of the brand and its continuing legacy both 'at home and away'. It has been apparent that the UK policing brand has absorbed and indeed benefitted from a goldrush of privatization. This in turn strengthened particular elements of the brand including through those security, police, and intelligence contractors who operated and transferred between Iraq and Afghanistan. Arguably there were other elements of UK policing that became somewhat diluted within these environments with the multiplicity of other international police present (see chapters 3 and 4). There has been a sense that the value of the UK policing brand has weakened at home (see chapter 2) while having strengthened overseas which is indicative of its enduring reification. Indeed, in the UK some of the policing practices transferred and their destinations have been perceived as controversial. This has brought challenging questions to the fore relating to the government's oversight not only of the private sector but of international policing *per se*. The growth in the private security industry has promoted a modicum of self-regulation through licensing and accreditation where government has failed to provide an official legislative framework. However, industry self-regulation may be perceived with a degree of scepticism when considering media and government concerns relating to policing expertise provided to countries with poor human rights track records and the need for additional scrutiny and official regulation. There has been a recent effort to account for government-funded aid and development projects as providing value for money for taxpayers through more rigorous internal and external evaluations, though this has not tackled the thorny issue of balancing overseas assistance (including policing) with UK government commercial and strategic interests. Here are critical lessons that should be learnt from the ease with which UK policing has been outsourced and whether in the longer term this may prove detrimental to the ongoing development of national policing values. In chapter 6 I turn to the UK government and police approaches to the delivery and oversight of international policing.

6
Promoting the UK Policing Brand
Coherence and Fragmentation

> ACPO International Affairs is a unique portfolio, representing the UK police service, supporting HMG with the ability to engage with affected and fragile states of importance. There is also that linked importance in retaining the reputation of the UK Police brand internationally and positioning UK police in high-ranking overseas posts. This provides HMG with cultural diplomacy as well as policing expertise.
> **Former Chief Constable Avon and Somerset and ACPO International Affairs portfolio holder, 2012**

It is clear that collectively, more can be done to maximise the benefits from effective international policing—be they protecting our people at home and abroad; projecting our global influence; or promoting our policing capability.

UK policing has a strong reputation with international recognition of its professionalism and performance. Our policing expertise and skills are in demand across the globe. The knowledge contained in police forces across the UK—and in the law enforcement sector as a whole—is recognised as highly valuable by our international partners.

We can use international policing to promote UK prosperity and policing capability, with UK policing's brand used to export our policing expertise. Not only will this increase capability in overseas states and organisations, it will also increase the skills of our own officers, who will bring their experiences back to UK forces and benefit local communities.

Brandon Lewis—former Minister
for Policing and the Fire Service, 2017

The delivery of international policing services has rested on the reputation of the UK policing brand, one that has prided itself on professionalism and excellence (Author interview with former ACPO IA portfolio holder, November 2012). Behind this, government security and development strategies have provided the necessary framework to encourage and facilitate that delivery. In 2008, ACPO supported the creation of a dedicated international portfolio ACPO IA alongside its administrative unit: the International Policing Assistance Group (IPAG). ACPO IA was replaced, following the advent of the NPCC in 2015, and rebranded as the JIPH. Governance arrangements have been provided by the NPCC in partnership with the UK government's National Crime Agency (NCA), the College of Policing, the National Police Coordination Centre, and the national CT network (Author interview with former senior police advisor, JIPH, February 2019). However, as this chapter outlines, despite attempts to centralize and standardize the promotion and delivery of international policing through institutional structures and accompanying policy, there have been shortcomings. Moreover, austerity and a global health crisis have resulted in a shrinkage in the number of serving officers deploying on international missions as compared to other EU countries (see appendix 1). UK policing support to the UN mission in South Sudan (UNMISS) and to NATO RSM in Afghanistan remained the last and most significant contributions the UK has made to multilateral missions to date (2021).

Building international policing strategy and doctrine

A number of key UK government strategies have driven the trajectory of international policing in the twenty-first century. In October 2010, the then coalition government published a national security strategy that underlined the importance in protecting national interests through the projection of 'influence abroad'. Building a secure and resilient UK 'in an age of uncertainty' required a range of security capabilities with an emphasis on the rule of law (HMG, 2010: 4). The accompanying SDSR set out how UK government would coordinate and integrate this approach to counter longer-term threats to the UK.[1] The following year, UK government (spearheaded by DfID, FCO, and MOD) published 'an integrated cross-government strategy to address conflict issues': the Building Stability Overseas Strategy (BSOS) which outlined the delivery of rapid crisis prevention and response in FCAS. This came partly in response to the projected increase in funding through official development assistance (ODA) and the commitments made in the NSS and SDSR the previous year. Continuing instability and conflict in the Middle East and North Africa provided some context to draw on lesson learning (including the Libyan intervention) from an international body of evidence. BSOS delivery included 'the capacity of law enforcement in parts of the world that suffer from instability and political upheaval which impacts on the UK': a 'joined up' approach that would theoretically permit a more rapid response from UK policing in partnership with other countries and international institutions (BSOS, 2010: 27–32).

The Police (Overseas Service) Act 1945 had as principal effect to permit UK police to 'serve abroad'. In 1994, new clauses and consequential amendments were made to ensure that police officers could deploy overseas and 'provide advice and assistance to international organisation[s] or institution[s]' (including the UN), or 'to any other person or body which is engaged outside the United Kingdom in the carrying on of activities similar to any carried on by the authority or the chief officer of police for its area'. Effectively this widened the scope of international policing and enabled, for example, UK police to undertake executive functions in Kosovo, although the clauses extended only to England, Wales, and Scotland and excluded Northern Ireland. This prompted David Trimble to raise the RUC's profile and the organization's importance within peacekeeping operations, to ensure that there were 'proposals to enable members of that force to serve overseas, because it has an enormous wealth of experience that many countries would find relevant' (House of Commons, debates, 1994: 156–8).

Since the mid-1990s, there has been a requirement that all *international policing* and *policing internationally* must be undertaken in support of UK government strategy. Police officers (and staff) (England and Wales) who

---

[1] The International Defence Engagement Strategy published in 2013 set out in practical terms how the UK government would implement the commitments within the SDSR.

provided international assistance (in its broadest sense), that is *outside UK policing activities* must be authorized to do so by their police organization, local police authority, and more recently PCC. This provision of 'advice and assistance overseas' comes under section 26 of the Police Act 1996,[2] which has recognized that the engagement of police officers for temporary service overseas can only be a voluntary arrangement, and that individuals cannot be required by their police authority or PCC to undertake these duties. Equivalent to the England and Wales section 26 legislative provisions were originally, in Scotland, section 12a of the Police (Scotland) Act 1967, and subsequently following the Police and Fire Reform (Scotland) Act 2012, the Police Service of Scotland (Temporary Service) Regulations 2013. In Northern Ireland, this has been covered by section 8 of the Police (Northern Ireland) Act 2000. All appointments have necessitated the approval of the Home Secretary (England and Wales), the Minister of Justice for Northern Ireland, and the Northern Ireland policing board, and in Scotland, the Scottish Police Authority (SPA) and Scottish minister for justice. Across each of the four nations, the appropriate duty of care provisions must be in place to ensure the 'safe engagement of serving officers'. ACPO IA in 2010, for example, revised a joint safety protocol under which arrangements to recruit, train, and deploy police to PSOs from English, Welsh, and Scottish forces and PSNI were regularized and reflected agreements reached between the different government departments. Concerns had been raised about the failure of some police forces with bilateral arrangements with other countries to fully recognize potential 'dangers' to their officers (ACPO IA, 2010).

Accompanying the emerging doctrine for international deployments have been the occasional guidance manuals developed by government departments (e.g. FCO, 2004a, 2007; HO, 2004, 2012, 2013), police institutions (e.g. ACPO IA, 2012) as well as numerous fact sheets and briefing notes (e.g. FCO, 2009). Essentially this material has outlined the key elements of the deployment process: recruitment and selection; pre-deployment training and administration; deployment and return and reintegration in the home force. It has covered financial and duty of care arrangements and clarified that the seconding department imbursed salaries (though not

---

[2] The provisions of this section are 'without prejudice to the [9 & 10 Geo 6. 17.] Police (Overseas Service) Act 1945 and section 10 of the [1980 c 63.] Overseas Development and Cooperation Act 1980. Words in s 26(8) repealed (17 June 2002) by International Development Act 2002 (c 1), ss 19, 20(2), Sch 4 (with Sch 5, par. 5); S I 2002/1408. Police Act 1996, c 16, Part 1, section 26(8).

International policing strategy and doctrine   163

regular pension contributions) during the secondment period which the FCO (2007) explained as:

> The FCO provides (and pays for) all necessary pre-deployment training, transport to and from the mission area, life insurance and emergency medical cover, and vaccinations. In addition to their salary, secondees may also receive a 'difficult post allowance', depending on where they are based and local working and living conditions (FCO, 2007).

Often written in an oversimplified form the early documentation gave little if any consideration to the realities of policing particularly within high-risk environments and the potential sacrifices officers would make: some faced challenges with their home force ceasing to make the necessary pension contributions as their salaries were being met by the FCO. In some cases, serving police topped up their own pension contributions with personal funds. This was the type of information that many felt was always presented in insufficient detail (Author interviews, 2010–2014).[3] Indeed, some of the earlier guidance material (FCO, 2007) appeared somewhat simplistic as outlined in the following quotation:

> Your working day is likely to be long and irregular. You will need to be self-sufficient in food and laundry, but the local community will help you and you may find a military base nearby which will offer 'home cooking'. Working conditions will not be ideal, but adequate. This is not the UK abroad and you should go with limited expectations of resources and conditions. This cannot be emphasised enough and that is why we only want people who genuinely like a challenge.

MDP who deployed to Afghanistan (see chapter 4) under the duty of care of the MOD provided guidance manuals that detailed security issues, operational safety within the Afghanistan context and were perceived by many officers as invaluable.[4] MDP developed a dedicated system of lessons

---

[3] A limited number of overseas guidance and related policy were developed by individual forces including Cleveland Police (2003), 'Seconded Officers/Police Staff including overseas deployment'—Corporate Policy; Hampshire Police (2007), 03800 Policy—Overseas Deployment of Police Officers, Version 3, last updated 6 June 2007. The ACPO IA lead at this time was CC Paul Kernaghan (Hampshire) which may have explained an emphasis on guidance material.

[4] These manuals are classified/restricted.

learning that drew on earlier and ongoing international policing experiences and was fed into MOD international policing doctrine.[5]

The SU from 2007 created a dedicated standby pool of deployable civilian experts (including police retirees) and serving police who had volunteered for a suitable mission. The SU later established a 'lessons team' and subsequently developed the 'what works series' that included 'toolkits' to support thematic or programmatic areas, in parallel with other guidance material for government officials, deployable civilian experts (including police) and contractors 'engaged in stabilisation'. In 2014, dedicated material on international policing was developed that drew on 'lessons on what it means to uphold and promote core policing principles in our overseas assistance, providing crucial insight into both 'what works' and the many challenges ...' including Libya, Afghanistan, and Sierra Leone (SU, 2014: 6). It has to date remained unchanged and yet key to lesson learning is that there is a regular information feedback loop that can be disseminated to all relevant parties. A lack of lesson learning doctrine has been a particular concern to those senior police who have overseas deployments and the need to 'maintain a level of professionalism and ability when working within countries requiring assistance ...'. This has necessitated up-to-date policing skills to enhance the mission mandate and its operational effectiveness and bolster corporate memory (Author interview with former ACPO IA portfolio holder, November 2012). UK policing's international corporate memory and the promotion of the brand has also been reliant on national policing institutions that deliver training, bilateral assistance, and the export of good practice.

National Policing Improvement Agency

The NPIA was established under the Police and Justice Act 2006 to provide expertise to all police forces across England and Wales. It stemmed from the merging of pre-existing 'improvement agencies', including the Central Police Training and Development Authority (CENTREX), the

---

[5] These manuals covered a range of issues relating to Afghan culture, context, history, and languages. MDP also developed 'Support 2 Operations' guidance manuals, e.g. MOD (2011). 'MOD Civil Servants on Operations: Guidance for Families', *Support 2 Operations*, August 2011, and MOD (nd) 'Safety and Security briefing for civilians in operational theatres', *Support 2 Operations*.

Police Information Technology Organization, and the National Centre for Policing Excellence amongst others. It operationalized on 1 April 2007 and was given a number of key objectives including the development of 'good practice', the sharing of an international understanding of policing issues' and the provision of a wide range of training support (Stelofox, 2008: 175). The NPIA's International Academy (NPIA IA) formerly housed at Bramshill in Hampshire was internationally renowned. Bramshill (which was subsequently closed in 2015) became a showcase for the UK policing brand. During its tenure, international police capacity building and leadership training greatly increased. The NPIA IA was entirely dependent on a public sector cost recovery model, which meant that all overseas projects were delivered on a contractual basis and the income generated provided the basis of all running costs. Additionally, the NPIA IA staff developed partnership working across wider UK policing and government departments to help facilitate the coordination of international policing and promote the UK policing brand nationally and internationally (Author interview with former head of the NPIA IA, May 2010).

The NPIA IA had a close working relationship with ACPO IA particularly during the period 2008 to 2012. Their strategic vision closely aligned: UK policing expertise was promoted internationally by NPIA IA and service delivery was enhanced by the coordination between the two police-led institutions. Proof alone was the NPIA IA's uptake of the International Policing Assistance Board (IPAB) referral process. By September 2009, only one year following the launch of NPIA IA, 72 per cent of the sixty-one referral cases had come from the academy alone (NPIA IA, 2010). ACPO IA acknowledged the 'pivotal role' that NPIA IA had played in supporting the 'the UK policing brand' and developing institution-wide collaboration (Author interview with former ACPO IA portfolio holder, February 2010). Yet the NPIA IA also provided a useful gateway for serving police to move into the private sector either at retirement or following a stint at Bramshill. Partly this was triggered by the business delivery model which revolved around three core strands: 'leadership' (training), 'executive operations' (programme management), and 'knowledge management' (strategy and transfer) and key for future police consultancy—the third strand—'advisory'. The international police advisory team comprised seconded UK police of superintendent rank (so-called international policing advisors) with regional responsibilities that included the EU, Africa, Middle East, and North Africa, Latin America, and Caribbean, Asia Pacific, and a specialist desk. Each international advisor was responsible for the 'client relationship, project and police consultancy management support' that aligned with the NPIA IA regional framework. This entailed the overseas marketing of operational training and development advisory services within their patch (Author interviews with international policing advisors, Bramshill, February 2011). In addition, in-country teams were embedded in Bahrain and Abu Dhabi where arguably the NPIA IA had the greatest bang for its buck. In July 2009, NPIA IA reported that UK policing had celebrated ten years of training 'excellence' in Abu Dhabi thanks to the close police relationships developed (NPIA, 2009). Indeed, many of the international policing advisors following several years of close working relationships with overseas police and governments slipped through the revolving door into private consultancy within *those countries* demonstrating the lucrative nature of UK policing and the international reputation of the brand (see chapter 5).

College of Policing

NPIA IA was replaced by the College of Policing International Faculty which outlined a strategic intent to continue the delivery of international policing through an international policing delivery plan. With the demise of Bramshill at the heart of international policing assistance, there has been a sense that training delivery, at least in the UK, has become more fragmented. Notwithstanding the drive by Police Scotland and PSNI to bolster their international reputation by bringing overseas police officers to their own training venues (see chapter 7). Nonetheless the CoP has sought to enhance police professionalism through their international activities (Author interview with former head of the JIPH and SU senior police advisor, 19 February 2019). However, the college has not always been fully cognizant of the potential risks arising from its international associations that might not align with government strategy and which could potentially damage the organization's reputation (College of Policing, 2016). Since 2010, there have been multiple controversies raised within media and civil society circles that related to UK police training within countries with a poor human rights track records. The CoP like the NPIA beforehand has come under media and civil society pressure to explain its involvement in countries that have included Egypt, Bahrain, and Saudi Arabia (see e.g. Foa, 2016). In 2016 and then 2017, *The Guardian* newspaper, for example, 'accused' the UK government of favouring commercial engagements over human rights. In one article it noted that the CoP had earned £3.3 million from international leadership training to twenty-three countries since 2012 and that eighty-nine per cent of income from that training emanated from countries where the death penalty existed. This had occurred despite a recommendation by the home affairs committee for adequate transparency and accountability surrounding international work (House of Commons Home Affairs Committee, 2016). The reality has been that between 2012 and 2018, Saudi Arabia remained the UK's biggest client for international leadership training spending approximately £1,466,515 with the NPIA IA and then with the CoP. This spend was almost mirrored by Bahrain, UAE, Oman, and Kuwait collectively (NPIA—CoP, 2018). In all income generated by the CoP from January 2013 to December 2020 for international training and assistance stood at a grand total of £20, 314.162 million (College of Policing, 2020). In response to these criticisms the NPIA, CoP, and also the HO have expressed the view that training has been designed to improve human rights compliance and an engagement with the topic, although campaigners against the death penalty and torture, including Reprieve and Index, have stated that there is a lack of evidence to substantiate this claim (e.g. see Wintour in *The Guardian*, 2016 and Amon in *The Guardian*, 2017).

The Overseas Security and Justice Assistance (OSJA) guidance was designed in 2011 to ensure UK overseas security and justice assistance work (including policing) met with the UK's human rights obligations and values and to mitigate against potential damage to an organization's reputation and professional integrity. Ensuring OSJA compliance was often described as 'patchy', with inadequate liaison between the FCO and wider UK policing. From 2013 to 2016, the records have suggested almost a complete lack of compliance from some police forces, who claimed the process itself was too unwieldy. Since the formal launch of the JIPH in 2017, attempts have been made to simplify the OSJA process through accompanying guidance notes as well as consulting more widely with UK policing particularly in relation to human rights issues. As such there has been an increase in uptake. The IPAB process has included a section on human rights compliance which requires an organization to judge whether there are 'serious concerns' that have related to the human rights record of the country to be visited; the human rights record of the institution that will receive assistance, and the necessary steps that will be taken to mitigate human rights risk that could arise from the activity (Author correspondence with JIPH, 2020). However, while the CoP has typically engaged with the IPAB referral process, there has been a sense of a fine line navigated between the commercial value of training and the decision as to proceed, or not, with international policing assistance within certain countries. In 2016, a HO affairs select committee enquiry openly suggested that:

[The] college has been put under pressure by the Home Office to raise revenue by providing overseas training. The committee raised concern that the provision of training on the basis of opaque agreements, sometimes with foreign government where some have been the subject of sustained criticism, threatens the integrity of the very 'brand of British policing' [sic] that the college is trying to promote (House of Commons Home Office Affairs Committee, 2016).

Despite this clear message, there has been no shift away from the provision of training and, in reality, there has been an increase in demand. One commercial reality for the UK policing brand has been that increasingly it has competed with other brands in the same places. These 'other' international providers have also sought an enhancement of their brand's reputation and commercial rewards. It would be tempting to assume that there has always been a degree of altruistic involvement when engaging with authoritarian states (and by extension their police institutions) on issues particularly relating to human rights and gender. While those UK police on the ground have stressed that their British policing values and purpose can be transferred through personal police encounters, the view held within government in relation to strategic interests and defence engagement may be somewhat different (Author interviews, 2015–2020). Despite this, it has been certain that the maintenance and promotion of the UK policing brand through UK police institutions has been integral to the work of ACPO IA and the JIPH.

Building international policing strategy

One key principle of international policing assistance has been the 'protection and enhancement of the UK policing'. Overseas activities have required oversight and scrutiny to ensure that the 'professional reputation of the UK police service' has been 'preserved, promoted and protected' (Author interview with former ACPO IA portfolio holder/CC Avon and Somerset, November 2012). This has not been without its challenges owing to the fragmented nature of both UK policing *and* government departments and resistance to the standardization of international policing delivery mechanisms.

The 2008 Policing Green Paper highlighted what it perceived as international policing activities and suggested that this could play a key role in reducing harm to the UK and making communities safer:

British policing, with the Office of Constable at its heart, is admired around the world for its excellence and its integrity; its operations and reforms have been studied internationally and British officers are stationed in over 30 countries, supporting and training forces in locations from Iraq to the Caribbean (HO, 2008: 5).

The same year, Paul Kernaghan, retired as Chief Constable of Hampshire Constabulary and ACPO IA portfolio holder and became the lead for the EU Coordinating Office for Palestinian Police Support. Kernaghan had considerably international policing experience. During his submission to the Iraq Inquiry, he voiced his disappointment that that 'seven years after Iraq, there appears to be little or no evidence of such a shift in official ministerial thinking' relating to the delivery of international policing assistance, to ensure that the 'UK can actually attract, train, deploy and retain officers properly equipped and rewarded for such important national security work.' Despite Kernaghan's criticism, his earlier recommendations to create a dedicated IPAB and its administrative IPAG hub had been actioned. This provided an 'important piece of the jigsaw' in the development of the necessary policies and procedures surrounding the future delivery of international policing which needed to be taken forward (Kernaghan, 2010).

Kernaghan, as ACPO IA lead, was replaced in 2008 by Avon and Somerset Chief Constable Colin Port. Port oversaw the management of the IPAG and its delivery arm: ACPO International Deployments, a 'centralized hub' administered by two seconded serving police. Its function was to provide an interface between ACPO, UK police forces, and government departments, including the SU deployment team that managed PSOs and stabilization missions, as well as coordinating the delivery of international policing through the IPAB processes. Established in July 2008 by the then Home Secretary Jacqui Smith, IPAB was (and has remained) a senior cross-governmental and policing advisory body originally chaired by the ACPO IA portfolio holder (Author interview with former IPAG secondee and Inspector Avon and Somerset Police, May 2010). Kernaghan's vision for the IPAB[6] was the first real attempt to coordinate the delivery of

---

[6] IPAB considered 'all non-investigative and non-operational assistance by UK civilian police forces to foreign states and international organisations, excluding certain areas where established liaison and coordination mechanisms already exist.... assistance from UK police services relating to ... police training, operational development and advisory support provided to foreign states by UK police forces and agencies ... peace support operations ... security

UK government and policing's professional interests overseas and to develop a strategic overview of UK aims in relation to international policing assistance. It also centred on the drive to centralize international policing through a referral process to provide guidance and assistance to the providers of international policing (Author interview with former ACPO IA portfolio holder/CC Avon and Somerset, November 2012).

In the early stages, there was some evidence of cross governmental-police agreement on important future strategies for international policing assistance that included an international policing assistance strategy (IPAS) published in March 2010. IPAS was an important piece of strategy in that it outlined how the delivery of international policing could be standardized and coordinated across all UK providers in the expectation that good practice could be exported. However, IPAS and the IPAB processes encountered difficulties in terms of adherence from across the UK international policing stakeholders. The uptake of the referrals process was far slower than expected: between April 2009 and March 2010 there were only fifty referrals from across all UK policing providers which was nonsensical given that the MPS alone had deployed internationally on over 300 occasions during the same period. It suggested a grave reluctance by UK policing to grant IPAB members scrutiny and oversight over what service was being delivered, by whom, where and why and, importantly to what accredited standard. This Port considered could at some stage damage the integrity of the UK policing brand and revealed the fragmented nature of UK policing (Author interview with former ACPO IA portfolio holder/CC Avon and Somerset, November 2012).

The difficulties in standardizing the processes of delivery were also revealing of the fragmented nature of strategic level decision-making by government departments without the involvement of senior police bodies when it concerned international policing. In 2009, for example, DfID, the FCO and MOD suggested that there should be a policy decision for the creation of a standby capacity of 500 to 1000 police available for immediate overseas deployment. This came without any reference to the HO, ACPO, individual chief constables and their police authorities who would legislate

---

and justice sector training, reform and development activities ... deployment/secondment of police officers and staff to ... build relationships and liaison mechanisms which improve operational capability ... strategic international engagement, in order to share best practice, develop doctrine and provide networking assistance to UK police forces and agencies (IPAB (2008), *Terms of Reference*).

on these sorts of matters and raised questions as to why ACPO was not seen as 'the voice of the police service' nor integral to the international policing *per se* (Author interview with former ACPO portfolio holder, 23 September 2011). The lack of a senior police voice and indeed presence at the government planning table was reminiscent of observations made during the Iraq Inquiry and in relation to Libya (see chapter 4).

Theoretically at that time, the IPAS had been an opportunity to promote coordination and consistency in the operational delivery of international policing assistance and to drive policy towards a 'mainstream role' ... 'to encourage police forces to make officers available for such work, and to recognize the career development opportunities international experience can offer' (ACPO IPAB, 2010: 4–5). The UK has remained out of step with many of its international partners, including some Scandinavian countries and Germany, where an international mission is perceived as part of a police career pathway and participation supported through incentives and a dedicated budgeting activity (Brown and Blair, 2016; Burdett and Sinclair, 2018). Moreover, an IPAS supported key government strategies including the NSS and BSOS. This was particularly important for ACPO IA where it was perceived that a fine line could be drawn between the '*export* of UK policing' and the '*provision* of UK policing expertise' to ensure suitability for a given context (ACPO IPAB, 2010: 7). It required IPAB to ensure that there were robust arrangements in place across a devolved UK policing structure with (at that time) over fifty individual forces and agencies to ensure effectiveness (Author interview with former IPAG secondee and Inspector Avon and Somerset Police, May 2010).

IPAG, however, was faced with increasing difficulties in embedding policy and process nationally and from a lack of sufficient resources and funding. Throughout 2010, IPAG survived on contributions from Avon and Somerset Police (the ACPO IA portfolio holder's force), the NPIA IA, and top-up funding that was actively sought across government (ACPO IA, 2011). Despite clear evidence of demand for UK policing internationally, referrals through the IPAB came at a snail's pace and consequently the IPAG encountered difficulties in mapping and logging international policing activities. The media criticisms surrounding UK policing in the Middle East and Libya (see chapter 4) had raised concern within ACPO of potential 'reputational damage', which reinforced the need for IPAB as a mechanism to bring a joined-up government and police approach to international policing. It was also complicated by the rising number of police retirees proffering their services overseas as 'representatives of UK policing' (Author interview with former ACPO IA portfolio holder, 28 May 2010).

One possible moment of real change came in 2011 with the IPAG's move from the NPIA IA (Bramshill) to London where it would be hosted by the SU and crucially funded through the Conflict, Stability and Security Fund (CSSF). While the SU focused on providing stabilization solutions (including policing) within FCAS, the demand for police advisors had increased from thirteen in August 2010 to twenty by July 2011. Moreover, the activities of the Security and Justice group based within DfID had also bolstered the number of police advisors to countries that included Afghanistan, Yemen, and the Sudan (Author interview with former SU senior advisor, 4 May 2012). DfID's management of security and justice sector reform programmes had been reinforced by the BSOS although there were challenges perceived by 2011 in supporting ongoing and future UNDP missions. By that time, UK policing no longer had the available capacity for overseas deployments: the 2010 emergency budget, growing austerity coupled with the first police and crime commissioner elections[7] in November 2012, dampened much of the enthusiasm for international policing. In particular, the efforts needed on the domestic front to ensure sufficient police capacity precluded UK police (particularly the senior ranks) from applying to multilateral missions. Consequently, support for multilateral missions waned within only one short-lived deployment to the UN mission in South Sudan (UNMISS) in 2014.

UK police in South Sudan: a missed opportunity

The deployment of five UK police officers to UNMISS from 2014 to 2016 has been the *last* UN deployment at scale to date (2021) and it has been questioned whether this trend can be reversed in the future. The curtailing of UK policing support to UNMISS ahead of a planned drawdown may have negatively impacted trust in the UK's ability to commit police to future UN missions. Yet stepping back in time, the UK had been the seventh

---

[7] Following the first election of PCCs, Colin Port wrote a briefing note outlining the importance of international policing. He stated that while a strategic policing requirement did not make specific reference in terms of providing international policing assistance 'could in turn disrupt the supply of Home Office Officers ... The supply of police officers for stabilisation purposes is recognised by HMG as being of strategic national importance' (Port, 2012).

largest police-contributing country in 2000 with 230 serving police officers serving within UN PSOs. Consequently, the UK had 'political as well as operational influence' in missions and at UN headquarters (Blair and Brown, 2016). This has since greatly diminished. From 2018 to 2019, there was a singular presence in Liberia of a senior officer deployed as police commissioner and one further officer seconded to UN headquarters. By 2021, the UK's commitment to UN missions had dropped to one officer deployed to UNMIK as a police liaison officer (Interpol). UNMISS has appeared as a missed opportunity to showcase elements of the UK policing brand through dedicated community policing projects.

In 2013, DfID provided funding for projects in South Sudan to assess the existence of 'community policing practices' and whether an official policy could be developed (SU, 2014: 47). The South Sudan National Police Service (SSNPS), formed in 2009, had no awareness of Western community policing practices. Despite this, the South Sudan Police Service Act (2009) had laid out provisions for community policing to support future police performance. By 2013, the SSNPS was encouraged to adopt a 'community policing ethos' by building the trust and confidence of local communities. This was poles apart from the policing realities across South Sudan where the police (many of whom had been recruited from the Sudanese army) were distrusted and feared by local communities in equal measure, and were a force rather than a service (Author interviews undertaken with UNMISS UK policing team members, 2014–2015). Within UNMISS sites, for example, SSNPS were not permitted entry and the mandate required the mission to 'protect civilians from physical violence' including those internally displaced people (IDP) living in UN protection of civilian (POC) sites. 'This duty applied to actual violence and to the threat of violence so required an immediate intervention and created an ongoing responsibility to protect the victim or other potential victims. The mandate also applied to the suspected perpetrator.' In 2014, the UN mandate focused exclusively on citizen security and safety and had no executive authority regarding policing or security issues (Dunster, 2018: 154).

UK police were given responsibility for the UNPOL Community Policing Team (CPT) and to implement what the UN described as 'community policing programmes' within IDP sites. More broadly, UNDP had an overarching mandate to reduce and prevent crime within and around sites; to combat the emergence of organized crime; establish crime patterns relating to serious crime and seek to prevent, and implement a community policing model through recognizable programmes that could subsequently be rolled out across South Sudan. At face value this appeared overly optimistic with conflict ongoing, the lack of a formal peace process, and difficulties in establishing co-operation with the SSNPS. UK police drove a strategy of engaging and empowering the IDP communities and the promotion of partnerships with all stakeholder groups which included the SSNPS. The CPT designed a solutions-based approach: visibility, engagement, and problem-solving based in consultations with IDP leaders. This would be achieved through training, workshops, and encouraging partnership working and performance management and communication (Author interviews with UNMISS CPT members, 2014–2015; Dunster, 2018; Gold, 2018).

In December 2014, the ICT presented a concept of operations (CONOPS) to UNDP and identified what they described as a 'community oriented policing strategy' and an operational plan. The policing strategy would first be introduced within the IDP POCs in Juba, then replicated across further POC sites, extended into areas deemed as safe for the voluntary return of IDPs and, finally across wider communities in South Sudan in collaboration with the SSNPS. The challenge to extending the strategy beyond the initial Juba site lay in the hostility between the IDPs, other local communities, and the SSNPS. From 2015, the ICT spearheaded the developed of workshops with SSNPS officers to focus on issues that related to HR, sexual and gender-based violence, child protection as well as community policing (UN, 2015; Gold, 2018). Yet the ICT (by which time included other international police) encountered a second challenge within the mission itself in that many UNPOL struggled with the basic concepts of community engagement, dialogue, and safety and how this aligned not only with the mandate but basic policing concepts. The ICT developed a support network across UNMISS to develop skills for all UNPOL officers delivering 'community policing' training and awareness. This included the sharing of good international practice and feedback on existing practices across UNMISS. Effectively this created a window of opportunity to build partnerships across international policing networks, to facilitate greater engagement within UNMISS, and to exchange knowledge and skills regardless of the country of origin. This was lost when the UK policing team withdrew suddenly from South Sudan in 2016 (Author interviews with UNMISS CPT members, 2019). Yet the 'quick wins' and wider lesson learning that UK policing has brought home has rarely been embedded within an international policing corporate memory despite the earlier vison of ACPO IA and the JIPH.

Joint International Policing Hub: 2015 to 2021

In 2016, Stephanie Blair and Maureen Brown posited that the UK was 'poised to re-engage' in international policing and to 'stop muddling through' the approaches that had been taken over the past decade. This necessitated 'a realistic and holistic UK government strategy on international policing and law enforcement' that aligned with national security objectives including the NSS. One positive they argued was the advent in April 2015 of the International Coordination Committee (ICC), as part of the JIPH–NPCC that provided the oversight and coordination of international policing assistance (Blair and Brown, 2016). The JIPH as the 2015 SDSR had noted would 'help fragile countries to access the best of British legal, policing and security expertise' (SDSR, 2015: para 5.123).

Until 2020, the JIPH had been 'hosted' by the tri-departmental SU and funded through the CSSF which was suggestive that its activities should focus primarily on countries that qualified for ODA. Its management and administration fell to two seconded police officers (one in a dual role as staff officer to the NPCC lead and strategic police advisor) and a civil servant. The JIPH benefitted from the considerable energy and vision of its architect (a mid-ranking MPS officer) to drive forward its development across government to safeguard the delivery and oversight—including through the IPAB referral processes—of international policing. New ventures that would arguably have been of strategic benefit to UK policing and government were watered down in the expectation that a *new* international policing strategy would be finalized—the original 2010 IPAS had been long shelved. However, even at the time of the JIPH's official launch in March 2017 this was no further forward, which prevented further expansion despite assurances from the then Policing Minister, Brandon Lewis, of the viability and importance of international policing assistance to the UK (Author interview with former head of the JIPH, February 2019).

JIPH police and civilian personnel sought to retain the JIPH as a *police-led institution* and to deliver international policing in alignment with government strategy,[8] despite a lack of international policing strategy agreed

---

[8] From 2016 to 2017 the JIPH coordinated UK police assistance to forty-seven countries globally as well as providing national guidance on deployments to UK and overseas police, law enforcement, and government organizations on a range of issues. From 2017 to 2020 it was posited for example that the UK would provide greater support for UN missions and at UN headquarters, would train international peacekeepers, provide more security and justice assistance, ensure that FCAS had greater access to UK policing expertise, that UK policing had

at ministerial level. However, increasing budgetary constraints and a misalignment between the SU's and the JIPH's objectives for what international policing activities constituted outside FCAS and stabilization missions, led to a rehoming in the HO in parallel with the ICDT then referred to as international capabilities team (ICT).[9] While the JIPH was originally placed within the international directorate, HO structures have been in continual state of flux. In 2021, the international directorate was replaced by International Strategy Engagement and Devolution which sits under Science, Technology, Analysis, Research, and Strategy (STARS), a horizontal HO structure. There are historic reasons for the JIPH's repositioning within the HO which, since the nineteenth century has been the traditional home of UK policing (Emsley, 1996), while the CO (1854 to 1966) had responsibility for the colonial police service (Sinclair, 2006), and a separate history from the Foreign Office (FO) (1782 to 1968). The *foreign* and *commonwealth office* (1968) has directed aspects of international policing on behalf of the FCO which have included advisory services, law enforcement, and police diplomacy and multilateral and bilateral capacity building. Therefore, prior to the FCO-DfID merger, the SU conveniently represented three government departments each with an overlapping and yet independent interest and approach to the delivery of international policing assistance. This included the MOD (which houses the MDP) and supported earlier PSOs and deployed to Afghanistan (see chapters 3 and 4). The recent governmental restructuring has impacted the JIPH and necessitated a realignment of its cross-government workings as highlighted by the 2021 integrated review. Moreover, with the advent of the International Strategy and Capabilities Unit, the number of government departments with an interest in the delivery of international policing has increased.

Since 2017, the HO has revitalized its approaches to overseas capacity building including policing and rule of law; fire and resilience; cyber security; borders, migration and asylum, and national risk and resilience. The HO policing team has employed a blended approach to capacity building: a combination of serving and retired police to deliver international police capacity building. The JIPH's move to the HO might 'close the gap' between the 2015 vision of expanding the delivery of international policing

greater influence across multilateral organizations, and had become a key bilateral partner with the EU post Brexit (Marsh, 2017: 3.6)

[9] In June 2021, the ICT was renamed the International Strategy and Capabilities Unit.

assistance through capacity-building programmes and emergency response which has included the new International Policing Response Cadre (IPRC).

International Policing Response Cadre

The IPRC stemmed from longstanding police-military relationships and support provided by both parties in times of national and international emergencies and crises. The IPRC has provided a 'cadre' of serving police held at 'very high readiness' (standby) for overseas deployment in support of Joint Force Headquarters (JFHQ). This *crisis policing response* (operational liaison and reconnaissance teams, humanitarian aid, disaster relief, and non-combatant evacuation operations) may provide a platform for future support of combat operations through the military's defence engagement.[10] Overseas deployments that require 'embedded police support' within the military has been referred to as the fusion doctrine or integrated approach (see Integrated Review, 2021), and may in the future create opportunities for police reform and SSR. There have been some parallels with the civil-military coordination that occurred during the PSOs in the West Balkans (see chapter 3) and during the interventions in both Iraq and Afghanistan (see chapter 4).

UK police first deployed with JFHQ in a training capacity in July 2008, but it was not until 2010, during a Joint Venture 10 exercise, that the relevance of civil-military co-operation within crisis environments was fully appreciated by both parties. Subsequently, the IPRC has been involved in international training missions including with the Kenyan and Ugandan rapid reaction forces to support preparedness for flood relief and cholera prevention, and support to military commanders in Somalia. One example that has exemplified the role played by embedded police within military operations was Libya in 2011 (see chapter 4) in relation to the evacuation of UK nationals. Rather than a 'search and secure' operation using armed capability, the policing response was to suggest (and this followed the deployment of a UK police officer to Malta) that the individuals should be

---

[10] Currently the IPRC has twenty-one members (sixteen deployable) drawn from three forces: Gloucestershire, Wiltshire and Avon, and Somerset with a recruitment process underway (2021) to expand to thirty from the south west region including Dorset and Devon and Cornwall (Author interviews and correspondence with IPRC member and Chief Supt Gloucestershire Constabulary, May 2020 and February 2021).

classified as missing persons (known as high risk 'misper'). As a result, an official report stated (2015) that:

> At the conclusion of Operation DEFERENCE, the military were so impressed with the value added by having an embedded policing presence (described by commanders as being a 'force multiplier') that a request was made to formally establish a police cadre of suitable officers to support all future JFHQ operations (JFHQ, 2015).

Over the past decade, the IPRC has sought candidates with the 'highest level of professionalism as representing UK Police PLC'. This has been interpreted as the assumption that an officer is considered an 'international policing experts within this area of expertise; (emergency and crisis response) and represents UK policing. The cadre has to date drawn officers from three forces, with a preference for those with either a military background or familiarity with a police-military environment. Serving police accepted into the cadre received dedicated training including HEAT, an annual IPRC training exercise, and training events through JFHQ both in the UK and overseas.[11] Each officer must commit to remaining on standby and be able to deploy within twenty-four hours of a call up. When the IPRC were called up in 2017, for example, to the British Virgin Islands (Tortola) following hurricane Irma, the police cohort arrived sixteen hours later.[12] The apparent success of that mission led to further requests, and in March 2020, a team deployed to Turks and Caicos, British Virgin Islands, and Cayman Islands to support the local police faced with potentially serious public disorder. The IPRC was given three core tasks: training assistance (familiarization of 'basic' public order); a principal point of contact between the British military and local policing (police-military co-operation), and a visible UK police presence to reassure local communities.[13] On return

---

[11] IPRC held five training events with JFHQ in 2021 including an exercise in Mozambique. Deployment to Oman to participate in Operation Sareera the largest of the British military exercises was evidence of an effective civil-military relationship.

[12] With the IPRC, a total of sixty UK police officers were deployed to Anguilla to support the Royal Anguilla Police Force and to the British Virgin Island to support the Royal British Virgin Islands Police Force. UK policing provided support in the maintenance of law and order and policing services and to British nationals within hurricane affected areas. NPCC 'British police arrive in the Caribbean to support Hurricane Irma recovery efforts', 11 September 2017. A total of fourteen UK police forces (approximately sixty officers) provided support with the relief efforts alongside Royal Marines personnel.

[13] NPCC had been asked for 200 UK officers but this was declined owing to the Covid-19 situation arising in the UK.

to the UK, the IPRC were placed on standby, though not deployed in response to the earthquake in Montserrat (July 2020) and the Beirut port explosion (August 2020) (Author interviews and correspondence with IPRC lead, 5 May 2020, 8 February 2021, and 23 March 2021). Over the past decade, the IPRC, despite limited capacity, has contributed to integrated police-military working, which has chimed with the recent drive to ensure frontline response cross-cutting capability and has raised the possibility of the growth in future 'police and defence engagement' within international environments (see chapter 8).[14]

Capacity building through the JIPH

The JIPH held both an administrative and a capacity-building role, and collaborated with a multiplicity of government and policing stakeholders. One recent example was a capacity-building project in Vietnam. Modern slavery and human trafficking have become a key thematic piece of work aligning with UK government criminal justice priorities as well as UK policing (HO, 2014).[15] In August 2017, the HO modern slavery unit established a fully funded multi-year programme on modern slavery and was approached by the JIPH for funding to set up a bilateral project; Vietnam was selected as a priority country. The following year JIPH representatives undertook scoping visits to Vietnam and Thailand, which included dialogue with international institutions, foreign governments, and non-governmental organizations and created an opportunity for UK policing to engage with modern slavery issues within an international context (JIPH, 2018a: 15). An MOU between Vietnam and the UK in 2018 led to a £500,000 grant from the HO modern slavery fund to provide training over a three-year period for investigation skills, evidence procedures, and development of

---

[14] By 2021 the IPRC was building collaboration through JFHQ, 77th brigade (support for hurricane response) and the specialized infantry group (overseas engagement and capacity building).

[15] See HO (2014), Modern Slavery Strategy, November 2014.

The aim of this Strategy is to reduce significantly the prevalence of modern slavery in the UK, as well as to enhance our international response. Modern slavery is often an international crime and requires a strong collaborative international response. This Strategy builds on and adapts the framework that has been successfully implemented in both our serious and organised crime and counter terrorism strategies. Modern slavery is a complex crime that takes a number of different forms. It encompasses slavery, servitude, forced and compulsory labour and human trafficking.

training manuals relating to human trafficking (Correspondence with the JIPH, May 2021).[16] In addition, two Vietnamese officers were seconded to Police Scotland to share good practice and support the human trafficking drive in the UK (Gibbons, 2021). By April 2021, the training provided in Vietnam by UK policing had been received by 600 police investigators, border officials, criminal prosecutors, and judges. In total twenty-four training courses were delivered in collaboration with the Vietnamese People's Police Academy (PPA), the British Embassy (Hanoi), and the JIPH in London. This provided unprecedented opportunities for UK policing to engage with the Vietnamese Police and develop collaborative working through in-country visits and networking (Author correspondence with JIPH, 2021).

Throughout 2020, COVID-19 impacted policing and law enforcement operations on a global basis and brought shifts in transnational crime activities as serious and organized crime adapted to new opportunities including, in particular, digital and cybercrime (Interpol, 2020). A 2020 JIPH report identified the challenges and opportunities for UK policing domestically and internationally through soft power approaches:

> There is a requirement to broaden the United Kingdom's (UK) reach into comparable overseas partnerships to develop our soft power with a focus on targeting transnational organised crime. The UK's experience has been that policing can support this most effectively by building relationships with other overseas law enforcement through training, secondments, capacity building, investigation collaboration, intelligence sharing, disaster and crisis management, and support. The police and partners, not only in the UK, must continually search for innovative practices to enhance capabilities at home (HO/JIPH, 2020: 1).

A partnership with the Asia region law enforcement management programme (ARLEMP): a joint initiative of the Vietnamese Ministry of Public Security, the Australian Federal Police, and the Royal Melbourne Institute of Technology in Vietnam, and the JIPH in 2020 collected data relating to

---

[16] UK policing has supported the Vietnamese modern slavery and human trafficking investigation training programme provided to the People's Police Academy. By April 2021, the programme had provided to training to 576 participants from 49 cities (250 police, 109 border guards, 122 prosecutors, and 95 judges; JIPH (2021b).

the management of the pandemic. This included the challenges faced by law enforcement and policing, best practices during Covid-19, the impact on transnational crime and possible next steps for law enforcement, and skills for preparedness and response for future pandemics, emergencies, and crises (ARLEMP, 2020). During the course of 2021, 'good practice' policing skills were circulated internationally with the aim of building a framework for future 'good' operational practice. In the UK, the ARLEMP findings were directly embedded into Operation Talla, the NPCC Covid-19 response programme. One key aim was to share outcomes globally in relation to the 'policing of pandemics' and, has included the global law enforcement and public health association which sit within the world health organization framework.

Both ARLEMP and the modern slavery programme widened the capacity-building and learning activities of the JIPH. However, the unit faced ongoing challenges in coordinating and mapping the delivery of international policing. From 2017 to 2018, the JIPH coordinated only eighty-seven referrals across in excess of sixty-two countries; from 2018 to 2019 this fell to seventy-three referrals across in excess of fifty-one countries, and, from 2019 to 2020, JIPH coordinated seventy-six referrals for fifty-eight countries. In 2020, referrals dropped sharply as a result of the pandemic although some views held have been that the IPAB referrals have not reflected the true number of international deployments. This has underlined the continuing fragmented nature of international policing whereby individual constabularies may operate independently of the referral processes including the OSJA. The referrals may only have captured 'substantive' international policing assistance activities including large capacity-building programmes whereas short-term training assistance and scoping activities may fall through the net (Author correspondence with the JIPH, 2021). In an almost complete reversal of fortunes, there are now fewer serving UK police overseas than at any time since the 1980s on long-term secondments with the recent (May 2021) drawdown from Afghanistan. The response to Hurricane Irma (as outlined earlier in this chapter) brought the IPRC and a cohort of almost sixty serving police from a range of constabularies on a short-term secondment although there has been nothing similar since. International policing has become almost entirely subsumed by bilateral international policing programmes managed by individual constabularies, the private sector, or a blended version of both.

Concluding comment

The governance, management, and vision for UK international policing has been challenged by the fragmented nature of government departments and UK policing in relation to *delivery*. Traditionally, international policing has been delivered by multiple departments: the FCO, DfID (now FCDO), the SU, the MOD, and the HO with often less than integrated ways of working and increasingly commercialization of these activities—and by extension the UK policing brand—have assumed greater importance. Fragmentation has increased as individual constabularies as well as commercial companies have sought to market their services overseas through the use of the UK policing brand. Partly this has emanated from historic bilateral partnerships but also through wider policing networks and diplomatic channels where there has been an interest in championing the UK policing brand (Allison, 2015).

The coordination and delivery of international policing has remained fragmented just as the UK policing brand has provided a range of different characteristics that may or may not be palatable for an international audience. Despite the valiant attempts of some senior police there has been a lack of consensus across government departments for a blueprint for international policing (Blair and Brown, 2016), and a new international policing strategy that can improve a 'state-based' delivery of international policing (Correspondence with the deputy head of the JIPH and HO strategic police advisor, February 2021).

Moreover, the UK policing landscape has changed significantly over the past decade. This has resulted in a sharp decline in the deployment of serving officers overseas (see annex 1) as local policing priorities have been brought into sharper focus. A lack of appetite for international work (despite the professional and personal benefits that this may offer) (Brown and Blair, 2016; Sinclair and Burdett, 2018) has been heightened by the notion that an international deployment has been seen as a career cul-de-sac, manifested, for example, by the very small numbers of police within the SU policing pool (around 45) as compared to some 500 a decade ago. The lack of cohesion in the delivery of a UK policing brand *per se* aside from the private sector, has extended to Police Scotland and Northern Ireland which is the subject of chapter 7.

7
Police Scotland and PSNI
New International Policing Agendas

> Scotland created Police Scotland and, Northern Ireland with the arrival of PSNI created the foundation for a new policing vision and a new culture... then came a new police brand in Scotland and Northern Ireland, which is partly tied in with all the independence stuff going on and, the drive to push forward a new organisation on the international scene.
> **Author interview with former ACC PSNI, 2020**

This chapter considers the international policing activities of Police Scotland and PSNI in the twenty-first century. Both organizations have contributed to the development of their own brands by increasing their international footprint, which has resulted in a greater fragmentation within the delivery of a multifaceted UK policing brand.

The emergence of the Police Scotland and PSNI brands were strengthened by political devolution. The creation of a Scottish Parliament and government in 1999 created new structural arrangements within law and order which impacted upon 'domestic' policing (Scott, 2011). Scottish policing became a 'devolved matter' where a tripartite partnership of central government, local government, and the original eight police forces 'arguably changed the balance of influence within that partnership' raising question around public accountability. A transformation occurred with the creation of Police Scotland on 1 April 2013, removing all the pre-existing structures of local police forces and continued a period of substantive reform (Fyfe and Terpstra, 2019), providing an impetus to develop international policing independently of policing in England, Wales, and Northern Ireland. This occurred in two ways: first Scottish police reform brought an experience and learning of change management, organizational, and cultural transformation that was then seen as applicable to wider international development agendas. Secondly, the crafting of Scotland's own international development strategy turned policy into practice by actively supporting an international policing agenda that could be owned by Scotland (as opposed to the UK). While to date there has been a greater push to develop and deliver brand 'Scotland' through international and commercial engagement, the post-2013 Police Scotland brand has remained under construction.

In Northern Ireland, the political breakthrough in April 1998, followed by the Good Friday agreement, saw occasional periods of devolved and direct administrative rule with the controversial issue of police reform dominating the political (and policing) agendas. In October 2006, the UK and Irish government intervened once again and drew up the St Andrews agreement, which resulted in an endorsement of PSNI by Sinn Féin and a commitment to power sharing within the Northern Irish assembly across the political party spectrum (Bryne, 2014). The (Northern) Irish element of UK policing has featured extensively in earlier chapters and has centred on semi-military and robust policing styles and expertise (see Ellison, 2007; Sinclair, 2012). In this chapter, I turn to the Northern Irish experience of SSR, and specifically the emergence of a 'new' 'Northern Irish Policing Model ... increasingly branded and promoted on the global stage' (Ellison and O'Reilly, 2008a: 331). In essence, the 'transformation of policing' in Northern Ireland, the implementation of these processes of change and the challenges and lessons learned from these processes provided a *template for change* for 'sharing peace building practice locally and internationally ... '(Bryne, 2014: i). This I discuss with reference to public order and community policing and their international transfer.

Promoting Police Scotland Internationally

The advent of Police Scotland

The policing reforms that created *a Police Scotland* have been described as 'some of the most significant' in the history of Scottish policing, and marked a drive towards greater centralization as compared to the continuing localism—forty-three constabularies—of policing in England and Wales (see Fyfe, 2014; Fyfe and Scott, 2013). This move towards centralization has been referred to as a fine balance between the centre and local areas, which had originated with the 1857 Police (Scotland) Act enforcing 'towns, burghs and counties to establish police forces'. As a consequence, there were eighty-nine police forces in Scotland by 1859, rapidly reducing to sixty-four by 1899, thirty-three by 1959 and then finally eight from 1975 to 2013: 'the eight "legacy" forces based in regional administrative areas were in place for four decades' (Davidson, Jackson, and Smale, 2016: 88–111). Yet has this reshaping and centralization of Scottish policing generated 'its own models of policing for the future or ... simply cop[ied] what is done elsewhere?' From the historical surveys undertaken, there may have been aspects of Scottish policing suggestive of a difference in approach to 'police work, activity and organisation in the northern part of the United Kingdom', *while adhering to the core tenets of UK policing* [author emphasis] that is 'policing by consent' (see chapter 2) (Donnelly and Scott, 2005: 1–4). Hugo Gorringe and Michael Rosie's (2010) suggested that there are policing activities which are considered essentially *Scottish*, including 'policing by consent' within a 'democratic' tradition, although they refuted the notion that there truly is a distinctive approach and mused that 'Scottish policing [...] *does* exist if only as a reassuring shorthand' and therefore requires careful scrutiny. (Gorringe and Rosie, 2010).

Behind this has been an identity and culture of Scottish policing informed by its historical development (Walker, 1999). Some Police Scotland officers have suggested that there are niche brand characteristics that have been resurrected as part of the Police Scotland brand 'offer' that have included the concept of localism, community engagement practices, and a distinctive approach to public order (Author interviews with Police Scotland officers, 2017 to 2019). The literature has tended to provide conflicting images of Scottish policing and questioned the existence of a dedicated Scottish brand. If a brand existed, was there a linkage with one of the original eight forces? Or was there a difference between policing within urban and rural areas? Or was the brand simply linked to a wider Scottish policing identity and the culture of the people of Scotland? These are some of the many complex questions that have been addressed within the literature. One explanatory issue has hinged on the concept of 'local policing'. The original eight regional forces generated what Scottish police considered to have been enhanced partnership working across local communities which was presented as quintessentially Scottish in style. Police Scotland, has always maintained the importance of a 'local' policing approach which has deep historic roots, despite decisions regarding local policing no longer being made at a local level but at a national level since the advent of Police Scotland (Fyfe, 2014). This Daniel Donnelly and Kenneth Scott (2011, 2nd edn) questioned prior to the amalgamation of the eight regional forces and asked whether:

> Policing in Scotland is any different from that which [is practiced] in the rest of the United Kingdom, ...[?] that whilst many Scottish police officers will say that it is, they would be unable to give a reason as to why or how. [However, policing in Scotland] reflects a much greater partnership approach, recognising that while the police may 'contribute', 'support' or 'assist' with many functions, theirs is not the sole role. The later priorities speak of 'public satisfaction', 'public confidence' and of policing which is 'ethical, accountable and transparent'. This reflects a clear awareness of the need to place Scottish policing in a much more collaborative position, both with other agencies and with the public (Donnelly and Scott, 2011:9).

Indeed, across Scotland, community safety and community engagement has resulted in an enhanced policing engagement with 'localism' including issues relating to social welfare (Crawford, 2009). While police amalgamation increased tensions between national policy and local priorities and had consequences for local policing, the Scottish Police Act made *local policing* a statutory requirement, despite the lack of certainty as to what it entailed and how it would be achieved (Terpstra and Fyfe, 2014). This concept of *local policing*, therefore, may have some resonance with the historical past, and has carried through in some form to the present day. (Davidson, Jackson, and Smale, 2016). Localism has been embedded within a Scottish policing culture and the political drive by the Scottish government to ensure that despite the amalgamation of the regional forces, a decentralized approach is adopted (Fyfe, 2014, and see Fyfe, et al., 2021). More recently this has correlated with Scotland's independence agenda; the drive to follow a different police reform path than in England and Wales, and to create a national Scottish identify (Terpstra and Fyfe, 2014).

Police Scotland has contributed to the building of this '*national* Scottish identity' (or brand Scotland) as well as the development of its own policing brand. A number of key strategic priorities were published in October 2016 with 'inclusion, prevention, response, collaborative working, accountability, adaptability and *localism*' [author emphasis] representing 'Scotland's high-level ambitions for what it expects its police service to be ... a service which works at an international level' (Police Scotland and Scottish Police Authority, 2017: 9). Once more localism had been eulogized, a concept whereby police engaged with the localities and their communities through openness, collaboration, and the appropriate dialogue through community policing (Matheson, 2014). This linked with Police Scotland's initial *branding* guidelines highlighted that 'the purpose of Police Scotland is to improve the safety and wellbeing of people, places, and communities in Scotland and that 'our focus is keeping people safe' to support Police Scotland in 'building' a 'solid and reliable brand that is high visible both in Scotland and overseas' (Police Scotland and Scottish Police Authority, 2013). The UK policing brand has benefitted from diverse forms of symbolic representation and heritage and this has also been true of Police Scotland. The Scottish Police college at Tulliallan Castle has become one symbol of Scottish policing, not only as the national policing college but also as Police Scotland's headquarters. It is at Tulliallan that Police Scotland's international development and innovation unit is housed that has steered international policing and the delivery of Police Scotland's international agenda.

A Scottish international development agenda

Scottish devolution 'represented the most radical change in the way Scotland [was] governed since 1707' (Keating, 2020: 11); the new system of government undertook public policy development that focused on decentralization including criminal justice and policing (Keating, 2010). The approach to international development within a devolved constitutional context also changed,[1] as the funds provided from the Scottish government's own budget grew an international development 'footprint' from 2005. The Scottish ODA spend has been included by UK government within its overall ODA return to the Organization for Economic Co-Operation and Development (OECD) and has counted towards the original 0.7 per cent GNI commitment. The Scottish government noted that this has been a 'key part of Scotland's global contribution within the international community',

---

[1] The term 'Scotland International' appeared as a title in P. Lynch (2020). 'Scotland International: Understanding Scotland's International Relations' in M. Keating (ed.). *The Oxford Handbook of Scottish Politics*. Oxford: OUP.

which has demonstrated Scotland to be a 'good global citizen' projecting core values of fairness and equality' (Scottish government, 2017).

In 2008, a *Scottish* international development policy was published establishing 'programmes of work'. This included Malawi where a £3 million annual fund was ring-fenced yearly with a formal acknowledgement of the 'special relationship and co-operation agreement between the two countries'. Additionally, funding was set out for the sub-Saharan Africa development programme, which included Zambia, Rwanda, and Tanzania and, the South Asia development programme including Pakistan, Bangladesh, and a number of Indian states (Scottish Government, 2008). From the onset, the Scottish government focused on specific regions and countries of strategic interest and, where partnerships had been established. Of importance was that 'inevitably, Scotland will learn and benefit from the experience of working partnership with developing countries, but these benefits will not detract from the development strategies and priorities identified by developing countries' (Scottish Government, 2008: 1–2). One argument advanced was the primary focus on developing 'international partnerships' particularly in countries where Scotland had pre-existing ties and, supporting development programmes in the 'countries of origin' of people who had migrated to Scotland (Author interview with Scottish government representative, international development department, February 2016).

Police Scotland published its own national and international development strategy in November 2015 in alignment with the Scottish government approach to international development and national priorities. Enshrined within Police Scotland's mission of 'keeping people safe', as set out in the Scottish Government's vision for community safety (Justice Board, 2018), was a ten-year policing 2026 strategy established between Police Scotland and the Scottish Policing Authority. The Scottish international development agenda (as distinct from the FCO or DfID international agenda) has directly impacted upon Police Scotland's own international approach and has contributed to building the Scottish policing brand. International policing has focused on 'international training and development'; 'providing specialist services, advice and support'; 'developing international collaborative partnerships', and 'developing police officers and staff through international actions' (Police Scotland, 2015) which:

> … will enable us to develop long term sustainable relationships that ensure where and when we decide to undertaken training and development, provide specialist services or support, and share best practice

that we are able to do this collaboratively and co-produce actions that deliver real outcomes or people, communities and countries. We will use an asset-based approach using *our Scottish Policing Model* [author emphasis] contextualized to meet country-specific needs, and our highly skilled and experienced officers and staff, and former officers and associates (Police Scotland, 2015: 7).

Police Scotland has since aimed at sharing 'best practice', learning and support provided for the 'stabilization of countries across the globe' with an emphasis on Scotland's priority countries (Author interview with former head of the international innovation and development unit, Police Scotland, February 2016).

Sustaining each of the priority areas has been dependent on Police Scotland 'winning' international policing projects either bilaterally or as part of a consortium bid. One recent strategy has been to target specific thematic groupings and countries where Scotland maintains an active interest as previously outlined. In 2016, there were four so-called 'zones of interest' that included CSSF countries (including Pakistan, Kenya, Sri Lanka, Malawi, India, Bangladesh, Nigeria, and Turkey); 'developing/emerging' countries (including for example Albania, Belarus, Bosnia and Herzegovina, Iceland, Kosovo, Macedonia, Montenegro, Serbia, Turkey); 'developed' countries (including the EU, USA, China, and Australasia and, finally, countries where communities had migrated to Scotland including refugee populations (for example: Syria, Libya, Afghanistan, Tunisia, Egypt, Ukraine, Georgia, Jordan, Moldova, Kuwait) (Correspondence with Police Scotland International Development and Innovation Unit, February 2016).[2]

Prior to 2013 and following the amalgamation of the eight regional forces, international work has been undertaken on a not-for-profit basis. This has occurred in two ways; either bilaterally between Scottish police/Police Scotland and an overseas police organization, or as a contribution to a wider UK policing where other stakeholders might be included. However, when joining a consortium, the existence of an independent Scottish policing brand might from an external perspective be subsumed within the overall UK policing brand (Author interview with former head

---

[2] Between 1 January and 31 March 2016, twenty-two police officers and staff were deployed on international policing projects to countries including Sri Lanka, Pakistan, the UAE, and the USA.

of the International Innovation and Development Unit, Police Scotland, August 2017).

Police Scotland has remained a non-profit making organization, recovering the full cost of international policing 'assistance' under contract from the relevant funding agency. Tulliallan Castle has increasingly become *the* location in which to showcase Scottish policing (Police Scotland, 2020). This has included training courses for international visitors and the hosting by Police Scotland of a wide range of 'senior and middle' command courses on behalf of the EU Police Service Training, and international policing police master classes, and police study visits from officers from across the developed and developing world (Correspondence with JIPH, August 2020). Capacity building (including training) and wider police reform has been the bedrock of Scottish international policing assistance. One very early example came in 2004, when a Scottish officer was deployed to the security sector development advisory team (SSDAT) in the FCO and, 'became involved in their first formal international development *policing* project (Guyana) from a Scottish perspective' (Author interview with former Chief Supt, Police Scotland, 13 February 2016). From 2007, support to the Sri Lanka Police Service (SLP) has become an important tranche of 'Scottish' international policing work.[3]

The Sri Lanka police

In August 2010, financial support provided by the South Asia economic development fund, through the Scottish government, supported the Scottish police college in building an 'extensive partnership involving the SLP, the Office of the Strategic Adviser in the Sri Lanka Ministry of Defence; The British High Commission in Sri Lanka; The Asia Foundation and the Scottish Qualifications Authority' (Milne and Thomson, 2012). A cessation

---

[3] UK government's SSDAT (FCO) developed policing projects in Sri Lanka from 2007 including assistance to the SLP to develop a dedicated 'strategic development division' to roll out a national community policing strategy. SLP officers from the strategic development division undertook training at the Scottish Police College at a time when Sri Lanka was seen as a FCAS with SLP involved with intrastate conflict. In 2009, PSNI was also requested to provide short term assistance in Sri Lanka to support the development of community policing drawing on their post-conflict experiences 'to support the community policing strategy' and 'to act as a 'critical friend'. Beyond a short scoping mission to Sri Lanka this was not taken any further forward (Author interview with former Supt PSNI who deployed to Sri Lanka in 2009, 14 April 2020).

in conflict between the Sri Lanka authorities and the Tamil Tigers in June 2009 had created post-conflict tensions between communities and security actors (including the SLP) and there was an urgent need to reconcile SLP with all local communities, ease local tensions, and ensure that public safety and law enforcement priorities were met. At the time the Scottish police college looked at possible community engagement strategies that might provide a solution to the SLP and Sri Lankan communities and became aware of the challenges that lay ahead. A former Chief Superintendent (2016) who deployed to Sri Lanka observed:

> We [the Scottish police college] were conscious that there is no model of community policing that can fit, that is transportable. What we wanted to do was to raise awareness within the police in Sri Lanka and the communities of what we thought community policing can be and can do. What community policing means in terms of the police being accountable to the public, what it means in terms of community safety, shared responsibility for social problems, what is means for local policing... although community policing has to be adapted to the needs of the country (Former Chief Supt and Police Scotland associate, February 2016).

In developing a community policing approach, the Scottish police college (and latterly Police Scotland) have managed the Sri Lanka programme since 2007. The approach taken has been through the deployment of strategic police advisors and police trainers to Sri Lanka (Sri Lanka Police College and the National Police Academy) in close collaboration with The Asia Foundation (a non-profit international development organization) with strong ties to SLP and the wider Sri Lanka communities. Building an awareness of the community policing 'philosophy' through training for SLP (including 'train the trainer') was underpinned by an international vocational award in community policing and the development of training manuals (Milne and Thomson, 2012). In parallel, wider police reform initiatives were undertaken by The Asia Foundation including Tamil language training for police, the institutionalization of community policing practices, evidence-based policy planning, countering gender-based violence, and supporting gender equality. The Sri Lankan context demonstrated that community policing projects required integration as an *approach* across all aspects of policing rather than being confined to the SLP's dedicated community policing units (Denney and Jenkins, 2013; The Asia Foundation, 2020).

Scottish policing engagement in Sri Lanka has not been without controversy. Contract renewal between the Scottish police college and SLP faced repeated criticism in the media and by civil societies regarding the provision of UK aid to a country where government officials have been accused of human rights abuses and war crimes. Police Scotland's activities in Sri Lanka in 2016 were described as 'hypocrisy' by the Labour Party with criticism in particular levied at public order training (see e.g. BBC News, 2016, 2021; *The Herald*, 8 September 2013, 3 August 2014). As earlier chapters have outlined, controversy over UK international police training has not been confined to Scotland alone. Rarely have the positive experiences of Police Scotland officers (and other UK police) in relation to international policing assistance, knowledge transfer *and* exchange been reported within the wider media circles. Nor have the discussions surrounding the human rights components required within each policing programme (including in this instance the SLP) and the concept of scrutiny been raised. Police Scotland officers have discussed their frustration at being unable to engage on elements of international policing practice (including the provision of human rights training) and to explore when and how change can and might occur. Indeed, the divergence of opinion surrounding international policing have always had the potential to derail a programme. Following the initial Scottish-funded Sri Lanka community policing programme from August 2010 to March 2013, the funding—which had amounted to £400,000—ceased. From that time funding came directly from the UK government's conflict prevention pool and then CSSF (Author interview with former lead International Development and Innovation Unit, Police Scotland, February 2017). Yet the flurries of criticism directed towards Police Scotland (and also wider UK policing) have continued and have more often than not focused on human rights issues. In 2018, the Scottish police authority and Police Scotland considered whether an equality and human rights impact assessment should be carried out to consider the wider ramifications of international policing assistance surrounded human rights issues. The 2018 findings reflected some of the more personal views held by Police Scotland officers:

> Many of the countries who seek international police assistance have a negative history of equality, diversity and human rights issues. In undertaking international training deployments, Police Scotland is positively contributing towards a more inclusive society in line with both UK and Scottish Government policy. The procedure has already facilitated

projects in Malawi, Sri Lanka, Saudi Arabia, Maldives, United Arab Emirates and Bhutan focussing on child abuse, gender-based violence, community safety and neighbourhood policing strategies, child protection, public order and human rights. The International Police Assistance Board (IPAB) and Government are gatekeepers within the authorisation process and systematically consider whether requests for assistance are in line with the UK's international objectives which in themselves will be subject to equality assessments (Scottish Police Authority and Police Scotland, 2018).

Police Scotland has continued its longstanding capacity building programmes in Sri Lanka as well as other countries. It has more recently developed specialist activities related to public and child protection and gender and sexual based violence which has aligned with much of the wider development thinking across UK government in relation to post-conflict stabilization (see e.g. SU, 2019), and has been reflected in the 'partnership' forged between Police Scotland and the Malawi Police Service.

The Malawi police

Scotland and Malawi have a history of shared engagement dating back to the colonial period. The linkage between both nations has been encapsulated within David Livingstone's journeys in the late 1850s and the Scottish missions that then took his name (Ross, 2014). From 2004, a small international development fund (of at least £3 million and typically over £7 million) was provided for bilateral Scotland-Malawi projects. The following year, Scotland and Malawi signed a co-operation agreement which became the basis of a formal partnership and set out a framework for funding provided by the Scottish government for *Scottish* organizations to collaborate with a Malawian partner (Wilson, 2019). It also allowed the Scottish executive to exploit a loophole within the Scotland Act to provide international development assistance, which had originally been listed as a reserved power for UK government. Since 2005, around £4.5 million of Scottish funding has been made available, bolstered by the Scottish government's growing commitment to international development (Wilson, 2019). During the build-up to the Scottish referendum in September 2014, the Scottish government made an explicit commitment to maintaining 0.7 per cent of an independent Scotland's GNI for international development (Scottish Government, 2013).

Providing international policing assistance to the Malawi Police Service has become part of the Scotland–Malawi development agenda. Malawi, a former British colony from 1891 to 1964 inherited at independence a quasi-military style of policing (Sinclair, 2006). It was not until 1994, when the country became a multi-party state, that the question of police reform was brought to the political table. The development of a strategic plan for policing was from 1996 supported by UK policing, with training and study visits funded by the FCO (Luhanga, 2001). The Police Scotland project with Malawi came in response to the Malawian government's 2016–2017 food insecurity response plan, following an acknowledgement of the risk of community violence in areas that had previously been affected by severe flooding. Food insecurity had caused widespread community displacement with women and children at particular risk of violence and abuse: 'sex for food cases have been variously reported, some women and girls were allegedly asked to give sex in exchange to be transported to safer zones by local water transport owners during floods [women and children] have no proper house hold protection, making them vulnerable' (Republic of Malawi, 2016: 15). The Police Scotland project had a longer-term aim of supporting the Malawi Police Service in tackling the challenges of violence, abuse, and sexual exploitation of women and children in disaster affected districts, as well managing the prevalence of gender-based violence amongst displaced communities. The approach was to share 'good practice from Scottish experiences' and provide specialist training and mentoring focused on public and child protection and gender-based violence. The project was also later transferred to both Zambia and Rwanda (Author interview with Det Chief Inspector, Police Scotland, 7 August 2017 who deployed to Malawi in 2017).[4]

Police officers were initially selected by the Scottish police college for short-term deployments to Malawi. Each officer was required to have had at least eight years of prior service and typically an experience of working within a family protection unit. This included the necessary skills relating to public protection, child protection, sexual offences including rape, and gender-based violence, which were described as 'focal points'. Small numbers of approximately four police were deployed on two-week missions over a period of several months to cover dedicated urban and rural areas in Malawi in support of the local police (Author interviews with Police Scotland officers

---

[4] The Scottish international development fund provided £498,000 funds to Police Scotland from 2017 to 2018 for gender-based violence and child protection training in Malawi and Zambia.

who had deployed to Malawi in 2017 including two sergeants, two inspectors, and one detective chief inspector, August 2017). The project began with an initial scoping in January 2017 and provided what was described as a 'blank canvas' for specialist officers to make recommendations, develop training programmes, and build partnerships with local police. The first deployments concentrated on the food distribution sites in Southern Malawi where violence against women and children had been reported following the flooding, and required Police Scotland officers to engage with their Malawian counterparts as well as a wide range of stakeholders.

While most officers had been selected for their experience in child and public protection, few had prior experience of an international mission and had volunteered to gain a different policing experience to back home. This experience was described by many as highly motivating although challenging, which 'took time to get our heads around'. This was particularly true of the cultural awareness and political sensitivity issues that most police faced in Malawi. However, there was also widespread recognition of the importance to *Scotland* in 'assisting countries that we have close links with', and that Police Scotland was building its own reputation overseas (Author interviews with Police Scotland officers, August 2017). From 2017 to 2019 the Scottish government supported a £10 million international development fund for 'partner countries' Malawi, Rwanda, Zambia, and Pakistan under which there were three dedicated funding streams: development assistance, capacity strengthening, and commercial investment initiatives. Police Scotland's projects fell under stream two with provision for £500,000 over a three-year period (2017 to 2019) in support of specialist training for tackling gender-based violence and improving child protection in Malawi, Zambia, and Rwanda. From 2019, the police partnership programmes in Malawi and Zambia were expanded to include 'marginalized groups such as women, children, those with disabilities, lesbian, gay, bisexual and transgender people and people with albinism' highlighted as particularly vulnerable (Author interviews with Police Scotland officers, August 2017).

The 'new' Northern Irish policing brand

From RUC to PSNI—reform and transformation

The RUC as described in earlier chapters developed from the early 1970s as an organization that prioritized security duties of a quasi-military nature

(Ellison and Smyth, 2000). The organization struggled to heal the rift within a deeply divided society, maintain community cohesion and to bring 'policing with the community' to all citizens (Mulcahy, 2006). The RUC, however, was no stranger to police reform and had been exposed to on-going attempts within the previous decade culminating in the Hunt Report in 1969 (O'Rawe, 2003; Topping, 2008). Hunt's recommendations were partially implemented before rapidly being overturned as Northern Ireland slid into chaos. In the intervening years it was widely acknowledged that *change* was required in policing for ,as Mary O'Rawe and Linda Moore (1997) commented, 'it [was] a difficult challenge for most institutions, and particularly police bodies imbued with a sense of tradition and organisational loyalty ...our research confirmed that not only is change possible, and indeed necessary, but that police themselves, once convinced of the need, can become active proponents of change (O'Rawe and Moore, 1997: 211).

At the time that O'Rawe and Moore published their detailed report 'Human Rights on Duty' outlining 'principles and practice which should inform and shape new policing arrangements', policing in Northern Ireland was faced with imminent change: 'dependent upon a combination of the right planning, a willingness to be open and accountable, good leadership and the right structures in place to manage change' (O'Rawe and Moore, 1997: 249). This became a real possibility following the 1994 ceasefires as the RUC was able through a 'cautious response as the violence subsided' to assume in some areas a more 'conventional community role (Ryder, 2000: 442). It was at this time that political leaders began a debate of the future role and size of the RUC. Subsequently the Northern Ireland Office, the Police Authority, and the RUC jointly establishing a fundamental review of policing (April 1995), led by the then CC Ronnie Flannagan. Certainly, the review was an attempt to 'define the level of policing Northern Ireland would need in the years ahead', to outline budget considerations although Flannagan was clear that his 'work would not be handcuffed to financial considerations only'. The collection of evidence from across the organization, the public sector, as well as perceived good practice from Ireland and other UK constabularies was an attempt to secure a 'radical blueprint for future policing ... the most sweeping policy and organizational shake-up in the history of the RUC which would turn the pyramid of command upside down ..' (Ryder, 2000: 452).[5] Fundamentally this was an attempt to

---

[5] Additionally, in 1997, a formal enquiry chaired by the former Norther Ireland Secretary Peter Brooke was held into the composition, recruitment, and training of the RUC which

bring the policing of Northern Ireland closely into line with *British* policing (Murphy, 2015), to erode the Irish/Northern Irish characteristics and inject a certain Britishness or civilianization. While Flannagan's review was subsequently 'frozen', 165 out of 175 recommendations in the subsequent Patten report mirrored those earlier identified in the fundamental review (Ryder, 2000).

The Patten report published in September 1999 was, however, the real instigator of change highlighting that policing in Northern Ireland 'was contrary to policing practice in the rest of the United Kingdom' which 'left the police in an unenviable position' (Patten Report, 1999: 2). Despite the commission having 'studied policing in other countries', they '[could] discover no model that can simply be applied to Northern Ireland' and that there were 'plenty of examples of police services wrestling with the same sort of challenges' (Patten Report, 1999: 3). On its publication, Patten stated that the report heralded a transformation rather than a disbandment of RUC (Mulcahy, 2008: 179), that this would be built upon concepts of best practice embedded deeply within the new organization. At the heart of the Patten report lay a human rights-based approach that would drive operational policing, which included a new oath of office, a code of ethics, and the integration of a human rights agenda within the training curriculum (Patten Report, 1999). This aligned with the Belfast agreement proposal that 'arrangements should be based on principles of protection of human rights and professional integrity' (Northern Ireland Human Rights Commission, 1999) and would feed directly into public order and community policing.

Policing with the community

Recommendation 44 of the Patten report outlined the development and delivery of a *policing with the community* strategy that further underpinned the police transformation process (Patten, 1999). The Patten commission addressed the problems of policing Northern Ireland's segregated communities through the concept of community policing: a 'genuine' police *and* community partnership which would entail collaborative working, 'the mainspring of police work'. This applied

---

resulted in a report published in 1998. The report was revealing in that it outlined the slow pace of change which was altered by the Patten Commission.

to all aspects of policing: 'police officers who are working closely with the communities they police will be much better to deal with the problems of parades, demonstrations or other events emanating from those communities or passing through their area' (Patten, 1999: 53). Mulcahy suggested that a focus oriented towards *policing* rather than the *police* transcended 'beyond the boundaries of traditional police-centred activities' (traditionally security focused) and provided 'scope for consideration of new partnerships'. Community policing would sit at the core of this new policing structure alongside accountability mechanisms, organizational structure, establishment, composition, recruitment, symbolism, and human rights (Mulcahy, 2008: 154–7). Patten, however, remained objective and did not refer to a complete lack of evidence of community policing in Northern Ireland. Indeed, the report referenced what the commission perceived as examples of good practice. This included a neighbourhood policing unit in the Langanside area of Belfast, which had operated during the 1990s throughout a volatile security situation and saw one of the architects, Sergeant Stephen Jones awarded the national policing award for community policing (Patten Report, 1999; Ryder, 2000). Following the Patten recommendations, PSNI adopted a so-called 'policing with the community' philosophy filtered through distinctive categories including accountability, empowerment, problem solving, partnership, and service delivery. While academic debate has tended to suggest that 'policing with the community' supported the 'politics of reform' rather than impacting 'meaningful change on the ground' (Topping, 2008: 391), from an organizational perspective it certainly contributed to something of a cultural shift and opened the longstanding debate relating to police-community confrontation that had largely dominated Northern Ireland (Bryne, 2014).

The implementation of Patten's 175 recommendations had been largely completed by May 2007 and confirmed by the oversight commissioner, and sat alongside over 1,000 recommendations put forward by the concomitant policing structures and bodies including the policing board, district policing partnerships, and ombudsman. This brought substantive organizational and 'high stakes' policing change (Murphy, McDowell and Braniff, 2016: 117) managed through a process of adaptive leadership internally and supported by external consultants. Change was described as a 'root and branch' transformation which challenged serving police in their day-to-day frontline policing: in 2009 it was estimated that almost 5,000 serving

PSNI officers were former RUC (Murphy, McDowell, and Braniff, 2016). The challenges surrounding police and justice transformation provided a springboard for wider discussion around police reform both nationally and internationally.

PSNI as a template for post-conflict change management

The peace process has been a *process* and Northern Ireland has remained a 'society in transition' since 1998 (Byrne, 2014). Police reform necessitated substantive *change* to the institutional structures and management and, in the operational behaviour of police *on the ground*. In discussions with former RUC–PSNI there has been acknowledgement that first, the acceptance that change was needed was required. Secondly, that the processes (initiated by Flannagan in his fundamental review and endorsed in the Patten report recommendations) impacted the 'new' PSNI in several ways: the removal of the symbolism that had been integral to RUC was a highly emotive and painful process that pushed some police into early retirement; institutional change brought *developmental concepts* to the organization through change management and fostered a degree of modernization and professionalism, where previously there had been a focus on securitization. Security policing had had budgetary constraints: 'after Patten we could spend money on computers like the mainland rather than bullet proof glass'. Thirdly, change created and made official multiple accountability structures, brought oversight and scrutiny embedding human rights and policing. Managing, learning from and the application of these processes of change provided a *template for change* that was perceived both internally and externally as a 'change model for policing' within FCAS and wider SSR (Author interviews with former senior RUC–PSNI officers 2018 to 2021).

The Patten report had only touched on international policing, recommending that Northern Ireland policing should co-operate more widely with other police services and credited the RUC with an international reputation; the officers 'had much to give as well as much to gain'. This provided opportunities 'to provide more training for overseas police services in their areas of excellence. Additionally, participation in PSOs, and other international policing opportunities, including secondments to Interpol and

Europol, were recommended (Patten Report, 1999: 101–4).[6] PSNI would then go on to benefit from what Graham Ellison and Conor O'Reilly (2008a) described as the 'overall context of Northern Ireland's "geo-branding" and efforts to enhance its reputational status internationally' (Ellison and O'Reilly, 2008a: 331). A concerted effort had been made by some Northern Ireland's politicians to use the experiences of the peace process 'as a model for ethnic troublespots around the globe ... a model for conflict resolution (Wilson, 2010: 3). Why not apply this to policing?

International investment had provided much needed support to Northern Ireland's economic environment; the private sector having encouraged direct foreign investment while remaining politically neutral throughout the Good Friday negotiations. International investment was also brought in under the auspices of Invest Northern Ireland (Invest NI), formerly the industrial development board, a government agency that actively promoted inward investment (The Portland Trust, 2007). Invest NI also supported the security sector *within* Northern Ireland, promoting 'businesses and organisations that are involved in delivering a range of security services from consultancy, intelligence gathering and training, through to forensic toxicology ... [these organizations] have developed cutting-edge products that are relied upon around the world to assist and safeguard police and fire fighters working in dangerous and hostile environments' (Invest Northern Ireland, 2014). By 2014, Invest NI listed fifty-eight companies that provided security expertise and consultancy services. This included Northern Ireland Cooperation Overseas (NI-CO), a not-for-profit public body dedicated to 'sharing the experiences of Northern Ireland's security sector including policing and institutional capacity building'. Additionally, NI-CO has had direct links with government departments and public sector institutions across the UK and Ireland and has provided training assistance, institutional capacity building, and consultancy across a diverse range of areas that have included agriculture,

---

[6] 'We also recommend that the British government should offer former reservists the opportunity to participate in British policing contingents in UN peacekeeping operations. Their skills, including firearms knowledge, could well be in demand in such operations. (Patten: 13:20) Several police services from Great Britain have participated in such operations in recent years as has the Garda Siochana. The RUC has not participated in the past, yet it has many skills which would be valuable in such situation. We recommend that the Northern Ireland Police should be ready to participate in future United Nations peace-keeping operations and we express the strong hope that they be invited to do so. We would also encourage the Northern Ireland police to seek out other international policing opportunities, for example secondments to Interpol and Europol' (Patten: 18.20).

healthcare, governance, justice, and policing, and consumer protection services (NI-CO, 2020). NI-CO has supported PSNI in building its international portfolio and reputation to generate income through policing services during a time of financial uncertainty and austerity. The trigger factor was certainly the changed processes undertaken as a result of the Patten recommendations as highlighted by a former PSNI chief superintendent (2011):

> The Report of the Independent Commission on Police Reform in Northern Ireland (Patten Report) is widely regarded as introducing unprecedented change into a policing organization. Having recently emerged from 30 years of conflict, the Police Service of Northern Ireland has had to deal with the challenge of building relationships with communities traditionally hostile to the police particularly at certain times of the year. We learnt many lessons as we worked through our own change process and some of these changes might be beneficial to police in other countries (Author interview with former Chief Supt RUC–PSNI, January 2011).

Over the past decade PSNI has supported policing programmes facilitated by NI-CO that have been approved by the Northern Ireland policing board and the department of justice. PSNI has deployed officers as part of the Northern Irish policing officer to Albania, Armenia, Bahrain, Bolivia, Croatia, Jordan, Kosovo, Lebanon, Oman, Venezuela, and Qatar amongst others and often through bilateral as opposed to multilateral programmes. In addition, RUC–PSNI police retirees (including those 'Patten leavers') have been selected specifically for their Northern Irish experiences and have worked as consultants across the Balkans, the Middle East, and South Asia although some returned to PSNI as civilian staff having taken an early retirement package.

As the reputation of PSNI spread internationally so the commercialization of that Northern Irish policing offer was developed. The concept of a PSNI brand, however, has been problematic for some RUC–PSNI retirees who have argued that sharing 'good practice' both nationally and internationally has been more important that the commercialization of the brand (Author interviews with former RUC–PSNI, 2015 to 2021). Certainly, from 2000, the opportunity to deploy large numbers of Northern Irish officers to the Balkans and then Iraq, was bolstered by Patten's recommendation that 'police numbers should be substantially reduced' from an establishment of

13,000 regulars, full and part-time reserves (Patten Report, 1999: 75).[7] With PSNI deemed too 'people heavy', the release of police cohorts to Kosovo was fortuitous and a useful starting point in demonstrating how the organization could be reduced. Subsequently and with every overseas programme, PSNI has also demonstrated how international policing can 'provide a lateral learning and professional development opportunity ... at no cost to the service and can bring additional learning for PSNI in terms of continuous improvement ... as well as support[ing] police services and justice ministries of the varies countries to address the challenges they face and enable them to work more effectively with other regional and international law enforcement and criminal justice agencies' (PSNI, 2015a: 1–5).

Supporting police reform in Bolivia and the Philippines

PSNI have engaged with international police reform and development driven by an experience of the processes of 'change' and wider lessons learning. One example was PSNI's engagement with the Bolivian police between 2005 and approximately 2011. Despite a so-called return to democracy in the late 1980s, governments in Latin America had been slow to prioritize police reform, rising levels of criminality and violence which the police had failed to curb owing more broadly to poor training, low levels of pay, and resultant corruption and criminal complicity. The literature has suggested that most Latin American police remained unpopular with the public and that high levels of citizen distrust were based on poor police efficacy, corruption, and excessive uses of force (see, for example, Dammert, 2019; Macaulay, 2012; Prado, Trebilcock, and Hartford, 2012).

Securing interest and funding for police reform in Bolivia emanated from an original request by the British High Commission to the FCO for support with improving civil-military co-operation. Following a period of escalating tensions between the police and the military in Bolivia, opportunities were identified to developing capacity-building projects in order to enhance civil-military co-operation, particularly within the context of public protest. One of the first PSNI officers to deploy to Bolivia suggested that the FCO made their original approach to the MPS, who in the spirit

---

[7] In 2001 (year 1) of the voluntary retirement scheme, 483 officers left between January and March 2001. From 2001 to 2002, 812 officers took the retirement package Hansard (2001).

of pick-and-mix within the UK policing brand pointed to PSNI as having more suitable experience for that particular context. The police-military team seconded initially to Bolivia included a serving PSNI officer, a serving military officer, and a military retiree and resulted in a collaborative PSNI-military training provided jointly to the Bolivian police and military, using the public order ACPO guidance manual 'keeping the peace' as a training benchmark. The support provided during this early phase was augmented by further requests for a community policing programme while PSNI were in-country delivering public order training. In particular, assistance was requested to improve police-community engagement and support the delivery of 'citizen security'. While this FCO programme was in financial terms comparatively small—approximately £500,000—it was described as 'ambitious' in the extreme. Initial scoping had revealed 'little evidence of a genuine understanding of the concept beyond simply being courteous and responding to calls for assistance. The officers [in Bolivia] were badly equipped and patrolled out of very basic station facilities.' The training delivered was based on presentations and engagement with local police commanders (Author interview with former Chief Supt PSNI 2011 who deployed to Bolivia and based on internal reports written at the time).

There is scant detail within the academic literature charting institutional police reform in Bolivia (as well as Paraguay and Uruguay). However, recent research (2019) has acknowledged that 'community policing ... has been a model of policing supported by major donors and multilateral agencies. The importation of concepts and its effects is an issue that requires further research, as in most cases the lack of adjustment to country-specific contexts has undermined results (Dammert, 2019). PSNI sought to pilot Northern Irish experiences of community policing within dedicated districts and to share lessons learned from a post-conflict environment and subsequent reform (2011):

> by the ... Patten Report [which] transformed the policing landscape, in Northern Ireland and has resulted in the PSNI being recognized as one of the most democratically accountable policing organizations in the world. We sought to use our knowledge of the significant change process that our own policing organization went through in order to demonstrate that a concentration on an ethos or philosophy of community policing needs to be complemented by structural and institutional change if the Bolivian police are to fundamentally change their

relationship with the community that they serve (Author interview with former Chief Supt PSNI, 2011).

In 2006, PSNI reported that from a programme perspective, there had been some signs of greater collaboration between the police and public through building on existing community networks and in working in schools, which had 'helped to reinforce the role of the citizen in their own security' (Author interview with former Chief Supt PSNI, 2011). Later research undertaken in Bolivia from 2013 to 2014 looked at local concepts of community policing. It suggested that the Bolivian community policing model sought to expand on the idea of 'civic groups', established in 1994, which included 'neighbourhood councils, school brigades for security and civil support groups to the police', and through community policing. This would include 'neighbourhood security brigades', embedded within the community and managed by the police 'whose task is to create a culture of public security and "peaceful coexistence of communities"...' (Jakobsen and Burr, 2019: 103–4).

The Patten reform agenda became an attractive proposition in some countries undertaking policing reform and there have been instances where the Patten report was exported as a template. In 2014, an independent commission on policing in the Philippines made up of local police representatives as well as externals including Royal Canadian Mounted Police officers, published details findings and recommendation for 'the reform of policing services in Bangasamoro and the wider Philippines community'. The introductory section noted that the Patten report had been 'used as a reference document and guide' and that acknowledgement was given to 'the authors of the Patten report for the tremendous assistance the report provided to the Independent Commission on Policing for the Bangsamoro'. The recommendations encapsulated within the report mirrored those outlined by Patten (ICP, 2014: 1–3) and were endorsed independently by RCMP within the report.

This perceived transfer of learning from PSNI to other police has also been part of a process of cross fertilization within wider UK policing. While knowledge transfer has always featured in UK policing, some senior PSNI have suggested that there was a rising interest across the UK of the PSNI experiences of policing public order post-Patten. PSNI officers became part of the ACPO (England, Wales, and Northern Ireland) national working group on public order from 2005. Some senior officers contributed to the updated 2010 'Keeping the Peace', a manual that renewed the guidance surrounding public order policing, drawing partly on PSNI's post-Patten experiences and the integration of human rights within use of force. The report outlined what it described as the 'distinctiveness of the original British style of policing' with core values that included accountability, discretion, impartiality, and independence, which included Northern Ireland (APCO ACPOS NPIA, 2010: 8). Her Majesty's Inspectorate of Constabulary (HMIC) too had surveyed PSNI during an inspection of public order policing in England, Wales, and Northern Ireland following serious concerns raised by government during the G20 London summit protests in April 2009. Then there was clear reference to a 'British model' (including Northern Ireland) although with far less consideration given to Scotland and the Scottish experiences of policing protest (see HMIC, 2009, 2011). The recommendations drew on 'core values of the British policing model' (in a similar vein to ACPO) included the 'adoption of a set of fundamental principles on the use of force which run as a golden thread through *all* [sic] aspects of police business', including a focus on human rights and sufficiently levels of accountability. This fed into concepts of 'the minimum use of force and the requirement for a measured and calculated route to escalation where the use of force is a possibility' (HMIC, 2009: 7). There was certainly an interest in Northern Ireland and the challenges faced when dealing with public order situations. Policing protest and managing public disorder *always* had the potential for higher levels of violence than the 'mainland', which necessitated different 'tactical solutions' including water cannon and plastic baton rounds (Author interview with former Chief Superintendent, PSNI and former public order ACPO advisor).[8] Yet the Patten report outlined the need to different tactical approaches to policing public disorder that included less 'lethal alternatives' to the plastic baton round which necessitated a wider range of equipment. The introduction of newer tactics was accompanied by 'rigorous training to ensure that all new technologies were used appropriately and safely and that officers could demonstrate that they were well aware of law, human rights and policy issues' following recommendations laid out in the Patten report (Author interview with former Sergeant RUC–PSNI, trainer and public order specialist, February 2011).

---

[8] PSNI key principles of policing public order and protest are enshrined in Police Service of Northern Ireland Manual of Policy, Procedure and Guidance on Conflict Management' (PSNI, November 2014) and Authorised Professional Practice for Public Order, College of Policing (2014).

Concluding comment

The UK policing brand (re)shaped from the start of the twenty-first century with Police Scotland and PSNI becoming added to the overall international offer. However, with the reforming of the UK policing brand came a fragmentation within the delivery of international policing across the four-nation state. The development of a Police Scotland *brand* was linked to Scotland's political trajectory following devolution and then the Scottish independence referendum. Within that came a drive to promote brand *Scotland* internationally. The amalgamation of the eight regional Scottish forces may have distilled regional characteristics but nonetheless Police Scotland has established a brand in its own right and one that has been exported internationally. The promotion of Scottish interests internationally has seen a slow but steady growth over the past eight years with a particular growth in bilateral projects within the priority countries. The organization benefitted from the Scottish government's international development agenda and the Scottish funding that was made available as well as wider UK ODA funding. The quest for international partnerships was bolstered by the governing Scottish Nationalist's party's drive for enhanced political autonomy and by opposing the Brexit referendum (Gethins, 2021). Promoting Scottish interests overseas has been part of this equation and has benefitted Police Scotland while the Police and Fire Reform (Scotland) Act 2012 outlined a possible framework for a standalone Scottish policing brand (see Fyfe, 2014; Thompson, 2019).

As the Scottish Government (and Police Scotland) have sought to promote the Scottish policing brand, so public bodies (and PSNI) have packaged the Northern Irish policing offer, which is 'not monolithic, but segmented and targeted towards a number of different "consumers" both domestically and internationally' (Ellison and O'Reilly, 2008a: 331). In 2021, the security and policing expertise rooted in conflict and post-conflict environments has largely been eroded and those RUC police retirees have left Iraq and Afghanistan. The RUC 'model' has been replaced by PSNI's *brand*, one built upon the *internal* experiences of transformational change within a lengthy post-conflict environment and the application of the lessons that accompanied that change. The original Irish semi-military model of policing has shifted towards civilianization, or as government and police have likened more recently to a 'British model' (ACPO ACPOS NPIA, 2010; HMIC, 2009, 2011). For a while, the RUC–PSNI brand co-existed: RUC police retirees became security, policing, and intelligence contractors in

Iraq and Afghanistan (see chapter 4) with some remaining within FCAS in 2021. Those RUC–PSNI officers who lived through the experiences of change management and institutional reform within a post-conflict environment have developed different skills and expertise for international transfer. As the RUC legacy has faded into memory so a PSNI brand has developed, fostered by public bodies and private companies that have actively promoted brand Northern Ireland which has included policing, justice, and security services. These transitions have revealed evidence of further cracks within UK policing, a brand that may have become more fragmented than at any time in its history. While there may be additional UK policing characteristics on offer internationally, the dichotomy *within the UK* has been an increased resistance to the centralization, co-ordination, and delivery of international policing and a tendency for separation within the four-nation state. Additionally, as international policing has grown as a commodity, so individual forces within England and Wales have sought out international opportunities either solo or as part of wider UK policing. The future trajectory of international policing may further fragment or there may be opportunities within a post-Brexit Global Britain agenda for synchronization as the chapter 8 considers.

8
'Global Britain' and the Future of International Policing Assistance

> UK international policing will be challenged as we move into the twenty first century. How can the UK deliver capacity building and assistance overseas without deploying serving officers? What role then for retirees and for the military if the UK is to participate in post-conflict stabilisation and reconstruction in what may be a more dangerous world?
> **Stabilisation Unit representative, 2020**

The UK's exit from the EU was finally completed on 1 January 2021 almost five years after the 2016 Brexit referendum and has represented one of the biggest challenges economically and politically since the Second World War (Chalmers, 2020a). Brexit collided with the Covid-19 pandemic, an even greater disruptor to global order, creating an acute health and economic crisis and further destabilizing an already weakened international rules-based system (Cimmino et al., 2020). Since the Brexit referendum, the UK has shifted its international position and embraced the concept of 'Global Britain', first used in an official capacity in 2016 by the then prime minister Theresa May.[1] Yet there has been something of a discrepancy between the national projection of 'Global Britain' and an international view held of the UK as a 'middle power'. On the one hand the UK's foreign and

---

[1] In June 2018, the Government launched a webpage that brought together key official documents relating to 'Global Britain'. The FCO noted the establishment of a 'new cross-HMG' Global Britain Board chaired by an FCO Director General as well as an FCO Global Britain taskforce 'to implement the expansion of the diplomatic network, take forward policy development and devise metrics for measuring progress'. Government ministers (including the then Foreign Secretary) continued to invoke the term regularly since that time, for example, 'Global Britain is leading the world as a force for good' Dominic Raab, FCO, 23 September 2019 (Robinson and Lunn, 2020).

Exporting the UK Policing Brand 1989–2021. Georgina Sinclair, Oxford University Press. © Georgina Sinclair 2022. DOI: 10.1093/oso/9780198743200.003.0009

security policy 'has moved in a more global direction' (Chalmers, 2020a: 3), but on the other hand, the UK's power has long been dwarfed by the US, EU, and China, and threatened by an international relations fragmentation in global trends. A weakening of global institutions which were once at the heart of this international order has contributed to an erosion of an earlier international rules-based system. Western multilateralism *per se* that was earlier reliant on a rules-based system has been challenged whether in relation to collective security, defence, or trade. With evidence that key international players including Russia, China, India, and Saudi Arabia have reoriented their foreign and securities policies towards a more nationalist and less-rules based stance, there has been some sense of a 'world that is moving in the opposite direction' (Chalmers, 2020a: 3).

Government restructuring, austerity, the pandemic, and cuts to overseas budgets from 2020 have had a noticeable impact. The UK aid budget, which had greatly augmented since 1990, had been one of the largest in the world (DfID, 2019). As described in the previous chapters, the earlier support for overseas interventions saw a goldrush of international policing. That era has passed. What are the future implications for international policing and how will the new (2021) government approaches (including the integrated and defence reviews (2021)) to security, defence, and development shape UK policing's support for bilateral and multilateral missions? Who will deliver international policing in the future? Will it remain the preserve of the corporate sector and a commercial enterprise for UK policing or will there be a (re)engagement with the UN, EU, and NATO? The challenges of policing at home may well place an emphasis on the further commercialization of policing *activities* rather than multilateral *assistance*. The recent and future direction of the UK's foreign, security, and defence agendas *will* impact UK policing and by extension international policing.

'Homeland First'? New challenges for UK policing in the twenty-first century

'UK policing today is under the microscope' stated a Deloitte 2019 report while a 'spike in serious violence and falling detection rates in some parts of the country have brought political focus onto the resilience of a model of policing that has long been the envy of the world' (Taylor, 2019: 1). Within the past decade, public safety and security challenges have been 'transformed by technology, globalisation ... [which] has contributed to a more complex landscape of crime and harm' with rising levels of crime including domestic violence, rape, child sexual exploitation, money laundering, cyber and digital crime, and narcotics trafficking (Muir et al., 2020: 3). In 2020, the NPCC with the Association of PCCs, categorically stated that policing would 'need to change' as 'globalisation continues to accelerate and present new challenges resulting in a rise in the complexity of the police task' (NPCC APCC, 2020). The 'problems' as identified within England and Wales (and could also be attributed in equal measure to Scotland and Northern Ireland) amounted to what the College of Policing (2020) described as:

> ... complex rather than merely complicated, which is to say they are fast-moving, cannot be broken apart and solved piece by piece, have little regard for established jurisdictional, bureaucratic or disciplinary boundaries and morph into new problems as a result of interventions to deal with them. Issues such as cybercrime, terrorism and organised crime transcend national borders and require cooperation both inside and outside government to solve. At the same time, many volume crimes are rooted in deeply entrenched social, economic and cultural problems, with policing just one of many actors responsible for their resolution. Few, if any, of these problems can be resolved by traditional, reactive policing approaches. Instead they require new approaches blending intelligence collection, data analysis, new technologies, specialist skills and problem-solving (College of Policing, 2020: 80).

A gap had opened between the commonly held perceptions of a twenty-first century policing brand and the reality, one that had moved beyond the 'traditional aims, values and ways of working' as a result of the contemporary threats (College of Policing, 2020: 80). Many of these deep-rooted issues have applied to policing *across the UK* where a 'transformation in the nature of the landscape of public safety and security requires us to think much harder and more imaginatively' (Muri and Walcott with Higgins and Halkon, 2020).

These challenges have been further exacerbated by an economic decline and the subsequent fiscal strategy of austerity. The UK's departure from the EU took place at a time of economic decline that has continued since the 2008 financial crisis, widening inequality between the north and south of the country and inducing a stagnation in productivity and real wages. Following the introduction of public austerity in 2010, the public sector faced financial challenges through budgetary cuts. While fiscal austerity realized a reduction in budget deficit (prior to the pandemic) the impact on public services was hugely significant (Chalmers, 2020a). There has been a decrease in the police budget of around twenty-two per cent across England and Wales, with most savings gained through the reductions in police officers, community support officers, and staff. By March 2015, the total police workforce had decreased by 14 per cent from 243,900 in 2010 to 209,500 in 2015; a reduction of approximately 34,400 personnel (HMIC, 2014 cited in Mann, Devendran, and Lundrigan, 2020). A decline in police numbers has overstretched frontline policing. While a prime ministerial pledge to recruit 20,000 new officers in England and Wales within three years was made, this has equated to roughly the same number lost during the ten years of austerity (*The Guardian*, 30 April 2020). Some commentators even suggested that the figure should more likely be 50,000 with many officers planning retirement or to leave the service owing to poor morale.

Reductions in police budgets have been made by reducing or spending less on goods and services and applying the 'same cost reductions across all budgets regardless of the importance of the specific area of policing'. Fiscal austerity has brought debate regarding police effectiveness and 'consequent implications for crime control and public protection' (Millie and Bullock, 2013 cited in Mann, Devendran, and Lundrigan, 2020: 630). A *Police Foundation* report noted that while funding had continued to fall, 'the policing mission' had augmented in its complexity and tasks (Higgins, 2020).

The economic issues have been worsened by a deepening global health crisis. The impact of the coronavirus crisis (while still ongoing at the time of writing) was described as having a 'profound but likely short term' impact which would increase pressure on UK policing (Walton and Falkner, 2020). The provisions of the Coronavirus Act (March 2020) gave the police powers to support health professionals after the UK was placed in lockdown. Additionally, the Health Protection (Coronavirus, Restrictions) (England) Regulations (March 2020) gave further police powers including dispersal of groups and fines for noncompliance (Muri and Walcott with Higgins and Halkon, 2020). Since 2020, the police have faced increased criticism over their handling of the pandemic lockdowns and public order issues (e.g. movement for Black Lives Matter, 'kill the bill' (police, crime sentencing, and courts bill 2021), and the vigil for Sarah Everard organized on 13 March 2021) with the BBC stating that public protest had become one of the 'hardest jobs in modern policing' (BBC, 2021).

In 2021, the government laid out that 'the precondition for Global Britain is the safety of our citizens at home and the security of the Euro-Atlantic region, where the bulk of the UK's security focus will remain' (Integrated Review, 2021: 14). The IR recognized the essential role of policing in ensuring UK domestic security from transnational threats including terrorism and serious and organized crime. In tackling these issues, government support was promised to further integrate the UK's counterterrorism capabilities by developing a new counterterrorism operations centre, bolstering the NCA capacity and through 'regional and local policing, and sustaining our international networks so that we are able to address the links between criminality from the local to international levels' (Integrated Review, 2021: 20, 32). Broadening and deepening integrated capability across government and the wider public sector has built on the 2018 NSCR fusion doctrine: 'coherent implementation by bringing together defence, diplomacy, development, intelligence and security, trade and aspects of domestic policy in pursuit of cross-government, national objectives' (Integrated Review, 2021: 19). However, any practical application of the fusion doctrine has remained a work in progress across government departments although across policing and wider law enforcement there has always been a degree of operational synchronization and informal networking.

As of mid-2021, UK policing faced multiple challenges that are knotty and difficult to address, a continuing if not increased pressure on budgets and staffing levels. Yet this came at a time when the government raised the importance of homeland first through the strengthening of the UK's security systems (including policing) to protect the public from growing transnational security threats (IR, 2021).[2] This future trend towards a strengthening of security responses to SOC and CT will necessitate a continued investment in police resource to ensure a balanced future operating environment (see e.g. College of Policing, 2020).[3] Meeting the ongoing

[2] 3,005 recruits joined as part of the government's uplift programme. In total, forces recruited 6,435 officers from November 2019 to March 2020 including recruitment planned before the programme was announced; 6,345 new police officers were recruited between November and March in England and Wales—3,005 of these were via the uplift programme. There are now a total of 131,596 officers, a 5 per cent increase on March 2019 in England and Wales (Grierson, 2020).

[3] The CoP 2020 Future Operating Environment 2040 report identified key challenges and ten trends: rising inequality and social fragmentation; an expanding and unregulated information space; changes in trust; technological change and convergence; harnessing artificial intelligence; workforce automation; larger, older, more diverse population; economic transitions; growing influence of no-state actors; climate change, environmental decline, and greater competition for resources (College of Policing, 2020).

security challenges—climate change, the pandemic, terrorism, and hostile state deterrence—may take up any of the available slack in policing as resources become increasingly constrained. With the UK out of the EU, there may be future challenges in managing homeland first, which will impact upon the delivery of international policing by the official state sector.

Exiting the European Union

Foreign, external security, and defence policy barely featured in the 2016 Brexit referendum campaign or the British government's lengthy pre-referendum report (Bond, 2020). Subsequently, the then Prime Minister Theresa May sought 'an ambitious partnership covering the breadth of security interests including foreign policy, defence [and] development' (UK Department for Exiting the European Union 2018: 51)—the political declaration that accompanied the withdrawal agreement highlighted an 'ambitious, close and lasting' security co-operation (Bond, 2020: 4). Despite the 'ambitions' outlined, there have been obstacles to renewing collaboration between UK policing and EU law enforcement agencies.

Operationally, security, law enforcement, and criminal justice had been key areas of collaboration between the UK and the EU, which following Brexit have required protracted processes of (re)negotiation. This has included all areas of judicial and criminal co-operation; extradition procedures (e.g. the European arrest warrant); policing and intelligence co-operation; management of the UK border system; and the relationship with Europol and the EU agency for criminal justice co-operation (Eurojust). Europol has been involved in 'international crime-fighting', encompassing counterterrorism, narcotics, human trafficking, child sexual exploitation and trafficking, financial crime, cybercrime, and the publication of threat assessments (see Rozée, Kaunert, and Léonard, 2013). Until 2018, Europol was led by Rob Wainwright (from the UK) who had been at the helm for nine years and included other seconded UK officers. UK policing had a long-standing linkage with Europol and had led on a number of thematic issues where the UK was seen as having specific expertise: modern slavery, human trafficking, cybercrime, and cigarette smuggling. In the past UK police were also seconded to Eurojust, an organization which has grouped national judicial authorities together to combat serious organized cross-border crime, coordinated EU-wide investigations and prosecutions of transnational crime, where the UK was seen as having an 'important and well-established role' (Author interview with UK police officers deployed to Europol, 9 December 2017).

While a trade and co-operation agreement was eventually finalized, the paltry access to EU criminal justice and security data raised concern in many quarters. This included access to EU data systems and data sharing tools and real 'gaps' which have resulted in protracted negotiations to find solutions to joint working. In March 2021, the House of Lords EU committee commended the fact that 'government has ... succeeded in avoiding an abrupt end of years of effective UK–EU joint working in these areas, which would have put the safety of citizens in the UK and across the EU at greater risk ... but there were grounds *for caution*' [author emphasis]. Access to European data systems and data-sharing tools had been built up over time to facilitate co-operation between EU Member States in policing and security and to ensure the exchange of wide-ranging information in real-time: suspects, extradition, missing persons, criminal records, DNA and fingerprint data, and so on. The UK was previously the second largest contributor to Europol's information systems, for example, and accessed roughly forty per cent of all data messaging. Over time the EU generated dedicated data systems including the Schengen information system II (SIS II) described as 'the most widely used and largest information sharing system for security and border management in Europe' (EU commission cited in House of Lords EU Committee, 2021b: 24), to which the UK had 'regrettably lost access' (2021b):

> ... Witnesses to past inquiries have repeatedly highlighted the vital role this system has played in supporting the operations of UK law enforcement agencies. At a joint evidence session held by the EU Justice and Home Affairs Sub-Committees in February 2020, Deputy Assistant Commissioner Richard Martin, of the National Police Chiefs' Council, told us that in 2019 UK police checked SIS II '603 million times' ... the fallback for UK police forces, to replace SIS II after the end of the transition period on 31 December 2020, was the Interpol I-24/7 database. Assistant Chief Constable Ayling described this as an arrangement that 'falls a long way short' of the benefits provided by SIS II (House of Lords EU Committee, 2021b: 24–5).

Other systems included Prüm for sharing databases on DNA profiles, vehicle registration data and fingerprints, passenger name record data to log individuals travelling to and from other members states and develop travel pattern analysis, and the European criminal records information system (ECRIS) which enabled real-time information exchange of criminal convictions across other Member States (HoC Home Affairs Committee, 2018). While the December 2020 agreement made provision for PNR data to be shared and for continued access to other systems, the UK no longer has any influence in shaping the development data collection and sharing tools (House of Lords EU Committee, 2021b: 5).

As of March 2021, detailed and complex negotiations were underway to establish data protection issues subjected to an EU enquiry into the UK's future data handling in alignment with EU data protection regulations. A myriad of other issues relating to law enforcement collaboration, 'the very "unsexy" side of Brexit' remained locked in negotiations, 'the stuff that may end up resulting in huge unforeseen consequences down the line' (du Preez, 2021). Within the UK, this has included serious issues arising from the Brexit border protocol which have impacted cross-border trade with implications for policing and security arrangements north and south of the Irish border. These post-Brexit challenges have placed the UK government's support for multilateral missions and operations on the backfoot and may extend to future EU, NATO, and UN missions and the future involvement of UK policing.

UK policing within EU, NATO, and UN missions

The earlier chapters described the UK's involvement in intensive military conflicts since the first intervention in the Western Balkans (chapter 3), followed by Iraq and Afghanistan (chapter 4), and smaller discretionary involvements in Sierra Leone and Libya (chapters 3 and 4), as well as later UN peacekeeping in South Sudan (chapter 6). Since the 1990s, UK police were regularly seconded to NATO, EU, and UN missions until 2016 when these activities sharply declined. Partly this was due to the decline in the numbers of police advisors seconded to the largest theatres—Iraq and Afghanistan—although Brexit provoked a debate in relation to defence, security, and policing and the EU-UK relationship.

The recent IR described the UK as a 'European nation', a 'leading European Ally within NATO, bolstering the Alliance by tackling threats jointly and committing our resources to collective security in the Euro-Atlantic region' (IR, 2021: 6). While the UK signalled a clear commitment to influencing wider EU security and defence policy, the military have been at the heart of the newer ways of this influence. The Germany–France–UK grouping (E3) has been suggested as a mechanism to strengthen the EU pillar within NATO for example, that lies at the heart of EU defence and has been reliant on the UK for twenty per cent of expeditionary capability (Wieslander, 2020). Yet there are key challenges ahead for the UK to translate military commitment into political influence within the EU, where the security agenda has no clear distinction between military and non-military issues (including policing) that have related to intervention, crisis management, and stabilization (Chalmers, 2017: 5–6). While EU Member States have actively supported NATO and EU-led missions and operations,[4] the UK has become more restrained and particularly where police support is concerned.

On exiting the EU, the UK was removed from the common foreign and security policy (CSDP) and the collaborative processes that take place between EU Member State embassies around the world and in Brussels. Although the UK has been removed from CSDP decision-making, it can theoretically contribute personnel (including police), military capabilities, and financial support across the EU's missions and operations where an increased European Defence Agency (EDA) budget, the development of a permanent structured co-operation (PESCO)—a programme for EU Member States to collectively enhance military capabilities for EU military operations—and the creation of a permanent EU operational headquarters for the planning of military operations without reliance on NATO, have demonstrated a growing interest (Jokela, 2020). The UK government's support for CSDP activities has not since 2016 been matched by the reality. By 2018, the UK had contributed to 25 of the 35 past or recent CSDP missions, with an average contribution of 15 personnel (military and civilian), which amounted to a mere 2.3 per cent of all EU Member States (House of Lords European Committee, 2018). As of mid-2021, there were no UK police seconded on EU missions.

One reason posited has been that EU missions have not held the same *strategic* value for the wider UK defence and security effort as would NATO, and have been 'merely something of a toolbox that we could mobilize to add value in a number of crisis or stabilization situations around the world, where you need to try to mobilize a mix of military, civilian, deployment,

---

[4] The EU runs both CSDP missions and operations. While civilian missions are always called 'missions', military tasks can be called either 'missions' or 'operations', depending on whether they contain an executive mandate (in which case they are termed an operation).

political and diplomatic tools' (House of Lords European Committee, 2018: 33). Yet the broadening and deepening of the UK military and security contributions to CSDP missions arguably would provide a useful tool in melding the 'benefits of joint capability development projects' moving forward (Jokela, 2020) and would promote engagement overseas across the military and policing space (see Integrated Review, 2021). UK policing had previously a record of collaboration with the EU not only through CSDP missions but through police training. The EU police and civilian service training (EUPCST) and previously the EU police services training ensured the collaborative development and delivery of training for police deploying internationally. A programme of continued participation has been approved by FCDO until 2022 which provides an opportunity for approximately three to four UK police to attend each training exercise. Further opportunities may present through a UK (HO) supported international masterclass, a consortium of six international policing and SSR organizations delivering learning and training within the higher international police echelons (Author interview with JIPH representative, March 2021).

As the earlier chapters have outlined, the UK has supported NATO missions and UN peacekeeping operations (see chapters 3, 4, and annex 1). The latest deployments that ended in 2021 included UK police support to the Ministerial Advisory Group—Interior (MAGI-I) under the NATO RSM umbrella in Afghanistan (Correspondence with JIPH, May 2021). UK policing has supported both NATO missions in Afghanistan since 2001 although any future involvement after August 2021 ceased. Certainly the UK government has expressed continued support for NATO missions moving forward and identified the 'risk of conflicts escalating' globally, that until at least 2030, armed conflict 'will remain prevalent and may increase unless concerted action is taken to address underlying political, social, economic and environmental drivers' (Integrated Review, 2021: 20). Whether serving UK police will be involved on a similar scale to NATO ISAF and RSM in Afghanistan remains less certain although there has always been an appetite to position individual senior police at the highest strategic levels.

The UK government remains a permanent member of the UN Security Council, although its operational engagement has become increasingly patchy. Despite this, the UN has clearly recognized the importance of policing 'across the entire peace and security spectrum, from conflict prevention and management to peacekeeping, peacebuilding and peace sustainment' (UN Security Council, 2016: 1). While the UK has no gendarmerie that it can deploy in a UN peacekeeping and typically FPU role, there has been recognition within government of the centrality of policing in preventing, mitigating, and potentially resolving violent conflict through early intervention, peacekeeping, and reconciliation (SU, 2019). As of 2021, UK policing has been included within the FCDO UN peacekeeping joint unit, deploying a superintendent as police advisor to the British peace support team in Africa (BPST(A), an integrated capacity to support UN and African Union peace support operations). There has also been joint working between the FCDO and the BPST(A) to develop an accredited training programme with the UN police division that would allow UK police to deliver UN police training. Although the involvement of UK policing has remained thin, there has been an aspiration within the JIPH and NPCC that the UK should support all multilateral missions: EU, NATO, and UN (Correspondence with JIPH, May 2021). Much of this will rest, however, on the appetite of chief officers and PCCs to release officers for international policing in the future.

Government mergers and overseas funding cuts

Deployments to multilateral missions and operations has been one aspect of international policing *assistance*. UK policing has provided international policing *activities* through UK government funded programmes although a decline in these programmes has occurred through cuts to overseas spending. Moreover, the FCO–DfID merger brought cuts to overseas funding in line not only with proposed government spend but an international reshaping of priorities (Chalmers, 2020b).

The 'new' FCDO was launched on 2 September 2020 following a lengthy period of consultation. The government's vision was for a 'new all-of-government approach if we are to secure our values and interests, reduce poverty, confront global challenges and be a stronger Force for Good [sic] in a changing world' (HoC, 2020: 1). Some commentators suggested that this was an FCO acquisition (or swallowing) of DfID rather than a merger (Chalmers, 2020b), which brought budgeting and governance challenges in its wake that would impact the security and development agenda (Author interview with former senior policing advisor SU, November 2020). The SU which had maintained a standby pool of police and other civilian deployable experts, has been subsumed by a newer structure to ensure 'effective use of our development resource ... central to the new Department's [FCDO] mission' (House of Commons, 2020).

In the November 2020 spending review, the conservative government announced that the 2021 aid expenditure would be reduced from 0.7 to 0.5 per cent, which sliced approximately 24 per cent in possible spend between 2020 and 2021 (Hughes, Tichell, Tyskerud, and Warwick, 2021). While overseas spending has remained high by 'international and historical standards', the figure in real terms is far smaller as the UK economy contracted during the pandemic with further 'more substantial reductions' predicted for the future (Hughes, Tichell, Tyskerud, and Warwick, 2021: 4). Leaked emails obtained by *Open Democracy* in March 2021 revealed the conservative government's plans to cut funding to some countries between fifty and ninety-three per cent. Aid budgets had already been cut in 2020: humanitarian aid to Yemen, for example, was purported to have been slashed from £164 to £87 million and the budgets for Afghanistan and Pakistan in 2021 had been threatened (Geoghegan, 2021) with some programmes terminated indefinitely (cited in Hughes, Tichell, Tyskerud, and Warwick, 2021). With a refocusing of the ODA strategic and thematic priorities[5] for 2021, and an international development strategy planned to establish the government's approach from 2022, it may be possible that programmes falling outside the series of seven strategic priorities will be replaced. Additionally, those countries no longer aligning with the UK's security, development, and foreign interests will no longer appear on the funding lists (FCDO, 2020). The general trends to reduce funding levels have brought some additional reductions within police reform and SSR programmes.

The FCDO 'merger' was a reminder of the conservative government's desired approach to integrated ways of working and the delivery of cross-cutting capability (Integrated Review, 2021). While overseas spending has been reduced, there may be an augmentation in the approaches to provide police-military co-operation within overseas crisis response and capacity building through wider defence engagement strategies.

---

[5] The 2021 ODA themes are climate change and biodiversity; Covid-19 and global health; girl's education; science, research, and technology; open societies and conflict resolution; trade and economic development, and humanitarian response and preparedness (FCDO, 2020).

Broadening military capabilities

The growing entanglement of foreign, security, and defence policies since the advent of the NSC in 2010 revived cross-government strategy while the fusion doctrine outlined a philosophy of improved ways of working. A more recent step change came in 2021 with the drive to be 'bolder in our ambitions' through a 'stronger collective strategy capability [which] is fundamental to successful, integrated implementation' (IR, 2021: 97). Theoretically this has necessitated a greater synchronization of activities and effect across government and wider stakeholders within the public and private sector. I suggest that this concept, if applied, could enhance police–military co-operation within an overseas context and that there are historical grounds for doing this.

The military's repertoire of activities has broadened over the past decade and has been reinforced by the 2021 defence review, that outlined a vision for the full spectrum of capabilities from warfighting to global defence engagement (Brooke-Holland, 2021). This approach chimed with wider defence engagement strategies outlined by the MOD and FCO *outside* of combat: conflict prevention, stability building, and gaining influence (MOD and FCO, 2017). Future defence engagement, it was suggested, would require greater agility to ensure that not only was the army prepared for possible combat but that it had the ability to 'oscillate' in the 'not combat' spectrum—homeland resilience and defence engagement that encompassed capacity building more broadly (Defence Review, 2021).[6] One challenge with this concept has been to understand the parameters within which defence engagement would begin and end, and where other security actors (including police) would be jointly involved. Prior military doctrine had framed the concept of 'integration': the new joint force 2025 doctrine outlined how the military could work with the whole of government and by extension increase capability within non-combat environments (MOD, 2016). A subsequent international development engagement strategy (2017), developed through collaboration between the MOD and the FCO, further demonstrated the government's commitment to broadening

---

[6] This has extended to hybrid operations within the 'poorly defined domain of the "grey zone"'. Whether due to the ambiguity of international law, the deniability of actions, or being completely hidden, attacks in the grey zone are designed to gain an advantage while ensuring the threshold of war is not reached. Cyber and chemical attacks have been used as grey zone tactics, espionage and disinformation (fake news) have been grey zone activities (Austin, 2020).

defence strategy towards *engagement* beyond military operations (FCO and MOD, 2017). In 2020 a further piece of military doctrine emerged, that focused on integration 'for advantage': across government, all national stakeholders and allies (MOD, 2020).

Police–military co-operation within conflict and post-conflict environments can be charted through the twentieth century. However, with the demise of colonial policing and the then RUC, both eminently suited to more robust semi-military policing styles and co-operating with the military, the UK policing brand has reoriented towards its English roots. Unlike most EU countries and other nations, the UK has no gendarmerie to fill the capability gap where a range of semi-military policing approaches are required (Sinclair and Burdett, 2018). As such UK international deployments have increasingly involved activities of a *civil nature* including: governance (e.g. counter-corruption, accountability, and transparency); political processes including peace and reconciliation; police and justice sector reform; the restoration of public services and infrastructure, broader institutional reform, and community safety and engagement. Yet owing to the high-risk environments in which most police have functioned overseas, collaboration with military and gendarmerie organizations has remained a necessity to ensure a synchronization of effect (Author interview with former Inspector, Thames Valley Police who deployed to Afghanistan 2019 to 2020, February 2021).

As discussed in chapter 2, the original Irish policing model transferred across the British empire as a mechanism for upholding colonial rule, while the commonwealth countries adopted a pick-and-mix approach within the English and Irish styles to suit their law and order maintenance requirements. Following the Second World War, colonial police forces became embroiled in the small wars and insurgencies of decolonization in collaboration with the British military and other security actors (Sinclair, 2006). Lindsay Clutterbuck (2015) in an examination of policing and counter-insurgency in Afghanistan reflected on this point:

> In the context of the UK, the origins and development of police and policing since the early nineteenth century are intricately linked to the need to deal with the outbreaks of insurgency, terrorism, and civil conflict that have occurred throughout the histories of Britain, Ireland, and in the wider British Empire. Colonial policing was often undertaken in concert with the military where there was both an understanding and a need for police-military engagement.... [British colonial police

engaged] in countering ten significant low-intensity conflicts that are generally accepted as 'insurgencies', plus a greater number of lesser engagements on a smaller scale and categorized as 'police actions'... upon examination, in at least eight of them the local civil [colonial] police and the British military operated together in a coordinated and integrated way and did so as a central plank of an overall COIN strategy.... In essence, for at least 50 years, the UK could rely on the presence of a recognizable police force and policing approach that could be built upon and restructured to counter any current outbreak of conflict (Clutterbuck, 2015: 440, 453).

The twentieth century experiences of the British army included large and small wars, counter-insurgency and counterterrorism. Low-intensity warfare (and later COIN) tactics were transplanted and used in Northern Ireland from the 1960s to the 1990s and 'labelled military aid to the civilian authorities' (Friesendorf, 2018: 71). The principles that informed this doctrine included an emphasis on 'civil-military' co-operation and was revisited by the military in the Balkans drawing on 'decades of experience in internal security missions (Friesendorf, 2018: 72) and shared 'Northern Irish' lesson learning from RUC–PSNI officers who deployed to BiH and Kosovo (Author interviews with former RUC–PSNI officers, 2010 to 2020). However, doctrine can only be relevant for so long and when the later involvement in Helmand came, 'the historical lessons of Malaya and Northern Ireland [became] 'a distant folk tale' (Egnell, 2011: 307 cited in Friesendorf, 2018: 203). Historical lessons should have been relearned through the right training, equipment, strategy, and doctrine (Friesendorf, 2018: 203). However, by that time, the UK policing brand had largely discarded its Irish semi-military characteristics as PSNI repivoted towards a concept of policing with the community (see chapter 7). MDP, the largest routinely armed national UK force had engagement in Afghanistan although its international policing corporate memory has since faded (Sinclair, 2015).

Cornelius Friesendorf (2018) undertook extensive field research in BiH, Kosovo, and Afghanistan, observing the tactics, approaches, and cultural mindset of the military (British, US, and German) and the Italian Carabinieri. One key issue to emerge was the 'unlikelihood' that an army could undertake the 'multiplicity of tactics' needed where 'protection of the people is pivotal' and when faced with wide-ranging challenges. There had to be a coordinated military–police approach to planning, operations, and exit strategies and generally the broader policing element necessitated the presence of a gendarmerie (Friesendorf, 2018: 20–1 and in discussion with the author). Friesendorf (2018) explained:

> When foreign soldiers are sent to war-torn countries, they often face problems other than conventional combat ... [exposure to] a variety of nonstate and par-state actors that lack the trapping of state institutions such as uniforms. These outfits include professional criminals, ragtag militias, child soldiers and gangs ... (Friesendorf, 2018: 18).

'Flexibility' and 'versatility' remained key in ensuring that the military could 'switch levels of force in a split second'. However, navigating between military tactics and quasi-policing activities (including public order, criminal investigation, and community engagement) remained 'impossible for the same organization to perform effectively two very disparate tasks because the organizational culture that makes it effective in achieving one is counterproductive in accomplishing the other'. The key was the harmonization of police–military activity which could be achieved through the use of a gendarmerie, special military forces who had received a different level of hybrid training to regular military and co-operation with civil police (Friesendorf, 2018: 20).

The UK government's strategic response to overseas crises and conflict has increasingly focused on 'early warning', 'rapid crisis prevention and response', and 'investing in upstream prevention' (BSOS, 2011: 18). While police have had a lesser role to play than the military, policing has increasingly been described as one of the pillars within crisis response and stabilization, particular in 'partnerships' with the military, other security actors, and local stakeholders (SU, 2014, 2017). Complex multi-organizational activities within messy conflict and post-conflict environments have become increasingly reliant on consistency, versatility, and transparency where planning, tactical approaches, and operational engagement may routinely overlap and merge (Friesendorf, 2018). Theoretically there has been a requirement for a shared understanding of the values and purpose of an 'engagement', outcome-based thinking and clarity around an exit strategy through collaborative working with an openness to lessons learning and their application within future scenarios (ICAI, 2018 and Author interviews with UK police who deployed to Afghanistan and Iraq, 2010 to 2020).

Policing–military co-operation has continued to exist within multilateral missions, under the police liaison umbrella and has been emphasized within stabilization operations. From a military perspective, these remain outside 'major combat' where military force can be one of the elements required to deliver security and contribute to stability. Importantly, all military and civilian (including police), international, and host nation security actors must collaborate to ensure effectiveness (SU, 2017: 5). However, through the prism of *defence engagement,* the military have been developing additional skills. When operating under the protect, promote, prepare agenda within security sector stabilization, for example, the military have taken on mentoring and capacity building of local security forces (including police). This for some UK police deployed to high-risk environments has been fraught with issues as to a perceived outcome of more militarized approaches to police training. For UK police, the military role should be a 'civil-military effort' in collaboration with local security actors and other international partners (Author interviews with UK policing, 2010–2020; SU, 2017: 4).

With large-scale military deployments (including Iraq and Afghanistan) having ceased, the British military have increased their light-footprint interventions (Watts and Biegon, 2017) and defence engagement priorities. In 2015, the national security strategy emphasized that transnational threats should be tackled 'upstream' and laid out the government's ambition for the military to be more engaged in non-combat missions (SDSR, 2015). As a result, some infantry battalions were reconfigured and given dedicated tasks in counterterrorism and supporting stabilization efforts in FCAS through training, mentoring, and advising. Two 'new' specialized infantry battalions were created in 2017, each with 300 personnel to undertake defence engagement overseas (Ares and Athena, 2016). Additionally, the army's 77th Brigade, a combined regular and reserve unit, has increasingly supported broader defence engagement. Civil–military co-operation has been a recognized feature: 'Integrate our efforts with those of other government departments, agencies, the police and our allies, including through collaborative work funded by the Conflict, Stability and Security Fund (CSSF)' (MOD, 2021a: 14).

The military have, as a consequence, also adopted a 'remote warfare' approach that is working 'by, with, and through' local forces who have engaged on the frontline against terrorist, extremist, and criminal groups (Karlshoej-Pedersen, 2018). As regards support to UN peacekeeping, aside from the military's long-standing contribution in Cyprus, there has been little involvement since the 1990s, which has somewhat paralleled UK policing. Following the cessation of the UK military (and police) deployment to UNMISS (South Sudan), the NSC agreed to deploy a UK army task group to the UN multidimensional integrated stabilization mission in Mali (MINUSMA). Established in 2013, this mission has sought to 'ensure security, stabilization and protection of civilians' which has included SSR, political dialogue and reconciliation, and the protection of human rights (UN, 2021). Mali has faced repeated waves of intrastate and regional conflict with the 'current conflicts [having become] multidimensional, more prolonged and increasingly dangerous' (Ares and Athena, 2016: 6). From 2019 to 2020, the 300-strong Light Dragoon task group undertook pre-deployment 'integration training' to provide 'reconnaissance and patrol tasks … to gather intelligence and engage with local Malian people … [which] is not a combat operation, nor is it a counter-terrorism operation' (MOD, 2020). The UK military in Mali have undertaken targeted 'cordon and search' operations for weapons and gathered intelligence to disrupt terrorist activities against local communities to ensure community security and safety (MOD, 15 May 2021 and Author interviews with MOD, June 2021). There may in the future be a role for UK policing in support of the military within EU missions and possibly operations should future governments be supportive of this approach.

Police engagement as a cross-cutting capability

The 2021 defence review highlighted the importance of domestic and overseas engagement for the UK's security actors in the face of 'more complex challenges'. This would be reliant on greater integration of 'efforts with those of other government departments, agencies, the police and our allies' (Defence Review, 2021: 15) and included greater use of hybrid models within disaster management and crisis response. The IPRC (see chapter 6) has been one element of UK policing that has provided a cross-cutting capability in support of the armed forces. Provided that there can be an increased flexibility in UK policing capacity moving forward, the IPRC will be slowly increased from its current pool of twenty-one officers and extended beyond its original hosts (Avon and Somerset, Wiltshire, and Gloucestershire) to other forces in England Wales. IPRC has been held at 'very high readiness' for deployment with the military in support of operational liaison and reconnaissance teams, humanitarian aid, disaster relief, and non-combatant evacuation operations. While this figure has appeared small from an outsider perspective, the importance has been in the significance of joint police–military capability and the perceived operational and integrated effectiveness that can be built into lessons learning for the future. The IPRC may become increasingly identified as integral to the UK's international policing offer and could in the future fill part of the gap left by RUC–PSNI officers. One particular characteristic common to both has been a familiarity with police–military co-operation in high-risk environments through the IPRC recruitment of police with familiarity of working with the military (Author correspondence with IPRC lead, May 2021). Theoretically, therefore, UK policing has provided *police engagement* which could interface with *defence engagement* in the future. However, international crisis and humanitarian response will always depend on additional police volunteers coming forward for short-term deployments outside from (although dependent on) IPRC. Crucially, there will need to be a consensus of opinion across the relevant government departments of the importance of retaining this type of international policing capacity which may now rest with the HO.

The JIPH (see chapter 6) moved from the SU to the HO in 2020, which has, in a similar manner to FCO-DfID developed police capacity-building programmes. More recently, senior police advisors (police retiree contracted through the HO) have been embedded within a host police overseas to provide strategic level support and 'reach back' into serving UK police as and when in-country training and mentoring has been required. This mix of retired (under contract to the HO) and serving policing has signalled a continued commercialization of the UK policing brand, and the flexibility to draw upon support from the public and corporate sectors (Author interviews with police retirees contracted to ICDT, 2019, and correspondence with the JIPH, May 2021). Similarly, the British military has a longstanding tradition of embedded 'loan service' officers (particularly within Middle Eastern countries and the Gulf States) along similar lines (see Yates forthcoming 2022). In the case of the UAE (see chapter 5), the model of embedding former UK policing within the local police was different in that the recruitment was undertaken by that country directly with the individual concerned *outside* of UK government (Yates, 2018). However, embedding senior police with an overseas police force whatever the mechanism has potential benefits for UK government in relation to wider diplomatic engagement, which can lead to enhanced engagement with local police and capacity-building opportunities.

In most overseas countries, including those where there are police capacity-building and development programmes, there are numerous diplomatic representations drawn from across the world. Police 'liaison' officers have 'inhabit[ed] the architecture of global policing and work in the transnational policing theatre of operations' across the operational and non-operational policing space (Bowling and Sheptycki, 2012: 78). UK government has placed 'national security' diplomacy as part of the toolkit to tackle threats to national security upstream (see Integrated Review, 2021: 46). The network of police liaison officers (including CT liaison officers) that have supported this have typically been drawn from across UK policing and law enforcement agencies. Officers are seconded to many of the UK embassies and high commissions and to the overseas territories. With a government pledge to expand the defence attaché and defence staff networks by one third to further 'defence diplomacy' overseas (Defence Review, 2021), there may be future opportunities to extend overseas police networks and increase opportunities for wider police diplomacy. This has come at a time when police liaison officers have been withdrawn from EU institutions and yet a government strategy for Global Britain has placed an emphasis on overseas strategic partnerships (IR, 2021). Besides, more broadly, international policing has always created opportunities to create informal and formal police and law enforcement networks, which have served as a foundation for closer operational working in the UK (Author interviews with UK police who have deployed overseas, 2010–2020).

Maintaining the UK policing brand

The spectre of austerity, the withdrawal from the EU, and the pandemic have placed greater emphasis on a homeland first culture (Chalmers, 2020a). The challenges faced by UK policing has increasingly taken up any of the remaining available slack in police resources, despite the conservative government's 2019 pledge for additional recruits. The pressure on frontline policing has demonstrated an ongoing reluctance by senior police and PCCs to release officers for overseas deployments beyond their own back yards. Consequently, future support for UN, NATO, and EU missions and operations will be squeezed and the appetite for international policing may hinge on the commercial nature of any activity. Yet the UK policing brand has revamped its value proposition over the past two decades as demonstrated by Police Scotland and PSNI (see chapter 7) and the corporate sector (see chapter 5). The brand has retained its niche value overseas; many of these characteristics have hinged upon Peelian concepts that have included policing by consent, community engagement, political independence, and accountability which has rested upon the mythology of UK policing. The paradox has been that a more robust proposition—the RUC—was eminently more suited to policing high-risk environments. The transformation from RUC to PSNI later provided a new and highly suitable value proposition. PSNI was held by overseas government and police alike as a success story having embraced the Patten reforms that included policing with the community and human rights (Author interviews with former RUC–PSNI, 2010 to 2020). Indeed, the concept of human rights (and community engagement) have since the 1990s become integral within SSR and later within defence engagement (Integrated Review, 2021; SU, 2019). In 2020, the UK introduced the Magnitsky sanctions system as a mechanism with which countries in violation of human rights could be targeted (IR, 2021: 16); one example of the importance placed on the integration of human rights within the UK's development agenda. Within police reform and SSR, this has included the safety and security of vulnerable and ethnic communities as well as the integration and progression of female police officers (SU, 2014, 2019).

Ensuring that the UK policing brand has remained an attractive international proposition has benefitted from *demand for the brand* within an era of interventions as well as the *resources to meet that demand*: the rise of the corporate sector. The large-scale interventions in Iraq and Afghanistan post-9/11 highlighted the critical role played by contractors in support of military operations and reconstruction who occasionally outnumbered serving personnel. As chapter 5 highlighted, armed and unarmed private security contractors (including UK military and police retirees) provided services that included guarding, security escorts, protecting fixed locations, as well as training for local police (and military). The recent interventions in Iraq and Afghanistan and subsequent post-conflict reconstruction efforts will be superseded by efforts to develop other parts of the Middle East, Africa, South Asia and beyond as the geography of threats changes direction. Clearly the corporate SSR sector (more broadly) will continue to flourish. Many companies have profited from the rapid commercialization of this sector and have not faced significant competitive pressures of the wider market. As 'market makers' some of these organizations had pre-existing relationships with government, the military, and the public sector and were able to create opportunities (through recent interventions) to establish or grow demand for products and services (Peltier, 2020). The revolving door between the public 'government' sector and the corporate world is well oiled. Yet there are important questions relating to the use of public funds ('taxpayers' money') in relation to the level of oversight. When extended to the use of the public funds to deliver the UK policing brand, there has been no government accreditation in place for individuals or for companies; the industry has continued to self-vet and self-regulate and to build professional standards as they see fit with international partners. Despite the UK government's increased emphasis on risk assessments, monitoring and evaluation, there has not been sufficient operational oversight of the corporate world (ICAI, 2018). The slippage from the official UK policing to the corporate policing world has demonstrated an element of extruded accountability and the delivery of the UK policing brand has been increasingly juxtaposed between the 'serving' and 'retired' policing sectors. International assistance or activities and lessons should in the future be drawn from the shortcomings and effectiveness of past efforts and embedded within the international policing offer.

For some time, serious concerns have arisen in relation to worthiness of overseas aid and the sustainability of overseas spending as the UK entered a period of economic decline in 2020 (Chalmers, 2020a). One key principle developed has been the effective oversight of the reform and development of local security forces not only by local civil authorities but also by international governments. Afghanistan and Iraq have been cases in point where serious issues have been raised relating to financial and resource wastages and lack of accountability. When, for example, it was calculated that $6 billion was spent on contractors to train the ANP (Schwartz and Swain, 2011), or that supposed payments for ANP salaries disappeared to ghosts within a corrupt governmental system and, indeed, that some local police were not paid for a period of time (SIGAR, 2019), it became apparent that financial aid can become a source of insecurity rather than security and affect a country's development (Byrd, 2010).

Growing the UK policing brand

Promoting the UK policing brand, ensuring oversight and coordination for the delivery of international policing, and retaining a corporate memory has been the primary responsibility of ACPO IA and then the JIPH (Author interview with former senior police advisor and JIPH lead, February 2019). The JIPH through its IPAB referral processes has sought to capture all international policing activities across UK policing. However, the failure of some forces to engage with this centralized police hub has prevented the creation of a complete historic record. Theoretically the JIPH sought to field 'daily' requests nationally and internationally that can be linked specifically to capacity building.[7] As such it continued to develop networks and respond to requests for information and advice across PSNI, Police Scotland, CoP, ACRO criminal records office, UK border force, NCA, and the International crime coordination centre (IPCC), as well government departments including the HO and FCDO and the security services and office for security and counterterrorism. International policing has been delivered across the spectrum of *assistance* and *activity* which can theoretically involve the whole-of-UK policing.

The drive to support the release of serving officers remained integral to the JIPH–NPCC and yet this has increasingly been thwarted by the lack of push from chief officers matched by the lack of pull from many serving officers. Many serving police officers have expressed a lack of understanding or interest in international policing, many perceive an international deployment as a career cul-de-sac rather than as a career game-changer. In cases where police have expressed an interest and have fulfilled the necessary rank and experience to deploy, professional and personal commitments have precluded their departure. UK policing, unlike many EU countries, has not as of 2021 formally recognized an international assistance deployment as part of an officer's ongoing career development and progression. The current discussions and development of the necessary training platforms and formal recognition through the CoP may well encourage more officers to come forward (Author correspondence with the JIPH, May 2021).

My own observations drawn from police who have deployed internationally over the past decade revealed the deep frustrations of so many on their return home. An international deployment gave rise to what many described as professional, leadership, managerial, and personal skills uplift that they perceived as beneficial not only for their own career trajectory but for the effectiveness of UK policing more broadly. An overseas deployment (of more than six months) has always required the considerable investment on the part not only the individual but also the UK government and the home constabulary. Earlier research projects have suggested, however, that the benefits of an overseas mission clearly outweighed the limitations

---

[7] During the financial year 2019 to 2020 the JIPH coordinated seventy-six substantive capacity-building assistance requests which translated into projects within fifty-eight countries (Author correspondence with the JIPH, May 2021).

and that new or improved professional skills acquired could be utilized. In particular, these were linked to *community engagement/policing* where exposure to a wider range of possible and new experiences reinvigorated the approaches taken when returning home, and enhanced local stakeholder dialogue; *cultural awareness and sensitivity* in relation to ethnic minorities and vulnerable communities following the new and challenging experience of policing with communities within FCAS; *managing hot spots* whereby the overseas experiences of providing security, safety, and engagement to communities within high risk environments supported new management and problem-solving techniques when faced with community tensions at home, particularly within ethnic and minority communities; *building and maintaining overseas networks* with other international police in relation to transnational threats and crime and criminal investigations; and developing leadership and managerial skills and building on policing skills already acquired in the UK (Emsley and Sinclair, ESRC, 2009–2015, and Author interviews, 2010).[8]

Concluding comment

The future direction of travel of international policing will certainly require an increased uptake from serving officers even if many of those officers then move into the corporate world. This may well involve blended government-to-government modes of delivery, whereby embedded senior police advisors (retired) contracted to UK government provide strategic level mentoring and advising for long periods and then utilize element of UK policing (serving) to deliver short periods of in-country training. This may be suggestive of a further shift towards international policing as a commercial *activity* rather the involvement in UN, EU, and NATO missions on a longer-term basis. However, despite the delivery mechanisms of international policing there has always been a sense of the continuing legacy of the UK policing brand within former commonwealth countries and those with close commercial and strategic ties to the UK. In the future, as the UK shifts its geopolitical axis following its departure from the EU and in a bid for Global Britain, new countries may come into the fold.

---

[8] Data has been collected and analysed in the UK from Author interviews with approximately 150 officers deployed overseas between 2009 and 2015. (Emsley and Sinclair, ESRC Ref No RES-000-22-3922).

This will, however, be reliant not only on the wider support of UK policing but the administrative core through which the vision, priorities, and governance of international policing (as outlined by government and police institutions) has rested: until very recently the JIPH–NPCC under the HO umbrella. Moving the JIPH from the SU to the HO may, on paper, have generated considerably more flexibility around access to policing ministers, which has the potential to increase recognition of what international policing *can do and will do*. Yet this will be highly dependent on a future overarching governmental international policing strategy that drives integrated approaches across the public–private sectors for a seamless and transparent delivery of international policing, that is deeply rooted in nineteenth-century policing and has created an enduring legacy.

Concluding Observations

> And what of UK international policing assistance now? How will the UK policing brand retain its global influence?
> **Chief Constable UK Police, 2021**

UK policing 'internationalized' from the early part of the nineteenth century through a circulation of police personnel, policing styles, skills, and equipment. It evolved from nineteenth-century English 'civil' and Irish 'semi-military' roots and spread across the British empire and commonwealth. I suggest that this historical trajectory contributed to the development of the UK policing brand and that this continued after 1989 through international policing 'assistance', 'co-operation', and 'activities' underpinned by interlocking historical trends discussed within the earlier chapters. Using the narrative of UK police practitioners to *tell their story* has been key in understanding the broad sweep of the how, the why, and the doing of international policing.

International policing has been delivered by the entire spectrum of UK policing (England, Wales, Scotland, and Northern Ireland) as well as the MDP, British Transport Police, military and services police. I have included many examples drawn from across UK policing, although with some greater degree of emphasis on the *traditional* rather than the *niche* police (predominantly MDP) and their overseas experiences within multilateral and bilateral missions and operations, which rested, although not exclusively, on the concept of non-operational policing. However, there were important examples (e.g. Kosovo and East Timor) when international police were given a mandate to assume full executive policing responsibility that included maintaining public order, conducting investigations, and undertaking special operations to allow the local (host-state) police and other law enforcement agencies to regain autonomy and self-sufficiency (UNDPKO, 2015). An exploration of international policing has revealed that there was often a fine line navigated within complex and high-risk environments between the operational and the non-operational. Many UK police with an overseas experience commented on occasions when they assumed a potential quasi-operational (rather than non-operational) support role when providing *assistance* (including mentoring and advising) to the local police. While assistance theoretically has included the provision of policing *support* through a *service* to a police recipient—an international exchange—this exchange has always been multilayered and complicated by the wide numbers of international police donors present. The official terminology has included the terms 'assistance', 'co-operation', and 'activities' but this has not fully captured the permanent shifting at ground level between the operational and the non-operational. Nor has there been adequate reflection related to the processes of *knowledge exchange* and *transfer* that occur between international police, local police, government, and wider stakeholders. These international experiences and policing exchanges have suggested that practitioners can interpret the world of international missions somewhat differently to the policymakers, government officials, and interested other parties. Many UK police expressed that the doing of policing within an international environment should be simplified to what police do at home—policing—while accepting that this will be challenged and constrained by the situational context, local police and communities, and being seen as 'outsiders'. The importance, however, lies in the need for greater acceptance by those operating outside the police network to appreciate that police typically can find common ground with other police the world over (Author interviews with UK police who deployed internationally, 2010–2020).

Police histories and 'back to the futurism'

I have used an historical lens to frame the evolution and export of the UK policing brand. There has been both a reality and a mythology surrounding the interpretations, discourse, and the 'doing' of UK policing that has continued to filter into the international delivery of the brand (and its return home) that has created an enduring legacy. An earlier traditional view held was that there was 'one "*police service*" [author emphasis] in England and Wales which sprang full formed in 1829 … the Metropolitan Police model [which] rapidly took over ... [as] a new departure for English policing ...' and spread across mainland UK (Emsley, 1999: 248). This English policing model became an 'institution of central symbolic importance, seen as embodying the very essence of English' (Critchley, 1978: 47). Juxtaposed against this *service*, in Ireland, Peel's earlier police reform experiment, the Irish Constabulary, was a model developed that paralleled the continental police *forces*: 'an admission that Ireland was different' and the population should be managed differently (Ellison and Smyth, 2000: 17). Yet the character of the UK policing brand emerged from an overlapping of the English and Irish 'models' that developed through the nineteenth and twentieth centuries both in their myths and through their realities. The styles employed as a result of this development provided policing and law and order enforcement that operated on a continuum between 'consent' and 'coercion'—the concept of consent having emerged from a Peelian mythology that has endured over time. Closer to the reality has been a cross-fertilization of these two broad models of policing criss-crossing the British Isles, empire, commonwealth, and beyond to meet expectations and needs of 'government' in response to a given context according to time, place, and events.

Over time the UK policing brand has been showcased and managed by the UK's police institutions including more recently Scotland Yard, the MPS, the NCA, and the NPCC, the forty-three constabularies in England and Wales, Police Scotland, and PSNI through variegated policing styles and approaches (Emsley, 1999). Particular favourites have included Peelian concepts of discretion, integrity, policing by consent, minimum force, and so on (Reiner, 1985). As my earlier research found, 'these early Whiggish [traditional] perspectives created a global professional police wisdom as British policing [has been] exported overseas' (Sinclair, 2016: 42). This congratulatory history has been all but preserved within the establishment and has continued to be exhibited within government and police policy and documentation *to this day* and used to maintain and promote the UK policing brand (Emsley, 2011; Lawrence, 2011; Sinclair, 2016a). The brand itself has comprised multiple characteristics that have been adopted, developed, and discarded over time. These have also been embedded within police reform and SSR policy and guidance material and more recently have broadened to include gender equality, human rights, accountability, diversity, and service delivery (SU, 2014: 16–20). Marketing what has been perceived as the best elements of British policing from government and public institutions in the UK internationally through the delivery of UK policing has added credibility and created buy-in over the long term.

A growing endorsement of the use of UK policing was reinforced by the pick-and-mix approach espoused by international governments and security actors who have sought out a particular civil or semi-military style that suited a given context (high- or low-risk environments). While this often centred on the export of the 'Peelian' favourite: community policing 'the police are the public and the public are the police' (see Brogden and Nijhar, 2005), there was also considerable need for the Northern Irish characteristics of the brand as we have seen in the Western Balkans, Iraq, and Afghanistan. Although in truth, as Emsley earlier commented, each police officer has always had the 'power of coercion, ... [although] they have generally preferred to act by consent'. It may be more realistic to 'conceive of the law and the police as multi-faceted institutions used by English people of all classes to oppose, to co-operate with, and to gain concessions from, each other' (Emsley, 1996: 256). This may have assumed that the image of the 'amicable bobby' has been a 'reality (for some) and a fiction (for others) but nonetheless a necessary fiction' as it has provided a basis for police legitimacy (Waddington, 1991: 4). Overall the softer sides of UK policing—policing by consent as illustrated by the bobby—have always held a particular attraction within official circles in the UK and overseas. This image may be increasingly at odds as the British public's vision on the 'bobby on the beat' has faded as a twenty-first century vision, as fewer officers are left to 'patrol the streets' and provide reassurance and police visibility (Emsley, 2009: 284).

Substantive reform no doubt lies ahead in England and Wales for a 'police service [that] was created to perform its task in a different age' (Muir et al., (2020): 52) through changes to culture and practice. As part of an ongoing (2020) strategic review of policing in England and Wales, Ian Loader has dissected the current 'police mission' and suggested that it was erroneous to 'default to the Peelian principles on the grounds that these offer a sturdy time-test guide as to what the police are to do and how they should go about it ...' (Loader, 2020: 3). Peelian principles have been integral to police mythology (Loader and Mulcahy, 2003) perhaps because 'the police like the Peelian principles because they make them feel good about the job they do and their place in society ... they operate mainly as a self-legitimation or branding device ... (Loader, 2020: 4). Yet while the reform of PSNI and Police Scotland has brought an overseas interest in police transformation more generally, it remains to be seen whether transformation in England and Wales will illicit the same response with police reform and SSR. Indeed, future changes in operational practices across wider UK may see a hardening in policing response within the management of public protest, specialist operations, and counterterrorism. The potential increased use of the military in support of homeland resilience may well widen the debate around militarization (see IR, 2021; MOD, 2021a). Should this involve UK policing then another phase of 'back to the futurism' might unfold where 'semi-military' approaches to policing will be deployed as a stark reminder of the UK's colonial past.

Moreover, those earlier colonial linkages are only now finally waning in former empire and commonwealth countries which earlier helped to develop and grow the UK police brand. One example is the Hong Kong police who retained an historic attachment to UK policing styles beyond the post-colonial period, continued to second Hong Kong police high flyers to the UK as well as retaining a tradition of serving 'expatriate' officers. In 1990, there were approximately 900 expatriate officers including former UK police with the last expatriate officers graduating from the Hong Kong police training school on overseas terms in 1994. With approximately fifty expatriate officers remaining as of 2021, the youngest is expected to retire in January 2028 (Leung, 2017). Hong Kong police scholars have acknowledged that a UK policing style has to some extent continued, despite an escalation in public order protest and street violence over the past few years. In particular, HKP discourse has maintained that 'consent' and 'police discretion' should remain integral to winning public support and that there is respect for 'soft skills' when employing street level tactics (Author correspondence with Lawrence Ho, March 2021; Ho, 2020a, 2020b).

The guardians of the UK policing brand?

The UK police brand has remained a powerful component of brand UK that has, at least until now, managed to retain a 'soft-power presence that currently far exceeds its population size or economic clout. The UK has grown used to leveraging its networks to amplify its power ...' (Hug et al., 2020: 3) The UK has always sought to generate competitive advantage and influence as a result of its soft-power approaches—it had been the biggest international aid donor for example—and has retained many of its historical connections through strategic and commercial interests. Moreover, there has always been that earlier reputation for sticking to an international rules-based approach and fair play. This has long pre-dated the twenty-first century (Chalmers, 2020a). Theoretically, UK policing has been integral to the export of UK soft power. However, this UK level of influence and international value can no longer be assumed as the UK's role in the world has changed. This has impacted upon the value of UK policing coupled with the challenges of competing with other police donors promoting their own policing agendas, including 'non-Western' players like Turkey, Russia, and China. These countries (and a growing number in the global south) have filled the gap left by Western states. When UK policing alone is considered, the number of serving officers who are interested in an overseas mission has fallen dramatically since 2010, with those deployed on multilateral missions having significantly reduced as the appendix tables show. Paradoxically while the UK's support for international aid dropped significantly in 2020, demand for policing assistance internationally has remained constant.

The (re)shaping of UK policing across the four-nation state has also impacted the delivery of the UK policing brand. As chapter 7 outlined, the advent of both PSNI and Police Scotland created something of a fragmentation in the overseas delivery of the UK policing brand. PSNI and Police Scotland's devolved governments' international agendas provided opportunities to market their own agenda internationally as distinct, though theoretically integral to UK policing. In particular, both organizations have promoted the police transformation and change management agendas, openly using the term 'brand' in association with Scotland or Northern Ireland rather than the UK. In the case of Scotland, there has been the added benefit of a dedicated international policing strategy in alignment with the Scottish government's international agenda. Within UK policing *per se*, it fell to the JIPH–NPCC to actively promote 'UK policing' domestically and overseas and, to capture international activities. However, the number of referrals to the JIPH through the IPAB remained comparatively small and it has been assumed that many are not reported, as individual constabularies market their own brand through bilateral policing projects. The true guardians of the UK policing brand may now be UK police retirees who have moved into the corporate world.

The rise of overseas contracting

The growth in the corporate security industry (including police contracting) coupled with a demand for SSR has reinforced the brand's value. There are tensions, however, between the risks and rewards for UK government and police as the corporate sector has assumed a greater importance. Deploying police contractors (and other military and service contractors) to high-risk environments essentially removes *risk* away from government, military, and police institutions particularly in relation to duty of care and cost issues. The extreme environments into which UK police deployed in the Western Balkans, East Timor, Iraq, and Afghanistan initially exposed the weaknesses and limitations of the government's approach to risk when deploying serving officers. Much of the criticism levied by police who deployed was that this prevented assistance being given on occasion owing to restrictions in place that related to duty-of-care issues. While support was provided by the military and PMSCs, the nature of these interventions was asymmetric and required extensive international military and police support to the local security forces. This required considerably more police personnel than could be deployed as well as a vast complement of contracted security personnel (including police/security contractors), logistical support, catering, vehicle maintenance, and so on. Former RUC–PSNI (particularly in Iraq) were well suited to this terrain, in part owing to their experience of high-risk environments and police–military co-operation although there were too few overall deployed (Author interviews with police contractors (UK police retirees), 2015–2020).

Since 2001, security contracting (particularly military) has grown exponentially with one view held by government officials and private companies that this has been a 'cost reducer' rather than a cost multiplier, and can increase the quality of services and goods offered. Yet herein lies a different risk. Typically, a lack of competitive pressure within the corporate sector may erode rather than enhance the quality of services provided (Peletier, 2020) for 'the market isn't always competitive because of who you know and that is certainly true of the policing world where companies gain notoriety and win contract after contract' (Author interview with police contractor deployed to Afghanistan, May 2020). Contracting has become big business and has continued to fill the combat, security, and service spaces within high-risk environments (Peletier, 2020). In lower risk environments, police capacity building has been bolstered by the corporate world as demonstrated by the ease with which police retirees have passed through the revolving door and secured ready employment. Despite being closely associated with the world of private security (and military services) for almost five decades, successive UK governments have shown little appetite to officially regulate this sector (Miller, 2020). That coupled with a growing reliance on contracts between industry and government has created processes of *self-regulation,* both national and international, and seemingly removed that element of risk from government. This has been demonstrated through the degree of hybridity that exists, whereby the public and private sectors have the flexibility to operate co-jointly overseas. One example would be the HO International Strategy and Capabilities Unit with its blend of police contractors and serving UK policing who collaborate in the delivery of police reform programmes. These hybrid networks have reflected the government's growing requirement for private sector spectrums to combat a growth in transnational threats including terrorism, serious and organized crime, and cybercrime (see IR, 2021). Within this there has been a recent growth in newer forms of police contracting focused on hard security and intelligence outsourced to police retirees.

Looking ahead, this new commercial UK police brand will need to be aligned with developments in the UK brand overall. The essence of brand UK is that it has upheld the highest possible Western and UK standards of professionalism alongside particular policing values and that it does so through a combined public-private approach. This has become of even greater relevance with the launch of the Global Britain initiative following the UK's departure from the EU (Chalmers, 2020a) and a reinvigoration of enlightened national interests (Gilmore, 2014). That the UK's Global Britain agenda has encompassed ethical responsibilities has ramifications for foreign, security, and development policies. Yet there has been a certain lack of clarity on the precise relationship between national interests and global ethical commitments, which has at times aligned a 'buccaneering' approach to free trade, with continued support for human rights, democratization and development (Gilmore, 2020: 26). The announcement of an increased use of targeted sanctions against individuals involved in human rights abuses, for example, employing the Magnitsky clause in the 2018 Sanctions and Anti-Money Laundering Act was applauded. Although inconsistencies between the UK's 'professed support for human rights and its pursuit of narrower national commercial interests have been consistently evident in its sales of weapons to regimes with exceptionally poor human rights records' (Gilmore, 2020). This has included international policing provided across the Middle East and South Asia, which has come under regular criticism in media and some government circles for the risk–reward trade-offs.

The UK police brand and the international policing agenda

UK policing has corporate memory of operational and non-operational policing through an internationalization of policing that began in the nineteenth century. Early policing assistance was a form of 'capacity building', from the deployment of UK police to the allied control commission in post-war Italy and Germany, to colonial police support for the localization of policing prior to independence within many colonies (Sinclair, 2006). As empire faded so UK 'international' policing support extended through the Cold War period and entered an era of 'new wars' from the early 1990s that included intrastate wars. This provided new opportunities as I have described not only for regular military and security actors but a wide range of PMSCs and PMCs (Kaldor, 2012). However, the geopolitical developments of the past two decades have demonstrated that 'the West is fading ... as the major driving geopolitical force in the world' (Burleigh, 2017: 369); the 2021 withdrawal from Afghanistan demonstrated a withering appetite for large-scale military interventions. Yet despite this, 'animosity among the world's most powerful countries risks crowding out multilateral efforts to manage crisis' (International Crisis Group, May 2021). Intrastate conflict and civil wars have continued and will continue in the future. They have and will always require an element of long-term stabilization and reconstruction effort.

The UK government (2021) expressed a commitment to 'act as a force for good in the world' through wider defence and development engagements and the reinforcement of existing international relationships and networks (MOD, 2021a). The glory days of large-scale Western interventions (including UK policing cohorts) may have been replaced by smaller missions. UN PSOs have become largely the preserve of the global south who have the capacity to provide FPUs as well as strategic level advisors. Peace operations have revealed the sheer complexity of policing required and typically necessitated the use of robust gendarmerie units that do not reflect those mythologized British values of policing by consent. Moreover, any accompanying security and justice programmes ('pure policing programmes') that could be managed by police have now been subsumed into much larger security programmes and farmed out to the private sector (Author interview with senior advisor SU, February 2020).

UK support for deploying serving officers on multilateral missions has waned; the initial enthusiasm demonstrated by UK policing through the international policing goldrush that occurred in BiH, Kosovo, Iraq, and Afghanistan were not adequately matched by a political reality to support international deployments moving forward. The criticism from the Chilcot Inquiry lingered on; why has there been a dearth of senior police at the military high table within operational planning for missions and why has there been no *new* international policing cross-governmental strategy that could enhance delivery of UK policing and promote brand cohesion? There has been a growing sense of the importance of *defence* engagement to the detriment of *police* engagement. As multilateral missions have become smaller within high-risk environments, so short-term deployment of specialized teams has increased (Author correspondence with Friesendorf, May, 2021). This could provide real opportunities for UK police with high levels of expertise to deploy for reduced periods of time thus allaying concerns of the loss of serving officers by senior police and PCCs. With a likelihood that in the future local host–state police will be taken to 'safe zones' outside the host country to receive training and mentoring, there will be the potential to reduce risk and duty-of-care issues associated with the deployment of serving police. However, despite attempts by JIPH–NPCC to promote, centralize, and standardize UK policing and lobby for these changes, austerity and the cuts to police budgets have seen a decline in the numbers of serving officers deploying on international missions since 2010. Just as the geopolitical context that the UK finds itself in has shifted away from unipolar dominance by the US and her allies, UK policing is at risk of losing its international policing corporate memory.

International UK policing: a fractured memory?

UK police have over time deployed into complex and volatile situations where the requirement for post-conflict reconstruction and stabilization has become central and has involved large-scale police reform programmes. This has involved a significant degree of police co-operation and overlapping of activities with a wide range of security actors where a common understanding of planning the approaches to be taken, policing activities, and the desired outcomes have been paramount. The extent of informal rather than formal knowledge exchange has been far greater within these situations—Iraq and Afghanistan have been prime examples. One criticism levied has been that 'we go through these cycles of constantly rebooting our memory and relearning. It is one thing that the British have yet to really get better at institutional memory. It is about better learning and retaining the knowledge so we do not have to relearn the mistakes we have made' (Farrell quoted in House of Commons Defence Committee, 2010: 33).

Yet UK policing has a history of knowledge transfer and exchange. British police not only 'policed' the empire but circulated and networked with other police as police 'knowledge' advisors across empire, commonwealth, and beyond and filtered these overseas policing experiences into the growth of a policing brand. The UK, in a similar vein to other European colonial powers, developed multifaceted policing styles to provide domestic and colonial (overseas) policing. Robust semi-military policing and an experience of COIN (including the military) were transferred from Malaya and Kenya to Northern Ireland, where this knowledge was grown until the late 1990s. RUC (RUC–PSNI) officers then contributed to a refining of corporate knowledge which further built the UK policing brand value for the interventions that occurred from the 1990s. Police who deployed internationally brought a *Northern Irish* experience of semi-military and divided society policing, as well as corporate knowledge of civilian–military co-operation within high risk and combat environments. Knowledge passed between the RUC and the British military may have been used to good effect in Kosovo and BiH when the corporate memory was still fresh and more often than not based on personal relationships. However, the knowledge of an earlier colonial and post-colonial doctrine of irregular warfare and COIN had passed by the time of Afghanistan (Friesendorf, 2018) and was transferred into the corporate world as former RUC–PSNI took specialized counter-intelligence and investigative expertise overseas. That corporate memory has now faded, as has the familiarity and experience of a close working relationship with the military and yet police–military coordination has been recognized as prerequisite to successful peacekeeping, stabilization, and capacity building (SU, 2014, 2019).

This point has demonstrated that an element of the UK policing brand—robust semi-military policing that may not have been out of place in Northern Ireland—has been lost, an element that was useful in filling a security gap within international missions that has continued to be filled by international gendarmerie forces. While this may be filled in the future through newer elements of UK policing including the IPRC and new approaches to policing CT, SOC, and cyber threats, there are emerging aspects of knowledge transfer and exchange that should not be underestimated moving forward. In particular, the policing experiences, skills, and knowledge of the global south that has been shared within an overseas environment. Their policing practices may have a 'violent (coercive) side' (Honke and Muller, 2016: 2) that clashes with traditional community policing approaches and yet the aspiration has been that these other approaches can be melded within the range of international policing activities and styles required. Previously, knowledge transfer occurred between some UK police and other international policing partners. Some, although not all, expressed their interest and willingness in learning from others and investing in policing practices at home (Author interviews with UK police, 2010–2020).

UK policing in 2020 and 2021 faced uncertainty as political and economic challenges brought about by the UK's withdrawal from the EU combined with a global health crisis. The twenty-first century UK policing brand has newer facets with the advent of PSNI and Police Scotland, but internally fragmented as Scotland and Northern Ireland have driven their own international agendas and looked to increase the commercial potential of their own policing brands. In England and Wales, the forty-three constabularies have continued to engage directly with the overseas market although there has been a renewed drive through the JIPH–NPCC to centralize international policing demand. While there has always been a degree of flexibility to pick-and-mix, the current trend set by PSNI and Police Scotland may reveal evidence of greater separation rather than cohesion within the wider UK international policing offer. This has been heightened by the UK's withdrawal from the EU and a possible future dissolution of the four-nation state. Rather than a future enhancement, this could see a fading of a UK policing brand built up through 200 years of blending 'civil' and 'semi-military' policing styles. When combined with the push towards privatization in SSR, it could also lead to further erosion of the historical and institutional memory of an internationalization that shaped the UK's policing journey.

It is hoped that this book has shed some light on these historical developments and will make a contribution to the ongoing academic and practitioner discourse regarding the myths and realities of a highly complex and long-lived policing brand. And, ultimately, that these snapshots of policing histories help capture some of that institutional memory to help guide the UK policing brand on its continuing global journey.

Postscript

As I write, the Kremlin's appetite for territorial aggression that led to an unprovoked attack on Ukraine threatens global stabilization and the advent of a more 'dangerous and capricious world' (Glenny, 2022). The UK has continued to provide support to Ukraine and may be drawn into newer imperatives to deter aggression should further crises break out across the Western Balkans, the Middle East, and Africa. A resurgence in authoritarian leadership coupled with a rebalancing of global power has signposted a clear move away from American unipolarity. The 'West' has emerged as somewhat isolationist, evidenced in part by the gradual relinquishing of that historic glaze of liberal democratic triumphalism. The continuing impact of the Covid-19 pandemic has generated further Western retrenchment and brought newer security issues linked to food, water, and climate change into sharper focus across the developing world. Learning the lessons from history has never been more important than it is today. This prompted some final reflections on the trendlines for the future as we leave an era of Western interventions, the 'forever war' in Afghanistan, and witness the expansionism of both Russia and China.

Millions of people from Ukraine join those from African and Middle Eastern countries on a trajectory towards Europe; a movement of peoples that will keep coming as conflict, poverty, socio-economic decline, and climate change drive them from their places of origin. The management of unprecedented numbers will require both an international and a coordinated security (and policing) response on a scale hitherto unseen. The need for security and development assistance will be unparalleled along these migration pathways despite a commonly held view that the Western age of interventions (including in Iraq and Afghanistan) is over.

The brutal end to an era of interventions in Afghanistan underlined the fundamental flaws in the Western approach to military intervention and subsequent 'state' capacity building; the realization (particularly after Afghanistan) that international stakeholders needed to be aware of what they were 'getting into' when combining military and security operations with development and reconstruction. Ongoing and future research will continue to dissect Afghanistan (and Iraq, Libya, and Syria) as well as wider intra and inter-state conflicts to draw out lessons. The extent to which learning will be implemented will be dependent on individuals with the ability and courage to 'draw together the strands of security, development, politics and economics, where the emphasis is on personal charisma and cultural and local knowledge coupled with an ability to understand the array of incentives shaping local actions, and to listen attentively rather than prescribe' (Killcullen and Mills, 2022: 180–1).

Meanwhile, the UK continues to shape its post-Brexit 'Global Britain' stance—which faces challenges both at home and abroad. The 2021 Integrated Review theoretically outlined a new security posturing, although the desire to be a global player has seemed overly ambitious. The apparent tilt towards the Indo-Pacific, as a reflection of the US 'pivot' towards Asia, has raised concerns as to how the UK could engage globally and support Europe military, how this could be reconciled with a significant reduction of the UK's international aid budget and a continued reduction in the size of the armed forces (Arnold, 2022). Indeed, how *will* the UK support the building of a 'global network of liberty' through its defence and security capabilities and international commitments including NATO and the EU? And what of any support from UK policing on the international stage as it faces ongoing challenges to the integrity and uniformity of the UK police brand?

Recent media reports have been particularly dismissive of UK policing and more recently focused on the stepping down of the first MPS female commissioner, Dame Cressida Dick and what has been construed as a total loss of public confidence in policing. In all likelihood the role of any future MPS commissioner will be increasingly challenged by the need to tackle issues related to misogyny, racism, and homophobia in the force, as well as the increased politicization that many police perceive of their role. The public discontent that has surrounded the Police, Crime, Sentencing and Courts Act 2022 is proof of disharmony between the public and the police. Indeed, the most recent in-depth analyses of the 'state of policing in UK' have outlined the wide-ranging challenges faced by police institutions and the need for change to prevent a crisis from occurring. It has been suggested that the UK policing brand (and particularly the model associated with England and Wales) remains firmly intact although needing an overhaul. In a recent report, Sir Tom Winser maintained that the British model of policing remains 'fundamentally different' to other policing models, encased within the core Peelian principle of *policing by consent*, which have more recently been exposed within newer initiatives related to 'community policing, restorative justice and procedural justice'. The report outlined how 'this experience reaffirms the continuing value of discretion, dialogue, and attention to the manner of police interactions, within the British approach. This contrasted markedly to the experience of policing in some other European countries ...'. Yet today 'the police sit at the *nexus of intractable social problems and high public expectations*' [author emphasis] (Muir, Higgins, Halkon, Walcott and Jeffrey, 2022: 19, 20, 82).

Declining police capacity and capability have the potential to further the ongoing crisis in policing and the ongoing recruitment of an additional 20,000 officers may not suffice to stem the tide of those officers retiring or leaving the service earlier than planned. As the March 2022 *Final Report for the Strategic Review of Policing* outlined, there are three core challenges: police capacity related to public safety demands; police capability linked to resourcing and the many capabilities required to meet policing demand and delivery; and the need for a different 'organisational platform'. (Muir, Higgins, Halkon, Walcott and Jeffrey, 2022: 10).

Arguably for the UK policing brand to survive, the structure of policing in England and Wales require reform—the forty-three-strong-force model in England and Wales can no longer be sustained moving forward in the twenty-first century, and the core mission and functions of what constitutes policing must be reviewed. Reinforcing the *brand value* of UK policing will necessarily require some mechanism of federalization (similar to Scotland and Northern Ireland) to ensure that a 'local to national to local' approach to policing can be delivered, which will strengthen approaches to international policing assistance in the future.

Bolstering operational capacity and capability in response to demand is, however, reliant on international (and particularly EU) police and law enforcement partnerships. There remain considerable challenges ahead related to agreements on law enforcement and criminal justice cooperation between the UK and the EU. The post-Brexit arrangements do not offer the same level of police and criminal justice collaboration (exchange of criminal data, involvement in EU law enforcement and criminal justice agencies, extradition provisions and so on) as before and maintaining close collaboration has proved particularly difficult to avoid a 'cliff-edge' departure. While an agreement related to 'law enforcement and criminal cooperation' has currently reached consensus between the EU and the UK, the details have yet to been finalized (HoL, 2021b). Difficulties remain for UK policing (and law enforcement more broadly) related to the management of serious crime now that the relationship with the EU has changed and this will certainly be reflected within future research.

And what of the future for UK policing and international development and security assistance? First, unless there is a sizeable inflation in policing capacity in the short-term, it remains unlikely that large cohorts of serving police officers will be released for international policing missions. Then there is the *why* and *so what* question of an international mission and the relationship with UK national and regional interests as well as the geographical proximity. Research emanating from post-9/11 interventions, the relevance, effectiveness, and value for money within broader security sector reform requires urgent consideration and should have a bearing on future missions. It is possible, however, that the current uncertainty surrounding future security arrangements in Ukraine and the Baltics (and with the geographical proximity) that there may more interest and flexibility in providing serving police for a future NATO mission. Where bi-lateral security and policing programmes are concerned, there will be ample opportunities for police retirees contracted by the UK government, commercial implementers, security organizations as well as overseas governments. Indeed, the UK policing brand will continue to provide a lucrative business model for police retirees as well as those police organizations who benefit commercially from deploying serving officers on short-term missions. UK policing (as well as the multifarious global policing brands) will seek out and widen commercial opportunities moving forward. The retired and serving sector will continue to work together, keeping the revolving door moving in a circular fashion and creating opportunities. Essentially the backbone of the UK policing brand comprising both the serving and retired sector, which will no doubt trade on its historical legacy for many years to come.

This book has helped chart the rise of privatized police contracting in the UK, as part of a broader trend of privatization in the military and security space across the West over the past three decades. Yet what happens when non-Western aligned countries enter the fray? The arrival of the Wagner Group, a Russian mercenary organization, in theatres of conflict across the Middle East and Africa is proof of the Russian private 'war' (combat) providers. Going forward, it may be the case that some governments may prefer to request the services of a quasi-mercenary organization to intervene directly, unencumbered by the bureaucracy and due diligence requirements of the West. Researchers must take seriously the repercussions of the drive towards privatization and the impact that this will have on international humanitarian law and human rights law commitments and, must look far more closely into the precise services that are being provided by the full range of security actors now before us. As global political and security structures continue to fragment, and then to re-order, it would be prescient to further our understanding of the role of state and non-state security and policing actors both 'at home and away'.

Georgina Sinclair
Greys Green, August, 2022

APPENDIX

Examples of UK police mission deployments

UK Police Overseas Deployments to UN, EU, and NATO missions 2011-2012[1]

Mission—Location	Nos Officers	Ranks	Force/Organization If known	Types roles
EUPol Afghanistan (Helmand)	3	1 Supt, 2 retired	MPS	Head of City Police & Justice Programme, Mentor/Advisor City Police (Lashkar Gah)_
EUPol Afghanistan (Kabul)	11	1 Ch Sup, 3 Supt, 4 Ch Insp, 1 D/Ch Insp, 1 D/Insp 1 retired	MPD, Northumbria, Hants., Warwicks, Herts, South Wales, Kent, West Yorks, Sussex	Deputy Head of Mission, Head of Police Staff College, Staff Officer, Head of City Police and Justice Prog, MOI mentor, Senior Training, CPJP Head,
NATO (NTMA) Afghanistan (Kabul)	5	1 ACC, 2 Supt, 2 Ch Insp	Sussex, Strathclyde, Northumbria, MDP, Hants.,	Chief of Police Trainers, Deputy Direc Training, Senior Police Advisor, Office Manager
PRT Afghanistan (Helmand)	19	All ranks	MDP	Police mentors and trainers

[1] NB. This information relates to officers deployed for HMG to UN, NATO and EU-led missions (peacekeeping, post-conflict states, fragile states, political missions). They are predominantly *serving officers*. This does not reflect the deployment of officers:

    For operational work seconded by their own forces (global).
    For temporary police assistance as agreed and seconded by their own forces (global).
    Retired offices working in Overseas Dependent Territories.
    Retired officers working in the private sector (global) (this number is substantial in comparison with the number of serving officers serving overseas).

Mission—Location	Nos Officers	Ranks	Force/Organization If known	Types roles
UN Sierra Leone (Freetown)	1	1 D/Supt	MPS	Counter Narcotics expert
EU (EUMM) Georgia	4	1 Insp, 1 DC, 2 PC	Lincs, MDP	Monitors
EU (EUCOPPS) Palestine	3	1 Ch Supt, 1 Ch Insp 1 retired	Northumbria, West Mercia	Senior Police advisor, Staff officer and liaison, Command and control expert
EU (EULEX) Kosovo	10	1 Ch Supt, 3 Ch Insp, 2 D/Ch Insp, 1 D/Insp., 3 PCs	Leics, Hants, Sussex, Avon & Somerset, Devon & Cornwall, Strathclyde, MDP	Head of police strengthening, Crime and Intel, Chief advisor to operations, D/Head Org Crime, Chief quality control, Intel Officer, Witness support unit
TOTAL	46			

UK Police Overseas Deployments to UN, EU, NATO, and bi-lateral missions 2019–2020

Mission- Location	Nos of officers	Types of roles
NATO RSM—MAG—I Afghanistan (Kabul)	5 (2 retired)	Senior police advisors to MOI
CSSF ISSAT Sierra Leone (Freetown)	2	Head of police reform
UN HQ (New York)	1	Senior police advisor
Total	10	

References

Aaker, D. A. (1996). *Building Strong Brands*. New York: Free Press.
Aaker, D. A. and Joachimsthaler, E. (1999). 'The Lure of Global Branding'. *Harvard Business Review*, November–December, 137–44.
ACPO ACPOS (2010). 'IPAB; Areas of Assistance within (and outside) the scope of the International Police Assistance Board'. *Briefing Note*.
ACPO ACPOS (2011). 'ACPO International Affairs: UK Police Assistance Overseas'. *Briefing Note*.
ACPO ACPOS (2012). 'ACPO International Affairs: UK Police Assistance Overseas'. *Briefing Note*.
ACPO ACPOS (2014). 'ACPO International Affairs: UK Police Assistance Overseas'. *Briefing Note*.
ACPO ACPOS NPIA (2010). *Manual of Guidance on Keeping the Peace*. Beds, Wyboston: Specialist Operations Centre.
ACPO IPAB (2010). *The United Kingdom's International Policing Assistance Strategy*. Volume 1. In association with FCO, NI Office, NPIA, HMRC, MOD, MPS, HO, SOCA, Cabinet Office, DFID, Association of Police Authorities and the Scottish Government.
Ahmad, A. (2016). 'Emiratis and expats can train to become Abu Dhabi community police officers'. *UAE*, 7 September 2016.
Ahrari, E. (2006). 'U.S. digs for 'long war''. *Asia Times*, 9 February 2006.
Aitchison, A. and Blaustein, J. (2013). 'Policing for Democracy or Democratically Responsive Policing? Examining the Limits of Externally Driven Police Reform'. *European Journal of Criminology*. 10(4): 496–511.
Akam, S. (2021). *The Changing of the Guard; The British Army since 9/11*. London: Scribe.
Albrecht, P. A. (2010). 'Transforming Internal Security in Sierra Leone: Sierra Leone Police and Broader Justice Sector Reform'. *Danish Institute for International Studies Report*, July 2010. Copenhagen: DIIS.
Albrecht, P. and Jackson, P. (2009). 'Security System Transformation in Sierra Leone, 1997–2007'. *Global Facilitation Network for Security Sector Reform*. Birmingham: University of Birmingham.
Al Mazrouei, H. and Pech, R. J. (2014). 'Expatriates in the UAE: Advance Training Eases Cultural Adjustments'. *Journal of Business Strategy*. 35(3): 47–54.
Amin, L. (2017). 'UK police earned millions training officers in repressive regimes'. *The Guardian*, 15 September 2017.
Amstel van N., and Rodenhäuser, T. (2016). 'The Montreux Document and the International Code of Conduct: Understanding the Relationship between International Initiatives to Regulate the Global Private Security Industry'. *Report*.

Geneva: DCAF. Amnesty International (2009). 'Amnesty questions human rights standards of P.S.N.I. training of Libyan police'. *Press releases*, 18 September 2009. Available at <https://www.amnesty.org.uk/press-releases/amnesty-questions-human-rights-standards-psni-training-libyan-police>.

Amstel, van N. and Rodenhäuser, T. (2016). 'The Montreux Document and the International Code of Conduct: Understanding the Relationship between International Initiatives to Regulate the Global Private Security Industry'. *Report*. Public-Private Partnerships Series, No. 1. Geneva: DCAF.

Anderson, D. M. and Killingray, D. (1991). (Eds.). *Policing the Empire: Government, Authority and Control, 1830–1940*. Manchester: Manchester University Press.

Anderson, D. M. and Killingray, D. (1992). (Eds.). *Policing and Decolonization*. Manchester: Manchester University Press.

Andreas, P. and Nadelman, E. (2006). *Policing the Globe; Criminalization and Crime Control in International Relations*. Oxford: Oxford University Press.

Ardemagni, E. (2019). 'The Abu Dhabi Policing Laboratory: Building Security. Forging Community'. *Civilianizing the State in the Middle East and Asia Pacific Regions: Middle East-Asia Project*, 16 July 2019. Available at: https://www.mei.edu/publications/abu-dhabi-policing-laboratory-building-security-forging-community.

Ares and Athena (2016). 'Is Britain braced for a return to peacekeeping ops?'. Issue 5: *United Nations*. Centre for Historical Analysis and Conflict Research, June 2016.

ARLEMP (2020). 'Asia Region Law Enforcement Management Program—ARLEMP Upskill—Pandemic Response and Preparedness'. *Briefing Note*.

Arnold, D. (1986). *Police Power and Colonial Rule, Madras, 1859–1947*. Oxford: Oxford University Press.

Arnold, E. (2022). 'Global Britain Strikes Back'. *Commentary*. RUSI, 27 January 2022.

Ascoli, D. (1979). *The Queen's Peace*. London: Hamish Hamilton.

Ashraf, M. A. (2007). 'The Lessons of Policing in Iraq—a Personal Perspective'. *Policing: A Journal of Policy and Practice*. 1(1): 1–4.

Austin, J. (2020). 'Grey Zone Deterrence—The key to a more secure future?'. *Analysis. UK Defence Journal*, 17 February 2020.

Baker, B. (2007). 'How Civil War Altered Policing in Sierra Leone and Uganda'. *Commonwealth and Comparative Politics*, 45(3): 367–87.

Baker, B. 'Sierra Leone Police Reform: the role of the UK government'. *GRIPS State-Building Workshop 2010: Organizing Police Forces in Post-Conflict Peace-Support Operations*, 27–28 January 2010.

Ball, N. and Walker, C. (2015). 'DFID Security and Justice Assistance: What Works?'. *Report commissioned by DFID*. London: HMSO.

Barrie, D. G. (2008). *Police in the Age of Improvement: Police Development and the Civic Tradition of Scotland, 1775-1865*. Cullompton: Willan.

Barth Eide. E. and Tanke Holm. T. (1999). 'Postscript: Towards executive authority policing? The lessons of Kosovo'. *International Peacekeeping*. 6(4): 210–19.

Barkawi, T. and Laffey, M. (2006). 'The Postcolonial Moment in Security Studies'. *Review of International Studies*, 32: 329–52.

Barker, A. (2004). *Shadows; Inside Northern Ireland's Special Branch*. London: Mainstream Publishing.

Barrie, D. G. (2008). *Police in the Age of Improvement: Police Development and the Civic Tradition of Scotland, 1775–1865*. Cullompton: Willan Publishing.

Barry, B. (2020). *Blood, Metal and Dust; How Victory Turned into Defeat in Afghanistan and Iraq*. Oxford: Osprey Publishing.

Barth Eide, E. and Tanke Holm, T. (1999). 'Postscript: Towards Executive Authority Policing? The Lessons of Kosovo'. *International Peacekeeping*, 6(4): 210–19.

Bayley, D. H. (1995). 'A Foreign Policy for Democratic Policing'. *Policing and Society*, 5(2): 79–94.

Bayley, D. H. (1999). 'Capacity-building in Law Enforcement'. *Australian Institute of Criminology*, 123: 1–4.

Bayley, D. H. (1997). 'The Contemporary Practices of Policing: A Comparative View' in National Institute of Justice. *Civilian Police and Multinational Peacekeeping—A Workshop Series: A Role for Democratic Policing*, 6 October 1997. Washington, D.C.

Bayley, D. H. (2001). *Democratizing the Police Abroad: What to Do and How to Do it*. Washington, D.C.: National Institute of Justice.

Bayley, D. H. (2006). *Changing the Guard: Developing Democratic Police Abroad*. Oxford: Oxford University Press.

Bayley, D. H. and Perito, R. (2010). *The Police in War: Fighting Insurgency, Terrorism, and Violent Crime*. Dulles, VA: Lynne Rienner Publishers.

BBC News (1995). 'British forces sent to Sarajevo'. *On This Day 1950–2005*, 23 July 1995. Available at <http://news.bbc.co.uk/onthisday/hi/dates/stories/july/23/newsid_2518000/2518249.stm>.

BBC News (2016). 'Police Scotland's overseas training work is 'hypocrisy'', 25 May 2016.

BBC News (2019). 'Policing resources at dangerously low levels, ex Scotland Yard chiefs warn', 5 July 2019. Available at <https://www.bbc.co.uk/news/uk-48878470>.

BBC News (2021). 'Sarah Everard: Met police chief will not resign over vigil scenes, 14 March 2021. Available at <https://www.bbc.co.uk/news/uk-56389824>.

Belfast Telegraph (2009). 'Fury over PSNI training for Libyans'. *Belfast Telegraph*, 18 September 2009. Available at <https://www.belfasttelegraph.co.uk/news/fury-over-psni-training-for-libyans-28495726.html>.

Betancourt, E., Bisca, P. M., Diamond, T., El-Badawy, E., Geer, R., Lavinal, O., and Wolfe, R. (2019). *Sharpening our Efforts; The Role of International Development in Countering Violent Extremism*. Center for Strategic and International Studies, USAID.

Biddle, K. (2000). *Conflict, Security and Development Group Bulletin*. Issue 5, March–April 2000: 1–4.

Biddle, K. (2007). *Oral History Program (interview by G. Peake): Policing*. Innovations for Successful Societies. National Academy of Public Administration and Princeton University's Woodrow Wilson School of Public Policy and Bobst Center for Peace and Justice, 5 December 2007.

Bjork, K. and Jones, R. (2005). 'Overcoming Dilemmas Created by the 21st Century Mercenaries: Conceptualising the Use of Private Security Companies in Iraq'. *Third World Quarterly*. 26(4–5): 777–96.

Blair, S. and Brown, M. (2016). 'Beyond Muddling Through: Towards a Blueprint for UK International Policing and Law Enforcement'. *The RUSI Journal*. 161(1): 62–9.

BMG Research (2019). 'Public Perceptions of Policing in England and Wales 2018'. *Project 1578*. Prepared for Her Majesty's Inspectorate of Constabulary and Fire and Rescue Services. Birmingham: BMG Research.

Bond, I. (2020). 'Brexit and External Differentiation in Foreign, Security and Defence Policy'. *Policy Briefs*. No. 2, September 2020.

Born, H., Caparini, M., and Fluri, P. (2002). (Eds.). 'Security Sector Reform and Democracy in Transitional Societies'. *Proceedings of the Democratic Control of Armed Forces Workshops at the 4th International Security Forum*. Geneva, November 15–17, 2000.

Bottoms, A. and Tankebe, J. (2012). 'Beyond Procedural Justice: A Dialogic Approach to Legitimacy in Criminal Justice'. *Journal of Criminal Law and Criminology*. 102(1): 119–70.

Bowling, B. (2009). 'Transnational Policing: The Globalization Thesis, a Typology and a Research Agenda'. *Policing*. 3(2): 149–60.

Bowling, B. and Sheptycki, J. (2012). *Global Policing*. Sage: London.

Boyd, G. and Marnoch, G. (2014). 'Capacity Building and the Afghan National Police Views from the Frontline'. *European Journal of Policing Studies*. 1(4): 251–73.

Bradford, B. and Jackson, J. (2011). 'Legitimacy and the Social Field of Policing'. 22 August 2011). Available at SSRN: https://ssrn.com/abstract=1914458 or http://dx.doi.org/10.2139/ssrn.1914458.

Brain, T. (2010). *A Future for Policing in England and Wales*. Oxford: Oxford University Press.

Bramati, L. (2020). *Iraq, 2003–2009: Lessons Learned from the Chilcot Commission, Where Stability Policing Could Have Made a Difference. Ten Considerations for Planners and Commanders*. Rome: Military Center for Strategic Studies.

Brand, D. (2010). *Iraq Inquiry Evidence of Douglas Brand OBE*. The Report of the Iraq Inquiry; Report of a Committee of Privy Counsellors. Volume III. Ordered by the House of Commons to be printed on 6 July 2016.

Brewer, J. D. (1990). *The Royal Irish Constabulary: An Oral History*. Belfast: Institute of Irish Studies, Queens University.

Brewer, J. D. (1990). *Inside the RUC*. Oxford: Oxford University Press.

Brewer, J. D. (1991). 'Policing in Divided Societies: Theorising a Type of Policing'. *Policing and Society*. 1(3): 179–91.

British Association of Private Security Companies (BAPSC) (2021). Available at <https://bapsc.org.uk/>.

Brodeur, J. P. (2007). 'High and Low Policing in Post-9/11 Times'. *Policing: A Journal of Policy and Practice*, 1(1): 25–37.

Brodeur, J. P. (2010). *The Policing Web*. Oxford: Oxford University Press.

Brogden, M. (1982). *The Police: Autonomy and Consent*, London: Academic Press.

References

Brogden, M. (1987a) 'An Act to Colonise the Internal Lands of the Island: Empire and the Origins of the Professional Police'. *International Journal of the Sociology of Law.* 15: 179–208.

Brogden, M. (1987b). 'The Emergence of the Police: The Colonial Dimension'. *British Journal of Criminology.* 27(4): 158–71.

Brogden, M. and Ellison, G. (2013). *Policing in an Age of Austerity; A Postcolonial Perspective.* London: Routledge.

Brogden, M. E. and Nijhar, P. (2005). *Community Policing: National and International Models and Approaches.* Cullompton: Willan Publishing.

Brooke-Holland, L. (2021). 'Defence Command Paper 2021: Summary'. *Briefing paper no. 9181.* House of Commons Library, 19 March 2021.

Brooking, S. (2011). 'Private Security Companies in Afghanistan, 2001–11'. In: Bijlert, M. and van Kouvo, S. (Eds.) *Snapshots of an Intervention. The Unlearned Lessons of Afghanistan's Decade of Assistance (2001–2011).* Afghanistan Analysts Network. Part II. Strengthening the Security Forces.

Brown, J., Neyroud, P., Loader, I., and Muir, R. (2013). *Policing for a Better Britain: Report of the Independent Police Commission,* June 2013. Available at: https://www.statewatch.org/media/documents/news/2013/nov/uk-police-commission-summary.pdf.

Brown, D. (2010). *The European Union, Counter Terrorism and Police Co-operation 1992–2007; Unsteady Foundations?* Manchester: Manchester University Press.

Brownsell, A. (2008). 'New Scotland Yard to license its brand'. *Campaign.* 4 December 2008.

Brunger, M. (2014). 'Exploring the Myth of the Bobby and the Intrusion of the State into Social Space'. *International Journal for the Semiotics of Law.* 27(1): 121–34.

Bryne, J. (2014). *Reflections on the Northern Ireland experience; The lessons underpinning the normalization of policing and security in a divided society.* Police Service of Northern Ireland, INTERCOMM and Saferworld, June 2014.

Brzoska, M. and Law, D. M. (2006). *Security Sector Reform in Peace Support Operations.* London: Routledge.

Bull, M. and Sinclair, G. (2012). 'Keeping the peace at home: the exchange of capacity in international and local policing forums'. Paper presented at *British Society of Criminology Conference.* Portsmouth, UK, July 3–7.

Burleigh, M. (2017). *The Best of Times, The Worst of Time: A History of Now.* London: Macmillan.

Byman, D. L. (2008). 'The Changing Nature of State Sponsorship of Terrorism'. *Analysis Paper.* No. 16, May 2008.

Byrne, J. (2014). 'Reflections on the Northern Ireland experience: The Lessons underpinning the normalisation of policing and security in a divided society'. *Policy Brief.* PSNI, INTERCOMM and Saferworld, June 2014.

Caparini, M. (2014). 'Capacity-Building and Development of Host State Police: The Role of International Police'. *Challenges Forum Occasional Paper No. 3,* May 2014.

Celador, G. C. (2007). 'The European Union Police Mission: The Beginning of a New Future for Bosnia and Herzegovina?' *IBEI Working Paper No. 2007/9.*

Çelik, F. B. (2020). 'Foreign Policy Decision-making in Operational Overlap: The UK's Policing Assistance in Afghanistan through the EU and NATO'. *European Security*. 29(4): 456–82.
Chalmers, M. (2017). 'UK Foreign and Security Policy after Brexit'. *Briefing Paper*, January 2017. London: RUSI.
Chalmers, M. (2020a). 'Taking Control: Rediscovering the Centrality of National Interest in UK Foreign and Security Policy'. RUSI Whitehall Reports, 10 February 2020. London: RUSI.
Chalmers, M. (2020b). 'Farewell Foreign and Commonwealth Office, Welcome Foreign, Commonwealth and Development Office'. *Commentary*, 16 June 2020. London: RUSI.
Chalmers, M. (2021). 'The Integrated Review: The UK as a Reluctant Middle Power?'. *RUSI Occasional Paper*, March 2021. London: RUSI.
Chalmers, M. and Jesset, W. (2020). 'Deferring Judgement—Whither the UK's Integrated Review and Defence? Commentary, 27 March 2020. London: RUSI.
Chanaa, J. (2002). *Security Sector Reform: Issues, Challenges and Prospects*. New York: Oxford University Press.
Chapleo, C. (2010). 'What Defines "Successful" University Brands?'. *International Journal of Public Sector Management*. 23 (2): 169–83.
Cimmino, J., Katz, R., Kroenig, M., Lipsky, J., and Pavel, B. (2020). 'A Global Strategy for Shaping the Post-Covid-19 World'. *Atlantic Council Strategy Papers*. Scowcroft Center for Strategy and Security.
Claassen, R. (2011). 'The Marketization of Security Services'. *Public Reason*. 3(2): 124–45.
Cleveland Police. (2003). 'Seconded Officers/Police Staff including overseas deployment'. *Corporate Policy*.
Clutterbuck, L. (2015). 'The Other Side of COIN; New Challenges for British Police and Military in the Twenty-first Century'. In: Johnson, R. and Clack, T. (Eds.). *At the End of Military Intervention; Historical, Theoretical, and Applied Approaches to Transition, Handover, and Withdrawal*. Oxford: Oxford University Press: 437–57.
Cockcroft, T. (2013). *Police Culture; Themes and Concepts*. London: Routledge.
Cole, P. with Mangan, F. (2016). 'Policing Libya; Form and Function of Policing since the 2011 Revolution'. *Report, Peaceworks 117*. Washington, D.C.: US Institute of Peace.
College of Policing (2014). *Authorised Professional Practice for Public Order*. 1 February 2014.
College of Policing (2020). *College of Policing International Income Generated from January 2013 to December 2020*. Available at: https://assets.college.police.uk/s3fs-public/2021-02/international_income_information_2013_20.pdf.
Colley, L. (1992). 'Britishness and Otherness: An Argument'. *The Journal of British Studies*. 31(4): 309–29.
Comber, L. (2008). *Malaya's Secret Police 1945–60: The Role of the Special Brand in the Malayan Emergency*. Victoria: Monash University/Singapore: ISEAS Publishing.
Cotton, S. K., Petersohn, U., Dunigan, M., Burkhart, Q., Zander-Cotugno, M., O'Connell, E., and Webber, M. (2010). *Hired Guns: Views About Armed*

Contractors in Operation Iraqi Freedom. RAND National Security Research Division: Sponsored by the Smith Richardson Foundation. Santa Monica, Ca.: RAND Corporation, MG-987-SRF, 2010. 19 July 2013.

Craig, P. (2008). *Undercover Cop; One Man's True Story of Undercover Policing in Ireland, the UK and Europe*. Dublin: Gill and Macmillan Ltd.

Crawford, A. (2006). 'Networked Governance and the Post-Regulatory State? Steering, Rowing and Anchoring the Provision of Policing and Security'. *Theoretical Criminology*. 10(4): 449–79.

Crawford, A. (2009). (Ed.). *Crime Prevention Policies in Comparative Perspective*. Abingdon: Routledge.

Crawford, A. (2014). 'The Police, Policing and the Future of the Extended Policing Family'. In: Brown, J. M. (Ed). *The Future of Policing*. Abingdon: Routledge: 173–91.

Critchley, T. A. (1967). *A History of the Police in England and Wales*. London: Constable.

Cortada, J. W. (2009). 'Power and use of context in business management'. *Journal of Knowledge Management*. 13(3): 13–27.

Curtis, R. H. (1871). *The History of the Royal Irish Constabulary*. Dublin: Moffat and Company.

Dammert, L. (2019). 'Challenges of Police Reform in Latin America'. In: Siedler, R., Ansolabehere, K., and Alfonso, T. (Eds.). *Routledge Handbook of Law and Society in Latin America*. New York: Routledge: Part II, Chapter 17.

Davidson, N., Jackson, L., and Smale, D. (2016). 'Police Amalgamation and Reform in Scotland: The Long Twentieth Century'. *Scottish Historical Review*. 95(1): 88–111.

Davies, C. (2011). 'Briton Danny Fitzsimons jailed in Iraq for contractors' murders'. *The Guardian*, 28 February 2011.

Day, G. and Freeman, C. (2003). 'Policekeeping is the Key: Rebuilding the Internal Security Architecture of Postwar Iraq'. *International Affairs*. 79(2): 299–313.

Deflem, M. (2004). *Policing World Society: Historical Foundations of International Police Cooperation*. Oxford: Oxford University Press.

Deflem, M. and Sutphin, S. (2006). 'Policing Post-War Iraq: Insurgency, Civilian Police, and the Reconstruction of Society'. *Sociological Focus*. 39(4): 265–83.

Denney, L. and Jenkins, S. (2013). 'Securing communities: the what and the how of community policing'. *Background paper*. London: ODI.

Den Heyer, G. (2011). 'New Public Management: A Strategy for Democratic Police Reform in Transitioning and Developing Countries'. *Policing: An International Journal*. 34(3): 419–33.

Denney, L. and Jenkins, S. (2013). 'Securing communities: the what and the how of community policing'. *Background paper*. London: ODI.

Dep, A. G. (1969). *A History of the Ceylon Police*. Volume II: 1866–1913. Columbo.

DfID (1999). 'Poverty and the security sector'. *Policy Statement*. London: SIPRI Library and Documentation.

DfID (2000). 'Security sector reform: Review of the role of external actors'. *Discussion Paper 2*, February 2000. London: DFID.

DfID (2011a). 'International Stabilisation Response Team (ISRT) Libya 20 May–30 June 2011'. *Report*.

DfID (2011b). 'Police and public security: update paper'. *Report by Senior Police Adviser*, Benghazi, 30 August 2011.

DfID (2012a). 'Libya Stabilisation Response 202486'. *Annual Review*, September 2012.

DfID (2012b). *Annual Review and Accounts 2012-13*. HC 12, 27 June 2013. London: The Stationery Office.

DfID (2019). *Statistics on International Development: Final UK Aid Spend 2018*, September 2019. London: The Stationery Office.

DfID, FCO, and MOD (2011). *Building Stability Overseas Strategy*. London: Crown Copyright.

Den Heyer, G. (2011). 'New public management: A strategy for democratic police reform in transitioning and developing countries'. *Policing: An International Journal*. 34(3): 419–33.

Dep, A. G. (1969). *A history of the Ceylon Police*. Volume II: 1866–1913. Colombo.

Diamint, R. (2002). 'Civilians and the military in Latin American democracies'. *Disarmament Forum No. 2*. Geneva: UNIDIR: 15–24.

Diamond, L. (1999). *Developing Democracy: Towards Consolidation*. London: The John Hopkins University Press.

Dinnen, S. (1997). 'The Money and the Gun Mercenary Times in Papua New Guinea'. *The Journal of Pacific History*. 32(3): 52–65.

Dinnen, S. (1999). 'Militaristic Solutions in a Weak State: Internal Security, Private Contractors, and Political Leadership in Papua New Guinea'. *The Contemporary Pacific*. 11(2): 279–303.

Donnelly, D. and Scott, K. (Eds.). (2005). 'Introduction: Policing Scotland'. In: *Policing Scotland*. Cullompton: Willan Publishing: 1–8.

Donnelly, D. and Scott, K. (Eds.). (2011). 2nd Edition. *Policing Scotland*. Cullompton: Willan Publishing.

Dowbiggin, H. L. (1928). 'The Ceylon Police and its Development'. *Police Journal*, no. 1: 203–17.

Duff, D. V. (1938). *Harding of the Palestine Police*. London: Blackie and Son Limited.

Duffield, M. (2007). *Development, Security and Unending War: Governing the World of Peoples*. Cambridge: Polity Press.

Duffy, J. (2013). 'Revealed: how Scots police trained Sri Lankan cops linked to human rights abuse'. *The Herald*, 8 September 2013. Available at: https://www.heraldscotland.com/news/13121850.revealed-scots-police-trained-sri-lankan-cops-linked-human-rights-abuse/.

Duffy, J. (2014). 'Human rights outcry as Scots police train Sri Lankan forces'. *The Herald*, 3 August 2014. Available at: https://www.heraldscotland.com/news/13173048.human-rights-outcry-scots-police-train-sri-lankan-forces/.

Dunigan, M., Carrie M., Farmer, R. M., Burns, Hawks, A., and Messan Setodji, C. (2013). *Out of the Shadows: The Health and Well-Being of Private Contractors Working in Conflict Environments*. Santa Monica, CA: RAND Corporation, 2013.

Dunn, P. W. D. (1951). 'The Role of the Police in a Democratic State'. *The Police College Magazine*. Special Volume. September 1951: 9–17.

Dunsby, J. (2015). 'The Changing Role of Contractors in Security Transition in Southern Afghanistan'. In: Johnson, R. and Clack, T. (Eds.). *At the End of Military*

Intervention; Historical, Theoretical and Applied Approaches to Transition, Handover, and Withdrawal. Oxford: Oxford University Press: 377–98.

Dunster, C. (2018). 'Managing Competing Risks Affecting Displaced Persons in a Conflict Environment: A Case Study from United Nations Policing in South Sudan'. In: Sinclair, G. and Burdett, R. (Eds.). *Mission Challenges, Lessons Learned and Guiding Principles: Policing with Communities in Fragile and Conflict Affected States; Lessons from the Field and Practitioner Perspectives*. Scottish Institute for Policing Research: 146–63.

Dziedzic, M. J. (2003). *The Public Security Challenge and International Stability Police Units*. US Institute of Peace.

Easton, M., Den Boer, M., Janssens, J., Moelker, R., and Vanderbeken, T. (Eds.) (2009). *Blurring Military and Police Roles*. Antwerp: Boom Juridische Uitgevers.

Egnell, R. (2010). 'Winning 'Hearts and Minds'? A Critical Analysis of Counter-Insurgency Operations in Afghanistan'. *Civil Wars*. 12(3): 297–315.

Ellison, G. (2007). 'A Blueprint for Democratic Policing Anywhere in the World?: Police Reform, Political Transition, and Conflict Resolution in Northern Ireland'. *Police Quarterly*. 10(3): 243–69.

Ellison, G. and Smyth, J. (2000). *The Crowned Harp: Policing Northern Ireland*. London: Pluto Press.

Ellison, G. and O'Reilly, C. (2006). '"Eye Spy Private High": Re-Conceptualizing High Policing Theory'. *The British Journal of Criminology*. 46(4): 641–60.

Ellison, G. and O'Reilly, C. (2008a). 'From Empire to Iraq and the "War on Terror": The Transplantation and Commodification of the (Northern) Irish Policing Experience. *Police Quarterly*. 11(4): 395–426.

Ellison, G. and O'Reilly, C. (2008b). '"Ulster's Policing Goes Global": The Police Reform Process in Northern Ireland and the Creation of a Global Brand'. *Crime, Law and Social Change*. 50: 331–51.

Ellison, G. and Pino, N. W. (2012). *Globalization, Police Reform and Development: Doing it the Western Way?* London: Palgrave Macmillan.

Ellison, G. and Sinclair, G. (2013). 'Entrepreneurial Policing? International Policing Challenges'. *Open Democracy*. Available at <http://www.opendemocracy.net/opensecurity/graham-ellison-georgina-sinclair/entrepreneurial-policing-international-policing-challe>.

Ellison, G. and Smyth, J. (2000). *The Crowned Harp: Policing Northern Ireland*. London: Pluto Press.

Emsley, C. (1985). '"The Thump of Wood on a Swede Turnip": Police Violence in Nineteenth Century England'. *Crime History Societies*.6: 125–49.

Emsley, C. (1991). *The English Police: A Political and Social History*. London: Harvester Wheatsheaf.

Emsley, C. (1996). *The English Police: A Political and Social History*. 2nd Edition. Harlow: Longman.

Emsley, C. (1999). 'Aspects of the History of Crime, Police and Policing in Europe since c. 1750'. *Doctor of Letters in History*. The Open University, Milton Keynes.

Emsley, C. (2009). *The Great British Bobby: A History of British Policing from 1829 to the Present*. London: Quercus Publishing.

Emsley, C. (2010). *Crime and Society in England, 1750-1900*. 4th Edition. Harlow: Pearson.

Emsley, C. (2011). 'Theories and Origins of the Modern Police.' Volume 1. In: Emsley, C. (Series Ed.). *The History of Policing*. Farnham: Ashgate.

Emsley, C. (2012). 'Marketing the Brand: Exporting British Police Models 1829-1950'. *Policing: A Journal of Policy and Practice*. 6(1): 43-54.

Emsley, C. (2014). 'Peel's Principles, Police Principles'. In: Brown, J. E. (Ed.). *The Future of Policing*. London: Routledge: 11-23.

Emsley, C. and Clapson, M. (2002). 'Street, Beat, and Respectability: The Culture and Self-image of the Late Victorian and Edwardian Urban Policeman'. In: Knafla, L. A. (Ed.). *Policing and War in Europe: Criminal Justice History*. Santa Barbara, CA: Greenword Press: 107-31.

Emsley, C. and Sinclair, G. (2009). 'Exploring UK policing practices as a blueprint for democratic police reform: the overseas deployment of UK Police Officers, 1989-2009'. ESCR RES-000-22-3922.

Emsley, C. and Sinclair, G. (2011). 'Bobbies Abroad'. *History Today*. 61(10): 49-51.

Farrell, T. (2017). *Unwinnable; Britain's War in Afghanistan 2001-2014*. London: The Bodley Head.

FCDO (2020). Policy Update, 25 November 2020.

FCDO (2021). *Statistics on International Development: Provisional UK Aid Spend 2020*, April 2021. UK Aid, National Statistics. Available at: https://assets.publishing.service.gov.uk/government/uploads/system/uploads/attachment_data/file/976923/Statistics-on-International-Development-Provisional-UK-Aid-Spend-2020a.pdf.

FCO (1999). *Daily Bulletin*, 11 November 1999.

FCO (2005). 'Iraq-UK Support to Civil Policing in Iraq-2005'. *Policy Brief* [Declassified], 21 February 2005.

FCO (2007a). *Peace support operations: Information and guidance for UK police personnel*. London: FCO, Police and Justice Team.

FCO (2007b). 'Foreign and Commonwealth Office International Policing: International Secondments Team Recruitment Pack 2007-2008'. *Fact Sheet*. London.

FCO (2009). 'Why does the UK contribute to peace support operations and other civilian missions?' Briefing Note. London.

FCO (2010). *A Strong Britain in an Age of Uncertainty: The National Security Strategy*. Cmnd 7953. London: HMSO.

FCO (2012a). *Freedom of Information Act 2000 Request Reference 0669-12*. 6 September 2012.

FCO (2012b). *The Overseas Territories; Security, Success and Sustainability*. Cmnd 8374, June 2012. London: HMSO.

FCO (2012c). 'Private Security Companies'. *Written statement to Parliament*. Volume 555: Debated on Monday 17 December 2021. UK Parliament: Hansard.

Federal Ministry of Interior Auswärtiges Amt (2006). 'Assistance for Rebuilding the Police Force in Afghanistan'. *Report*. Federal Ministry of Interior. 2006: 1-17.

Fedorowich, K. (1996). 'The Problems of Disbandment: The Royal Irish Constabulary and Imperial Migration, 1919-29'. *Irish Historical Studies*. 30(117): 88-110.

Foa, M. (2016). 'British Government is covering up its assistance to torturers and killers worldwide'. *Open Democracy*, 25 November 2016.
FO (1950). 371/81498.
FO (1952). 371/103407.
FO (1962). 371/166726/DV1015/2/G.
FO (1964). 371/175483.
Foa, M. (2016). 'British Government is covering up its assistance to torturers and killers worldwide'. *Open Democracy*, 25 November 2016.
Foreign Affairs Committee. (2016). 'Libya: Examination of intervention and collapse and the UK's future policy options, Session 2016–17'. *House of Commons Paper*. HC 119, 14 September 2016.
Fulham, G. J. (1981). 'James Shaw-Kennedy and the Reformation of the Irish Constabulary 1836–1858'. *Eire-Ireland*. 16: 93–196.
Franklin, D. (2008). *Derek Franklin Memoir*. (Unpublished).
Friedman, J. (2011). *Building Strategic Capacity in the Police: Sierra Leone, 1998–2008*. Innovations for Successful Societies. Princeton University.
Friesendorf, C. (2011). 'Paramilitarization and Security Sector Reform: The Afghan National Police'. *International Peacekeeping*. 18(1): 79–95.
Friesendorf, C. (2012). 'International Intervention and the Use of Force; Military and Police Roles'. *SSR Paper 4*. Geneva: Geneva Centre for the Democratic Control of Armed Forces (DCAF).
Friesendorf, C. (2018). *How Western Soldiers Fight: Organization Routines in Multinational Missions*. Cambridge: Cambridge University Press.
Friesendorf, C. and Krempel, J. (2011). 'Militarized versus Civilian Policing: Problems of Reforming the Afghan National Police'. *PRIF-Report No. 102*. Frankfurt: Peace Research Institute. (Trans. Lynn Benstead).
Fyfe, N. (2014). 'Observations on Police Reform in Scotland'. *British Society of Criminology Newsletter*. 74: 8–12.
Fyfe, N. (2014). 'Different and Divergent Trajectories?' in Brown, J. (Ed.). *The Future of Policing*. Abingdon: Routledge: 493–517.
Fyfe, N. R., Anderson, S., Bland, N., Goulding, A., Mitchell, J., and Reid, S. (2021). 'Experiencing Organizational Change During an Era of Reform: Police Scotland, Narratives of Localism, and Perceptions from the "Frontline"'. *Policing: A Journal of Policy and Practice*. 15(1): 263–76.
Fyfe, N. R. and Scott, K. B. (2013). 'In Search of Sustainable Policing? Creating a National Police Force in Scotland'. In: Fyfe, N. R., Terpstra, J., and Tops, P. (Eds.). *Centralizing Forces? Comparative Perspectives on Contemporary Police Reform in Northern and Western Europe*. The Hague, The Netherlands: Eleven: 119–35.
Fyfe, N. R. and Terpstra, J. (2019). 'Great Expectations? Assessing the Creation of National Police Organisations in Scotland and the Netherlands'. *International Journal of Police Science and Management*. 21: 101–7.
Gaddis, J. L. (2002). *The Landscape of History: How Historians Map the Past*. Oxford: Oxford University Press.
Garland, D. (2001). *The Culture of Control: Crime and Social Order in Contemporary Society*. Oxford: Oxford University Press.

Garton Ash, T. (2009). '1989 changed the world. But where now for Europe'. *The Times*, 4 November 2009.

Gaston, E. L. (2008). 'Mercenarism 2.0? The Rise of the Modern Private Security Industry and Its Implications for International Humanitarian Law Enforcement'. *Harvard International Law Journal.* 49(1): 221–48.

Gaub, F. and Walsh, A. (2020). 'Relationship Therapy: Making Arab Police Reform Work'. *Chaillot Paper 160*, November 2020.

Geoghegan, P. (2021). 'UK government accused of 'grotesque betrayal' as full foreign aid cuts revealed'. *Open Democracy UK: Investigation*, 5 March 2021. Available at: https://www.opendemocracy.net/en/opendemocracyuk/uk-government-accused-of-grotesque-betrayal-as-full-foreign-aid-cuts-revealed/.

Gerrard, B. (1977). 'The Gloucestershire Police in the Nineteenth Century'. *M. Lit.*, University of Bristol.

Gethins, S. (2021). *Nation to Nation: Scotland's Place in the World*. Edinburgh: Luath Press Ltd.

Gibbon, S. (2021). 'Tackling modern slavery: A UK-Vietnamese collaborative approach to combat human trafficking'. Feature. *Policing Insights*, 4 May 2021.

Gilmore, J. (2014). 'The Uncertain Merger of Values and Interests in UK Foreign Policy'. *International Affairs*. 90(3): 541–57.

Gilmore, J. (2020). 'Developing domestic foundations for a values-based UK foreign policy'. *Article*. The Foreign Policy Centre.

Ginifer, J. (2005). 'Armed violence and poverty in Sierra Leone: a case study for the Armed Violence and Poverty Initiative'. *Report*. Bradford, Centre of International Cooperation and Security, Department of Peace Studies, University of Bradford. AVPI Case Studies.

Glenny, M. (2022). 'Talking to the Russian people is the only way out of this hell'. *The Sunday Times*, 13 March 2022.

Gold, J. (2018). '"Nyagoa"—from Somerset to South Sudan: Community Policing in a Conflict Zone, August 2014–May 2016'. In: Sinclair, G. and Burdett, R. (Eds.). *Mission Challenges, Lessons Learned and Guiding Principles: Policing with Communities in Fragile and Conflict Affected States; Lessons from the Field and Practitioner Perspectives*. Scottish Institute for Policing Research: 83–6.

Goldsmith, A. and Dinnen, S. (2007). 'Transnational Police Building: Critical Lessons from Timor-Leste and Solomon Islands'. *Third World Quarterly*. 28(6): 1091–109.

Goldsmith, A. and Sheptycki, J. (2007). (Eds.). *Crafting Transnational Policing*. Oxford: Hart Publishing.

Gorringe, H. and Rosie, M. (2010). 'The "Scottish" Approach? The Discursive Construction of a National Police Force'. *The Sociological Review*. 58 (1): 65–83.

Grabosky, P. (2009). 'Police as International Peacekeepers'. *Policing and Society*. 19(2): 101–5.

Greene, J. R. (2014). 'New Directions in Policing: Balancing Prediction and Meaning in Police Research'. *Justice Quarterly*. 31(2): 193–228.

Greener, B. K. (2009). *The New International Policing*. Basingstoke: Palgrave Macmillan.

References

Greener, B. K. (2020). 'Local Legitimacy in Peacebuilding: Pathways to Local Compliance with International Police Reform'. *International Peacekeeping.* 27(5): 859–63.

Greener, B. K. and Fish, W. J. (2013). 'Police–Military Interaction in International Peace and Stability Operations; Working Towards Guidelines for Action'. *Civil-Military Working Paper 1–2013.* Australian Civil-Military Centre/Australian Government. Canberra, ACT.

Grierson, J. (2020). 'More than 3,000 extra officers join police as part of Johnson pledge'. *The Guardian*, 30 April 2020.

Groenewald, H. and Peake, G. (2004). 'Police Reform through Community-Based Policing'. *Philosophy and Guidelines for Implementation,* September 2004. International Peace Academy and New York: Saferworld/International Peace Academy.

Haider, H. (2009). *Topic Guide on Conflict.* Governance and Social Development Resource Centre.

Hamilton, A. and Moore, L. (1995). 'Policing a Divided Society'. In: Dunn, S. (Ed.). *Facets of the Conflict in Northern Ireland.* London: Palgrave Macmillan: 187–98.

Hampshire Police (2007). *03800 Policy–Overseas Deployment of Police Officers.* Version 3. Last updated 6 June 2007.

Hansard (2001). 'Northern Ireland: RUC Funding'. Volume 626 cc 1371–3. HL Deb 17 July 2001.

Hansen, A. S. (2002). *From Congo to Kosovo: Civilian Police in Peace Operations.* Oxford: Oxford University Press.

Harris, A. T. (2004). *Policing the City: Crime and Legal Authority in London, 1780–1840.* Columbus: Ohio State University Press.

Hart, J. (1951). *The British Police.* London: Allen and Unwin.

Harwich, C. (1961). *Red Dust; Memories of the Uganda Police 1935–1955.* London: Vince Stuart Ltd.

Hassan, H. (2010). 'Foreign police officers arrive to make expats feel at home'. *The National*, 4 April 2010. N UAE. Available at: https://www.thenationalnews.com/uae/foreign-police-officers-here-to-make-expats-feel-at-home-1.526861.

Hawkins, R. (1966). 'Dublin Castle and the Royal Irish Constabulary, 1916–1922'. In: Williams, D. T. (Ed.). *The Irish Struggle 1916–1926.* London: 167–81.

Heiduk, F. (2011). 'Policing Mars or Venus? Comparing European and US Approaches to Police Assistance'. *European Security.* 20(3): 363–83.

Heinemann-Grüder, A. and Grebenschikov, I. (2006). 'Security governance by internationals: The case of Kosovo'. *International Peacekeeping.* 13(1): 43–59.

Held, D. and McGrew, A. (2007). *Globalization/Anti-Globalization; Beyond the Great Divide.* 2nd Edition. Cambridge: Polity Press.

Hendrickson, D. and Karkoszka, A. (2002). *SIPRI Yearbook, 2002: Armaments, Disarmament and International Security.* Stockholm: Stockholm International Peace Research Institute.

Henry, A. and Mackenzie, S. (2012). 'Brokering Communities of Practice: A Model of Knowledge Exchange and Academic–Practitioner Collaboration Developed in the Context of Community Policing'. *Police Practice and Research.* 13(4): 315–28.

References

Herlihy, J. (2005). *Royal Irish Constabulary Officers: A Biographical and Genealogical Guide, 1816–1922.* Dublin: Four Courts Press Ltd.

Hewitt, P. (1999). *Kenya Cowboy; A Police Officer's Account of the Mau Mau Emergency.* London: Avon Books.

Higgins, A. (2020). 'Policing and the Public: Understanding Public Priorities, Attitudes and Expectations; The Strategic Review of Policing in England and Wales'. *Insight Paper 1.* London: The Police Foundation. 17 February 2020.

Hill, R. S. (1986). *Policing the Colonial Frontier: The Theory and Practice of Coercive Social and Racial Control in New Zealand, 1767–1867.* Wellington, N.Z.: Historical Publications Branch, Dept. of Internal Affairs.

Hill, R. S. (1989). *The Colonial Frontier Tamed: New Zealand Policing in Transition, 1867–1886.* Wellington: GP Books.

Hill, R. S. (1995). *The Iron Hand in the Velvet Glove: The Modernisation of Policing in New Zealand, 1886–1917.* Wellington, N.Z.: Historical Publications Branch, Dept. of Internal Affairs in association with the New Zealand Police.

Hill, R. S. (2019). 'Coercion, Consent and Surveillance: Policing New Zealand, 1914–1918'. In: Campion, J., Lopez, L., and Payen, G. (Eds.). *European Police Forces and Law Enforcement in the First World War.* London: Palgrave Macmillan: 243–53.

Hillyard, P. (1997). 'Policing Divided Societies: Trends and Prospects in Northern Ireland and Britain'. In: Davies, F. P. and Jupp, V. (Eds.). *Policing Futures; The Police, Law Enforcement and the Twenty-First Century.* London: Palgrave Macmillan: 163–85.

Hinton, M. S. and Newburn, T. (2008). (Eds.). *Policing Developing Democracies.* London: Routledge.

HM Government (2010). *A Strong Britain in an Age of Uncertainty: The National Security Strategy.* Cmnd 7953, October 2010. London: HMSO.

HM Government (2015). *National Security Strategy and Strategic Defence and Security Review 2015: A Secure and Prosperous United Kingdom.* Cmnd 9161, November 2015. London: HMSO.

HM Government (2018). *National Security Capability Review; Including the Second Annual Report on Implementation of the National Security Strategy and Strategic Defence and Security Review 2015.* March 2018. London: HMSO.

HM Government (2017). *Overseas Security and Justice Assistance (OSJA): Human Rights Guidance.* Available at: https://assets.publishing.service.gov.uk/government/uploads/system/uploads/attachment_data/file/583304/OSJA_Guidance_2017.pdf.

HM Government (2021). *Global Britain in a Competitive Age: The Integrated Review of Security, Defence, Development and Foreign Policy.* CP 403. London: HMSO.

HMIC (2011). 'Policing Public Order; An Overview and Review of Progress against the Recommendations of *Adapting to Protest and Nurturing the British Model of Policing*'. *Report,* February 2011.

HMICFRS (2022). *State of Policing–The Annual Assessment of Policing in England and Wales 2021.* London: Her Majesty's Chief Inspector of Constabulary.

Hoffman, B. (2006). *Inside Terrorism.* New York: Columbia University Press.

Holdaway, S. (Ed.). (1979). *The British Police.* London: Edward Arnold.

References

Holdaway, S. (Ed.). (1983). *Inside the British Police*. Oxford: Basil Blackwell.
Ho, L. K. K. and Chu, Y. K. (2012). *Policing Hong Kong 1842–1969: Insiders' Stories*. Hong Kong: City University of Hong Kong Press.
Ho, L. K. K. (2020a). 'Rethinking Police Legitimacy in Postcolonial Hong Kong: Paramilitary Policing in Protest Management'. *Policing: A Journal of Policy and Practice*. 14(4): 1015–33.
Ho, L. K. K. (2020b). 'Legitimization and De-Legitimization of Police: in British Colonial and Chinese SAR Hong Kong'. *Journal of Inter-Regional Studies: Regional and Global Perspectives*. 3: 2–13.
Holmqvist, C. (2005). 'Private Security Companies; The Case for Regulation'. *SIPRI Policy Paper No. 9*. Stockholm International Peace Research Institute, January 2005.
Home Office (1999). *The Government's Proposals for Regulation of the Private Security Industry in England and Wales*. Cmnd 4254, March 1999. London: HMSO.
Home Office (2004). *Overseas Deployment Manual for Police Officers*. Updated 25 May 2004.
Home Office (2008). *From the Neighbourhood to the National: Policing our Communities Together*. Cmnd 7448, July 2008. London: HMSO.
Home Office (2010). *Policing in the 21st Century: Reconnecting police and the people*, London: HMSO.
Home Office (2012a). *Overseas Deployment Information for Police Officers*, June 2012.
Home Office (2012b). *The Overseas Territories and the Home Office*, April 2012. London: HMSO.
Home Office (2014). *Modern Slavery Strategy*, November 2014. London: HMSO.
Home Office (2016). 'College of Policing–International Policing Unit'. *Final Report v2.0*. Home Office Internal Audit, 25 November 2016.
Home Office (2019). *Annual Report and Accounts 2018–19*. HC 2193, 6 June 2019. London: HMSO.
Hönke, J. and Müller, M. M. (2012). 'Governing (In)security in a Postcolonial World: Transnational Entanglements and the Worldliness of "Local" Practice"'. *Security Dialogue*. 43(5): 383–401.
Hönke, J. and Müller, M. M. (2016). (Eds.). *The Global Making of Policing: Postcolonial Perspectives*. London: Routledge.
Hough, M. (2003). 'Modernisation and Public Opinion: Some Criminal Justice Paradoxes'. *Contemporary Politics*. 9(2): 143–63.
House of Commons (1999). *Written answers to questions international development*. Volume 329: Debated on Wednesday 14 April 1999. UK Parliament: Hansard.
House of Commons Foreign Affairs Committee (2002). 'Private Military Companies'. *Ninth Report of Session 2001–02*. HC 922, 1 August 2002. London: The Stationery Office.
House of Commons (2016). 'Lessons still to be learned from the Chilcot Inquiry'. *Tenth Report of Session 2016–17*. House of Commons Public Administration and Constitutional Affairs Committee. HC 656, 16 March 2017. London: The Stationery Office.

House of Commons (2020). 'Merging success: Bringing together the FCO and DFID'. Government Response to Committee's Second Report. *Sixth special report*, 24 September 2020. London: The Stationery Office.

House of Commons Defence Committee (2005). 'Iraq: An Initial Assessment of Post-Conflict Operations'. *Sixth Report of Session 2004-05*. Volume 1. HC 65-1, 24 March 2005. London: The Stationery Office.

House of Commons Defence Committee (2012). 'Operations in Libya'. *Ninth Report of Session 2010-2012*. HC 950, 8 February 2012. London: The Stationery Office.

House of Commons Home Affairs Committee (2016). 'College of Policing: three years on: Government and College of Policing responses to the Committee's Fourth Report of Session 2016-17'. *Fourth Special Report of Session 2016-17*. HC 678, 13 September 2016. London: The Stationery Office.

House of Commons Home Affairs Committee (2018). 'Policing for the future'. *Report, together with formal minutes relating to the report*, 22 October 2018. London: The Stationery Office.

House of Commons Home Affairs Committee (2018). 'Home Office preparations for the UK exiting the EU'. *Twelfth Report of Session 2017-19*. HC 1674, 7 December 2018. London: The Stationery Office.

House of Commons Select Committee Foreign Affairs (2000). 'Kosovo'. *Fourth Report*. Session 1999-2000, 23 May 2000. London: The Stationery Office.

House of Commons Select Committee Foreign Affairs (2002). 'Private Military Companies'. *Foreign Affairs–Ninth Report*, 23 July 2002. London: The Stationery Office.

House of Commons Select Committee Foreign Affairs (2016). 'Libya: Examination of intervention and collapse and the UK's future policy options'. *Third Report of Session 2016-17*. HC 119, 14 September 2016. London: The Stationery Office.

House of Lords European Union Committee (2016). 'Brexit: future UK-EU security and police cooperation'. *7th Report of Session 2016-17*, 16 December 2016. London: The Stationery Office.

House of Lords European Union Committee (2018). *Brexit: Common Security and Defence Policy missions and operations*. London: The Stationery Office.

House of Lords European Union Committee (2021a). *Future UK-EU Relations*. Lords Select Committee. London: The Stationery Office.

House of Lords European Union Committee (2021b). 'Beyond Brexit: policing, law enforcement and security'. *25th Report of Session 2019-21*. HL Paper 250, 26 March 2021. London: The Stationery Office.

House of Lords Select Committee on Defence (2005). *Examination of Witnesses (Questions 227/239)*, 26 January 2005. London: The Stationery Office.

Hug, A., Baldoumas, A., Chakrabortty, K., and Sriskandarajah, D. (2020). (Eds.). *Finding Britain's Role in a Changing World; Building a Values-based Foreign Policy*. The Foreign Policy Centre and Oxfam.

Huggins, M. (1998). *Political Policing: The United States and Latin America*. Durham, NC: Duke University Press.

Hughes, B. (2021). 'PSNI rolls out branding changes a year after previous proposals ditched due to backlash'. *BelfastLive*, 23 June 2021. Available at <https://www.belfastlive.co.uk/news/psni-rolls-out-branding-change-20884077>.

Hughes, S., Tichell, I., Tyskerud, Y., and Warwick, R. (2021). 'The UK's reduction in aid spending'. *IFS Briefing Note BN322*. The Institute for Fiscal Studies, April 2021.

Hunt, C. T. (2015). *UN Peace Operations and International Policing: Negotiating Complexity, Assessing Impact and Learning to Learn*. London: Routledge.

Ignatieff, M. (1979). 'Police and People: the Birth of Mr. Peel's Blue Locusts'. *New Society* 49: 443–5.

Imlah, A. (2017). 'Assemblages of networks, partnerships and friendships in international development: the case of Malawi and Scotland'. *PhD thesis*. Glasgow: University of Glasgow.

Independent Commission for Aid Impact (2019). ICAI Annual Report 2018 to 2019. *Report to Parliament's International Development Committee*. June 2019.

International Crisis Group (2005). 'Bosnia's Stalled Police Reform: No Progress, No EU'. *Europe Report No. 164*, 6 September 2005.

International Crisis Group (2010). 'The Rule of Law in Independent Kosovo'. *Europe Report No. 204*, 19 May 2010.

International Crisis Group (2021). 'Slivers of Hope in the Middle East'. *Crisis Watch; The President's Take*, 2 June 2021. Available at: https://www.crisisgroup.org/content/slivers-hope-middle-east.

International Development Act (2002). 'UK Public General Acts'. *The National Archives*. Available at: https://www.legislation.gov.uk/ukpga/2002/1/contents.

Interpol (2020). 2nd Edition. 'Covid-19 Pandemic; Protecting Police and Communities'. *Guidelines for Law Enforcement*. November 2020.

Invest Northern Ireland (n.d.). 'Security Specialists: Local companies, international reputations for excellence and innovation'. *Brochure*.

Inwood, S. (1990). 'Policing London's Morals: The Metropolitan Police and Popular Culture, 1829–1850'. *London Journal*. 15: 129–46.

Iqbal, J. (2019). 'It will take a royal commission to sort out our policing' *The Times*, 27 December 2019. Available at <https://www.thetimes.co.uk/article/it-will-take-a-royal-commission-to-sort-out-our-policing-8q2rqgc2r>.

Iraq Inquiry (2016). *The Report of the Iraq Inquiry: Executive Summary*. Report of a Committee of Privy Counsellors. HC 264, Ordered by the House of Commons to be printed on 6 July 2016. London: HMSO.

Isenberg, D. (2007). 'A Government in Search of Cover: Private Military Companies in Iraq'. In: Chesterman, S. and Lehnardt, C. (Eds.). *From Mercenaries to Market, The Rise and Regulation of Private Military Companies*. Oxford: Oxford University Press: 82–93.

Isenberg, D. (2009). *Shadow Force: Private Security Contractors in Iraq*. Westport, Connecticut: Praeger Security International.

Jackson, P. and Beswick, D. (2018). (3rd Edition). *Conflict, Security and Development: An Introduction*. London: Routledge.

Jackson, J., Bradford, B., Stanko, B., and Hohl, K. (2013). *Just Authority? Trust in the Police in England and Wales*. London: Routledge.

Jackson, J., Hough, M., Bradford, B., Hohl, K., and Kuha, J. (2013). 'Policing by Consent: Understanding the Dynamics of Police Power and Legitimacy'. *Policing by Consent: Topline Results (UK) from Round 5 of the European Social Survey*. ESS Country Specific Topline Results.

Jackson, J. and Sunshine, J. (2007). 'Public Confidence in Policing: A Neo Durkheimian Perspective'. *British Journal of Criminology*. 47(2): 214–33.

Jakobsen, L. J. and Buur, L. (2019). 'The Blurred (In)security of Community Policing in Bolivia'. In: Diphoorn, T. and Grassiani, E. (Eds.). *Security Blurs: The Politics of Plural Security Provision*. Routledge. Routledge Studies in Anthropology No. 51: 100–17.

Jalali (2016). 'Afghanistan National Defense and Security Forces: Mission, Challenges, and Sustainability'. *Report*. Washington, D.C.: United States Institute of Peace.

Jeandesboz, J. (2017). 'European Border Policing: EUROSUR, Knowledge, Calculation'. *Global Crime*. 18(3): 256–85.

Jeffries, C. (1938). *The Colonial Empire and Its Civil Service*. Cambridge: The University Press.

Jeffries, C. (1952). *The Colonial Police*. London: Max Parrish.

JIPH (2018a). *Modern Slavery Fund: Vietnam Policing Scoping Visit, 29 Jan–5 Feb 2018*.

JIPH (2018b). *Modern Slavery Fund: Vietnam Policing Scoping Visit, Follow-Up–10–18 April 2018*.

JIPH (2021a). 'Another Successful Delivery of Human Trafficking Investigation Skills in Vietnam'. *Briefing Note*.

JIPH (2021b). 'Vietnamese Modern Slavery and Human Trafficking Investigation Training Programme'. Report on the evaluation workshops carried out on 7th and 8th April 2021.

Johansen, A. (2017). 'Future Trends in Historical Research on Policing: Towards Global and Interdisciplinary Perspectives'. *Crime, Histoire and Sociétés / Crime, History and Societies*. 21(2): 113–21.

Johnson, R. and Clack, T. (2015). (Eds.). *At the End of Military Intervention; Historical, Theoretical, and Applied Approaches to Transition, Handover, and Withdrawal*. Oxford: Oxford University Press.

Johnston, L. (1992). *The Rebirth of Private Policing*. London: Routledge.

Johnston, L. (1999). 'Private Policing in Context'. *European Journal on Criminal Policy and Research*. 7: 175–96.

Johnston, L. (2006). 'Transnational Security Governance'. In: Wood, J. and Dupont, B. (Eds.). *Democracy, Society and the Governance of Security*. Cambridge: Cambridge University Press: 33–51.

JFHQ (2015). 'SOR for Home Office (HO) Police Support to Joint Forces Headquarters (JFHQ)'. 20151008-CivPolSOR.doc.

Jokela, J. (2020). *Stronger Together? The Impact of Brexit on Security and Defence Cooperation*. European Policy Centre.

Jones, D. J. V. (1983). 'The New Police, Crime and People in England and Wales, 1829–1888'. *Transactions of the Royal Historical Society*. 33: 151–68.

Jones, S. and Chulove, M. (2009). 'Contractor held for murder of fellow Briton and Australian in Baghdad'. *The Guardian*, 9 August 2009.

Jones, S. J., Wilson, J. M., Rathmell, A., and Riley, K. J. (2005). 'Iraq'. In: *Establishing Law and Order after Conflict*. Santa Monica, CA: RAND Corporation.

Kaldor, M. (2012). *New and Old Wars: Organized Violence in a Global Era*. (3rd Edition). Cambridge: Polity Press.

Kapferer, J-N. (2004). *The New Strategic Brand Management: Creating and Sustaining Brand Equity Long Term*. London: Kogan Page.

Karlshoej-Pedersen, M. (2018). 'The True Cost of Defence Engagement'. *Blog*. Oxford Research Group: Breaking the cycle of violence, 14 June 2018.

Kaspersen, A. T., Eide, E. B., and Hansen, A. S. (2004). 'International Policing and the Rule of Law in Transitions from War to Peace'. *Policy Paper No. 4–2004*. Norwegian Institute of International Affairs.

Keating, M. J. (2010). *The Government of Scotland: Public Policy Making after Devolution*. Edinburgh: Edinburgh University Press.

Keating, M. J. (2020). (Ed.). *The Oxford Handbook of Scottish Politics (Oxford Handbooks)*. Oxford: Oxford University Press.

Keller, K. L. (1993). 'Conceptualizing, Measuring and Managing Customer-based Brand Equity'. *Journal of Marketing*. 57: 1–22.

Kernaghan, P. (2010). 'Witness Statement to the Iraq Inquiry', 9 June 2010 and 23 July 2010. *The Report of the Iraq Inquiry; Report of a Committee of Privy Counsellors*, 6 July 2016. Volume V. London: HMSO.

Killcullen, D. and Mills, G. (2022). *The Ledger: Accounting for Failure in Afghanistan*. London: Hurst and Company.

Kinsey, C. (2006). *Corporate Soldiers and International Security: The Rise of Private Military Companies*. London: Routledge.

Kinsey, C. (2022). 'A step too far: how the ICoCA actions could unintentionally help to privatise war (Part Two)'. *Defence-in Depth Blog*, March 2022.

Klein, N. (2007a). *The Shock Doctrine: The Rise of Disaster Capitalism*. London: Penguin.

Klein, N. (2007b). 'Disaster Capitalism: the Economy of Catastrophe'. *Harpers*. 315(1889): 47–88.

Klein, N. (2008). *The Shock Doctrine: The Rise of Disaster Capitalism*, London: Penguin Books.

Klockars, C. (1985). *The Idea of Police*. Beverly Hills, CA: Sage.

Koenig, D. J. and Das, D. (2001). *International Police Co-operation: A World Perspective*, New York: Lexington Books.

Koncak, D. (2018). 'Rethinking Community Policing in International Police Reform: Examples from Asia'. *SSR Paper 17*. London: Ubiquity Press/Geneva: DCAF.

Koski, C. M. (2009). 'Afghanistan at a Crossroads: The Quest for Democratic Policing in a Post-9/11 Era'. *Police Practice and Research: An International Journal*. 10(4): 317–32.

Krogstad, I. G. (2012). 'Security, Development, and Force: Revisiting Police Reform in Sierra Leone'. *African Affairs*. 111(443): 261–80.

Laan van der F., Goor van de L., Hendriks, R., Lijn van der J., Meijinder, M., and Zandee, D. (2016). 'The Future of Police Missions'. *Clingendael Report*, February 2016.

Laffey, M. and Nadarajah, S. (2016). 'Securing the Diaspora: Policing Global Order'. In: Hönke, J. and Muller, M.-M. (Eds.). *The Global Making of Police: Postcolonial Perspectives.* London, UK: Routledge: 114–31.

Latham, R. (2001). *Deadly Beat: Inside the Royal Ulster Constabulary.* London: Mainstream Publishing.

Lawrence, P. (2011). (Ed.). 'The New Police in the Nineteenth Century'. Volume II. In: Emsley, C. (Series Editor). *The History of Policing.* Farnham: Ashgate.

Leung, C. (2017). 'Is there a future for foreign police officers in Hong Kong'. *South China Morning Post*, 5 November 2017.

Levine D. H. (2010). 'Rule of Law, Power Distribution, and the Problem of Faction in Conflict Interventions'. In: Sellers M. and Tomaszewski T. (Eds.). *Ius Gentium: Comparative Perspectives on Law and Justice*, 3: 147–75. Springer Nature Switzerland AG: Springer.

Loader, I. (1999). 'Consumer Culture and the Commodification of Policing and Security' *Sociology*. 33(2): 373–92.

Loader, I. (2002). 'Governing European Policing: Some Problems, and Prospects'. *Policing and Society*. 12(4): 275–90.

Loader, I. (2020). 'Revisiting the Police Mission'. *Insight Paper 2*. The Strategic Review of Policing in England and Wales. The Police Foundation, March 2020.

Loader, I. and Mulcahy, A. (2003). *Policing and the Condition of England: Memory, Politics and Culture,* Oxford: Oxford University Press.

Loewenstein, A. (2015). *Disaster Capitalism: Making a Killing out of Catastrophe.* London: Verso.

Lowe, W. J. and Malcolm, E. L. (1992). 'The Domestication of the Royal Irish Constabulary, 1836–1922'. *Irish Economic and Social History*. XIX: 27–48.

Luhanga, I. J. (2001). 'Policy formulation in Malawi: case of police reform 1995–2000'. *PhD thesis*. Wellington, NZ: Victoria University of Wellington.

Lutterbeck, D. (2005). 'Blurring the Dividing Line: The Converging of Internal and External Security in Western Europe'. *European Security*. 14(2): 231–53.

Macaulay, F. (2012). 'Cycles of Police Reform in Latin America'. In: Francis, D. J. (Ed.). *Policing in Africa.* New York: Palgrave Macmillan: 165–90.

Macoun, M. J. (1996). *Wrong Place, Right Time: Policing the End of Empire.* London: The Radcliffe Press.

Magee, K. (1991). 'The Dual Role of the Royal Ulster Constabulary in Northern Ireland'. In: Reiner, R. and Cross, M. (Eds.). *Beyond Law and Order: Criminal Justice Policy and Politics into the 1990s.* London: Macmillan: 78–91.

Makki, S., Meek, S., Musah, A. F., Crowley, M., and Lilly, D. (2001). 'Private Military Companies and the Proliferation of Small Arms: Regulating the Actors'. *Biting the Bullet Briefing Papers. Briefing 10.* London: British American Security Information Council (BASIC), International Alert, and Saferworld.

Malawi Office of the Vice President (2016). *2016/2017 Food Insecurity Response Plan.* The Republic of Malawi: Department of Disaster Management Affairs.

Malcolm, E. (2005). *The Irish Policeman, 1822–1922: A Life.* Dublin: The Four Courts Press.

Mann, M. (1997). 'Has Globalization Ended the Rise and Rise of the Nation-State?'. *Review of International Political Economy*. 4(3): 472–96.

Mann, N., Devendran, P., and Lundrigan, S. (2020). 'Policing in a Time of Austerity: Understanding the Public Protection Paradox through Qualitative Interviews with Police Monitoring Officers'. *Policing: A Journal of Policy and Practice*. 14(3): 630–42.

Manning, P. K. (2010). *Democratic Policing in a Changing World*. Boulder, CO: Paradigm.

Marenin, O. (1998). 'The Goal of Democracy in International Police Assistance Programs'. *Policing: An International Journal of Police Strategies and Management*. 21(1): 159–77.

Marenin, O. (2005). 'Building a Global Police Studies Community'. *Police Quarterly*. 8(1): 206–21.

Mark, R. (1978). *In the Office of Constable*. London: Collins.

Marsh, A. (2017). 'Update on International Police Assistance'. *Agenda Item: 7*. Chief Constables Council. 18 October 2017.

Mastrofski, S. and Lum, C. (2008). 'Meeting the Challenges of Police Governance in Trinidad and Tobago'. *Policing: A Journal of Policy and Practice*. 2(4): 481–96.

Matheson, M. 'Policing in Scotland Is Continuing to Perform Well'. *Police Oracle*, 2015. Available at: <http://www.policeoracle.com/news/Policing-in-Scotland-is-continuing-to-perform-well_90487.html>.

Mathias, G., Kendrick, D., Peake, G., and Groenewald, H. (2006). 'Philosophy and Principles of Community-based Policing'. *Community Policing Study*, 3rd Edition. Serbia, Belgrade: SEESAC.

Mathieu, F. and Dearden, N. (2005). 'Corporate Mercenaries: The Threat of Private Military and Security Companies'. *Report*. London: War on Want.

Mawby, R. C. (2013). *Policing Images: Policing, Communication and Legitimacy*. Abingdon: Routledge.

Mawby, M. C. and Worthington, S. (2002). 'Marketing the Police–From a Force to a Service'. *Journal of Marketing Management*. 18(9–10): 857–76.

McDonald, H. 'Amnesty calls for tighter controls before training foreign police'. *The Guardian*, 23 February 2011. Available at <https://www.theguardian.com/uk/2011/feb/23/amnesty-training-foreign-police>.

McFate, S. (2008). 'Securing the Future: A Primer on Security Sector Reform in Conflict Countries'. *Special Report 209*, Washington, D.C.: United States Institute of Peace.

McFate, S. (2015). 'PMSCs in International Security Sector Reform'. In: Abrahamsen, R. and Leander, A. (Eds.). *Routledge Handbook of Private Security Studies*. London: Routledge: 118–29.

McFate, S. (2016). 'The Evolution of Private Force'. In: Berndtsson, J. and Kinsey, C. *The Routledge Research Companion to Security Outsourcing in the Twenty-first Century*. London: Routledge: 65–76.

McLaughlin, E. (2007). *The New Policing*. London: Sage.

Meek, S. (2003). 'Policing Sierra Leone'. In: Malan, M. et al. (Eds.). *Sierra Leone–Building the Road to Recovery*. Pretoria, SA: Institute for Security Studies: 105–16.

Merlingen, M. and Ostrauskaite, R. (2005). 'ESDP Police Missions: Meaning, Context and Operational Challenges'. *European Foreign Affairs Review* 10: 215–35.

Michalopoulos, C. (2020). *Ending Global Poverty: Four Women's Noble Conspiracy*. Oxford: Oxford University Press.

Miller, C. T. (2009). 'U.S government private contract worker deaths and injuries'. *ProPublica*, 23 September 2009. Available at: https://projects.propublica.org/tables/contractor_casualties.html.

Miller, C. T. (2010). 'Disposable Army: this year, contractor deaths exceed military ones in Iraq and Afghanistan'. *ProPublica*, 23 September 2010. Available at: https://www.propublica.org/series/disposable-army.

Miller, P. (2020). *Keenie Meenie: The British Mercenaries who Got Away with War Crimes*. London: Pluto Press.

Miller, W. (1977). *Cops and Bobbies*. Chicago: University of Chicago Press.

Millie, A. and Bullock, K. (2012). 'Re-imagining Policing Post-austerity'. *British Academy Review*. 9: 16–18.

Milne, G. and Thomson, G. (2012). 'Scottish Policing and Policy Transfer: Developing a Sustainable Model of Community Policing in Sri Lanka'. *SIPR Briefings*. No. 11. The Scottish Institute for Policing Research, March 2012.

Ministry of Defence (2011). 'MOD Civil Servants on Operations: Guidance for Families'. *Support 2 Operations*, August 2011. Ministry of Defence, Braintree: Wethersfield.

Ministry of Defence (n.d.). 'Safety and Security Briefing for Civilians in Operational Theatres'. *Support 2 Operations*. Ministry of Defence, Braintree: Wethersfield.

Ministry of Defence (2016). 'Shaping a Stable World: the Military Contribution'. *Joint Doctrine Publication 05*. Swindon, Ministry of Defence Shrivenham: Development, Concepts and Doctrine Centre.

Ministry of Defence (2020a). *Introducing the Integrated Operating Concept 2025* (IOpC 25). Swindon, Ministry of Defence Shrivenham: Director Development, Concepts and Doctrine Centre.

Ministry of Defence (2020b). 'The British Army has arrived in Mali: Here's what you need to know about the deployment'. *Voices of the Armed Forces*. Available at <https://medium.com/voices-of-the-armed-forces/the-british-army-has-arrived-in-mali-heres-what-you-need-to-know-about-the-deployment-b639c37a647e>.

Ministry of Defence (2021a). *Defence in a Competitive Age*. CP 411. March 2021. London: HMSO.

Ministry of Defence (2021b). HL Deb. CW UIN HL474, 1 June 2021.

Ministry of Defence Police (2012a). 'Ministry of Defence Police: International Policing'. *Overview*. Braintree: Wethersfield.

Ministry of Defence Police (2012b). *PowerPoint Presentation Overview*. Braintree: Wethersfield.

Ministry of Defence Police and Guarding Agency (2012). *Annual Report 2011–2012* Braintree: Wethersfield.

Mobekk, E. (2005). 'Identifying Lesson in United Nations international policing missions'. *Policy Paper—No. 9*. Geneva Centre for the Democratic Control of Armed Forces (DCAF).

Monk, R. (2011). *Written Correspondence with Author*.

Montgomery, R. and Griffiths, C. T. (2016). 'The Use of Private Security Services for Policing'. *Research Report: 2015-RO14*. Public Safety Canada: Research Division.

Morgan, P. (1998). 'Capacity and Capacity Development–Some Strategies'. *Note prepared for the Political and Social Policies Division*. Policy branch, CIDA, October 1998.

Muir, R., Higgins, A., Halkon, R., Walcott, S., and contributions from Jeffrey, B. (2022). 'A New Mode of Protection' Redesigning policing and public safety for the 21st century'. *The Final Report of the Strategic Review of Policing in England and Wales*. London: The Police Foundation, March 2022.

Mulcahy, A. (1999). 'Visions of Normality: Peace and the Reconstruction of Policing in Northern Ireland'. *Social and Legal Studies*, 8(2): 277–95.

Mulcahy, A. (2006). 'Trust, Accountability and the Police'. Studies: *An Irish Quarterly Review*. 95(377): 31–9.

Mulcahy, A. (2008). 'Community Policing in Contested Settings: The Patten Report and Police Reform in Northern Ireland'. In: Williamson, T. (Ed.). *The Handbook of Knowledge-Based Policing: Current Conceptions and Future Directions*. Chichester: John Wiley and Sons Ltd: 117–37.

Mulcahy, A. (2013). *Policing Northern Ireland; Conflict, Legitimacy and Reform*. Abingdon: Routledge.

Muri, R. and Walcott, S., with Higgins, A., and Halkon, R. (2020). 'Public safety and security in the 21st century'. *The first report of the strategic review of policing in England and Wales*, July 2020.

Murphy, J. (2013). *Policing for Peace in Northern Ireland; Change, Conflict and Community Confidence*. Basingstoke: Palgrave Macmillan.

Murphy, J. (2015). 'Tracking Change in Northern Ireland Policing: Temporal Phases and Key Themes'. *Policing: An International Journal of Police Strategies and Management*. 38(1): 117–31.

Murphy, J., McDowell, S., and Braniff, M. (2016). 'Historical Dialogue and Memory in Policing Change: the Case of the Police in Northern Ireland'. *Memory Studies*. 10(4). https://doi.org/10.1177/1750698016667454

Murray, T. (2007). 'Police-Building in Afghanistan: A Case Study of Civil Security Reform'. *International Peacekeeping*. 14(1): 108–26.

Murray, W. and Scales, Jr., H. J. (2003). *The Iraq War: A Military History*. Cambridge, Mass: Belknap Press of Harvard University Press.

Muthien, B. and Taylor, I. (2002). 'The Return of the Dogs of War? The Privatization of Security in Africa'. In: Hall, R. B. and Biersteker, T. J. (Eds.). *The Emergence of Private Authority in Global Governance*. Cambridge: Cambridge University Press: 183–201.

Nadelmann, E. A. (1993). *Cops across Borders: The Internationalization of US Criminal Law Enforcement*. University Park, PA: Penn State Press.

Nalla, M. K. and Prenzler, T. (2018). (Eds.). *Regulating the Security Industry: Global Perspectives*. London: Routledge.

National Police Chiefs Council (2016). *Policing Vision 2025*.

National Police Chiefs Council (NPCC) and Association Police and Crime Commissioners (APCC). (2020). *Policing Vision 2025*. Available at: https://www.npcc.police.uk/documents/Policing%20Vision.pdf.

National Security Council (2005). *National Strategy for Victory in Iraq. November 2005*. Washington, D.C.: The White House.
NATO (2010). *The International Academy Bramshill Annual Report Summary–2009–2010*.
NATO (2016). *Allied Joint Doctrine for Stability Policing*. AJP-3.22. Edition A, version 1, July 2016. NATO/OTAN: NATO Standardization Office.
Nebreda Martell, J. D. (2016). 'The Role of Gendarmeries in Peacebuilding Operations'. *MSc in Conflict and Security Studies*. London: Kings College.
Neild, R. (2001). *Democratic police reforms in war-torn societies*. Washington, D.C.: Washington Office on Latin America.
Newburn, T. (1999). 'Understanding and preventing police corruption: lessons from the literature'. *Police Research Series Paper 110*. London: Research Development Studies.
Newburn, T. (2011). 'Reading the Riots: The riots and policing's sacred cow' . *The Guardian*, 6th December 2011. Available at <http://www.guardian.co.uk/commentisfree/2011/dec/06/policing-sacred-cow-reading-riots>.
NI-CO (2021). Northern Ireland Co-operation Overseas. Available at <https://nico.org.uk/>.
Nogueira, P. (2012). *Sanulus: Diario de Missao em Timor-Leste*. Lisbon: Chiado Editora.
Northern Ireland Human Rights Commission (1999). *Response to the report of the independent commission on policing in Northern Ireland (The Patten Report)*. Northern Ireland Human Rights Commission, November 1999. Available at: https://nihrc.org/uploads/documents/advice-to-government/1999/patten-policing-report-november-1999.pdf.
Norton-Taylor, R. (2011a). 'British government approved sale of crowd control equipment to Libya', *The Guardian*, 20 February 2011. Available at: https://www.theguardian.com/world/2011/feb/20/british-crowd-control-equipment-libya.
Norton-Taylor, R. (2011b). 'Libya's 'mission creep' claims as UK sends in military advisors'. *The Guardian*. 20 February. Available at https://www.theguardian.com/world/2011/apr/19/libya-mission-creep-uk-advisers
Nossal, K. R. (2001). 'Global Governance and National Interests: Regulating Transnational Security Corporations in the Post-Cold War Era'. *Melbourne Journal of International Law*. 2(2): 459–76.
NPCC (2020). *NPCC International*. Web page available at: <https://www.npcc.police.uk/NPCCBusinessAreas/International.aspx>.
NPIA (2009). *Annual reports and accounts 2008/09*. HC 738, 13 July 2009. London: HMSO.
O'Brien. K. A. (2000). 'PMCs, Myths and Mercenaries: The Debate on Private Military Companies'. *RUSI Journal*. 145(1), February 2000. London: RUSI.
ó Ceallaigh, T. (1966). 'Peel and Police Reform in Ireland, 1814–18'. *Studia Hiberrica*. 6: 25–48.
OECD (2005). Security Sector Reform and Governance. A DAC Reference Document, DAC Guidelines and Reference Series. Available at: https://www.oecd.org/fr/cad/securitysystemreformandgovernanceoecddacguidelinesandreferenceseriesdacnewssept-oct2005.htm.

O'Rawe, M. and Moore, L. (1997). *Human Rights on Duty; Principles for Better Policing–International Lessons for Northern Ireland*. Committee on the Administration of Justice.

O'Rawe, M. (2007). 'Human Rights, Transitional Societies and Police Training: Legitimating Strategies and Delegitimating Legacies'. *Journal of Civil Rights and Economic Development*. 22(1): Article 5: 199–65.

O'Rawe, M. (2009). *Security System Reform and Identity in Divided Societies: Lessons from Northern Ireland*. Research Brief. International Center for Transitional Justice. Available at: https://www.ictj.org/sites/default/files/ICTJ-Identities-SSR-ResearchBrief-2009-English.pdf.

OECD. (2005). Security Sector Reform and Governance. A DAC Reference Document, DAC Guidelines and Reference Series.

OECD. (2015). *Handbook on Combating Corruption*. Vienna: OSCE.

OECD. (2017). *OSCE Guidebook Intelligence-Led Policing*. Vienna: OSCE.

O'Reilly, C. (2010). 'The Transnational Security Consultancy Industry: A Case of State–Corporate Symbiosis'. *Theoretical Criminology*, 14 (2): 183–210.

Osland, J. S. (2017). 'An Overview of the Global Leadership Literature'. In: Mendenhall, M. E., Osland, J., Bird, A., Oddou, G. P., Stevens, M. J., Maznevski, M., and Stahl, G. K, *Global Leadership; Research, Practice and Development*. 3rd Edition. London: Routledge: 57–117.

Overseas Development and Co-operation Act 1980 (repealed). Ch. 11 (1) to (4). 'Overseas service by police officers'. UK Public General Acts delivered by The National Archives. Available at: https://www.legislation.gov.uk/ukpga/1980/63/part/III/1991-02-01.

Palmer, S. H. (1988). *Police and Protest in England and Ireland 1780–1850*. New York: Cambridge University Press.

Palou-Loverdos, J. and Armendariz, L. (2011). 'The Privatization of Warfare, Violence and Private Military and Security Companies: A Factual and Legal Approach to Human Rights Abuses by PMSC in Iraq'. *Report*. Barcelona: Nova Innovacio Social.

Parris, H. (1961). 'The Home Office and the Provincial Police in England and Wales–1856–1870'. *Public Law*: 230–55.

Paterson, B. (n.d.). 'British in East Timor'. *Personal Notes*.

Pattison, J. (2014). *The Morality of Private War: The Challenge of Private Security and Private Military Companies*. Oxford: Oxford University Press.

Palou-Loverdos, J. and Armendariz, L. (2011). 'The Privatization of Warfare, Violence and Private Military and Security Companies: A Factual and Legal Approach to Human Rights Abuses by PMSC in Iraq'. *Report*. Barcelona: Nova Innovacio Social.

Peake, G. and Marenin, O. (2008). 'Their Reports Are not Read and their Recommendations Are Resisted: The Challenge for the Global Police Policy Community'. *Police Practice and Research*. 9(1): 59–69.

Peltier, H. (2020). 'The Growth of the 'Camo Economy' and the Commercialization of the post Post-9/11 Wars'. *20 Years of War; A Costs of War Research Series*, 30 June 2020. Watson Institute, Brown University.

Percy, S. (2009). 'Private Security Companies and Civil Wars'. *Civil Wars*. 11(1): 57–74.
Perito, R. M. (2011). 'The Iraq Federal Police; U.S. Police Building under Fire'. *Special Report*. Washington: United States Institute of Peace.
Perrin de Brichambaut, M. (2009). IFSH (Ed.). *OSCE Yearbook 2008*. Baden-Baden.
Philips, D. and Storch, R. D. (1999). *Policing Provincial England 1829–1856. The Politics of Reform*. London: Leicester University Press.
Pino, N.W and Waitrowski, M.D. (2006). (Eds.). *Police Reform in Developing and Transitional Societies*, Ashgate.
Pippet, G. K. (1938). *A History of the Ceylon Police*. Volume I: 1795–1870. Columbo.
Police Act (1996). UK Public General Acts 1996 c. 16. Delivered by The National Archives. Available at <https://www.legislation.gov.uk/ukpga/1996/16/contents>.
Police Advisory Board (2013). *Guidance on Police Officer and Staff Secondments*; Agreed by the Police Advisory Board for England and Wales, December 2013.
Police Oracle (2021). 'Dyfed-Powys chief to become Commissioner of Virgin Islands force', 26 January 2021.
Police (Overseas Service) Act 1945. 1945 Chapter 17 9 and 10 Geo 6, 20 December 1945. UK Public General Acts delivered by The National Archives.
Police Scotland (2015). *National and International Development Strategy*, November, 2015.
Police Scotland (2020). *Freedom of Information Request: IM-FOI-2020-0429*, 10 March 2020.
Police Scotland (2021). International Development and Innovation Unit. Available at: <https://www.scotland.police.uk/about-us/police-scotland/police-scotland-college/international-development-and-innovation-unit/>.
Police Scotland and Scottish Police Authority (2017). '2026 Serving a Changing Scotland'. *10 year strategy for policing in Scotland*. SPA/2-17/02, 20 June 2017.
Port, P. (2012). *Briefing Note–Police and Crime Commissioners: The Integrated Approach*, 19 November 2012.
Poynting, S. and Whyte, D. (2012). 'Counter-Terrorism and the Terrorist State'. In: Poynting, S. and Whyte, D. (Eds.). *Counter-Terrorism and State Political Violence: The 'War on Terror' as Terror*. London: Routledge: 1–19.
Prado, M. M., Trebilcock, M., and Hartford, P. (2012). 'Police Reform in Violent Democracies in Latin America'. *Hague J Rule Law*. 4: 252–85.
Preez du, D. (2021). 'Loss of access to EU security data post-Brexit is "concerning"'. *Blog*. Diginomica, 26 March 2021.
Pritchard, A. and Sinclair, G. (2013). 'International Police Assistance: "Globalising UK Policing Practices"'. In: Neyroud, P. (Ed.). *Policing UK 2013: Priorities and Pressures: A Year of Transformation*. London: Witan Media Ltd: 100–102.
Private Security Industry Act (2001). *UK Public Gender Acts 2001 c. 12.*, 11 May 2001. Delivered by The National Archives.
PSNI (2009). 'Secondment to Sri Lanka 2009'. *Letter*, 9 February 2009 PSNI. *Freedom of Information Request*, F-2015- 00034.
PSNI (2011). 'Information relating to sending PSNI officers to Libya'. *FOI Request: F-2009-03181*.

References

PSNI (2014). *Manual of Policy, Procedure and Guidance on Conflict Management* (de-restricted from November 2014). PSNI.

PSNI (2015a). 'PSNI Training Assistance to Other Countries for Last 5 years'. *Freedom of Information Request*, F–2015–02237.

Purdon, P. (2016). 'Literature and Global Policing'. In: Bradford, B., Jauregui, B., Loader, I., and Steinberg, J. (Eds.). *The SAGE Handbook of Global Policing*. London: Sage: 136–53.

Rao, S. (2013). 'Community policing in fragile and conflict-affected states'. *GSDRC Helpdesk Research Report 997*. Birmingham: GSDRC and University of Birmingham.

Rawlings, P. (2002). *Policing: A Short History*. London: Routledge.

Rawlinson, K. (2016). 'British police criticised for lack of transparency in Bahrain training deal'. *The Guardian*, 29 August 2016. Available at: https://www.theguardian.com/law/2016/aug/29/british-police-criticised-for-lack-of-transparency-in-bahrain-training-deal.

Reiner, R. (1985). *The Politics of the Police*. London: Wheatsheaf Books Ltd.

Reiner, R. (1995). 'Myth vs. Modernity: Reality and Unreality in the English Model of Policing'. In: Brodeur, J.-P. (Ed.). *Comparisons in Policing: An International Perspective*. Aldershot: Ashgate: 16–49.

Reiner, R. (2010). *The Politics of the Police*. 4th Edition. Oxford: Oxford University Press.

Reinke, H. (2009). 'Crime and Criminal Justice History in Germany: A Report on Recent Trends'. *Crime, Histoire et Sociétés/Crime, History and Societies*. 13(1): 117–37.

Reith, R. (1938). *The Police Idea*. Oxford: Oxford University Press.

Reith, R. (1940). *Police Principles and the Problem of War*. Oxford: Oxford University Press.

Reith, R. (1943a). 'Preventative Principle of Police'. *Journal of Criminal Law and Criminology*, 34(3): 206–9.

Reith, R. (1943b). *The British Police and the Democratic Ideal*. Oxford: Oxford University Press.

Reith, R. (1948). *A Short History of the Police*. Oxford: Oxford University Press.

Reith, R. (1952). *The Blind Eye of History; A Study of the Origins of the Present Police Era*. London: Faber and Faber.

Richards, A. and Smith, H. (2007). 'Addressing the role of private security companies within security'. *Journal of Security Sector Management*. 5(1): 1–14.

Robinson, T. and Lunn, J. (2020). 'Brexit reading list: Global Britain'. *Briefing Paper. No. 8338*. House of Commons Library, 28 January 2020.

Rohwerder, B. (2016). 'Lessons learned from security-related programming in stabilisation and conflict-affected contexts'. *Helpdesk Research Report*. GSDRC Applied Knowledge Services. Birmingham: GSDRC and University of Birmingham.

Ross, K. R. (2014). 'A Very Definite Radicalism: The Early Development of the Scotland-Malawi Partnership 2004–09'. In: Adogame, A. and Lawrence, A. (Eds.). *Africa in Scotland, Scotland in Africa*. NL, Leiden: Brill: 307–25.

Rowe, M. (2007). (Ed.). *Policing beyond Macpherson: Issues in Policing, Race and Society*. Cullompton: Willan Publishing.

Rozée, S., Kaunert, C., and Léonard, S. (2013). 'Is Europol a Comprehensive Policing Actor?'. *Perspectives on European Politics and Society*. 14(3): 372–87.

Rubinstein, R. A. (2010). 'Peacekeeping and the Return of Imperial Policing', *International Peacekeeping*, 17(4): 457–70.

Ryder, C. (2000). *The RUC, 1922–97: A Force under Fire*. London: Arrow Books.

Rynn, S. with Hiscock, D. (2009). 'Evaluating for security and justice: Challenges and opportunities for improved monitoring and evaluation of security system reform programmes'. *Report: Security and justice sector development*. Saferworld, December 2009.

Saferworld (2006). 'The Ten Principles of Community-Based Policing'. *Handout*.

Sannerholm, R., Quinn, S., and Rabus, A. (2016). 'Responsive and Responsible; Politically Smart Rule of law Reform in Conflict and Fragile States'. *Report*. Folke Bernadotte Academy, Sweden.

Sarre, R. and Prenzler, T. (2000). 'The Relationship between Police and Private Security: Models and Future Directions'. *International Journal of Comparative and Applied Criminal Justice*. 24(1): 91–113.

Scheye, E. and Peake, G. (2005). 'To Arrest Insecurity: Time for a Revised Security Sector Reform Agenda'. *Conflict, Security and Development*. 5(3): 295–327.

Schmeidl, S. (2010). 'The Good, the Bad, and the Ugly—The Privatized Security Sector in Afghanistan'. In: *Afghanistan's Security Sector Governance Challenges*. Geneva: Geneva Centre for the Democratic Control of Armed Forced (DCAF). 45–77.

Schmeidl, S. and Karokhail, M. (2009). 'Prêt-a-Porter States: How the McDonalidization of State-Building Misses the Mark in Afghanistan'. In: Fischer M. and Schmelzle, B. (Eds.). *Building Peace in the Absence of States: Challenging the Discourse on State Failure.*. Berlin: Berghof Handbook Dialogue Series, Berghof Research Centre for Constructive Conflict Management: 67–78.

Schofield, S. (2008). 'The Risks of Department of Defense Outsourcing'. *Contract Management*. 48, September 2008.

Schooner, S. L. (2008). 'Why Contractor Fatalities Matter'. *38 Parameters*. 78–91.

Schwartz, M. and Swain, J. (2011). 'Department of Defense Contractors in Afghanistan and Iraq: Background and Analysis'. *CRS Report for Congress*. R40764. Congressional Research Service.

Scott, K. B. (2011). 'Politics and the Police in Scotland: The Impact of Devolution'. *Crime Law Soc Change*. 55: 121–32.

Scottish Government (2008). *Scottish Government International Development Policy*, 7 May 2008. Available at: https://www.gov.scot/policies/international-development/.

Scottish Government (2013). Scotland's Future; Your Guide to an Independent Scotland. Available at <https://www.gov.scot/publications/scotlands-future/pages/15>/.

Scottish Government (2017). *Contribution to International Development Report 2017–2018*. Scottish Government. Available at: https://www.gov.scot/binaries/content/documents/govscot/publications/progress-report/2018/09/contribut

ion-international-development-report-2017-18/documents/00539841-pdf/00539841-pdf/govscot%3Adocument/00539841.pdf.
Scottish Government (2021). 'Community Safety'. *Policy*. Available at https://www.gov.scot/policies/community-safety/.
Scottish Police Authority (2013). *Police Scotland/Branding*. Available at <http://www.spa.police.uk/assets/126884/175734/item15-police-scotland-branding>.
Scottish Police Authority and Police Scotland (2018). 'Equality and Human Rights Impact Assessment (EqHRIA)'. *Summary of Results*, 18 June 2018. Available at: https://www.scotland.police.uk/spa-media/rurnifmr/cyber-kiosk-toolkit-eqhria-external.pdf.
Security in Complex Environments Group (SCEG). (2021). Available at <https://www.sceguk.org.uk/>.
Sedra, M. (2010). (Ed.). *The Future of Security Sector Reform*. The Centre for International Governance Innovation (CIGI). Canada: Waterloo, Ontario.
Seely, B. and Rogers, J. (2019). 'Global Britain: A Twenty-First Century Vision'. *Global Britain Programme*, February 2019. London: The Henry Jackson Society.
Serewicz, L. (2002). 'Globalization, Sovereignty and the Military Revolution: From Mercenaries to Private International Security Companies'. *Int. Polit.* 39: 75–89.
Service, T. (2017). 'Community Policing in Challenging Environments'. *Working Paper No. 51*. Coginta.
Shearing, C. D. (1997). 'Toward Democratic Policing: Rethinking Strategies of Transformation'. *National Institute of Justice Research Report*. Policing in Emerging Democracies: Workshop Papers and Highlights, Washington, D.C., 14–15 December 1995.
Shearing, C. D. (1992). 'The Relations between Public and Private Policing'. In: Tonry, M. and Morriss, N. (Eds.). *Modern Policing*. Chicago, IL: University of Chicago Press: 399–434.
Shearing, C. D. and Stenning, P. (1983). 'Private Security: Implications for Social Control'. *Social Problems*. 30(5): 493–506.
Shearing, C. D. and Stenning, P. (1987). *Private Policing*. University of Michigan: Sage Publications.
Sheridan, A. M. (2009). 'A Thematic Review of the UK Approach to International Policing: Peace Support Operations'. *MSc in Policing*. Canterbury Christ Church University, February 2009.
Sheptycki, J. W. E. (1995). 'Transnational Policing and the Makings of a Postmodern State'. *British Journal of Criminology*. 35(4): 613–35.
Sheptycki, J. W. E. (1998). 'The Global Cops Cometh: Reflections on Transnationalization, Knowledge Work and Policing Subculture'. *The British Journal of Sociology*. 49(1): 57–74.
Sheptycki, J. W. E. (2000). *Issues in Transnational Policing*. London: Routledge.
Sheptycki, J. W. E. (2003). *In Search of Transnational Policing*. Aldershot: Ashgate.
Sheptycki, J. W. E. (2010). 'The Constabulary Ethic Reconsidered'. In: Lemieux, F. (Ed.). *International Police Co-operation: Emerging Issues, Theory and Practice*. Cullompton: Willan Publishing: 298–319.
Shilston, T. G. (2010). 'Getting it right and getting it wrong: personal reflections on police development in Afghanistan'. *Working Paper Series 26*. 1–17. International

Police Executive Symposium/Geneva Centre for the Democratic Control of the Armed Forces.
Short, C. (1998). 'Security, Development and Conflict Prevention'. *Speech at the Royal College of Defence Studies*, London, 13 May 1998.
SIGAR (2019). 'High-Risk U.S. Reconstruction Program Areas in Afghanistan'. *Statement of John F. Sopoko, Special Inspector General for Afghanistan Reconstruction*, 3 April 2019.
Sinclair, G. (2006). *At the End of the Line: Colonial Policing and the Imperial Endgame*. Manchester: Manchester University Press.
Sinclair, G. (2008). 'The 'Irish' Policeman and the Empire: Influencing the Policing of the British Empire–Commonwealth'. *Irish Historical Studies*. XXXVI (142): 173–87.
Sinclair, G. (2011a). The Sharp End of the Intelligence Machine': The Rise of the Malayan Police Special Branch 1948–1955. *Intelligence and National Security*. 26(4): 460–77.
Sinclair, G. (2011b). 'Globalising British Policing.' Volume IV. In: Emsley, C. (Series Editor). *The History of Policing*. Farnham: Ashgate.
Sinclair, G. (2012). 'Exporting the UK Police Brand: The RUC-PSNI and the International Policing Agenda'. *Policing: A Journal of Policy and Practice*. 6(1): 55–66.
Sinclair, G. (2015). '"Insider"/"Outsider" Policing: Observations on the Role of UK Police (MDP) in Afghanistan and the Application of "Lessons Learnt"'. In: Clack, T. and Johnson, R. (Eds.). *Transition, Handover and Withdrawal, Historical, Theoretical and Applied Approaches to Exit*. Oxford: Oxford University Press: 414–37.
Sinclair, G. (2016a). '"British Cop or International Cop?" "Global" Makings of International Policing Assistance, 1999–2012'. In: Honke, J. and Muller, M.-M. *The Global Makings of Policing: A Postcolonial Perspective*. London: Palgrave Macmillan: 132–49.
Sinclair, G. (2016b). 'Identifying the Challenges, Lessons Learned and Good Practices for Effective Policing with Communities in Fragile and Conflict-Affected States'. *SIPR Briefings*, No. 17.
Sinclair, G. (2016c). 'Disentangling the "Golden Threads": Policing the Lessons from Police History'. In: Bradford, B., Jauregui, B., Loader, I., and Steinberg, J. (Eds.). *The SAGE Handbook of Global Policing*. London: Sage: 29–46.
Sinclair, G. and Burdett, R. (2018). (Eds.). *Mission Challenges, Lessons Learned and Guiding Principles: Policing with Communities in Fragile and Conflict Affected States; Lessons from the Field and Practitioner Perspectives*. Scottish Institute for Policing Research.
Sinclair, G. and Williams, C. (2007). '"Home and Away": The Cross-Fertilisation between "Colonial" and "British" Policing, 1921–85'. *The Journal of Imperial and Commonwealth History*. 35(2): 221–38.
Sindall, K. and Sturgis, P. (2013). 'Austerity Policing: Is Visibility More Important than Absolute Numbers in Determining Public Confidence in the Police?'. *European Journal of Criminology*. 10 (2): 137–53.

Singer, P. W. (2004). *Corporate Warriors: The Rise of the Privatized Military Industry.* Ithaca, NY: Cornell University Press.

Singer, P. W. (2007). 'Can't Win with 'Em, Can't Go To War without 'Em: Private Military Contractors and Counterinsurgency'. *Foreign Policy at Brookings.* Policy Paper No. 4, September 2007.

Skeppstrom, E. (with contributions from Gabrielsson Kjäll, G.). (2016). *The SSR Adviser's Handbook.* FBA.

Skinner, M. (2008). 'Counterinsurgency and State Building: An Assessment of the Role of the Afghan National Police'. *Democracy and Security.* 4(3): 290–311.

Souhami, A. (2007). 'Understanding Institutional Racism: the Stephen Lawrence Inquiry and the Police Service Reaction'. In: Rowe, M. (Ed.). *Policing beyond Macpherson; Issues in Policing, Race and Society.* Cullompton: Willan Publishing: 66–88.

Smith, B. (2011). 'UK relations with Libya'. *Standard Note SN/IA/5886.* International Affairs and Defence Section. House of Commons Library, 2 March 2011.

Smith, F. W. (2010). *Statement of Colin FW Smith QPM, Assistant Chief Constable (Ret'd) to the Iraq Inquiry*, 25 June 2010. Archived on 23 November 2017. The National Archives.

Smith, G. (2009). 'Conceptualizing and Testing Brand Personality in British Politics'. *Journal of Political Marketing*, 8(3): 209–32.

Smyth, J. (2002). 'Community Policing and the Reform of the Royal Ulster Constabulary'. *Policing: An International Journal*, 25(1): 110–24.

Smith, P. T. (1985). *Policing Victorian London: Political Policing, Public Order, and the London Metropolitan Police.* London: Greenwood Press.

Souhami, A. (2007). 'Understanding Institutional Racism: The Stephen Lawrence Inquiry and the Police Service Reaction'. In: Rowe, M. (Ed.). *Policing beyond Macpherson; Issues in Policing, Race and Society.* Cullompton: Willan Publishing: 66–88.

Sri Lanka Campaign for Peace and Justice. (2021). 'UK Engagement with Sri Lanka: Improving Human Rights or Endorsing Impunity?' *Blog*, 18 January 2021.

Stabilisation Unit. (2010). 'Responding to Stabilisation Challenges in Hostile and Insecure Environments: Lessons Identified by the UK's Stabilisation Unit'. November 2010.

Stabilisation Unit (2014). 'Policing the context: Principles and guidance to inform international policing assistance'. *What Works Series*, March 2014.

Stabilisation Unit (2018). 'Countering Violent Extremism in Fragile and Conflict Affected States'. Report. Stabilisation Unit, December 2018.

Stabilisation Unit (2019). *The UK Government's Approach to Stabilisation. A Guide for Policy Makers and Practitioners.* Stabilisation Unit, March 2019.

Stelfox, P. (2008). 'National Policing Improvement Agency (NPIA)'. In: Newburn, T. and Neyroud, P. (Eds.). *Dictionary of Policing,* Cullompton: Willan Publishing: 175–6.

Stenning, P. (2009). 'Governance and Accountability in a Plural Policing Environment—The Story so far'. *Policing: A Journal of Policing and Practice.* 3(1): 22–33.

Stenning, P. and Shearing, C. (2015). 'Privatisation, Pluralisation and the Globalisation of Policing'. *Research Focus*. 3(1): 1–8.

Stenson, J. (2015). 'Police Scotland Ridiculed over "Branding" Guide'. *The Scotsman*, 11 April 2015. Available at: https://www.scotsman.com/news/police-scotland-ridiculed-over-branding-guide-1507821.

Stingo, V., Dziedzic, M. J., and Barbu, B. (2012). (Eds.). *Stability Policing; A Tool to Project Stability*. Norfolk, Virginia: NATO Headquarters Supreme Allied Commander Transformation.

Stoker, D. and Westermann, E. B. (2018). 'Expeditionary Police Advising: Some Causes of Failure'. *Small Wars and Insurgencies*. 29(5–6): 964–80.

Stone, D. (2012). 'Transfer and Translation of Policy'. Policy Studies. 33(6): 483–99.

Storch, R. (1975). 'The Plague of the Blue Locusts: Police Reform and Popular Resistance in Northern England 1840–57'. *International Review of Social History*. 20: 61–90.

Storch, R. (1976). 'The Policeman as Domestic Missionary: Urban Discipline and Popular Culture in Northern England 1850–1880'. *Journal of Social History*. IX. 4: 481–509.

Suroush, Q. (2018). 'Assessing EUPOL Impact on Afghan Police Reform (2007–2016). *Report*. EUNPACK and AREU: Afghanistan Research and Evaluation Unit.

Taylor, D. (1997). *The New Police in Nineteenth Century England: Crime, Conflict and Control*. Manchester: Manchester University Press.

Taylor, J. (2019). 'Policing 4.0; Deciding the future of policing in the UK'. *Report*. London: Deloitte.

Technavio (2019). 'Private Security Services Market by Service, End Users, and Geography—Global Forecast and Analysis 2019–2023'. *Report*, September 2019.

Temporal, P. (2004). *The Brand Advantage: Public Sector Branding in Asia*, Times Editions.

Terpstra, J. and Fyfe, N. R. (2014). 'Policy Processes and Police Reform: Examining Similarities and Differences between Scotland and the Netherlands'. *International Journal of Law, Crime and Justice*. 42(4): 366–83.

The Asia Foundation (2020). *Supporting Community Policing and Police Reform*. Colombo: The Asia Foundation.

The Independent Commission on Policing for Northern Ireland (1999). 'A New Beginning: Policing in Northern Ireland'. *Report*. (Patten Report). September 1999.

The New York Times (2006). 'America's Shame; Torture in the Name of Freedom'. *The New York Times*, 20 February 2006. Available at <https://www.nytimes.com/2006/02/20/international/europe/torture-in-the-name-of-freedom.html>.

The Police Foundation (2020). 'Public Safety and Security in the 21st Century'. *The First Report of the Strategic Review of Policing in England and Wales*, July 2020.

The Portland Trust (2007). *Economics in Peacemaking: Lessons from Northern Ireland*. London: Portland Trust.

The Royal Irish Constabulary Manual; or Guide to the Discharge of Police Duties (6th Edition) (1909). Dublin: HMSO.

The Times (2019). *Letters to the Editor*, 5 July 2019.

Thompson, M. K. (2019). 'Brexit, Scotland, and the Continuing Divergence of Politics'. *The Midwest Quarterly*. 60(2): 141+.
Thompson, R. (1978). *Defeating Communist Insurgency: Experiences from Malaya and Vietnam*. London: Palgrave Macmillan.
Thruelsen, P. D. (2010). 'The Taliban in Southern Afghanistan: A Localized Insurgency with a Local Objective'. *Small Wars and Insurgencies*. 21(2): 259–76.
Topaktas, G. (2016). *Policing Peace Operations: Filling the Security Gap between Military and Police*. New Brunswick, NJ: Rutgers University.
Topping, J. R. (2008). 'Community Policing in Northern Ireland: A Resistance Narrative'. *Policing and Society*. 18 (4): 377–96.
Tosh, J. (2000). *The Pursuit of History*. 3rd Edition. Harlow: Pearson Education Ltd.
Troebst, S. (1998). 'Conflict in Kosovo: Failure of Prevention? An Analytical Documentation, 1992–1998'. *ECMI Working Papers No. 1*. May 1998.
Tyler, T. R. and Jackson, J. (2013). *Popular Legitimacy and the Exercise of Legal Authority: Motivating Compliant, Cooperation and Engagement*. New Haven: Yale University Press.
UK Government (2021). 'UK troops seize Daesh arms cache in Mali peacekeeping operation'. *Blog*, <www.gov.uk>, 15 May 2021.
UN (2000a). 'United Nations Transitional Administration in East Timor'. *East Timor Update*, March 2000.
UN (Peacekeeping) (2000b). *Report of the UN Panel on Peace Operations*. (Brahimi Report) UN Doc A/55/305-5/. Available at: https://peacekeeping.un.org/en/report-of-panel-united-nations-peace-operations-brahimi-report-a55305.
UN (2017). 'Overview of the global study on national legislation covering private military and security companies'. *Report to the 36th session of the Human Rights Council*, 20 July2017. Working Group on the Use of Mercenaries.
UN (2021). *MINUSMA Fact Sheet*. United Nations Multidimensional Integrated Stabilization Mission in Mali. Available at <https://peacekeeping.un.org/en/mission/minusma>.
UN-CMCoord (n.d.). *UN-CMCoord United Nations Humanitarian Civil-Military Coordination Field Handbook*. V1.0. Geneva: United Nations.
UN Department of Safety and Security (2012a). 'Armed Private Security Companies'. Chapter IV. *Security Management*, Section 1, 8 November 2012.
UN Department of Safety and Security (2012a). 'Security Management System'. *Security Policy Manual*. 8 November 2012.
UN Department of Safety and Security (2012b). *Guidelines on the Use of Armed Security Services from Private Security Companies*. Annex A—Statement of Works, 8 November 2012.
UNDP (2009). *Capacity Development: A UNDP Primer*. New York: United Nations Development Programme.
UNHRC (2018). *UN Human Rights Special Procedures (2018)* 'Mercenarism and Private Military and Security Companies'. 2018/40. Geneva: United Nations.
Unsworth, M. (1999). 'RUC officers to be sent to Kosovo as part of British peacekeeping effort'. *The Irish Times*, 2 August 1999. Available at: https://www.irishtimes.com/news/ruc-officers-to-be-sent-to-kosovo-as-part-of-british-peacekeeping-effort-1.212640

US National Security Council (2005). *The National Strategy for Victory in Iraq*. National Security Council, November 2005.
Vaitilingam, R. (2021). 'After Brexit: the impacts on the UK and EU economies by 2030'. *LSE Blog*, 25 January 2021.
Van Veen, (2020). 'Like it or not: coercive power is essential to development'. *Blog*, OECD Development matters, 23 October 2020.
Varisco, A. E. (2014). 'The Influence of Research and Local Knowledge on British-led Security Sector Reform Policy in Sierra Leone'. *Conflict, Security and Development*, 14(1): 89–123.
Verhage, A., Terpstra, J., Dellman, P., Muylaert, E., and Van Parys, P. (Eds.). (2010). 'Policing in Europe'. (CPS *(Journal of Police Studies)* Series).
Vernon, P., O'Callaghan, S., and Holloway, K. (2020). 'Achieving durable solutions by including displacement-affected communities in peacebuilding'. Joint submission by the Swiss Federal Department of Foreign Affairs and HPG to the High-Level Panel on Internal Displacement. *Policy Brief 77*, May 2020.
Vinh, N. (2007). 'Current Trends in Intelligence Outsourcing Affect Work Force Stability'. *Signal Magazine*, 1 December 2007.
Voelz, G. J. (2009). 'Contractors and Intelligence: The Private Sector in the Intelligence Community'. *International Journal of Intelligence and Counter Intelligence*, 22: 586–613.
Waddington, P. A. J. (1982). 'Towards Paramilitarism? Dilemmas in Policing Civil Disorders'. *British Journal of Criminology*. 27: 37–46.
Waddington, P. A. J. (1991). *The Strong Arm of the Law*. Oxford: Oxford University Press.
Waddington, P. A. J. (1999). *Policing Citizens: Authority and Rights*. London: UCL Press.
Waldren, M. (2007). *Armed Police: The Police Use of Firearms since 1945*. Cheltenham: The History Press.
Walker, N. (1999). 'Situating Scottish Policing'. In: Duff, P. and Hutton, N. (Eds.). *Criminal Justice in Scotland*. Farnham: Ashgate Publishing: 94–114.
Walton, R. and Falkner, S. (2019). 'Rekindling British Policing: A 10-Point Plan for Revival'. *Report*. London: Policy Exchange.
Walton, R. and Falkner, S. (2020). *Policing a pandemic; the challenges of maintaining law and order during the Coronavirus response*. London: Policy Exchange.
Wang, H., Xiong, W., Wu, G., and Zhu, D. (2018). 'Public–Private Partnership in Public Administration Discipline: A Literature Review'. *Public Management Review*, 20(2): 293–316.
Ward, P. (2004). *Britishness since 1870*. London: Routledge.
Watts, T. and Biegon, R. (2017). 'Defining Remote Warfare: Security Cooperation'. *Remote Control Project*. London: Oxford Research Group.
Weinberger, B. (1995). *The Best Police in the World: An Oral History of English Policing*. Scolar Press.
Wieslander, A. (2020). 'How France, Germany, and the UK can build a European pillar of NATO'. *Atlantic Council*, 23 November 2020.
Weiss, R. P. (2007–08). 'From Cowboy-Detectives to Soldiers of Fortune: The Recrudescence of Primitive Accumulation Security and its Contradictions on the New Frontiers of Capitalist Expansion'. *Social Justice*. 34(3–4): 1–9.

Weitzer, R. J. (1985). 'Policing a Divided Society: Obstacles to Normalization in Northern Ireland'. *Social Problems*. 33(1): 41–55.

Weitzer, R. J. (1987). 'Policing Northern Ireland Today'. *The Political Quarterly*. 58(1): 88–96.

Weitzer, R. J. (1995). *Policing under Fire: Ethnic Conflict and Police–Community Relations in Northern Ireland*. Albany, NY: State University of New York Press.

Whetton, C. I. (2000). UK Government Assistance to the Police in Developing Countries. *Crime Prevention and Community Safety: An International Journal*. 2(2): 7–24.

Whitaker, B. (1964). *The Police*. Harmondsworth: Penguin.

White, N. D. (2016). 'Regulation of the Private Military and Security Sector: Is the UK Fulfilling it Human Rights Duties?'. *Human Rights Law Review*. 16: 585–99.

White, S. (2016). 'Iraq Inquiry: 'Seeds for bloody anarchy sown' by Iraq Invasion, says former police advisor'. BBC News, 7 July 2016. Available at <https://www.bbc.co.uk/news/uk-northern-ireland-36733634>.

White, S. (2018). 'Policing Reforms in the Aftermath of Conflict: Justice and Security Sector Reform Lessons from Northern Ireland for Peacebuilding and Countering Violent Extremism—A Practitioner's Perspective'. *Policy Brief*. Global Center on Cooperative Security.

Whitman, R. (2020). 'The UK's European diplomatic strategy for Brexit and beyond'. *Politics and International Relations News*, 28 February 2020.

Wilder, A. (2007). 'Cops or Robbers? The Struggle to Reform the Afghan National Police'. *Issues Paper Series*. Afghanistan Research and Evaluation Unit, July 2007.

Williams, C. A. (2008). 'Constables for Hire: The History of Private "Public" Policing in the UK'. *Policing and Society*. 18(2): 190–205.

Williams, C. A. (2011). 'Police and Policing in the Twentieth Century'. Volume III. In: Emsley, C. (Series Editor). *The History of Policing*. Farnham: Ashgate.

Wilson, B. R. L. (2019). 'Scotland, Malawi and the post-development critique: an analysis of power and equality in international development'. PhD thesis. Glasgow: University of Glasgow.

Wilson, R. (2010). *The Northern Ireland Experience of Conflict and Agreement: A Model for Export?* Manchester: Manchester University Press.

Wintour, P. (2016). 'Human rights work has been downgraded by Foreign Office, says MPs'. *The Guardian*, 5 April 2016. Available at <https://www.theguardian.com/politics/2016/apr/05/human-rights-work-has-been-downgraded-by-foreign-office-say-mps>.

Wintour, P. (2016). 'May acknowledges human rights issues in seeking Gulf trade deal'. *The Guardian*, 5 December 2016. Available at <https://www.theguardian.com/law/2016/dec/04/theresa-may-urged-to-address-human-rights-concerns-trade-deal-gulf>.

Wisler, D. (2007). 'The International Civilian Police Mission in Bosnia and Herzegovina: From Democratization to Nation-Building'. *Police Practice and Research*. 8(3): 253–68.

WO (1945). 204/8933.

Yates, A. (2016). 'Western Expatriates in the UAE Armed Forces, 1964–2015'. *Journal of Arabian Studies*. 6(2): 182–200.

Yates, A. (2018). 'Contracted Foreign Advisors in the Abu Dhabi Police Force: Explaining their Enduring Presence, 2002-2015'. In: Stoker, D. and Westermann, E. B. (Eds.). *Expeditionary Police Advising and Militarization: Building Security in a Fractured World*. Solihull: Helion and Company Limited: 294-311.

Yates, A. (2022). *Invisible Expatriates: The contribution of Western military professionals to the UAE Armed Forces*. Unpublished manuscript.

Zandee, D., Deen, B., Kruijver, K., and Stoetman, A. (2020). 'European Strategic Autonomy in Security and Defence: Now the going gets tough, it's time to get going'. *Clingendael Report*, December 2020.

Index

For the benefit of digital users, indexed terms that span two pages (e.g., 52–53) may, on occasion, appear on only one of those pages.

Figures are indicated by *f* following the page number

Abu Dhabi
   example of private security policing 127
   role of UK police retirees 151–56
Afghanistan
   fundamental flaws in Western approach 245–46
   informal information exchange 242–43
   international police capacity building
      deployment of serving and retired UK police 97–98
      global policing exchange 98–99
      invasion in response to 9/11 96
      police capacity building and technical assistance 98
      role of Afghan National Police 96–97
   MDP military integrated approach to MMA
      approach to risk 104–5
      cessation of integrated services training 105
      concept of district level operations 104*f*
      conceptual approach 103–4
      January 2008 and March 2013 103
   private/corporate security sector
      building intelligence management systems 144–50
      hard security and strategic advising 139–44
      human rights and other abuses 136–37
   rise of overseas contracting 238–39
   significant UK contributions 160
   training, mentoring, and advising ANP
      challenges faced by international 'Western' police 101
      democratic (community) policing 100
      gender discrimination 102
      leading role of military 101
      need for police-led reform 99–100
      problems with corruption 101–2
      recruitment of superintendents and senior commanders 100
      reputation of British policing 100
      slow pace of reform 102–3
Armed police *see* **firearms**
Assistance
   to DfID 22
   failure at government level to prioritize UK international policing assistance 94–95
   growth in Western support for aid and development assistance 6
   Iraq
      failure to consult UK police 107
      first formal request for UK police assistance 107–8
   'new all-of-government approach' 218–19
   non-operational assistance 20
   to other countries 22
   peace support operations and overseas development assistance 35
   peacekeeping policing 68–69
   police capacity building and technical assistance in Afghanistan 98
   'protection and enhancement of UK policing' 168
   security and justice sector 21
Association of Chief Police Officers (ACPO)
   see also **Joint International Policing Hub (JIPH)**
   close working relationship with NPIA IA 165–66
   growing the UK policing brand 229–30

Index

Association of Chief Police Officers (ACPO) (*cont.*)
  International Affairs portfolio 95, 159
  replacement by NPCC 8

'Back to the futurism'
  concluding observations 234–37
  historical framework
    corporate security sector growth 35–37
    overview 33
    pre-1989 UK policing brand development 33–34
    SSR, aid, and development 34–35
  Sierra Leone 89–91
Balkans *see* Western Balkans
Bolivia
  PSNI support 201, 202–5
Brand management
  application of corporate branding techniques to public services 7–8
  part of a wider UK government strategy 7
  Scotland Yard 8
  UK policing generally 8–9
Brand Scotland 186–87, 189–90, 206–7
Brexit
  completion of UK's exit from EU 208–9
  impact on external security, and defence policy 213–15
  impact on Western-led interventions 215–18
  impetus for Scotland's drive for enhanced political autonomy 206
  political and economic uncertainty 244
  shaping of post-Brexit 'Global Britain' 246
  shift of UK police brand 5, 208–9
British colonial police
  alternative system of policing 44–45
  complications from earlier policing institutions 45
  emphasis on retaining a semi-military model 45
  twentieth century police discourse 48
British Transport Police 5, 12, 94–95, 233–34

Capacity building
  Afghanistan 98
  'engine of development' 32
Global Britain 208
JIPH
  administrative and a capacity-building role 179–80
  impact of COVID-19 180
  joint initiatives in Asia 180–81
  modern slavery programme 181
  requirement to broaden UK overseas reach 180
  ongoing crisis in policing 247
  Sri Lanka police service 193
Capacity development
  defined 32–33
Ceylon Police
  debate between colonial administration and police commissioner 46–47
  experimentation with both models 45–46
  transformation to 'civilians in uniform' 47
'Civil/ English' model
  alternative system of policing 44–45
  Ceylon Police
    debate between colonial administration and police commissioner 46–47
    experimentation with both models 45–46
    transformation to 'civilians in uniform' 47
  cross-fertilization of approaches across empire 47–48
  historical framework 33
  iconic 'bobby' 33–34
College of Policing (CoP)
  see also National Policing Improvement Agency (NPIA)
  close working relationship with NPIA IA 8, 129–30
  development of professional and accountable policing throughout the world 136–37
  entrepreneurial policing 139
  overseas security and justice assistance work 167
  overseas training to raise revenue 168
'Colonial/ Irish' model
  British colonial police
    complications from earlier policing institutions 45
    emphasis on retaining a semi-military model 45
    twentieth century police discourse 48

Ceylon Police
  debate between colonial administration and police commissioner 46–47
  experimentation with both models 45–46
  transformation to 'civilians in uniform' 47
cross-fertilization of approaches across empire 47–48
historical framework 33
iconic 'bobby' 33–34
Irish Constabulary
  hierarchical division between officers and other ranks 43–44
  Peel's first policing experiment 42–43
myths and realities 38
Community policing
  Afghanistan 100
  Bolivia 204
  concepts to theorize and operationalize SSR 28–30
  East Timor 88
  inappropriate to Iraq 112–13
  international 'tasks' 21
  Iraq 113–14
  'new' Northern Irish policing brand 197–99
  part of peacekeeping policing 31
  Police Scotland 186
  South Sudan
    'community oriented policing strategy' 174
    UNPOL Community Policing Team (CPT) 173–74
  Sri Lanka police service 191
Confidence *see* **trust and confidence in policing**
'Conflict entrepreneurs' 67
Consent *see* **policing by consent**
Corruption
  Afghanistan 101–2
  Iraq
    need for situational awareness 116
    particular challenge 115–16
    police with fingers in everything 116
    preparation for the UK's drawdown 117
    support from international police 117

Data sources *see* police voices
Democratic policing
  Afghanistan 100
  concepts to theorize and operationalize SSR 28–30
  inappropriate to Iraq 112–13
  Western research literature 22
Diversity
  critical issues for UK government 119–20
  expertise required internationally 26–27
  focus of all SSR programmes 102
Divided society policing
  deployment of RUC in Western Balkans 76–79
  Northern Ireland
    attractiveness of overseas deployment 58–59
    the 'divided society model' 57
    history of turbulence and conflict, 57
    strong Protestant link with RUC 58

East Timor
  community policing 88
  high levels of violence 87–88
  in-country risk assessment for the FCO 85
  initial deployment of UK police 85
  need for experience of hostile environments 86
  need for flexibility and innovation 87
  rise of overseas contracting 238–39
  tension within the UK policing brand 88
'**Entrepreneurial policing**'
  core manifestations
    ad hoc consultancies 138
    engagement with public and government institutions 139
    establishment of private security consultancies 138–39
  need for police institutions to compete within market place 129–30
  private/corporate security sector 9
  seamless movement of police 17
  terminology 8
Expeditionary policing 5, 84–85, 93
  see also **Western-led interventions**

Firearms
  deployment of RUC in Western Balkans 79–81
  Iraqi police 110–11, 112–13
  private security firms 137, 144

Index

Firearms (*cont.*)
  requirement for armed capability in Libya 124
  UK policing after 9/11 107–8
  UN peacekeeping operations 199–200

Gender
  Afghanistan 102
  critical issues for UK government 119–20
  focus of all SSR programmes 102
Global Britain
  broadening of military capabilities 220–25
  continuous reshaping post-Brexit 246
  future challenges 5, 208
  future direction of travel of international policing 231–32
  impact of Brexit 208–9
  impact of Brexit on external security, and defence policy 213–15
  impact of Brexit on Western-led interventions 215–18
  'new all-of-government approach' to assistance 218–19
  new challenges -homeland first 209–13
  new security posturing 246
  police engagement as a cross-cutting capability 225–27
  relevance of public-private approach 240
  UK police brand
    growing the UK policing brand 229–31
    maintaining the UK policing brand 227–29
Global policing 24–26, 98–99, 226–27, 248
Global policing exchange
  Afghanistan 98–99
  emergence 25

Herzegovina *see* **Western Balkans**
Historical framework
  'back to the futurism' 234–37
  myths and realities *see* **myths and realities**
  Police Scotland 185–86
  pre-1989 UK policing brand development 33–34
  private/corporate security sector
    focus on 'mercenaries' 36–37
    growth of the private military and security industry 130
  impact of neoliberalism 35–36
  overview 128–29
  research methodology 9, 10–11
  revisionist histories 50–51
  Scotland's support for Malawi Police Service 193
  security sector reform
    benefits from rise of SSR 34
    New Labour's international development policy 34–35
    peace support operations and overseas development assistance 35
  UK police brand
    overview 6–7
    three discernible trends 6
    two broad policing models 33
  Whig histories 49–50
Homeland first
  maintaining the UK policing brand 227–28
  new challenges for Global Britain 209–13
Human rights
  Afghanistan 102
  critical issues for UK government 119–20
  expertise required internationally 26–27
  focus of all SSR programmes 102
  impact of drive towards privatization 248–49
  'new' Northern Irish policing brand 197
  private security contractors 136–37

International policing
  benefits from effective international policing 159
  benefits from rise of SSR 34
  benefits of collective action 159
  building international policing strategy
    creation of dedicated IPAB 169–70
    difficulties facing IPAG 171–72
    difficulties of standardization 170–71
    IPAG's move from the NPIA IA 172
    key principle of international policing assistance 168
    Policing Green Paper 2008 168–69
    some agreement on important future strategies 170
    UK out of step with international partners 171
  challenges faced by UK policing 18

Index

challenges to governance, management, and vision 182
corporate memory of policing through internationalization 163–65
  delivered by the entire spectrum of UK policing 233–34
  delivery of UK police brand 160
  failure at government level to prioritize UK international policing assistance 94–95
  form of 'brand management'
    application of corporate branding techniques to public services 7–8
    part of a wider UK government strategy 7
    Scotland Yard 8
    UK policing generally 8–9
  a fractured memory 242–44
  fragmented coordination and delivery 182
  future of international development dependant on capacity 248
Global Britain
  broadening of military capabilities 220–25
  future challenges 208
  future direction of travel of international policing 231–32
  growing the UK policing brand 229–31
  impact of Brexit 208–9
  impact of Brexit on external security, and defence policy 213–15
  impact of Brexit on Western-led interventions 215–18
  maintaining the UK policing brand 227–29
  'new all-of-government approach' to assistance 218–19
  new challenges -homeland first 209–13
  police engagement as a cross-cutting capability 225–27
global policing 24–26
historical framework of UK police brand 6
International Policing Response Cadre (IPRC) *see* **International Policing Response Cadre (IPRC)**
internationalization of UK policing
  appeal of Irish police experience 59–60
  continuing involvement in Africa 63
  continuing involvement in Asia 62–63
  new brands in 21st century 63–64
  post-war police missions in Europe 61–62
  sense of 'back to the futurism' 65
  strong global resonance of UK brand 59
  wide circulation of advisors in early 20th century 60
Joint International Policing Hub (JIPH) *see* **Joint International Policing Hub (JIPH)**
key UK government strategies
  deployment of police to serve abroad 161
  financial and duty of care arrangements 162–63
  importance in protecting national interests through 'influence abroad' 160–61
  MDP guidance manuals 163–64
  occasional guidance manuals 162–63
  oversimplified form of early documentation 163–64
  requirement for UK strategy support 161–62
  standby pool of deployable civilian experts 164
meaning and scope
  assistance to DfID 22
  assistance to other countries 22
  assistance to peace support operations (PSO) 21
  assistance to security and justice sector 21
  exclusion of missions led by international institutions 20–21
  international engagement 22
  international 'tasks' 21
  non-operational assistance 20
  other overseas police visits 22
  support from police advisors 22
  umbrella term 19–20
means by which the UK can project global influence 19
  as part of a larger process of development 15
peacekeeping policing
  benefits to participants 66

294 Index

International policing (cont.)
    chasm between theoretical concepts and on-the-ground activities. 68–69
    classification of participants 66–67
    concluding comment 92
    'conflict entrepreneurs' 67
    East Timor 85–88
    effectiveness 68
    overview 16
    realistic expectations 69
    Sierra Leone 89–91
    uniqueness of post-Cold War period 67–68
    Western Balkans 69–85
  promotion of cohesion within government and policing 17
  reliance on partnerships 247–48
  role of police voices 12–13
  Scotland's development agenda
    Malawi police service 193–95
    not-for-profit basis 189–90
    Police Scotland's own strategy 188–89
    'programmes of work' 188
    public policy development of devolved government 187–88
    Sri Lanka 190–93
  theoretical underpinnings 5–6
  transnational policing 23–24
  UK police in South Sudan
    community policing 173–74
    deployment of five UK police officers 172–73
    funding from DfID 173
  Western-led interventions *see* **Western-led interventions**
  Western research literature
    mushrooming of police reform 22–23
    transnational, global, and international strands 22
  as a whole-of-UK policing 17
International Policing Response Cadre (IPRC)
  element of crosscutting capability 181
  future role in security policing 167
  high-level candidates 178–79
  relevance of civil-military co-operation 177–78
  response to Hurricane Irma 181
  support for police-military relationship 177

Iraq
  failure at government level to prioritize UK international policing assistance 94–95
  informal information exchange 242–43
  police corruption
    need for situational awareness 116
    particular challenge 115–16
    police with fingers in everything 116
    preparation for the UK's drawdown 117
    support from international police 117
  post-invasion planning and policing
    creation of new IPS 106
    delays in seconding police officers overseas 109
    effects on UK foreign and security policy 106
    failure to consult UK police 107
    first formal request for UK police assistance 107–8
    slow and inadequate inclusion of UK police 108
  pre-deployment preparation
    challenges on arrival 112–13
    community policing 113–14
    engagement in high-profile activities 114
    failure to provide adequate pre-deployment briefings 112
    inadequate mission subsistence allowance 111
    intelligence activities 114–15
    lack of a standby pool of serving UK police 111
    mentoring and advising provincial police chiefs 114
    time lag between an application and release 111–12
    UK police held posts as senior 'civilian' police advisors to MOI 114
  primary responsibility retained by military 95
  private/corporate security sector
    building intelligence management systems 144–50
    growth of the private military and security industry 132–33
    hard security and strategic advising 139–44

human rights and other abuses 136–37
towards private sector regulation
in UK 135
rise of overseas contracting 238–39
training and advising the Iraqi police
establishment of a civilian police
advisory team (109–10
policing resources available 110
quasi-gendarmerie training 110–11
Irish Constabulary
hierarchical division between officers and
other ranks 43–44
Peel's first policing experiment 42–43

Joint International Policing Hub (JIPH)
see also **Association of Chief Police
Officers (ACPO)**
capacity building
administrative and a capacity-building
role 179–80
impact of COVID-19 180
joint initiatives in Asia 180–81
modern slavery programme 181
requirement to broaden UK overseas
reach 180
focus until 2020 175
guardian of UK's international policing
brand 129–30
international policing assistance 20–21
oversight and coordination
of international policing
assistance 175
police-led institution 175–76
rebranding of ACPO IA 160
revitalized approach since 2017 176–77
simplification of OSJA process 167

Kosovo *see* **Western Balkans**

Libya
post-intervention stabilization
avoidance of wide scale humanitarian
crisis 121
'caretaking' role of UK police 122
creation of new institutions 123
drive to promote cross-government
working 121–22
focus on strategic planning 124
formal advisory role of UK
police 122–23
heavy conflict during 2011
uprising 121
impact of anti-government
protests 120–21
need for robust policing
approaches 124
request for a UK policing model 120
UK police brand 123–24
urgent requirement for armed
capability 124
relevance of civil-military
co-operation 177–78
UK police and strategic intent
diplomatic relations after murder of
Yvonne Fletcher 118
excellent government to government
relationship 119
media controversy with
Amnesty 119–20
origins of Libya's police 118
senior police as strategic advisors 118
UK engagement with core policing
departments 118–19

Malawi Police Service
history of shared engagement with
Scotland 193
Scotland-Malawi development 194
selection of officers for
deployment 194–95
Metropolitan Police Service (MPS)
commonly held beliefs rooted in
history 39
origins 40
showcasing of UK police brand 235
Military police
co-operation in West Balkans 81–82
concurrent jurisdiction in Afghanistan,
Iraq, and Libya 151
Iraq
abuse by US military 132–33
lead role 109
recruitment 107
turning point in US military
operation 146–47
need for coordinated military-police
approach 222–23
Ministry of Defence Police (MDP)
fault lines within 93
guidance manuals 163–64

296 Index

Ministry of Defence Police (MDP) (*cont.*)
  integrated approach to MMA in Afghanistan
    approach to risk 104–5
    cessation of integrated services training 105
    concept of district level operations 104f
    conceptual approach 103–4
    January 2008 and March 2013 103
  international 'niche' policing 82–85
  opportunities in private security after retirement 150–51
  part of wide spectrum of international policing 233–34
  relationship with Home Office 93
Models
  necessary starting point 14
  terminology 13
  tools for exploring the past 14
  use of specific references and documentation 15
  use of term 'British' 14–15
Myths and realities
  British colonial police
    alternative system of policing 44–45
    complications from earlier policing institutions 45
    emphasis on retaining a semi-military model 45
  Ceylon Police
    debate between colonial administration and police commissioner 46–47
    experimentation with both models 45–46
    transformation to 'civilians in uniform' 47
  colonial policing 38
  commonly held beliefs rooted in history 39
  cross-fertilization of approaches across empire 47–48
  divided society policing in Northern Ireland
    attractiveness of overseas deployment 58–59
    the 'divided society model' 57
    history of turbulence and conflict, 57
    strong Protestant link with RUC 58
  five key historical trendlines 38–39
  history of nineteenth century 'new' policing 40
    conceptual distinctions adopted by public and historians 41–42
    creations of the bureaucratic nineteenth-century state. 40
    difficulties of police reform 42
    important development in law enforcement 41
  internationalization of UK policing
    appeal of Irish police experience 59–60
    continuing involvement in Africa 63
    continuing involvement in Asia 62–63
    new brands in 21st century 63–64
    post-war police missions in Europe 61–62
    sense of 'back to the futurism' 65
    strong global resonance of UK brand 59
    wide circulation of advisors in early 20th century 60
  Irish Constabulary
    hierarchical division between officers and other ranks 43–44
    Peel's first policing experiment 42–43
  mismatch between public discourse and police hopes 39
  new brands and enduring myths
    'distinctive historical place' of UK policing 54
    public's trust in policing 54–56
  overview 16
  period of 'detraditionalization' and 'diversification' 39–40
  police voices 11–12
  policing by consent 51–54
  revisionist histories 50–51
  Whig histories 49–50

National Crime Agency (NCA)
  commonly held beliefs rooted in history 39
  delivery of international policing services 160
  entrepreneurial policing 139
  growing the UK policing brand 229–30
  'Homeland First' 212
  rebuilding of the Afghan intelligence agency 97–98
  showcasing of UK police brand 39, 235

National Police Chiefs Council (NPCC)
  difficulties with centralization and standardization of UK policing 242
  drive to support the release of serving officers 230
  replacement of ACPO 8
  showcasing of UK police brand 235
  support for multilateral missions 217–18
National Policing Improvement Agency (NPIA)
  see also College of Policing (CoP)
  close working relationship with ACPO IA 165–66
  delivery of bespoke training packages 121–22
  development of professional and accountable policing throughout the world 136–37
  establishment 164–65
  guardian of UK's international policing brand 129–30
  linkage between the UK and the UAE 152–53
  not-for-profit organization 119–20
  replacement by CoP 166–67
  visit to Libya 118–19
New Police
  conceptual distinctions adopted by public and historians 41–42
  creations of the bureaucratic nineteenth-century state. 40
  difficulties of police reform 42
  important development in law enforcement 41
Northern Ireland
  deployment of RUC in Western Balkans
    armed policing capability 79–81
    peacekeeping role 73–75
    value of divided society policing 76–79
  divided society policing in Northern Ireland
    attractiveness of overseas deployment 58–59
    the 'divided society model' 57
    history of turbulence and conflict, 57
    strong Protestant link with RUC 58
  fragmentation of UK police brand 206
  internationalization approaches and brand offer 63–64

internationalization of UK policing 59–60
Irish Constabulary
  hierarchical division between officers and other ranks 43–44
  Peel's first policing experiment 42–43
'new' Northern Irish policing brand
  community policing 197–99
  from RUC to PSNI 195–97
  part of wide spectrum of international policing 233–34
police contracting in Iraq and Afghanistan
  building intelligence management systems 144–50
  hard security and strategic advising 139–44
PSNI
  effect of political devolution 183–84
  foundation for new policing vision and culture 183
  impact of increased international activity 183
  police reform in Bolivia and the Philippines 202–5
  from RUC to PSNI 195–97
  template for post-conflict change management 199–202
  targeting of different consumers 206–7
  use of models 14–15

Peacekeeping policing
  benefits to participants 66
  civilian police as key component 31–32
  classification of participants 66–67
  concluding comment 92
  'conflict entrepreneurs' 67
  East Timor
    community policing 88
    high levels of violence 87–88
    in-country risk assessment for the FCO 85
    initial deployment of UK police 85
    need for experience of hostile environments 86
    need for flexibility and innovation 87
    tension within the UK policing brand 88
  effectiveness 68
  evolution of peacekeeping culture 30–31

298　Index

Peacekeeping policing (*cont.*)
　historical framework　34–35
　increasing subject for study　30–31
　overview　16
　realistic expectations　69
　Sierra Leone
　　dedicated programme of police reform　89–90
　　issues relating to risk　90–91
　　process of state-building　91
　　rotation of UK police within UN missions　89
　theoretical stabilization by military　31
　uniqueness of post-Cold War period　67–68
　Western Balkans
　　ad hoc approaches to assistance　70–71
　　armed policing capability　79–81
　　creation of UNDPKO　69
　　deployment of RUC　73–75
　　impression of chaos　71–72
　　increasingly cluttered security and development landscape　69–70
　　Ministry of Defence Police　82–85
　　police-military co-operation　81–82
　　requirement for an international police presence　72–73
　　UK provision support　70
　　UN's initial brief　71
'Peelian principles'　1, 4–5, 10–11, 39, 50, 236–37
Philippines　204
Police corruption *see* corruption
Police Scotland *see* Scotland
Police Service of Northern Ireland (PSNI) *see* Northern Ireland
Police voices
　individual snap shots of their international policing experiences　12–13
　oral testimonies and observations　11–12
　primary and secondary interviews　12
　UK police service　11
Policing by consent
　mutual consent　51–54
　New Police　41
　overlapping of styles and activities　4
　Peelian principle　4–5
　traditional model of policing　51
　Whig histories　49

Private/corporate security sector
　Abu Dhabi
　　as an example　127
　　role of UK police retirees　151–56
　Afghanistan
　　building intelligence management systems　144–50
　　hard security and strategic advising　139–44
　connection between public and private policing
　　entrepreneurial policing　138–39
　　'police assemblage'　137–38
　'entrepreneurial policing'　9
　　core manifestations　138–39
　　need for police institutions to compete within market place　129–30
　　seamless movement of police　17
　　terminology　8
　focus on security and police contractors　128
　global phenomenon　128
　growth of the private military and security industry
　　benefit of engaging consultants　130
　　decline of quasi-informal mercenary groups　131–32
　　historic backdrop　130
　　intervention in Iraq　132–33
　　post 1989 surge of contracting　131
　　security as a valuable and valued commodity　132
　historical framework
　　focus on 'mercenaries'　36–37
　　impact of neoliberalism　35–36
　　overview　128–29
　historical framework of UK police brand　6
　impact of private-public partnership　157–58
　importance　127
　international opportunities after retirement　150–51
　Iraq
　　building intelligence management systems　144–50
　　hard security and strategic advising　139–44
　　link to the ongoing commercialization of public policing　129–30

new commercial UK police brand 240
overview 17
rise of overseas contracting 238-40
Russian private 'war' providers 248-49
strengthening of UK policing brand 157
towards private sector regulation in UK
  creation of self-regulation 135-36
  human rights and other abuses 136-37
  impact of Sandline affair 134
  intervention in Iraq 135
  little Government appetite for
    regulation 133-34
  Private Security Industry Act 2001 137

Research methodology
export of UK policing 9-10
historical and sociological approaches 9
interpretation of police history 10-11
role of police voices
  individual snap shots of their
    international policing
    experiences 12-13
  oral testimonies and
    observations 11-12
  primary and secondary interviews 12
  UK police service 11
use of models
  necessary starting point 14
  terminology 13
  tools for exploring the past 14
  use of specific references and
    documentation 15
  use of term 'British' 14-15
Western research literature
  mushrooming of police reform 22-23
  transnational, global, and international
    strands 22
Revisionist histories 50-51
Royal Ulster Constabulary (RUC)
attractiveness of overseas
  deployment 58-59
the 'divided society model' 57
peacekeeping policing
  armed policing capability 79-81
  deployment in Western Balkans 73-75
  value of divided society policing 76-79
police contracting in Iraq and
  Afghanistan
  building intelligence management
    systems 144-50
  hard security and strategic
    advising 139-44
from RUC to PSNI 195-97
strong Protestant link 58

Scotland
fragmentation of UK police brand 206
international development agenda
  Malawi police service 193-95
  not-for-profit basis 189-90
  Police Scotland's own strategy 188-89
  'programmes of work' 188
  public policy development of devolved
    government 187-88
  Sri Lanka 190-93
internationalization approaches and
  brand offer 63-64
internationalization of UK policing 59
part of wide spectrum of international
  policing 233-34
Police Scotland
  building of brand Scotland 186-87
  effect of political devolution 183-84
  enhanced policing engagement 186
  foundation for new policing vision and
    culture 183
  greater partnership approach 186
  historical development 185-86
  impact of increased international
    activity 183
  international development
    agenda 188-89
  significance of reforms 184-85
promotion of Scottish policing
  brand 206-7
support for Malawi Police Service
  history of shared engagement 193
  Scotland-Malawi development 194
  selection of officers for
    deployment 194-95
support for Sri Lanka police service
  capacity building 193
  community policing 191
  criticism in media and by civil
    societies 192-93
  urgent need post-conflict 190-91
use of models 14-15
Scotland Yard
brand management 8
centrality in police reputation 11

300 Index

Scotland Yard (*cont.*)
  commonly held beliefs rooted in history 39
  showcasing of UK police brand 235
Security sector reform (SSR)
  benefits for international policing 34
  complications due to number of donor countries 27–28
  concepts to theorize and operationalize SSR
    community policing 29–30
    democratic policing 29
    focus on good practice 30
    overview 28–29
  critical gap in the UK government's approach to SSR 125
  drive to improve aid effectiveness 26–27
  growth in Western support for aid and development assistance 6
  New Labour's international development policy 34–35
  peace support operations and overseas development assistance 35
  responses to Western-led interventions 27
  rise of overseas contracting 238–40
  Sierra Leone
    dedicated programme of police reform 89–90
    process of state-building 91
  transformation of security sector system 26
  Western research literature 22–23
Sierra Leone
  dedicated programme of police reform 89–90
  issues relating to risk 90–91
  process of state-building 91
  rotation of UK police within UN missions 89
South Sudan
  community policing
    'community oriented policing strategy' 174
    UNPOL Community Policing Team (CPT) 173–74
  deployment of five UK police officers 172–73
  funding from DfID 173
  significant UK contributions 160

Sri Lanka police service
  capacity building 193
  community policing 191
  criticism in media and by civil societies 192–93
  urgent need for support post-conflict 190–91
Support, monitoring, advising, reporting, and training (SMART) model 69

Transnational policing 23–24
Trust and confidence in policing
  all-time low in late 20th century 55–56
  continued erosion in 21st century 56
  reliance on consent and legitimacy 54–55

UK policing
  challenges faced by UK policing 18
  changing landscape 182
  dismissive recent media reports 246–47
  'distinctive historical place' 54
  future of international development dependent on capacity 248
  history of knowledge transfer and exchange 243
  iconic 'bobby' 33–34
  internationalization of UK policing
    appeal of Irish police experience 59–60
    continuing involvement in Africa 63
    continuing involvement in Asia 62–63
    new brands in 21st century 63–64
    post-war police missions in Europe 61–62
    sense of 'back to the futurism' 65
    strong global resonance of UK brand 59
    wide circulation of advisors in early 20th century 60
  'internationalized' from early days 233
  key subject of book 18
  police voices 11
  reputation abroad 100
  uncertainty after Brexit 244
UK policing brand
  Afghanistan 101
  brand management 8–9
  building international policing strategy
    creation of dedicated IPAB 169–70
    difficulties facing IPAG 171–72
    difficulties of standardization 170–71

Index 301

IPAG's move from the NPIA IA 172
key principle of international policing assistance 168
Policing Green Paper 2008 168–69
some agreement on important future strategies 170
UK out of step with international partners 171
competition with other brands 168
cooperation with Police Scotland 189–90
delivery of international policing services 160
fragmentation 206
fragmented coordination and delivery of international policing 182
in Global Britain
  growing the UK policing brand 229–31
  maintaining the UK policing brand 227–29
historical framework
  overview 6–7
  three discernible trends 6
  two broad policing models 33
impact of devolution 238
international policing agenda 241–42
international policing as a whole-of-UK policing 17
International Policing Response Cadre (IPRC) *see* **International Policing Response Cadre (IPRC)**
Joint International Policing Hub (JIPH) *see* **Joint International Policing Hub (JIPH)**
key subject of book 18
knowledge transfer and exchange 243–44
Libya 120, 123–24
myths and realities *see* **myths and realities**
need for reform 246–47
new commercial UK police brand 240
powerful component of brand UK 237–38
pre-1989 UK policing brand development 33–34
promotion of UK prosperity and policing capability 159–60
strengthening through corporate and military sectors 157
strong global resonance 59
tension exposed in East Timor 88
theoretical underpinnings 5–6
three different policing systems in 21st century 63–64
UK police in South Sudan
  community policing 173–74
  deployment of five UK police officers 172–73
  funding from DfID 173
use of models 14

Ukraine
advent of a more 'dangerous and capricious world' 245
movement of peoples towards Europe 245

Western Balkans
ad hoc approaches to assistance 70–71
armed policing capability 79–81
creation of UNDPKO 69
deployment of RUC 73–75
impression of chaos 71–72
increasingly cluttered security and development landscape 69–70
Ministry of Defence Police 82–85
police-military co-operation 81–82
requirement for an international police presence 72–73
rise of overseas contracting 238–39
role of UK in conflict hotspots 94
UK provision support 70
UN's initial brief 71

Western-led interventions
Afghanistan
  international disunity and disarray 96–99
  MDP military integrated approach to MMA 103–5
  training, mentoring, and advising ANP 99–103
concluding remarks 124–26
failure at government level to prioritize UK international policing assistance 94–95
fault lines within stakeholders 93
fundamental flaws exposed in Afghanistan 245–46
historical framework of UK police brand 6

Western-led interventions (*cont.*)
  impact of 9/11 94
  impact of Brexit on UK role 215–18
  impetus for SSR 27
  Iraq
    police corruption 115–17
    post-invasion planning and policing 106–9
    pre-deployment preparation 111–15
    training and advising the Iraqi police 109–11
  Libya
    post-intervention stabilization 120–24
    UK police and strategic intent 118–20
  overview 16
  primary responsibility retained by military 95
  replacement by smaller missions 241–42
  role of UK in conflict hotspots 94
  whole-of-government approach with advent of SU 95–96
Whig histories 49–50